Contents

Women of the House

Women's household work in Ireland 1926–1961

Discourses, Experiences, Memories

CAITRIONA CLEAR

IRISH ACADEMIC PRESS
DUBLIN • PORTLAND, OR.

First published in 2000 by
IRISH ACADEMIC PRESS
44, Northumberland Road, Dublin 4, Ireland

and in the United States of America by
IRISH ACADEMIC PRESS
c/o ISBS, 5804 NE Hassalo Street,
Portland, OR 97213–3644
Website: www.iap.ie

British Library Cataloguing in Publication Data
Clear, Caitriona
   Women of the House : women's household work in Ireland, 1926–1961: discourses,
   experiences and memories. – (Women in Irish history)
   1. Women – Ireland – Social conditions 2. Housekeeping – Ireland – History –
   20th century
   I. Title
   640.9'415
   ISBN 0–7165–2714–6 (hardback)
   ISBN 0–7165–2717–0 (paperback)

Library of Congress Cataloging-in-Publication Data
Clear Caitriona, 1960–
   Women of the house : women's household work in Ireland, 1926–1961 : discourses,
   experiences, memories / Caitriona Clear.
       p. cm. — (Women in Irish history)
   Includes bibliographical references and index.
   ISBN 0–7165–2714–6 (hbk.) — ISBN 0–7165–2717–0 (pbk.)
    1. Women—Ireland.   2. Ireland—Social conditions.   I. Title.   II. Series.

HQ1600.3 .C5 2000
305.4'09415—dc21   99–088161

Typeset in 10.5 pt on 12 pt Ehrhardt
by Carrigboy Typesetting Services, County Cork
Printed by Creative Print and Design (Wales), Ebbw Vale

Acknowledgements

The historian who uses personal testimony sometimes feels like a curious little girl sitting quiet and unnoticed in the corner while the women are talking and sometimes like a mad doctor cutting up bodies and reassembling them! I hope that I have used the testimony people were good enough to supply me with in a way that is respectful to the life stories they told me, and while the finished product cannot hope to match these stories for vividness and colour, I hope that it is something other than a Frankenstein's monster. The book could not have been written without these contributions, and research was a very pleasant as well as an interesting task. The generosity and hospitality of the contributors would have to be experienced to be believed. Limitations on time and other demands meant that I did not meet everybody who responded, but I felt warmed, as well as informed, by the enthusiasm and intelligence of all the responses both written and oral. So the biggest thanks goes to the people, at least three of whom are now *ar shlí na fírinne*, who gave freely of their time, energy and vast store of memories. Anonymity is guaranteed, but I have advised people of their pseudonyms and hope they will recognise their testimony if they read the book.

Professor Mary E. Daly of University College, Dublin, supervised this book in its original incarnation as a PhD thesis; she always understood the pressures that delayed its production, but was amazingly prompt, thorough and helpful in her comments and criticisms, and supportive when it mattered. Special thanks to Mary Clancy, whose ground-breaking work on Free State women has been an inspiration, and with whom I've had many long and enlightening conversations on twentieth-century Irish women. Maria Luddy has long been a friend and a support since the days of the Feminist History Forum, and her comments on this manuscript were extremely helpful. Over the years I've benefitted in many ways from knowing Dympna McLoughlin, Margaret MacCurtain, Cliona Murphy, Mary Cullen, Maura Cronin, Caitriona Beaumont, Marie Boran, Mary O'Dowd, Bernadette Whelan, John Logan, Mona Hearn, Ann Colman, Alan Hayes and Eilís Ward, and I thank them all too. Needless to say my opinions, like my mistakes, are my own and none of these good history friends should be held responsible for any or all of them! Thanks also to several classes I taught in Women's Studies and Women's History in University College, Galway, at degree and diploma level, since 1991, and to Ann Lyons of National University of Ireland, Galway, Women's Studies Centre. Thanks to my colleagues in the History Department in Galway, 1991–96 – Gearóid MacNiocaill, Tom Bartlett, Gearóid O Tuathaigh, Nicholas Canny, Steven Ellis, Dáibhí O Cróinín, Phil Faherty – and to Niall O Ciosáin for some comments on sources and many conversations on the uses of oral and personal testimony. Anne Byrne, agricultural journalist, sent me on some very useful material. Thanks also to the National Library of Ireland, the National Archives and the James Hardiman Library of University College, Galway (now known as the National University of Ireland, Galway) and Emer Madden in the Arts Faculty, National University of Ireland, Galway, and Maura O Cróinín for some vital work with the disc at the very end. Thanks also to National University of Ireland, Galway, for a sabbatical year 1997–98 which enabled me to get the bulk of the thesis rewritten as a book. Thanks to Ursula Gavin in Cathal Brugha St. College library, for all her help.

In a work like this the personal and the professional debts are very hard to disentangle one from the other. My mother Kathleen Clear was always on the lookout for books and items that might interest me, and lent me her personal archive of cookery and household books; thanks to her and to my father, Paddy Clear, for rearing all of us with a vivid and immediate sense of the past. I would also like to thank my aunts Sr Eileen Synnott and Sr Carmel Synnott and my uncle and aunt Tom and Brigid Synnott for the help they gave, and the interest they have always taken. On the other side of the family, I must mention my aunt Mary Clear, my late grand-aunt Agnes Ryan who died in 1995 and my cousin Eithne McCormack for conversations about Dublin and social work in the 1940s and 1950s. My parents-in-law, Paddy and Bríd Lenihan, were also very interested and always ready with stories and insights too. Moving on to my own generation, Síle de Cléir was of tremendous professional and personal help to me in her capacity as folklorist, librarian and sister; my other sisters and brother – Eileen Clear, Máire Flannery and Larry de Cléir – were also a great support, as were good friends Gráinne Lenihan, Eilín Ní Fhlaithbheartaigh, Carol Nash and Elizabeth Tilley. Finally, thanks to Pádraig Lenihan for everything really – encouragement, humour, empathy, criticism, forbearance, fags. Donncha Lenihan is older than this piece of research, Manus is about the same age as it, Cora elbowed it out of the way for a while and Síle only surfaced when it was all over. They slowed up the work considerably, but I would not have had it or them any other way.

EXPLANATORY NOTE

Throughout this work, the use of a pseudonymous first name and an initial (e.g. Larry K., Josephine E.) indicates that the personal testimony provided by that contributor is being referred to. This avoids clogging up the text and the notes with references to the tapes, letters and documents which are in the author's possession, and transcripts of which were included in the thesis upon which this book is based. If a full name is used, then that is a real name referring to written or oral testimony provided by somebody other than a contributor, and it is duly acknowledged. Short biographies of contributors to the project are provided in Section A of the Bibliography, while an explanation of sources and methodology is provided in Appendices 1 and 2.

List of Tables

List of Illustrations

Introduction

There is a child at her side.
The tea is poured, the stitching put down.
The child grows still, sensing something of importance.
The woman settles and begins her story.

Believe it, what we lost is here in this room
on this veiled evening.
The woman finishes. The story ends.
The child, who is my mother, gets up, moves away.

In the winter air, unheard, unshared,
the moment happens, hangs fire, leads nowhere.
The light will fail and the room darken,
the child will fall asleep and the story be forgotten.

From: Eavan Boland, 'What We Lost'[1]

Peering out at us in all their variety from behind census figures and statistics of birth, disease and death; whispering insistently to us in books, documents, letters and voices, the women and men of the past will not let the light fail or the room darken. The fear that their story will be forgotten motivated me to write this book; the vigour and vividness of people's memories of women's household work in the past kept me going when the subject slipped out of my grasp and challenged me to define it. I pinned it down, disentangling *writings about* these unpaid women workers, from these workers' own experiences. No sooner had I done this than I realised that people's memories of personal experience are coloured by their own priorities and values – that opinions as well as facts are inscribed in memory, influencing what is remembered and what is forgotten. Another difficulty was that the experiences of these workers were so diverse that finding common threads of experience was a daunting task. I dealt with this difficulty by putting the work itself at the centre of the inquiry, and for this reason I concentrated as much as possible on women who would have done most, or all, of their own household work, unaided by household staff – lower-middle class and working-class women of the house, and women from nearly all sizes of farm. I left out the experience of Travellers because I believe that they deserve a complete study of their own, which would take account of their traditions, customs and language. Neither did I look at the experience of upper-

I

middle class women who had domestic servants for all or most of the period, as this really belongs in an in-depth study of domestic service. Besides, almost all (89%) of the people who answered my appeal gave information on houses in which there were no servants – the others had at most one servant, more often than not one who came in every day.

Women who performed household work in their own houses constituted the largest block of adult women in the first forty years of Irish independence.[2] Almost all of the social initiatives and preoccupations of the new state in its first forty years rested on assumptions about these women's work and its meaning for the family, the community and the state. Local authority houses were built by the Cosgrave government, but it was not until the 1930s that a major building programme was undertaken by Fianna Fáil, at its height building 12,000 new houses a year with piped water, flush toilets, gardens and other facilities to ease the work of the woman of the house.[3] Non-contributory widows' pensions were finally introduced in 1936, after almost a decade of pressure from the Society for Mothers' Pensions.[4] Voluntary and local authority maternity and child health schemes were growing in number year by year.[5] Children's allowances – payments of half a crown a week for every third and subsequent child – were introduced in 1944, and extended to every second child from 1952.[6] The introduction of better provisions for widows of persons dying intestate came in 1954, and the Married Women's Status Act (1956) gave married women equal legal status with their husbands.[7] A nationwide nutrition survey was initiated by the Department of Local Government and Public Health in the early 1940s, and the first Household Budget Inquiry reported in 1950–1.[8] After a rocky start, in 1953 the new Department of Health eventually succeeded in making free health care available for the majority of mothers and babies up to six weeks.[9]

Fixed, if not always accurate or even internally consistent, ideas about women and household work lay beneath initiatives and recommendations on both men's and women's employment; the exclusion of married women from white-collar public service work, complete by 1933, and the discriminatory treatment of women in the Conditions of Employment Act (1936) are the most obvious examples of this.[10] Neither, however, must we forget the constant recommendations by government commissions and women's organisations in the 1940s that girls be trained as domestic servants, when it should have been clear that Irish girls and women were forsaking this kind of work in huge numbers.[11] High rates of female emigration from the early 1940s drew attention not only to the men left behind who were thus bereft of potential wives, and the homes never set up, but also to the middle-class women deprived of cheap domestic labour and forced to do their housework unaided. Concern about population decline, which reached a head in the early 1950s, prompted redefinitions of both women's and men's relationship to household work. The focus on farm women's work in particular was sharpened, and calls for women's work to be eased by the servicing of rural dwellings with water and electricity grew ever louder.[12]

Women and the households for which they were notionally responsible were central to all of these concerns. If the tenement-dwelling mother struggling to keep her family alive was the strongest indictment of the greed of property and the indifference of legislators, the farm woman carrying buckets of water and cooking over a fire was seen, more and more, as a shameful reminder of rural conservatism and indifference to women's needs. There were other images in elite and popular media – the wasteful, ignorant mother who needed to be taught how to cook and clean and maintain her family's health; the pleasure-loving young wife who needed to be reminded sharply of her responsibilities; the young (by definition urban) stay-at-home housewife who needed to be told what to buy and how to use what she bought; the wise and practical wife and mother who needed the guidance of her wiser and more practical husband; the woman deprived of adequate medical care in pregnancy and childbirth, and in the 1950s, the young woman boarding the ship for England who could not be expected to marry in Ireland without guarantees of a better life. Not only the employment policies and the health and social welfare initiatives, but also the very anxieties, fears, hopes and compromises of the new state could be summed up with reference to these images of women.[13] Household work and those performing it were therefore very important. Yet, not only was women's household work not officially described as 'gainful employment', it was rarely discussed or described in detail by those who made public pronouncements on, and decisions about, these issues. Furthermore, the women who were returned in the census as 'engaged in home duties', and many others besides who took charge of a house – married, single or widowed, of all ages from the teens to the nineties – did not, as a rule, speak in public or publish their opinions and preoccupations. It need hardly be pointed out that they did not form a trade union.

The temptation to find out 'how it all began', is, Michelle Rozaldo reminds us, an occupational hazard of feminist scholarship.[14] For the generation of feminists writing since the early 1970s, the particularly tenacious social subordination of women in modern Ireland, if it did not 'all begin' in the first forty years of independence, was certainly consolidated in these years. A recent generation of writers has reminded us that the new state attacked women's recently established citizenship. Women were exempted from jury service, married women barred from public service white-collar work, including National teaching, and women's access to factory employment was restricted in 1935. Article 41.2 of Eamon de Valera's Constitution of 1937 identified all women with motherhood and domesticity. Anthropological and fictional evidence of female subordination and drudgery in rural life, the falling number of Irish women returned in the census as gainfully employed in these forty years and the high numbers of female emigrants from the mid-1940s are produced as evidence of a social environment that was particularly unfriendly to females of all ages and conditions. Pronouncements by high-profile figures such bishops and politicians on women's duties complete this picture; Eamon de Valera's St Patrick's Day speech of 1943 with its reference to comely maidens is seen as the high watermark of idealisation/oppression.[15]

The most recent, authoritative history of modern Ireland written by J.J. Lee (one of the contributors to the first volume of Irish women's history), invokes a short story by William Trevor to convey the plight of women in Ireland in the 1940s:

> If the comely maidens would laugh, it would be the bittersweet laugh of liberation through emigration from a sterile society where the Bridies left behind would be glad to settle, their girlhood dreams dashed, for the Bowser Egans.[16]

This amounts to a suggestion that those who stayed behind to marry in rural Ireland from the 1940s to the late 1950s were forced to settle for selfish, immature, alcoholic husbands, and that rural Ireland had become a 'sterile society' for women in these years. Jenny Beale describes farm women's lives in terms of their unremitting hard work, remoteness from other women, lack of running water and electricity and, in keeping with Arensberg and Kimball's perception, clear subordination due to separate spheres of male/female work. She also suggests that the coming of water and electricity to the country, and urban life in general, was no great improvement on rurality for women in the home as far as authority and fulfilment were concerned.[17] Catherine Rose, in one of the founding texts of second-wave Irish feminism, had already commented on the 'hardship and drudgery' of the farm woman's daily round and noted that while the winter was a slack season for men's work, there was no corresponding relaxation in women's routines.[18] Amy Wieners' short survey of the literature on (undifferentiated) 'rural' women in Ireland assumes that 'rural' women have traditionally been subordinate and powerless, using a definition of power as located in ownership of property, access to paid work and education.[19] Deborah Simonton, in the most recent survey of European women's work, refers almost parenthetically to what has now become established 'fact' – the Irish farm woman's low status and low self-esteem.[20]

The aspects of rural life that are seen by Beale, Rose, Lee, Wieners and others as having been most oppressive to women in these years are their extreme hard work, separate sphere of work from men, overt subordination to men, lack of facilities and services (water and electricity), isolation from other people (especially other women), and lack of real choice in marriage partners, topped by the all-pervasive oppression of the Roman Catholic Church. Domesticity and powerlessness are seen as synonymous by some commentators, in line with the founding texts of secondwave twentieth-century feminism.[21] Evelyn Mahon attributes the 'failure of Irish women to shed the hegemony of the Catholic Church' to the fact that Irish women are not, for the most part, 'integrated into the economy' because between a half and two-thirds of Irish women are and have always been 'engaged in home duties'.[22] Her underpinning assumption that women working in the house are not 'integrated into the economy', and that this state of life in and of itself makes them docile and easily cowed, might well be true, but it should at least be questioned. That is one of the things which this book sets out to do.

It is impossible, however, to disagree with Beale's description of the first half century of independence as 'fifty years of inequality'.[23] The attacks on Irish women as workers and citizens are well-documented, as is the unease of several politicians, bishops and others in public life with women outside what was believed to be their proper sphere. Some writers see in the succession of anti-women measures a grand ideological design. Maryann Valiulis's explanation of the state's attitude to women in the first two decades of independence as a typically post-colonial 'gender ideology' is defensible, but her attention to the colourful ins and outs of political debate and bishops' pronouncements on this subject assign to what she calls 'the established powers' a homogeneity of opinion on women which just did not exist.[24] There was, on the contrary, a variety of published opinion on the subject of women in public life from churchmen and politicians (male and female), as well as from journalists; women in public life had their defenders as well as attackers.[25] Indeed, it is possible to read Valiulis's several articles on this subject and not to be aware that Irish women not only had the parliamentary vote in this period, but also sat in both houses of the Oireachtas. Her claim that women's 'political, economic and reproductive rights' had been so curtailed by 1937 'that women were *explicitly barred* from claiming for themselves a public identity' (italics mine) is a magnificent overstatement, and one which is belied by the small but significant number of highly-respected women in public life.[26] The parliamentary vote was taken away from women in Germany, Spain and Poland in the 1930s; it had never been granted to women in France, Portugal and Italy, and women were barred from many kinds of work in these countries in this period. Bars against married women and gender specific labour legislation were in place in most western countries, including Britain and the USA.[27] Catherine Rose's account of women and politics in Ireland never mentions that Irish women were among the first in Europe to be fully enfranchised, some six years before women in Britain. And closer examination of the changes in the kind of census-designated gainful employment lost and gained by women over this period (see Chapter One), challenges the claim that women were coerced 'back into' the 'domestic sphere' by the new state.[28]

The idea that there was a 'domestic ideology' in Ireland in the first decades of independence crops up everywhere. Food historian Regina Sexton refers to 'those kitchen-bound Free State women', and playfully renames a recipe from the only state-published cookbook (first published in 1924 and republished, unchanged, over the following decades), 'De Valera's Pie'.[29] The introduction to the most recent collection of articles on women's history in Ireland comments that 'the dominant ideology of the Irish Free State, as exemplified by the Constitution, placed women in the home as mothers and housekeepers'.[30] If ideology is defined as a set of beliefs underpinning a nation or a political system, did the attacks on women's citizenship and employment rights in Ireland in the 1920s and 1930s constitute an ideology? I will be arguing in the next four chapters that they did not, and that the attacks – substantial as they were – were piecemeal and inconsistent. Married women were not barred from factory or service work, or from the learned professions, or from midwifery, shopkeeping, farming and labouring. They were not compelled to take domestic science at school. They lived in a political system that enabled females to compete in school–leaving and matriculation examinations on equal terms with males, and to aspire to the highest political offices in the land, when women had been barred from such equality in many European states.

It is tempting, when looking at the past, to see patterns where none exist. Frances Gardiner traces the damage to women's rights from the death of feminist James Connolly in 1916, to the banning of contraceptive information in the Censorship of Publications Act 1929, to the Conditions of Employment Act (1936) and the 1937 Constitution. She comments:

> This constitutional vision of the role of woman in Irish society as fulltime wife and mother in an indissoluble marriage tallies with the earlier resistance to the enfranchisement of women. Political activism would be completely at variance with this comfortable home-maker role.[31]

She goes on to cite the 'public furore' which greeted the Mother and Child scheme as another example of the state's repressive attitude to women. This is a tempting progression, but it does not add up. First of all, it is true that the doomed signatories of the 1916 Proclamation were, almost to a man, feminists and supporters of equal citizenship, unlike the first Free State government, but it is hugely significant that W.T. Cosgrave's government did not dare to renege on equal citizenship.[32] Secondly, divorce and contraception were not issues that enjoyed inevitable support among feminists either in Ireland or in many other countries – democratic or fascist – in the 1930s. Up to the 1960s many feminists and others were deeply worried about the eugenic implications of much advocacy of contraception. Besides, there were, Clancy tells us, other identifiably feminist issues on which Irish women in public life, including TDs and Senators, fought and on which they courageously confronted what were seen to be men's interests – the age of consent and men's duty to maintain illegitimate offspring, for example.[33] The defeat of the Mother and Child scheme proposed by Dr Browne certainly indicates that mothers' and children's health was seen as secondary to other considerations, but some points must be borne in mind. This was a state scheme in the first place; it was drawn up without any female consultation whatsoever, and its architects even attempted (unsuccessfully) to remove the autonomy and eradicate the distinctive identity of that very important all-female profession, trained midwives.[34] This is not to imply that either this Bill, or its luckier 1953 successor, were irrelevant to women's lives; both were far more relevant than the 1937 Constitution.

The Constitution drawn up by Eamon de Valera and accepted by a narrow majority of the Irish electorate in 1937 is often believed to have contributed, more than anything else, to women's inequality in twentieth-century Ireland. Constitutional lawyer Yvonne Scannell states that it was 'rooted in a patronising and stereotyped view of womanhood'. She reminds us, however, that this document reaffirmed mothers' guardianship rights, and that there are at least six articles in it which 'can be used, directly or indirectly, to vindicate women's rights'.[35] Mary Daly goes even further, suggesting that Article 41.2 should be

"Will yiz shut up, all o' yiz, while your father's explainin' me position under the New Constitution!"

1. 'Will yiz shut up'. *Dublin Opinion*, September 1937: This seems to be an ironic comment by Charles E. Kelly on the special position, indeed, of the hard-pressed and obviously authoritative working-class mother, and on the presumption of the Constitution in reinforcing such authority. There is also the less comfortable suggestion that the idea of the Dublin working-class woman having any political importance is itself hilarious for Kelly. Whatever the interpretation, the cartoon shows us that Article 41.2 was, for whatever reason, considered comical by some contemporaries.

viewed as 'acknowledging the importance of women's lives and work within the home, giving status to many members of society who were otherwise ignored'.[36] The extent to which Article 41.2 was a recognition of anything is unclear, but this is a point of view which bears consideration. De Valera's irritation at feminist opposition to the Constitution suggests that he did not inhabit a political environment that was entirely indifferent to women's views: indeed, he told the late Professor T.P. O'Neill that Ivy Pinchbeck's *Women Workers and the Industrial Revolution* (1933) had had a major impact on his thinking and forced his attention onto protecting Irish women and children from the worst effects of what he hoped was Ireland's industrial revolution.[37] The fact that de Valera felt the need to invoke a feminist authority for his reference to women in the Constitution is indeed significant.[38] Nor must we forget that the Constitution was accepted by only a narrow majority of the Irish electorate. While there is no way of determining the sex breakdown of voters, some women could have used their votes to oppose this attempt to dilute their citizenship. Nor were there any more attacks on women's citizenship and employment after 1937, despite suggestions in the 1940s, for example, that women's emigration should be controlled.[39] Lest it be thought that an attempt is being made here to gloss over the serious attacks on women's work and citizenship, I should reiterate that there was strong and overt hostility to women throughout this period. However, this was not always expressed as a desire to immure women in the house; it was not always directed at women in paid work and public life, and it did not always come from people who were conservative on other social issues. It was not internally consistent enough to be called an ideology.

The historian must remember, in any case, that what was said and written about women, and recommended for women, is only half of the story. The other, arguably more important, half is how these women themselves experienced their working lives. Chapter One will look at the statistical background – numbers, ages, marital status – and will place women of the house firmly in the context of women's paid work. Chapters Two, Three, and Four will be concerned mainly with writing about women's household work and the attitudes of people who wrote, spoke in public, legislated and addressed women in publications aimed at them. Chapter Five looks at changes in the experience of pregnancy and child-birth, seen against the background of medico-social discourses. Chapter Six looks at some aspects of infant feeding from the point of view of mothers, and Chapters Seven and Eight continue to focus on experience by looking at the day's work and how it differed from place to place, and at structures of authority and control over resources within households. The basic question this book will try to answer is a simple, and perhaps a naïve, one: did life get better or worse, harder or easier for Irish women performing household work in their own houses in these forty years?

Oral evidence and personal testimony of many kinds will be used in this work. People's eyes on 'the past' tell us not only about lived experience, but about 'social memory' – how things are remembered and what is prioritised in memory.[40] The methodology of oral evidence/personal testimony used here will be discussed according to how the evidence is used, but a summary of the basic practices and assumptions is set out in Appendix 1.[41] A descriptive pseudonymous list of the contributors to the project is given in Section 1 of the Bibliography.

REVIEW OF THE RESEARCH

Marilyn Boxer and Jean Quataert, courageously attempting an alternative women-centred periodisation of history, set 1890 as a key starting date in a new era for women – the beginning of state intervention in women's household and reproductive work.[42] From this date onwards, initially in a haphazard, ad hoc way, European governments monitored, supervised, and sometimes even recompensed, to varying degrees, women's work in childbearing, infant rearing and housekeeping. There were many reasons for the escalation of public concern about high infant mortality and the chronic poor health of many children and adults. The introduction, in most European countries, of compulsory schooling, brought children together and subjected them to the everyday observation of people who were often of a different social class. Schools were also places where infectious diseases and vermin could spread very quickly, so public education more or less demanded some form of health intervention. At the same time, imperialism and the nationalism of large and small nations believed the health of the 'race' to be of vital importance, for reasons of national security and national 'greatness'. Growing unemployment and the 'new' trade unionism of the unskilled forced attention upon the poor living conditions of many working-class people – living conditions that were believed to be conducive to bad health and degenerative diseases. Socialists and social democrats demanded that governments provide safety nets of some kind for these people in the form of social benefits. Catholic social action, given a boost by the papal encyclical of 1891, *Rerum Novarum*, also insisted on the need for social benefits.[43] The ongoing debate about the need to 'protect' women workers in certain kinds of industry, which led in some countries to sex-specific labour legislation, reinforced the belief that the health of the working classes depended to a great extent upon women's health.[44] Prominent women, who took part in all of these campaigns and debates, whether as a result of political (including feminist) conviction, philanthropic bent or religious activity – and sometimes all three together – used the vocabulary of women's difference from men. They stressed the importance of women's maternal function, actual and potential, to reinforce their arguments on behalf of working-class women and women in general, as well as to bolster their own authority as spokeswomen.[45] The safety net of social benefits as it has developed in most European countries over the past century or so, therefore, grew up not only out of nationalist concerns, social-democratic pressure and the economic and social conditions of the time, but also owed something to the specific intervention of women in all of these areas.

Some historians emphasise the controlling and supervisory impulses behind government and voluntary initiatives in the area of women's work and welfare, although they acknowledge that such initiatives boosted the power of female welfare workers. The term 'maternalism' is used to describe this kind of public life for women who were often, though not always, feminists. Others,[46] while they are often extremely critical of public health and welfare initiatives, lay more emphasis on the measurable progress made in public health and particularly in the health of mothers and children, as a result of all these developments. All agree that, for better or for worse, the dawn of the twentieth century saw a strengthening conviction that governments should play some part – remunerative, admonitory, educational – in women's household and reproductive work. The growth of mass electronic communications, rapidly rising literacy levels and a vigorous manufacturing and retail sector brought attention to bear upon the buying and spending habits of women of the house. The advertising of food, patent medicines and goods for the home produced, it is suggested, an anxious 'home-maker' devoted to her family's health and comfort.[47] High male unemployment, economic depression and social tensions caused resentment towards women in the paid workforce, and thus the identification of 'woman' with 'home' was opportunistically intensified. Furthermore, women doing household work were central to the state's identity, its definition of itself, and matters affecting these non-worker workers touched on crucial, and contested, questions about the state's relationship to individuals and to households – issues like health, housing, schooling and employment.

There was, therefore, in all countries, a public construction of women that gave priority to their household and familial function. When we try to look at the everyday working lives of these women in their own houses, therefore, we have to clean away several layers of the dust and grease of prescription and opinion. We cannot just discount such prescription, as it certainly had an impact on people's lives by way of government measures – benefits, legislation, prohibitions and subsidies, and it might also have influenced people's way of looking at the world in more subtle ways, prompting, for one thing, resistance and hostility to such authorities. The everyday realities of household work – how it was carried out, what it meant to women – is another story entirely, a story which some courageous historians have attempted to write, and whose existence has been an example to this historian.[48]

There are many difficulties with this kind of research. The first difficulty is that faced by most researchers into social history – the problem of sources. This is not really a problem at all. While there are some areas of experience that might remain disappointingly and tantalisingly beyond reach, the archive for the study of these workers is to be found in the censuses of population, the vital statistics and the various inquiries and commissions set up by government and in every oral or written personal testimony on the subject in this period. There is also an overwhelmingly large body of published opinion on these workers, and of exhortations and admonitions to them. The problem with sources is not so much uncovering them as trying not to limit oneself to one particular kind of source. Overcoming the first difficulty leads to the second: how do we interpret and evaluate all this data? It is easy enough to distinguish between, for example, the advice of a magazine and the practice of the woman in the house – we must also interrogate the observations of sympathetic contemporaries about these workers, and recognise that this applies not only to published sources but, in a slightly different way, to people's memories. The third difficulty lies with the historian, who must, as far as possible, keep her or his own opinions about what the subjects of the research should, or should not, have believed, valued and aspired to, out of the process. Joanna Bourke, while she acknowledges that the domestic rhetoric of social reformers owed something to upper and middle-class attempts to control the lives of poorer people, argues that Irish women, from the late nineteenth century, were consciously taking control of the domestic sphere:

> By the turn of the century, more women had decided that they were in a position to invest a higher proportion of their work-time within the household, and for many of these women, this was an investment worth making.[49]

Whatever the truth of this assertion, the very suggestion that women might have found working in the house meaningful and satisfying in itself, is anathema to many late-twentieth-century feminists. There are encouraging signs of change: the most recent sociological essay on Irish women devotes an entire chapter to women working full-time in the home, discussing the realities of their lives in their economic, social and emotional contexts.[50] However, at the time of writing, the National Women's Council prioritises the traditional second wave feminist aim of getting women out of the house to work full-time, by stating directly that the economic dependency of the full-time woman at home is undesirable.[51] We cannot evaluate women's household work in the past or in the present unless we at least question the assumption that work outside the house is necessarily, and of itself, empowering and liberating for women, and that work inside it is necessarily, and of itself, confining and limiting. Nor must we fall into the opposite assumption that the experiences of housework, motherhood and family maintenance are and were universally positive and their meanings shared by all women at all times and at all social levels. Ideas about women's innate nurturing and home-making capabilities have been given a boost by the 'cocooning' consumerism of the 1990s and can be called upon to service increasingly time-consuming male working lives, to say nothing of right-wing family models based around male authority and female submission.[52]

WOMEN OF THE HOUSE

A small but significant difficulty can be disposed of immediately: what will we call the subjects of this research?

One of Hanna Sheehy Skeffington's last public acts was to write a short article for the first issue of *The Irish Housewife*, the annual publication of the newly founded Irish Housewives' Association (of which Sheehy Skeffington's daughter-in-law Andrée was a founder member). Many feminists of Hanna's generation were involved in, or kindly disposed towards, this new organisation.[53] The article was published after Hanna Sheehy Skeffington's death in 1946. In it she applauded the young organisation, but lamented the use of the word 'housewife'; why, she asked, was there no word or phrase in English to compare with the French *menagère* or the Irish *bean a'tighe*?[54] This gave me some ideas about terminology. The women who were mainly responsible for the caring and life-maintaining tasks upon which sustainable human life depends were variously known throughout this period as housewives, home-makers, mothers, wives and sometimes, by those who believed that women's supposedly immanent domestic vocation should dominate everything else in their lives, simply as women. They were usually referred to in the singular, in ordinary conversation in Ireland, as 'the woman of the house'. With thanks to one of the founders of modern Irish feminism, this is the term I have decided to adopt and to use, with minor variations, throughout this study. 'Home-maker' is certainly an accurate working description of the kind of worker we are talking about – somebody whose work repeatedly made and remade the home. However, as a description it was too often used in this forty-year period, in Ireland as elsewhere, to refer to women who were seen to work only in their own households for it to be useful for our purposes. Besides, how often was it used by these workers to describe themselves? 'Housewife' has the same exclusivity about it, and furthermore, it was and is almost always used, rightly or wrongly, to refer to married women only, and usually to urban married women. Just as there were married women whose working lives incorporated work within the household and outside it, there were single and widowed women working outside the household and within it. My chosen term has the advantage of being both general and specific – a woman of the house is any woman who is seen to be in charge of certain functions within a house, those to do with the organisation and performance of its everyday nurturing and recreational functions. 'Woman of the house' also has the advantage of being a direct translation of the Irish *bean a'tighe*; *teach* (of which *tighe* is the genitive case) translates as house, building, shop, region, kingdom, family and line of descent;[55] it does not carry the same meaning as the English word 'home'. This is not to say that conceptions of 'home', as distinct from house or household, did not exist in Ireland at this time: it is merely to warn us against assuming that they were universally held, or that they are a constant throughout history.

It could be argued that the term 'woman of the house' is as value-laden as all the others because it might be taken to imply that every house has or should have a woman responsible for it, and because it carries connotations of authority and expertise, or subjugation and confinement, depending upon your point of view. Its use is not intended to convey either of these meanings in this work, but bearing in mind how difficult it is to find a description of these workers that is descriptive rather than prescriptive, this is about the best that can be done. Also, and very importantly, it is the closest to normal usage. The workers who are the focus of this study are women who had primary responsibility for the daily maintenance of a dwelling and of the lives of its members, through gathering and preparing food, organising the living space, looking after clothing, and often, physically and culturally, reproducing – bearing and rearing children – in addition to this work. Sometimes they also worked outside the household for pay, or performed income generating work within it. If they did so, such engagement does not seem to have cancelled out their responsibilities in the household, though it might have reordered priorities in that work. They were urban and rural, upper-middle class lower-middle class, and working class; as stated earlier, the emphasis in this study is on women who would have had to do most or all of their own household work unaided by paid domestic servants. The term 'woman of the house' in this study will be used mostly in the plural; the clumsy sounding phrase 'women of the house' will warn us against too readily accepting the collective identity assigned to these workers, not only by those who sought to confine and limit them, but also by those who tried to defend them, in the years covered by this study.

CAITRIONA CLEAR
Galway
March, 2000

CHAPTER ONE

'Engaged in Home Duties':
Statistical Background

The biggest and most important social change in independent Ireland up to the 1960s was arguably the acceleration and final completion of a population movement that had been happening gradually since the nineteenth century – the flight from agricultural occupations. Other related changes were the improvement in living standards on the land and in the towns and cities, the falling marriage rate and falling population, the rise in white-collar and shop employment, and an increased participation in second-level education. The occupational and other tables in the censuses of 1926, 1936, 1946 and 1961 provide us with a rough guide to some of these changes as they affected women's work, paid and unpaid.

PATTERNS OF PAID WORK 1921–61

A comprehensive, full-length survey and analysis of women's paid work in Ireland in the decades after independence has yet to be written, though brave attempts have been made to fill in some of the gaps in our knowledge.[1] The main source of numerical information about women's paid work are the occupational tables of the censuses of population of 1926, 1936, 1946 and 1961.[2] This source has its shortcomings. It does not take into account the part-time and informal, though crucial, earnings of women who might not have been officially designated as 'gainfully occupied'. Still, it gives us a broad outline of trends.

The number of adult Irish women (aged 12 and over in 1926, aged 14 and over thereafter) described by the census as 'gainfully occupied' fell by 16% between 1926 and 1961. At the earlier date, 30.5% of all adult females were 'gainfully occupied', at the later, 28.6%. (The equivalent figures for males were 83.3% and 82.3%). Table 1.1 illustrates this.

A cursory glance at the falling percentages of women gainfully occupied, and then at those engaged in home duties, could lead to the rapid-fire conclusion that a new post-colonial state, nervous about its identity, was ushering women out of paid work and back into the home. Cursory glances can be deceptive. The two sectors that saw the most dramatic decline over this forty-year period were domestic service and assisting relatives in agriculture. In agriculture the decline was underway, steadily and inexorably, from the 1890s, though it

Table 1.1: *The main female occupations and areas of work, according to the censuses of 1926, 1936, 1946 and 1961**

| | Total Working Population | | |
Year	Total AF	Total FGO	% FGO to AF
1926	1,127,077	343,894	30.5
1936	1,072,204	351,367	32.7
1946	1,081,362	334,862	30.9
1961	1,001,095	286,579	28.6

| | Agriculture (see also Table 1.2) | | |
Year	No.	% of FGO	% of AF
1926	121,957	35	10.8
1936	106,723	30	9.9
1946	81,526	24.3	7.5
1961	42,111	14.6	4.2

| | Domestic Service | | |
Year	No.	% of FGO	% of AF
1926	87,553	25.4	7.7
1936	86,102	24.4	7.6
1946	78,522	23.4	7.2
1961	39,971	13.9	1.3

| | Shop Service | | |
Year	No.	% of FGO	% of AF
1926	17,382	5	1.5
1936	19,879	5.6	1.8
1946	21,450	6.4	1.9
1961	24,670	8.6	2.4

| | Industry | | |
Year	No.	% of FGO	% of AF
1926	32,601	9.4	2.8
1936	36,532	10.3	3.4
1946	35,252	10.2	3.2
1961	43,496	15.1	4.3

* FGO = females gainfully occupied: AF = adult females (12+ in 1926, 14+ thereafter)

	White-Collar/Secretarial (includes post-office and telephonists)		
Year	No.	% of FGO	% of AF
1926	17,679	5.1	1.5
1936	25,425	7.2	2.3
1946	32,602	9.7	3.0
1961	48,442	16.9	4.8

	Professions		
Year	No.	% of FGO	% of AF
1926	29,505	8.5	2.6
1936	32,937	9.2	3.0
1946	36,806	10.9	3.4
1961	41,176	14.3	4.1

	Engaged in Home Duties	
Year	No.	% of AF
1926	550,147	48.8
1936	552,176	51.4
1946	589,461	54.5
1961	601,392	60.0

accelerated after 1946. The fall in the number of domestic servants was slower up to 1946, which made the subsequent rapid decline all the more noticeable. There were 72% fewer domestic servants in Ireland in 1961 than in 1926, and 65% fewer women working in agriculture; the decline in these areas was indeed dramatic. Assisting relatives were informal-contract (often unpaid) employees on their own family farms; domestic servants were employees in other people's houses. Far more dramatic than the rise in the proportion of adult women 'engaged in home duties', then, was the decline in the proportion of adult women for whom 'the home' – their own or somebody else's – was a site of gainful employment. Women were patently not being chased out of the work-force and 'back into' the 'home'; female assisting relatives were, on the contrary, leaving a workplace which was also a home, and domestic servants were leaving other people's houses to emigrate or to work in other sectors.

The largest single group of females gainfully occupied in 1926 and 1936 were assisting relatives on farms, and these also made up the majority of women in agriculture. (See Table 1.2.) Female farmers were in a minority and farmers' wives were not counted as assisting relatives but deemed to be 'engaged in home duties'. In 1946 and 1961 the proportion of female farmers to the total women in agriculture had risen, due to the fall in the number of assisting female relatives. There was always a slightly higher proportion of female farmers on smaller rather than larger farms. Most were widows and single women, running farms on their own, though, as will be seen below, there was a higher than average proportion of married women farmers in their own right in Mayo. In

1926 and 1936 the majority of female farmers were over 35, and about one third were over 70 in 1936. Farmers' daughters in 1926 and in 1936 were mostly under 44, and clustered in the 20–24 age-group in all sizes of farms. Other female relatives were predominantly single also, in these years most were aged between 34 and 54, spread fairly evenly throughout most sizes of farm. These patterns did not change for the agricultural workforce in 1946 – at this date 74% of female farmers were widows and 90% of all female farmers were over 45. What is striking – if predictable – about farmers' daughters in this year is that the smaller the farm, the younger the daughters seem to have been in leaving it. Other female relatives, mostly single, were far fewer in number and, where they existed, lived on farms of between 15 and 100 acres – farms that would have been able to feed them and unable to do without their assistance. In 1961 there was an intensification of these trends, when well over two-thirds of the women in agriculture were ageing, widowed farmers, and the less than a fifth who were daughters were almost all in their late teens and early twenties.

Throughout the period males made up the vast majority – never less than 70% – in all sectors of agriculture, whether as farmers, assisting offspring, other relatives or labourers. This obscures the farmer's wife or the sister or daughter who ran the house and the farmyard and who was usually heavily involved in the remunerative work of the farm. By counting these women as 'engaged in home duties' instead of as assisting relatives, the census was giving to understand that there was a substantial difference between the female assisting relative and the farm woman of the house.

The decline in numbers of domestic servants is the other contributory cause of the falling size of the female workforce over this period. For at least half of the period, however, about a quarter of Irish paid workers, and roughly 7% of the adult female population, performed household work in other people's houses. In the 1930s and 1940s, and even the 1950s, commentators of all socio-political persuasions insisted that domestic service was an ideal employment for girls and women of a certain class. The Commission on Youth Unemployment in 1951 reiterated the oft-uttered suggestion that proper training, wage-scales and other supports should be put into practice so as to encourage girls to take up this occupation, but girls and women at this stage were turning away from domestic service in droves.[3]

White-collar secretarial and office work (I have added telephonists and post-office clerks into this category) saw a striking increase (174%) in their number of women workers in the forty years after independence. (Refer to Table 1.1.) They comprised 5% of the paid female workforce in 1926 and 17% in 1961. They made up almost 5% of adult females at the latter date, compared to 1.5% in 1926, though it should be remembered that the adult female population of 1961 was notably smaller than that of 1926. Women in industrial work increased in number by over a third in this period, and these workers, mostly in textiles and apparel factories but some in bookbinding, food processing and light electrical manufacturing, made up 15% of the female workforce in 1961. Women

Table 1.2: *Adult females in agriculture according to census occupation data, 1926, 1936, 1946, 1961*

Year	Total Adult Females in Agriculture total AF in AG	% of total in AG
1926	121,957	22.5
1936	106,723	20.9
1946	81,526	17.6
1961	42,111	10.7

| | Farmers | | |
Year	as % total F	as % AF AG	as % FGO
1926	18	39.5	14
1936	17.9	43.5	13.2
1946	16.8	51.5	12.5
1961	13.8	69.1	10

| | Farmers' Daughters/Daughters in Law | | |
Year	as % total O	as % AF AG	as % FGO
1926	25.9	43.8	15.5
1936	23.4	42.1	12.7
1946	18.8	35.4	8.6
1961	10.4	19.7	2.9

| | Farmers Other Relatives | | |
Year	as % total OR	as % AF AG	as % FGO
1926	31	14.9	5.3
1936	26.7	13.3	4
1946	21	11.2	2.7
1961	14.5	12	1.4

F = farmers; AF AG = adult females in agriculture; O = offspring; OR = other relatives
FGO = females gainfully occupied

teachers, nurse-midwives, nuns and other professional workers increased by 39.5% from 1926 to 1961, making up almost as large a proportion of the female workforce as industrial workers in 1926, 1936, 1946 and 1961. Shop service was one of the most rapidly growing sectors for Irish women, yet, contrary to what might be expected, shop assistants were a much smaller group, proportionately, than white-collar office, professional and industrial workers throughout the period. This might be because in small businesses the domestic servant could have doubled as the shop assistant. The number of female shopkeepers and their proportion to the workforce remained fairly steady throughout the period, though it rose slightly between 1946 and 1961.

These forty years wrought great changes in women's working lives. Going by the census, the average working (i.e. gainfully occupied) woman in 1926 and 1936 was a single or widowed woman working on a farm (not, it must be repeated, a farmer's wife, who was not deemed to be gainfully occupied), or a domestic servant. In 1961 she was more likely to be a clerk-typist or a factory worker. The workforce of which the latter workers were representative was a smaller one in proportion to the total population. Emigration had taken away tens of thousands of girls and women over the previous decade and a half. Conclusions about gains made by Irish women in certain sectors of paid work must bear this fact firmly in mind. What must also be borne in mind is that 'home duties' or unpaid work were absorbing more and more women as these years went by. A true picture of women's work, paid and unpaid, can be made by looking at the proportion of women in each sector to the total adult female population. There are quite obvious problems with this – not all adult females were employed, or employable (there were invalids, people in institutions, students), but these problems are offset by one major advantage. Such an analysis allows us to take women 'engaged in home duties' into the reckoning and it shows us that they were, according to the census, the single largest 'group' in the adult female population in every date looked at. (See Table 1.1.) Female professional workers, despite the fact that their numbers rose steadily by nearly two-fifths over this period, still made up only 1.5% *more* of the adult female population in 1961 than they had in 1926, and even in the sector which experienced the most dramatic growth of all, white-collar secretarial work, the numbers never exceeded 5% of the total adult female population. Women described as 'engaged in home duties', on the other hand, made up 48.8% of this population in 1926, 51.4% in 1936, 54.5% in 1946 and 60% in 1961. Their numbers at all times exceeded the numbers of women in the paid workforce.

There are several ambiguities about the 'engaged in home duties' category of worker. The census is no doubt the best and the most complete numerical guide to a number of aspects of Irish life in this period, but this is not to say that it is a mirror of reality and of everyday life, nor is it a value-free source. Information given to the census was elicited, collected and presented by the census-takers, who had their own ideas of what constituted certain categories of worker. Nowhere is this more striking than in their categorisation of women whose principal occupation was the work of the household. In the first place, by having a category 'engaged in home duties', the census enumerators were giving to understand that such an avocation existed. Common sense and observation might have prompted this recognition; 'invisible' as women's household work often is, its existence cannot be denied. The designation 'engaged in home duties', however, and the decision to place this category in the 'not gainfully occupied' section of the occupational tables, suggest a certain way of looking at the work of women of the house. How are 'duties' different from 'work'? And, as said earlier, how was the formally unpaid, home-based work of a farmer's wife, for example, different from the formally unpaid, home-based work of that farmer's daughter or sister, who was counted as gainfully occupied? In homes where the wife and mother worked for gain outside the home, was nobody, then, engaged in home duties, even when no servants were employed? Conversely, in houses where a servant or servants relieved the woman of the house of what would have been seen as her responsibilities, did the latter consider herself to be engaged in home duties? If she had no paid work, she certainly seems to have done so, and so did the census. In sibling farm households, how was it determined whether sisters keeping house for whichever brother was the principal farmer were assisting relatives or engaged in home duties? Presumably respondents picked definitions of themselves and their function, or had it picked for them by whoever filled out the census form, but this and other designations were picked from a fixed menu provided by the information accompanying the census. Did 'engaged in home duties' adequately describe what women believed to be their work and function in the household? Other occupational descriptions give more of an idea of what the work entailed for women, except for agriculture but even here, workers are broken down into farm size, an acknowledgement that the work and income of a farm varied significantly according to the size of the holding. Common sense would seem to suggest to us that 'home duties' would vary widely according to socio–economic level and even geographical location, yet the census makes no attempt to classify people engaged in home duties along these lines.

The only way in which the census-takers acknowledge that 'engaged in home duties' is in some way a problematic job description is by stipulating, in the 1926 census and thereafter, that only in households of six members or more can more than one member be counted as thus engaged.[4] This meant that if the mother of a family was being helped, full-time, by her eldest daughter or sister (or son or brother!), the second person would not be counted by the census as 'engaged in home duties' unless there were more than six people living in the house. Though this was a praiseworthy attempt by the census-takers not to hide female unemployment inside the category of 'home duties', by making this stipulation at all the census was giving to understand that it had some idea of what constituted a 'weighting' of home duties. Care and maintenance of four other persons – young, old, sick, well, male, female; no distinction is made between stages and states of life that could have called for varying levels of care – is considered a valid workload for one person. This does not mean, however, that one person looking after eight persons is considered a double worker, or six persons, a worker and a half! And workload, as in the day-to-day performance of life-maintenance tasks, does not seem to have been a consideration. No recommendation is made about not counting domestic servants' employers as engaged in home duties.

Furthermore, because the census lists only primary occupations, people whose census-designated principal occupation was outside the home and who still had primary responsibility for the care, maintenance and, sometimes, the reproduction, of household members, are not included under this heading. All of this underlines the difficulty in arriving at a true numerical evaluation of women of the house in Ireland in this period. All of the married women could be taken, and a household responsibility inferred, but this would leave out single women who made up a substantial, if declining, number of women listed by the census as engaged in home duties.

WOMEN, WORK AND MARITAL STATUS

In 1926, 24% of all adult females engaged in home duties were single, in 1936 22%, in 1946 21.2%, in 1951 16.5% and in 1961 13.5% – from a quarter to just over an eighth in 35 years. (See Table 1.3).
The dramatic decline between 1946 and 1961 shows how rapidly emigration and migration absorbed women who had no prospect of paid work in Ireland. In 1926, the proportions of single women to the total women of the house grew larger with age. For example, 38.3% of all single women in the 45–54 age-group were engaged in home duties compared to 21% of those aged 18–19. This

Table 1.3: *Single women 'engaged in home duties': ages and marital status according to the censuses of 1926, 1936, 1946 and 1961.*[5]

Year	Women engaged in Home Duties		
	% M	% S	% W
1926	68	24	8
1936	69	22	9
1946	69.5	21.2	8.3
1961	73	13.5	13.5

Year	Single women Engaged in Home Duties as % of in Every Age Group				
Year	% TSW	12–13	14–15	16–17	18–19
1926	23	0.8	8.2	18.8	21
1936	24	–	7.9	14.4	16.8
1946	25	–	14.7	–	–
1961	20	–	–	5.7	–

Year	20–24	25–34	35–44	5–54	55–64	65+
1926	0.6	30.6	37.5	38.3	36.9	26.3
1946	19	26.5	35.7	38.6	40.6	35.4
1961	9.9	20.5	30.3	34.7	39.4	44.5

M = married S = single; W = widowed TSW = total single women implies that at the earliest census date, looking after a house (whether on one's own or with another person also thus engaged in a household of six or more members) was not necessarily something that single women did while they were biding their time waiting for a job or marriage. The 1936 figures are roughly similar: 22% of all women engaged in home duties are single, but 24% of all single women in the population are thus engaged, and again, the older (up to age 70) the age-cohort of single women, the greater the percentage of them who were engaged in home duties. The big change happened, as can be seen, between 1946 and 1961. There was a dramatic decline in the proportion of those engaged in home duties who were single by the latter date (13.5%), and a less dramatic decline in the proportion of single women in Ireland who were thus engaged (to 20%) which suggests that it was less normal for single women at this stage to tend house. A look at the ages shows that there is even more than ever a clustering of single women in the older age groups. The population of single women of the house was ageing and not being replaced. Furthermore, it was far more common in 1926 to find the daughter of a big family at home helping her mother, or rearing a family in the absence of her mother, than it was in 1961. The fact that the proportion of single women in their teens and early twenties keeping house were in noticeable decline as early as 1936 indicates the growing acceptability of, and opportunities for, paid work for young women. Falling maternal mortality in the 1940s, and improvements in mothers' health[6] so that fewer demands were made on single female relatives, were partly responsible for the long-term decline in the number of young and middle-aged single women running houses at all ages.

Never less than 90% of married women, however, were listed as engaged in home duties throughout the period, and as time went on, more married women were thus describing themselves, or being described thus by the census; 90.3% of all married women in 1926, rising to 93.7% in 1961, the major increase happening in the years 1946–61. (See Table 1.4).

Table 1.4: *Married Women Engaged in Home Duties:*
% of TMW in every age group

Year	% TMW	16–17	18–19	20–24	25–34
1926	90.3	76.6	77.8	85.9	90
1936	90.7	78	84.6	89.8	92.4
1946	90.7	——82.0——		86.2	91.8
1961	93.7	——89.8——		91.8	94.8

Year		35–44	45–54	55–64	65+
1926		88.9	83.9	75.2	40.4
1936		93	92.5	92.8	74.6
1946		93.5	92.7	92.4	77.3
1961		94.8	93.3	92.9	91.7

An analysis of the age-groups shows that while single women over 35 were more inclined than younger single women to be full-time in the home, the greatest proportion of married women in home duties were consistently in the 25–45 age-group – ages when women would have had young families, and thus have been unable to work outside the home. Right up to 1961, however, there were slightly fewer teenage married women and women over 65 or 70 engaged in home duties than those in between. This might suggest that teenage married women had to work because of particularly severe economic need, or that employers, if they were taking on married women at all, preferred younger women. These teenaged matrons were too young to have been teachers, farmers, shopkeepers, midwives or hold any of the professional or propertied livelihoods which had a comparatively high representation of married women. Although few in number, their existence is noteworthy because many of these young married women must have been mothers, and this suggests that motherhood as such did not necessarily stop women from working for wages. Youth unemployment was a serious social problem by the end of the 1940s; these women might have been working outside the home because of the the low pay or unemployment of teenage husbands.

What is even more striking is that the proportion of married women of all ages who were engaged in home duties rose, significantly, from 1926. The married woman who defined herself primarily as a worker of some sort was obviously not unknown in the 1920s, particularly among those aged from 35 up – an age when there were enough older children to help with housework, perhaps. The majority of women in gainful employment were either young, or single, or both. In 1936, 63% of saleswomen in shops, for example, were under 29, and most, in all age groups, were single which suggests that many shops operated an informal marriage bar. In 1951, the vast majority of telephonists, typists and factory workers were single and in their late teens and twenties. There was, in this year, a striking number of married teachers over 45. These were women who had qualified before the marriage bar came into effect on 1 January 1933 and to whom it did not apply. As far as the census is concerned, most married women worked for no wages in their own homes. Some of these women might well have had, as Mary Daly suggests,[7] informal sources of income and might not have chosen to reveal this on the census form. There was a small decline between 1926 and 1961 (roughly, the beginning and the end of the period) in the proportion of married women who were gainfully occupied, but a more noticeable drop of almost two percentage points in the female workforce who were married. See Tables 1.5a and 1.5b.

Married women made up such a small percentage of the female workforce throughout the period that it might seem pointless to be investigating them in depth, but closer examination shows significant change as far as married women's work was concerned. One of the most striking changes is the sharp decline between 1926 and 1946 in the percentage of white collar (i.e. office) women workers who were married. In 1926 in Ireland as a whole, 12.6% of these workers were married, and in some parts of the country – Mayo, Tipperary South,

Table 1.5a: *Percentage in Each Conjugal Category who are Gainfully Occupied, 1926, 1946, 1961*

| | Saorstat Éireann/Ireland | | |
	1926	1946	1961
Married	5.7	5	5
Widowed	42	32	26
Single	46	53	56.3

Table 1.5b: *Percentage of Gainfully Occupied Females in Each Conjugal Category, 1926, 1946, 1961*

| | Saorstat Éireann/Ireland | | |
	1926	1946	1961
Married	6.9	6.7	5
Widowed	16	13	15
Single	77	80.3	80

A closer look at the census reveals where these shifts, big and small, occurred. See Appendix III.

Leitrim, Kilkenny and Clare – married women made up between a fifth and a quarter of all women working in this field. Nor was this always connected to a low level of female employment; in Kilkenny, Tipperary South and Mayo, the percentage of adult females who were in paid work approximated to, or exceeded, the national figure. In six out of eight other counties where married women made up more than 17% of white-collar workers in this year, there was also high female employment. Dublin City, the four Dublin boroughs and Waterford City had particularly low representation of married women in white-collar work in this year, and though married women were more common in this work in the cities of Limerick and Cork, they were by no means as plentiful as they were in the counties cited above. By 1946 the devastating impact of the marriage bar can be seen. The impact of the marriage bar against women National teachers, effective on those who qualified from 1933 onwards, is not as immediately apparent, perhaps because a woman who qualified as a teacher in 1932 still had on average 40 years service ahead of her, married or single. Married women professionals – teachers, doctors, midwives, veterinary surgeons and other professions – were most likely to be found, in 1926, in parts of the country where female employment was in general, low, such as Kerry, Leitrim, Mayo, Roscommon and Cavan, and this pattern was even more marked in 1961. The cities had, throughout the period, the lowest percentage of women in the professions who were married. This was because of the concentration of institutional employment for medical professionals, the proliferation of nuns – by definition professional, and by definition single! – and the preference given in hiring teachers in Catholic and Protestant schools to single women. What is notable about the twenty years between 1926 and 1946 as far as married women in the professions were concerned, is not the slight decline in some regions, but the rise in the percentage of married women professionals in Limerick (City and County), Tipperary North and South, Cork (County), Clare, Wicklow, Meath, Longford, Galway, Waterford (City and County), Sligo, Donegal and Monaghan – over half the country, in terms of surface area if not population. This could be explained by the departure of many single midwives to Britain during and after the war, and a consequent greater representation of married women. By 1961 the effects of the marriage bar (revoked three years earlier though it was) on National teaching were apparent. Only in Donegal, Cavan and Leitrim in this year did the percentage of female professionals who were married reach or exceed – and then, not by much – 20%. All three counties were areas of low female employment in general. There was also a greater representation of married women in service work in 1961 than there had been in 1926 and 1946. By 1961, most service was institutional service – hotel or hospital work – and in the cities of Dublin, Dun Laoghaire, Cork and Waterford, married women seem to have picked up these job opportunities, such as they were. As far as industry was concerned, the majority of female workers were, as in all sectors, single, but Offaly, Clare, Tipperary South, Longford, Kilkenny, Tipperary North and Laois had between 19% (Offaly and Clare) and 14% (Laois) of their industrial female workers married in 1926. There is not necessarily a connection between a low level of female employment generally and a high representation of married women in this year. These were mainly workers in textiles, garments and leather, with some food processing in the cities. In the cities of Waterford and Limerick, 12% of the industrial female workforce were married in 1926. In the cities of Dublin and Cork, however, the percentages were five and six, respectively. The big surprise in 1926 was Donegal, where one would expect, going by other evidence, to find a high proportion of women, regardless of marital status, describing themselves as industrial workers: only 7% of female industrial workers in this county in 1926 were married. The fact that this rose to 10% in 1946 suggests that it was not the wives of seasonal migratory labourers who were describing themselves as workers in their own right in 1946, or the proportion would have been higher. The 1946 figure can be explained by the absence of husbands on temporary migration, but such absences would have been even more marked in 1926. Could it owe something to women's changing self-definition? By 1961 there is a definite connection between comparatively high percentages of married women in industry and low levels of female employment generally. Louth is one striking exception; here, 12% of female industrial workers were married in 1961, (the national figure was 7.6%) and 34% of adult women were employed, compared to 28.6% nationally.

Married women who were farmers and shopkeepers might be seen as operating independently of economic and social change, insofar as their existence depended to a large extent upon inheritance from parents or relatives. This might be true of widows, but married women defining themselves as businesswomen must have had husbands in some other line of work. In the west, for example, it was quite common for inheriting women to work the small farm while their husbands worked for wages locally or away from home, and this would account for the 19% of all women farmers who were married in Mayo in 1946 (the national figure was 6.5%). In 1961, all the Leinster counties bar Louth, and Clare, Limerick, Tipperary North and South, Waterford, and Galway and Mayo saw a rise in the percentage of female farmers who were married. These were not marginal agricultural areas; in parts of the country characterised by smaller farms (all the Connacht counties except Galway and Mayo and the three Ulster counties), there was a fall in the percentage of married women who were farmers. This could be explained by the emigration of the 1950s and the abandonment of near-subsistence farming. The rise in the more prosperous areas could indicate that more farms were being passed on to daughters, or that women who inherited farms were becoming loth to sign them over to their husbands – perhaps because those husbands had work elsewhere or perhaps because of increased self-confidence. The same could, perhaps, be said of shopkeepers: the percentage of female shopkeepers who were married rose everywhere except Carlow, Dun Laoghaire, Longford, Clare and Tipperary North, over this period.

Married women's work changed over these decades. The national figures are very heavily influenced by the fact that Dublin City contains between a quarter and a third of the population. This reminds us that most employment for women was destined for single women and was located in urban areas. The married woman worker in the cities was most often in low-paid, often freelance or casual service work. Outside the cities, married women workers were more likely to present as independent, authoritative figures; the midwife, teacher, farmer and shopkeeper were important figures (regardless of farm or shop size) in the rural or small town communities they served, as was the dressmaker, an industrial worker.

This survey is introductory only. Further research into patterns of women's work, whether married, single or widowed, will have to take a regional approach and evaluate information from the census in the light of local economies, customs and demographic patterns.

CONCLUSION

In one sense, the census tells us nothing we do not already 'know' about women's work in Ireland in the first four decades of independence. We 'know' that the numbers, and proportions, of adult women in paid work fell significantly; we 'know' that the largest single 'group' of women was made up at all times of those who were engaged in home duties. While marriage bars certainly had an impact on the employment of middle-class women, the real decline in women's remunerative work happened because of the long-term, gradual departure of girls and women from familial agricultural work, and the first slight, then accelerated, rejection by women of domestic service. Together, these occupations accounted for over 60% of women gainfully occupied in

1926, and for almost 23% in 1961. Work in industry, shop service, white-collar work and the professions absorbed a greater percentage of the female workforce by default, but the workforce was a smaller one. Those leaving the land and domestic service might well have been setting up houses of their own; they are more likely to have had at least an interval of better-paid work before they did so. However, this work was more likely to be in Britain than in Ireland, a fact which the shrinking female workforce makes clear.

Almost as important as the information that the census gives us, however, is the way it packages this information. By describing this work as 'duties' and including those who performed it under the 'not gainfully occupied' heading along with students, invalids, retired people, pensioners and the unemployed, and by giving it a certain 'weighting', the census was, effectively, expressing an opinion about the work. It was only one of many opinions expressed over these years, and the next three chapters will attempt to discuss some of the other opinions, attitudes and perspectives.

A Specialised Vocation? Perceptions of Women, Domesticity and Public Life 1923–43

In particular the state recognises that by her life within the home, woman gives to the State a support without which the common good cannot be achieved.

Article 41.2, Bunreacht na hEireann, 1937

I think that you ought not to put forward being a woman as a specialised vocation.

Edward Coyne, SJ, to women's organisations giving evidence to the Commission on Vocational Organisation, 1940[1]

INTRODUCTION

The year 1923 saw the fragile beginnings of peace and a return to normal life; 1943 saw the Oireachtas agreeing to introduce children's allowances, and a new tone emerging in public discussions about women of the house and their relationship to political life and employment. As already mentioned in the Introduction, historians and others have paid most attention to the kind of public construction of the 'domestic woman' which they see as having been embodied in the 1937 Constitution and lamented by some bishops in their Lenten pastorals in the 1930s. There were, however, a number of themes in writing about women, the house and public life in these twenty years, and there were also feminist organisations and women's organisations that addressed this issue. The utterances of some bishops and some statesmen which have been represented for us as typical of the era, took place against this background of debate – a debate when mainly women, but also some men, in public life, tried to redefine women's relationship to both the domestic and the political.

'CAN IRISH GIRLS COOK?' THE GOAL OF DOMESTIC AND MATERNAL COMPETENCE

'Of late the energies of the young women of Ireland have been absorbed in politics,' wrote Katharine Tynan in *The Voice of Ireland* (1924), a showcase publication of the new regime with articles on history, landscape, literature, art and other aspects of contemporary Ireland. Tynan admitted that there was room for women in politics, but believed that over-involvement by women in politics in recent years had led to neglect of 'sweeter and more pressing matters'. These were the care of the household and what Tynan saw as necessary improvements there. She lamented what she saw to be the poor standards of housekeeping in Ireland, wondering how much drinking in Ireland was due to 'the cold hearth and the miserable feeding at home'. She called for Irish women to learn to love housecraft and other Irish women to set about teaching it.[2] Government and voluntary bodies had been encouraging such 'improvement' for almost thirty years at this stage. The Department of Agriculture and Technical Instruction (1898), and before that the Congested Districts Board (1891), the Women's National Health Association (1907) and the United Irishwomen (1911), aimed to provide lower-middle class, working-class, small farming and labouring women, urban and rural, with information and advice on hygiene and nutrition, so as to improve living conditions of rural life and to thereby stem emigration and migration. *The Irish Homestead*, George Russell's journal which was the unofficial organ of the broad based movement towards agricultural reform and social improvement in the early twentieth century, regularly lamented the 'monotony' of the tea, bread, potatoes, bacon and cabbage diet of the country people, and recommended more variety.[3]

Tynan's remarks about the neglect by women in nationalist politics of matters to do with the 'improvement' of hearth and home were grounded in reality. Women in nationalist, labour and suffrage political movements had paid little, if any, attention to women's work in the household, concentrating on the attainment of national independence and of civil equality with men. The ideal of domestic improvement seems to have been associated with the constructive unionism of the earlier period, at least as far as politics and public life were concerned. The Irish Countrywomen's Association, successor to the United Irishwomen, rebutted with amusement this impression of their association as run by 'ladies of the manor', or as Myles na Gopaleen called them, 'tweedy old dears with ascendancy notions'.[4]

In the spring of 1938 a hapless clergyman, Canon Davis from Galway, remarked in print that the 'girls' he was employing as servants were unable to cook anything other than very basic dishes. The controversy that followed these inflammatory remarks burned steadily for at least four weeks in the 'Our Readers Are Writing' letters column in the *Irish Independent*, and in news columns as well. (Some of the letters were very informative about diet and will be referred to again in the section on women's own experiences.) What concerns us at this point is the flood of opinions, most of them signed by nicknames or initials.

Most of the letters were literate, pithy and vigorously expressed:

> Sir – May I as a cook of 17 years' experience say a few words in defence of Irishwomen. How dare our obviously ignorant critics rant in such a fashion about the women who are responsible for the happiest homes in the world, let them say what they like about hotel cooks, but let our women alone. Almost every woman of my acquaintance is quite a good cook of the food she can afford.[5]

This reference to women being able to cook the food they could afford was a common one:

> Considering the dreadful home life of most Irish country women, they do splendidly for their men and their families.

So wrote Rose Green from Cavan, who was not afraid to sign her name.[6] 'A Sympathiser with our Girl Cooks' remarked that 'our learned and overfed folks' could not expect complicated French cooking from a girl who came from 'a respectable cottage home', and stated that:

> If those girls got the education, which is their legal right, all this mud-throwing would not disgrace our papers.[7]

'Cook-General' pointed out that it was difficult to do complicated dishes on the open fire, and that the 'country housewife' who has to cook for animals as well as family was hardworked:

> . . . and as she is often only too thankful for the bare necessities of life, she has neither the inclination nor the time for thinking out new dishes.[8]

E. Carter also believed that the criticism of Irish cooks was 'futile and unfair' – there should be schools set up to train girls as cooks and in housework.[9] Mrs Kate Rohan, a returned exile, agreed, accepting that diet had to change to introduce more healthy variety, but insisting that Irish 'colleens' could learn as quickly as anybody how to do this.[10] Kathleen Maguire née Ferguson, an author of several books on cooking and housekeeping in the early years of the century and a pioneer of cookery teaching in Ireland, however, did little to banish the image that some might have had of cookery instruction as linked with Unionism when she recommended that a certain other subject be sacrificed for compulsory domestic science:

> Make domestic science compulsory for girls, and leave out compulsory Irish, and you will have a very different country, though to say this would be resented.[11]

'Disgusted' had little faith in modern ways, in education or in Irish women's financial skills:

> How many can properly bake the good old soda cake?
> How many can serve up a properly prepared and cooked dinner of bacon and cabbage? Not many, except in the country districts, where the women still are women.
> Three ladies whom I know recently attended a full course of cookery lessons and brought home all the gossip of the town . . . How many girls

contemplating marriage ever work out on paper beforehand their weekly budget? Not many. The magic tin-opener seems to be the 'hope' of many of them.[12]

'L.C' was even more blunt:

> The average housewife in the homes of farmers and workingmen does not cook. She does not even try to, and worse still, she does not even serve or prepare food reasonably cleanly.[13]

Though this correspondence was originally about servants, its terms rapidly extended to all Irish women. It is useful because it contains all the period's evaluations of the skills of Irish women of the house – that they were ignorant, dirty and wasteful; that they were merely ignorant, and that the responsibility for remedying this ignorance did not lie with them; that poverty and bad conditions, not ignorance, were responsible for their shortcomings; that some of the old ways were good, and some of the new; that Irish women of the house should not be criticised at all. 'Disgusted', above, is expressing a minority viewpoint when he or she looks back to the old ways as best, identifies urbanisation, modern life (tin-openers) and laziness as the reasons for bad cooking and deplores domestic education as a waste of time. Her or his comments on contemporary women of the house are like the acid ones proffered by Máire Ní Néill, a retired Wexford schoolteacher, to the Folklore Commission in 1940, as summed up in her crisp remark: 'God sends the food but the devil sends the cooks.'[14] There was such an association of modernity with desertion of household skills that the high take-up by office workers, factory workers, 'stay-at-home girls' and others of domestic economy evening classes run by the Dublin Vocational Education authority in 1931 was considered newsworthy by the *Irish Press*. An official involved was quoted as saying: 'Contrary to the general opinion about girls today, the girls really like the classes in domestic economy.'[15] Clancy notes that Kathleen Browne, TD, in the 1920s, believed that modern girls were woefully unprepared for marriage. Browne recalled the days when being able to make a husband's shirt was one of the qualifications for that state.[16]

The voices calling for greater advice and guidance for the woman of the house were legion. Novelist and trade unionist Annie M.P. Smithson who was a public health nurse in Dublin's inner city in the 1910s and 1920s, blended understanding of the terrible conditions under which slum-dwelling mothers laboured, with horror at their ignorance:

> They (the 'little ones') are handicapped from birth; their mothers are over-worked and under-nourished . . . They suffer too, more than they need, through the ignorance of their parents – the want of knowledge in all that pertains . . . to motherhood, is simply appalling among our poorer classes. With the best intentions in the world, they go the wrong way entirely in the case of their children. 'Child Welfare' and all that it means

– proper feeding and clothing, sunshine and fresh air, cleanliness, discipline and training – all this is hard to teach to the average woman in our tenements.

Smithson goes on to lament the way children of barely one year get 'the run of the table, same as ourselves', are left in the care of children barely older than themselves, and fed ice-cream and sherbet off barrows in summertime. The remedy is to get mothers to attend Baby Clubs, where the mothers can also consult the doctors and nurses about their own health.[17] In the conference between public health and public assistance authorities in 1930, the emphasis was on mothers being educated to take responsibility for their children's health. 'The mothers of the state are the most potent factors for good in the nation's health,' remarked Dr H. O'Neill from Westmeath, and many other doctors agreed with him. Dr J. MacCormack from Monaghan, for example, urged that mothers should be encouraged to attend school lectures on health where there would be 'little headlines' written on the board for them about 'cleanliness, rest, sunlight, fresh air, proper diet'.[18]

The woman of the house was seen to need guidance in more than health matters, however. Brigid Redmond, Fine Gael TD, echoed Katharine Tynan's devastating criticism of Irish women when she opined in 1937 that:

> The daily wastage of food on many small holdings resulting from women's ignorance of household management would maintain many a starving family in comparative comfort.

Redmond went on to provide information on the Irish Countrywomen's Association, which she hoped would be instrumental in a reorganisation of rural household economies. Redmond, as we shall see in the next chapter, was one of those TDs who supported payment of children's allowances being made to the mother in 1943–4, but support for the domestic empowerment of women does not stop her stating that 'very few [countrywomen] know their jobs or how to make the most of their resources'. For this she blames the ready availability of ready-made goods and 'a wrong sense of values, derived from highly urbanised, industrialised communities'.[19] Life-long feminist and academic Mary Hayden made a similar point about urban working-class women in 1940:

> The workman's wife buys her loaf from the baker; treats her family (unfortunately) to dinners the chief ingredients of which have been extracted from cans, smears her children's bread with bought jam.

Hayden used this, which she characterises as a vastly reduced workload for the average woman of the house ('unless she has small children, she has not nearly enough to do' [!]) as an argument for getting women to participate more in public life, but this does not detract from her judgmental tone, or her right to judge in the first place.[20] When Dr James Deeny, later Chief Medical Officer in

Ireland, but at that stage a GP in Lurgan, Co. Armagh, read a paper in Dublin on the (generally bad) state of health of 205 married women mill workers in Lurgan, he provoked plenty of comment from the floor about women's health and family subsistence in the Republic of Ireland.[21] In the discussion following, Dr H. Kennedy (who had already contributed to the 1930 conference on public health), blamed what he believed to be the white-bread-and-tea staple diet of urban people for poor health, and urged a return to the traditional milk and potatoes diet of working-class rural Ireland.[22] Miss Amy Lisney, of the well-known auctioneering family, said that she would like to 'state the case of' the working-man's wife, who had no outlet outside the house, no club, no school, nobody to organise hers. In effect:

> Poverty was not altogether her fault. It was brought about by a lot of things like bad housing, and was a condition local authorities must now study. It was not either the lack of necessary housing. She had known houses side by side where the incomes were the same, £2.10s a week. In one case the house was untidy, the children ill and husband irregular in his work. Next door they seemed to have more and the house was clean and tidy. That shows that one must educate this huge class of women and teach them how to manage.[23]

Dr Deeny, however, had just shown in his paper on Lurgan women that it was often those who seemed to be doing well materially who were anaemic and sickly, the stress of 'managing' having taken such a toll of their health. Dr Deeny's survey is not immediately relevant to the subject under discussion, taking place as it did not only under a different jurisdiction, but in the very different conditions of the historically industrialised north-east. However, everything Deeny did was of huge relevance to independent Ireland, because he became the Chief Medical Officer in the early 1940s, and his experiences in the north no less than in the country in general informed his policies, as his autobiography shows. In any case, his Lurgan survey was one of a number of medico-social enquiries into women's health in this period which highlighted the poor health of working-class mothers and drew attention to the pressures on them. Two doctors who carried out a survey of fifty pregnant wives of unemployed men in Dublin's Rotunda hospital in 1939, found that only 6% of these women were eating enough protein, only 8% had adequate calorie intake, and all were anaemic.[24] As far as 'managing' was concerned, Charles Clancy-Gore's survey of expenditure and family budgeting on a local authority housing estate in Dublin in 1943 concluded that it was beyond the capacity of the average housewife to spend money in the manner recommended by experts. This was because she was faced with over-priced local shops, inadequate storage space for food, lack of transport and other obstacles to buying wisely and in bulk, not least of which was the scarcity of money. Clancy-Gore had the figures and the tables to prove what other observers over the previous twenty years had grasped from observation or intuition.[25] Fr T.F. Ryan SJ reminded the *Capuchin Annual* readers as early as 1930 that poor women were doing more than their best:

THE IRISH PRESS, MONDAY, SEPTEMBER 14, 1931

SOME IRISH MOTHERS AND THEIR CHILDREN by DOROTHY MACARDLE

IRISHMEN are said to be sentimental about their mothers, and no wonder. No wonder at all in a man who grew up in a small, struggling home, and who, looking back, must realise what a miracle of patience and courage was the mother who kept the grace of God about her children in such a pitiless world.

Given a natural chance at all, the Irish mother will do that. You will see Irish children ragged and barefoot, thin-faced and hungry, but it is seldom that you will find in Ireland a cowed or dispirited child. The youngsters in the meanest streets have a gaiety that can turn a broken box into an Alfa Romeo, a pile of rubble into a playing-field, a heap of clay into a kingdom of delight. And their mothers are managing, sometimes on twelve shillings a week.

It was in North Cumberland Street that I saw joyous games being played in a "derelict site" loaded with rubbish and stones. The children might have been playing on green grass under trees, had Dubliners cared enough. It was a neighbouring streets that I saw homes which, one would imagine, should break the heart of even the bravest mother and the spirit and health of even the sturdiest child.

"WE ARE SEVEN."

Mrs. Doherty is fortunate. She has two rooms and they receive one pound a week of Relief. There are seven children. Her husband has been out of work a long time, and the eldest girl is out of work now, but there is a son who sells papers, when a few shillings can be spared to buy "stock" with, and makes a profit of fourpence a dozen on sales; there is a girl who goes to tin slob-lands and finds cinders and sticks.

Their room is at the top of the house and though it is hard on the children to climb up the steep stairs with water, and down again with the bucket to empty it, it is good to have air. Tidy children, the seven of them must be. It is a pleasure, after mounting the filthy broken staircase, to open their door and see boards scrubbed as clean and bed-covers as snowy, as boards and bed-covers can be. But Mrs. Doherty's face is as white as her sheets.

THE ONE-ROOM HOUSE.

For top floor-back rooms the rent here is five shillings or more. In a single room that costs five shillings a week, Mrs Farrell lives with her husband, their bay, and a boy aged two. By selling papers her husband earns ten or twelve shillings a week. When the rent is paid and the Burial Society subscription, they have, at best, six shillings a week between the four of them for clothing, fuel and food. The baby looked sickly, but the Child Welfare Association was giving them milk for it and it may live. It is only the fittest who survive, probably, to play games among the rubble and stones.

The woman who lives in the basement next door had had ten children, she told me, but some of them were still-born and others died. Four, the oldest six years old, are living with the mother and father in that cellar like room. The rent is four and six pence a week. Her husband, she boasted, "has lovely hands;" he does paper-handling when he can get orders, but there have been none for a . . . . marble mantlepiece, and there are two beds, a table and some boxes—nothing else. The other things are in pawn. She is dark, thin woman, with a face like Leonardo's Madonna; her health is breaking down.

Her husband has been unemployed for so long that his unemployment benefit is exhausted. They have seven-teen and six pence in Relief money. There is three shillings rent to pay. Five children already lived in that room with them, and a few weeks ago, in that room, a sixth was born. They were to be evicted that week, but were granted a respite.

It will be hard for them to find a cheaper room. Mrs Boyle could manage better with the relief money, pay rent, and keep the place cleaner, but that she feels so weak still, and the children are all so young.

ONE SHILLING A DAY.

There is a widow in another part of the city who has two little boys. They are doing well at school now, are ambitious, and full of great plans about the things they will buy for their mammy when they are big. She is to have breakfast in bed every morning and bottles of scent. Quite how well she has earned it, they can never know.

She goes out daily to do house-work . . . ment fund and no union. Young girls go out and do all the work of a house and the family washing for three shillings a week. She can mend, do upholstery and painting, clean, wash and cook, and has a hoard of curious

knowledge applicable to every domestic crisis. She has been offered a shilling a day.

STORES FOR THE WEEK

When Billy, the younger boy, was born, she nursed him for a year, and during that year she drew relief money; twelve and sixpence a week. Then she gave up the relief, put the children in the Nursery every day, and went out to work, and presently was earning the same amount. She could have managed very well on that but for the high rents.

Getting her money on Friday she would lay in stores for the week; two pounds of sugar, half a pound each of butter and margarine, which she mixed, Jam and tea; a stone of potatoes; coal. These, with gas for light, and milk and a loaf every day, rest about eight and fivepence a week.

With the rest she would get, one day, rice; another, an egg on an onion to mix with mashed potatoes; or a scrap of lap of mutton for fourpence-halfpenny, or three pennyworth of . . . . Domestic workers have no unemploy-liver to make a stew. They could have had food enough to keep well on, the three of them, and fuel, for the ten shillings a week; and she could make clothes for them all out of old garments given her by her employer.

THE PROBLEM OF RENT,

There remained the problem of rent. For a room in any of the respectable streets six or seven shillings was asked. In the back streets you would get a room for four or even three shillings, but "No Children Taken" was the

answer at door after door. It was only in a place hard to let because it was so dilapidated that she get in, for three shillings, with two little boys.

I visited them in a room in Charlemont Street one winter, when Joey was ill. The fire could not be kept burning because the grate was broken: the east wind could not be kept out because the window did not shut; chill blasts crawled over the rotten flooring; the ceiling sagged dangerously over the beds; the wall-paper was peeling and stained with damp. And I saw them in summer, when the mother was ill, in a back kitchen—a dark, airless room with a stone floor, where beetles swarmed and she thought that she heard rats.

She was too ill to work. She had to be taken to hospital for an operation. We got the children into a Convalescent Home.

BETWEEN LIFE AND DEATH.

The mother lay between life and death at the time when we heard that, owing to influenza, the Convalescent Home had been evacuated. It was in the Union that we found there—two fright-ened, lonely, lost little boys. Had we not been able to keep that news from her, I think she would have died. But she lived; paid the rent; saved the home.

To keep the home together, if it is only a cellar, to "make out somehow." keep out of the Union—that is the resolve that sends men every day for years to the Labour Exchanges and sends women searching for the shop . . .

HAPPY IN SPITE OF ALL.—Children at play in a Dublin tenement street.

2. Some Irish Mothers and Their Children. *Irish Press* September 14, 1931. This article is typical of a kind of crusading social journalism evident in the first year or so of the *Irish Press*, the paper owned by Eamon de Valera. Dorothy Macardle, prominent Republican historian was a keen de Valera supporter who was not afraid to criticise him for his attitude to women in the 1937 Constitution. This article shows that her feminism, like that of most feminists in Ireland at this time, was rooted in concern for the material conditions of life for working-class women.

It is a woman's task to keep the home clean and to keep a tenement room in a constant state of cleanliness requires greater physical endurance and more dogged perseverance on the part of a woman than almost any other task that could be imposed upon her. How unreasonable it is that we should expect cleanliness from all.

He also drew attention to the interdependent nature of neighbourly relationships: 'It is no unusual thing for a poor woman to give literally every penny she has to another who is momentarily worse off'.[26] Dorothy Macardle, writing in the early 1930s, described conditions that 'should break the heart of even the bravest mother and the spirit and health of even the sturdiest child'. One woman, whose husband and eldest daughter were a long time unemployed, lived with seven children in two rooms on £1 a week relief, and whatever her son made selling papers (4d per dozen sold). She was a good housekeeper and her place was spotless, but, Macardle noted: ' [her] face is as white as her sheets'.[27]

The answer, some women's organisations believed, was to get women organised in some way to put pressure on local and national government. It was this belief that united Catholic and Protestant women in a variety of organisations in the 1930s, 1940s and 1950s. In order to understand not only the values of these organisations, but reactions to them, it is necessary to look first of all at other perceptions of women, work and the home in these years.

MAINLY CATHOLIC PERSPECTIVES ON FEMINISM, WOMEN'S WORK AND THE HOME

Irish women, claimed Alice Curtayne in 1933 in a talk entitled 'The Renaissance of Woman', had been granted equal citizenship in 1922 'without any appearance of concession and without their having had to lift a finger to secure it'. This ignorance of the Irish suffrage movement is unusual in a journalist and novelist born in Ireland in 1901. Curtayne acknowledged that there had been a struggle for the female franchise in Britain and in America; she characterised this as 'the story of our time that everyone knows'. Her lecture was not so much an attack on what she called 'secular feminism', as an insistence that much of modern feminism was only a fulfilment of Catholic and Irish traditional respect for women legally, spiritually and vocationally. She admired the American suffrage movement in particular for its audacity and its tenacity, but she questioned the value of identical educational programmes for males and females, and in common with many of her contemporaries, deplored the effect of urban life and office work on young women's health and welfare.[28]

Less than ten years earlier, 'Eithne', writing on feminism in *The Irish Monthly*, showed what might have been some familiarity with, and hostility towards, the home-grown feminist movement. In 1925, in the second of a series of articles entitled 'Where Are You Going To My Pretty Maid?', she distinguished between two varieties of feminism – revolutionary feminism and Christian feminism.

'Eithne' characterised the former as advocating abolition of every social distinction between the sexes, while Christian feminism asked only for 'the suppression of certain social and legal abuses which paralyse women's action in certain well-defined circumstances'. Christian feminists had succeeded, she argued, in nearly all their aims, but the revolutionary feminist remained:

> She speeches in thoroughfares, she wrangles in newspapers, she flings her fool arguments into Sunday journals, plays and novels. She is always ready to go shouting to jail – a martyr to the cause![29]

The only Irish women going to prison for political causes in the 1920s who immediately spring to mind are Republican women who, while they might have been feminists, were not being imprisoned for feminist causes. Was 'Eithne' referring to the militant Irish suffragists who had been sent to prison at the high point of the suffrage agitation before 1914? Perhaps, but significantly enough, 'Eithne' was equally emphatic about her other adversaries, those she called anti-feminists:

> 'Woman's sphere is the home,' says the anti-feminist dogmatically. Nonsense. Wherever infancy has to be mothered, pain tended, pity and sympathy poured out, sorrow lightened, hungry hearts appeased, hope brought to the dejected, the pillow of death smoothed – there woman is 'at home', there is her sphere.[30]

This is the 'equality in difference' argument, virtually the same as that which was used by many of the first wave feminists who sought to justify women's involvement in public life on the grounds of their particular expertise in matters of private and public morality.[31] The 'Where Are You Going To . . .' series dealt for the most part with perennial matters of advice to girls and young women – about friendships with the opposite sex, working and living in lodgings, modesty in dress, amusements.[32] It is striking to see, in the midst of all this, the question of women's function in public life addressed, just as it is significant that Curtayne's lecture was published by the Anthonian Press, a Catholic company, with an imprimatur by the Bishop of Ferns.

Maryann Valiulis takes her evidence for 'the ecclesiastical construction of the ideal Irish woman', (domestic, subservient and out of public life) mainly from Lenten pastoral letters,[33] claiming: 'The prelates (sic) agreed that women should be denied access to the public arena'.[34] Examination of a variety of Catholic writers over these decades, however, shows that no one ideal Catholic woman existed, and that there was strong support from many Catholic writers for women's involvement in public life and their participation in the workforce. Those who feared that women's political and economic emancipation would come to no good – and they never doubted that this emancipation was a reality – were always careful to utter support for emancipation in some of its forms. This support seems to have been motivated by a faith in the transforming power of women in politics. The *Catholic Bulletin* in 1923, commenting on falling population and rising 'individualism' in France, suggested that the female franchise, if and when it was introduced there, would go a long way toward tempering the trend toward 'individualism' and 'paganism'.[35] The widely read *Irish Messenger of the Sacred Heart*, produced by the Society of Jesus, which had probably the widest readership of any periodical in Ireland by the 1930s, had a similar wariness about women's involvement in careers and public life in 1930. Note, however, the writer's care not to condemn such advances:

> During recent years, in many countries, notably in England, there has been a movement for what is called the 'emancipation' of women. As a result of the persevering efforts of a resolute group, women have secured access to careers and positions that were hitherto closed to them, and they now vote on an equality with men. But it is a lamentable fact that during all these same years there has existed also a change in another direction, a gradual lessening of respect for the sanctity of marriage which leads directly to the degradation of women. 'Women have acquired the vote and have discarded the vow' is the way in which the situation has been summed up by a Protestant preacher in England.

The editorial went on to hail Jesus Christ as the prime emancipator of women (a common theme in Christian writing about women), to point to unstable marriages and childlessness as results of more recent attempts at their emancipation. Predictably enough, he also hit at the 'excessive cult of pleasure', a ready target always in those days of a bewildering variety and novelty of accessible mass entertainment.[36] But the use of the words 'persevering' and 'resolute' to describe feminists suggests a certain sympathy with, and admiration for, them; there were plenty of negative terms he could have used instead. In 1937 the *Irish Messenger of the Sacred Heart*, in the person of Fr Stephen J. Brown, SJ came back again to the question of women's emancipation and its links with rampant materialism. This time employment was treated much more specifically:

> But the modern world that would repudiate in horror the name of Communism is scarcely better [than Communist Russia]. It sneers at marriage . . . it would 'emancipate' women from the household and the care of children, it scoffs at authority in family life . . . And even when you have a good-living Christian family there are modern conditions not a few that tell against home life. There are the employments of mothers and daughters, keeping them, no less than the men, absent from home.[37]

Fr Brown believed that the employment outside the home of daughters was also interfering with home life, but note his suggestion that men being kept away from the home was a necessary evil too – his ideal was the one often promoted in the pages of the 1930s *Messenger* of the rural family working the land together. Maire MacGeehin (who also called herself Máire NicAodháin), later a member of the

Commission on Vocational Organisation, and a translator of childrens' books, summed up this attitude in 1937. Commenting that the Irish were 'naturally God-loving and God-fearing because of their close communion with nature which is the mirror of God', she used the metaphor of invasion and subjugation to describe the move from the country to the towns, and emigration:

> We cannot close our eyes to the fact, however, that never before was the danger so imminent of the peaceful penetration of ideas foreign to our creed and our traditions . . . If our race withstood the onslaughts of the invader for over 700 years it was because each generation renewed its vigour in the soil of Ireland. Now a more wily invader is luring our people from their allegiance to the soil and to their traditions, and it is the onslaughts of this invader that we of the Catholic Action movement are out to withstand.[38]

This sentiment links MacGeehin, who supported women in public life (as we shall see when looking at her addendum to the CVO report) and took a practical interest in the day-to-day lives and working conditions of women of the house, with those who were more pessimistic about women's involvement in politics and the workplace. Such links were common.

Nor was harking back to a lost or mythical past an inevitable element of discourse about women in Ireland in this twenty-year period. Some Lenten pastorals might have told parents to lay the lash across the backs of disobedient daughters, but others reflected contemporary childcare advice when they urged parents not to be too aloof or austere with their children. Parents were reminded in the pastoral letter of Dr Dignan, bishop of Clonfert, in 1934, published in the *Connacht Tribune*, that:

> A good education for a girl is better than a dowry, and parents ought to give the best education possible to their daughters as well as to their boys.

He went on to recommend that because girls' 'natural place' was in the home, mothers should instruct them in housekeeping, but this was not to be the sum total of their education.[39] Throughout this period, nobody – neither feminists, anti-feminists or neutrals – dissented from the view that girls needed to be trained in housework. However Dr Dignan's recommendation that education should be provided in preference to dowries would seem to suggest a belief that preparation for the job market was more important than an inducement to marriage; it was a very modern viewpoint.

Dr Dignan, given his views on women and the home, would probably have agreed with Fr W.P. MacDonagh, SJ, (1938).[40] Fr MacDonagh believed in excluding women from the professions and recommended, on the grounds of simple justice, equal pay for equal work. MacDonagh sees those responsible for the removal of women's social and political disabilities as 'nobly-inspired'. He goes on, however, to quote Chesterton in support of his claim that women are actually freer in the home than in the office or factory, and concluded: 'The true emancipation of the modern woman must consist in freedom from the necessity of earning her own bread'.[41] In common with de Valera's Constitution of 1937, he used the terms 'woman' and 'mother' interchangeably. He also nominated the man as the 'natural head of the family'. Professor Mary Hayden was given ample space to respond to Fr MacDonagh's views, and to the anti-feminist views of Fr Hunter Guthrie in the same magazine in 1940. Fr Guthrie, while he would have been in broad agreement with MacDonagh about women and the home, went much further and blamed women's involvement in public life and neglect of the home for a myriad of social ills. Professor Hayden, herself a Catholic and involved in a number of Catholic social action programmes in Dublin city, disposed of Guthrie's views on the falling standard of public morality by citing many instances of a rising standard due to women's involvement in politics. She also argued presciently, if perhaps a little prematurely, given the state of domestic technology in Ireland at that time, that modern appliances were rendering women's continuous presence in the home redundant, and that women as a matter of justice should be involved in all kinds of public life. She certainly resorted to the argument about women's moral superiority in political and public life, but argued that because of this, women's political and economic equality should be developed rather than curtailed.[42]

The Catholic social ideal on the eve of the Second World War was that of a society full of families presided over by males, with its public life full of men *and* women imbued with Catholic ideals about the family and public morality. L'Observateur, with his or her usual keen eye on France, noted with approval in the *Catholic Bulletin* in 1938 the removal of certain civil and legal disabilities from French women, and their elevation to the same legal status as their husbands. He also noted other reforms 'not only consistent with modern ideas on the rights of women, but with the authoritative teachings of the *semaines sociales*'. The Catholic Church in France, L'Observateur went on to say, had always been 'friendly to the political and civil aspirations of the educated woman eager to serve society'. However, L'Observateur, while welcoming the scrapping of the obedience obligation in the French marriage code, was glad to note that the woman was still obliged to live with her husband, and was worried to see that wives could take husbands to court to revise the latter's rulings (an indication that authority should still hold) on matters such as the wife's profession.[43] The dominant social Catholic, Irish perspectives on women's relationship to household work and to public life in the 1930s and 1940s are summed up in the *Report of the Commission on Vocational Organisation* (1943).[44]

'HOME-MAKERS' AND 'COUNTRYWOMEN': THE COMMISSION ON VOCATIONAL ORGANISATION 1940–43

The CVO was appointed by Eamon de Valera in 1939 to enquire into the possibility of developing some kind of vocational organisation of society, along the lines of the corporate state in Italy and Portugal, while preserving democracy. J.J. Lee states that de Valera came under intense pressure from social Catholics in his circle, many of whom had had a hand in drafting parts of the Constitution, and that he could find no convincing reason, therefore, not to accede to the demands of senators Michael Tierney and Frank MacDermot, in 1938, that such a Commission should be set up.[45] Vocationalism, or the political organisation of citizens along the lines of vocation or calling, had been suggested by Pius XI in *Quadragesimo Anno* as a possible reorganisation of society so as to promote class harmony.[46] In Ireland vocationalism was eagerly welcomed by leading social activists and intellectuals – some Protestants like Louie Bennett,[47] and the Reverend Dr Irwin, among them – as a middle road between fascism and communism. The Commission heard evidence from 174 organisations, societies, trade unions, professional bodies and interest groups (including six women's organisations) from 1939 to 1941, and it published its report in 1943. There were three female commissioners, two of whom (Lucy Franks and Bennett) were Protestant, a fact that reflects the disproportionately high profile of Protestant women in public life in Ireland.

The Report of the Commission on Vocational Organisation was not taken seriously by government, and the National Vocational Assembly over which the Report spent so much time, never came into existence. However, the Report must be taken seriously by historians as a mission statement of mainstream-progressive Irish social thinking – mainly Catholic thinking – in the 1940s. As far as women were concerned, the Report took women's participation in the democratic process for granted. There were no recommendations to lay lashes across female backs, no perorations against cinemas and dance halls, or indeed, against women workers. Women's trade unions, which gave evidence to the Commission, were heard in the same matter-of-fact way as male trade unions. Idealisation of women's household and maternal work was conspicuous by its absence, although the Report did make recommendations about women 'engaged in home duties', or 'home-makers', as it called them. It was not the Commission that had coined this term, however, but the women's organisations, representatives of 'home-makers', that gave evidence to the Commission purportedly on behalf of all women 'engaged in home duties'.

The sessions in which women's organisations gave evidence to the Commission on Vocational Organisation have been discussed elsewhere[48] so it is not proposed to go into great detail here.

Four organisations gave evidence on behalf of those who were not gainfully occupied and yet worked: the irony of this census designation was not lost on any of those giving evidence. The Irish Countrywomen's Association (see Appendix C for details about all four organisations) gave evidence in a long session on its own, in which it was encouraged to speak at length about what it saw as the unusual position in which country women – mainly though not exclusively farm women – were placed as both producers and consumers, maintainers of the house and remunerative workers on the farm or holding. The delegates, led by Muriel Gahan, claimed that the ICA played a very important part in training women for public life and giving them confidence in public speaking and organisation. The need for a separate female organisation was affirmed. Fr John Hayes, founder of Muintir na Tire and a long-time supporter of rural electrification and aquafication for the woman's sake, asked if the ICA would not consider coming in with Muintir. He was worried about the fact that the women seemed to be leaving Muintir na Tire and going in with the ICA, and was concerned because Muintir guilds needed women: 'they are really more necessary than the men in the rural areas'. But he appeared to concede the point that women needed a separate organisation. The ICA delegates, while tactfully not agreeing with his suggestion that Muintir was 'severely masculine', went on to say that in mixed organisations, men did most of the talking and women were left out. As mentioned earlier, the delegates laughingly countered suggestions that they were all 'ladies of the manor' or that what they did was 'a form of rural slumming'. Theirs was a democratic organisation, they insisted, in which women of all social classes were equal. They acknowledged, however, that the organisation had not made much headway in the poorer rural areas.[49]

The other three organisations that gave evidence to the Commission, in a joint session, were also accused of 'slumming', but in a far less tentative or good-natured way. The session at which the the Joint Committee comprising the National Council of Women in Ireland, the Joint Committee of Women's Societies and Social Workers and the Catholic Federation of Women's Secondary School Unions (see Appendix C) gave evidence was so unsatisfactory for the three delegates, Lucy Kingston, Winifred O'Hegarty and Vera Dempsey, that they issued another memorandum to the Commission afterwards, clarifying what they had intended to say. These three delegates were urging that 'home-makers' as such be given a strong voice on the proposed National Vocational Assembly. When pressed, the delegates came up with a two-pronged definition of 'home-maker'. This designation covered women of the house who needed everyday help in their rearing of children – practical help like crèches for children of working mothers – but also advice on mother craft, infant care and hygiene generally. However, 'home-makers' were also women in voluntary organisations who helped these other women, and were in a position of superior authority and, it is suggested, expertise to them. One would imagine that this kind of cross-class co-operation, undertaken voluntarily and promoting class harmony, would have been exactly the kind of initiative that vocationalism would have taken to its bosom. This was not so, or at least, not in the case of women of the house. One difficulty of this session was that the chairman, Bishop Michael Browne, spent so much time interrupting the women, and even disparaging them, that the reader's attention is deflected away from some of the real problems of definition of 'home-makers' and onto the women's difficulty in actually finishing their sentences. Browne objected first of all to the idea that working-class mothers needed training in how to look after infants. He accused the women's organisations of being 'ladies of leisure' and described their activities as 'slumming'. He flatly contradicted them and opined that all they were interested in was getting women out of the home to work, and he suggested that most women preferred to leave political matters to the men.

Other Commissioners at the session, Fr Edward Coyne, Louie Bennett and Protestant Bishop Dr Harvey, tried to get the women to answer straightforward questions about what they wanted and why they wanted it. Fr Coyne did uncover a central problem with the Joint Committee's definition of home-maker when he asked what exactly a home-maker was, and if it was a term which was synonymous with woman: this was where he warned the delegates that they should not 'put forward being a woman as a specialised vocation'. As good feminists – and feminist was a term to which the three women proudly laid claim in this hostile atmosphere – the delegates could not disagree with that! After all, three years earlier, feminists such as Lucy Kingston had been objecting to just such an idealisation, a conflation of the terms 'woman' and 'mother' in de Valera's Constitution. And Kingston seemed to be indulging in just such idealisation when she said somewhat immoderately in response to some particularly pointless and ignorant questioning from Browne, that the war in Europe was the result of 'masculine statesmanship; the women cannot be blamed'. Throughout the session the delegates used the terms 'woman/women' and 'home-maker' interchangeably. And when Browne accused them of slumming, by assuming authority over poorer women, they did not have a convincing answer for this charge.[50]

In the Report, published in 1943, the introduction to the session dealing with persons 'engaged in home duties' comments that the three organisations 'deserve special mention for the able manner in which they gave evidence before this commission.'[51] It is an odd comment, and one which is not made about any other organisation. If, as J.J. Lee states, the Report was mainly written by Fr Edward Coyne, then the remark can be understood as a kind of apology for the way the session had gone – was Coyne appalled and, as another Catholic priest, embarrassed at Browne's manners? The best apology of all, of course, would have been to give the 'home-makers'' representatives what they had asked for, namely ample representation on a proposed National Vocational Assembly. They were not granted such a voice: an allowance was made for the co-option of a 'home-maker' representative onto the NVA, should it be needed. The Report made detailed and full recommendations about how the 'home-makers' should organise at parish level:

> a separate and largely autonomous section [should] be formed for the wives, mothers and young women of the parish as representing the needs and interests of the family or household as such, especially the more purely domestic side.

This group would organise 'the women of the parish' by providing courses in things like domestic hygiene and poultry-rearing, improving the water supply and the medical services and also doing something about prices and marketing. It would also monitor entertainment and endeavour to maintain 'a high standard of decency in public life'. These organisations would, in turn, lead to the formation of larger county federations which would in turn nominate representatives to national boards 'where the social and economic interests of the home require a competent advocate'. 'Countrywomen', women in charge of a house on farms or in the country generally (a definition prompted by the representations of the Irish Countrywomen's Assocation), were to be included in this, though women farmers and female assisting relatives could be represented on agricultural panels, as could women in any other trade or profession.[52]

It was the under-representation of 'home-makers' on the proposed National Vocational Assembly that caused two of the Commissioners, Máire MacGeehin (or Máire F. NicAodháin, as she signed herself), and G.H.C. Crampton (a building contractor and regular contributor to the sessions of the Statistical and Social Inquiry Society), to produce addenda to the Report. NicAodháin/ MacGeehin, a Commissioner whose attendance record was excelled only by that of the Chairman, Bishop Michael Browne of Galway, Reverend Dr Irwin and Stephen O'Mara, argued that if women were organised at local level, their organisation at national level should pose no great problems either. She proposed that a National Council of Home-makers should be set up, comparable to the other vocationally-based National Councils which were proposed. The allowance for co-opting the 'home-makers' onto the proposed National Vocational Assembly was 'practically worthless', she believed, both because the co-opting body would not have the requisite knowledge to enable it to select suitable representatives, and because the number of seats allotted could be as low as one, out of 120, and that not a permanent seat. 'Home-makers', she argued, needed a minimum of five out of 120 seats. She also called for a bias towards home-making in the training of girls.[53] Mr Crampton agreed with the substance of NicAodháin's addendum but he went further in his suggestion that 'home-makers' should occupy no less than fifteen out of the 120 seats on the proposed Assembly.[54]

The Report had gone as far as it would go, however, and discomfort with a certain kind of women's public activism can be discerned in the following extract:

> To avoid possible misconceptions, it may be well to remark that we must not be taken as implying that the wives and mothers of Ireland are an oppressed class which has no means of voicing its claims and obtaining the redress of its grievances. They have the same democratic rights as men, can elect representatives and influence local councils and the Oireachtas, if they are so minded. In regard to conditions in the home and the efficiency of their agricultural production, they can persuade the male members of the household to improve conditions, for they are not more helpless, silent and unassertive than women in other countries. One of the principal functions of organisation is to inform those engaged in home duties as to the improvements which could be made by themselves in housekeeping, rearing of children, and other duties, to convince them of the value and feasability of improved methods, and to arouse their enthusiasm for higher standards. As in other vocations, progress is impeded when people are satisfied with low standards, ignorant of better

methods, and hopeless or indifferent as regards effort. The purposes of organisation should be, among other things, to develop in present and future mothers a higher estimate of the dignity of their vocation, a more complete knowledge of all that pertains to the full and happy performance of their duties, and a realisation of the improvements that can be secured by concerted action.[55]

The extraordinary thing about this comment is that men had the same rights of citizenship as women, and yet nowhere did the Commission use this fact to dismiss or diminish potential problems in the organisation of males in any vocational group. The very purpose of the Commission was, after all, to address what were seen to be the shortcomings of people's representative power in democracy. The mention of women's supposed influence over their menfolk suggests the Commissioners' belief that men's consent and co-operation is crucial for women to improve conditions in their houses. The reference to women in other countries is obviously meant to forestall any suggestions that Irish women might be particularly oppressed and indicates that the Commission was defensive about such suggestions. The obligation to instruct and to improve is also forcefully emphasised, as if there has been enough talk about rights and now it is time to talk about duties. Taken as a whole the passage sounds a note of exasperation with women's advocates, one which cancels out the earlier apology. There is an adherence, moreover, to the view of women, particularly 'home-makers', as essentially dependent upon their menfolk, with the tremendous additional advantage of political equality. This dual mandate, it is implied, imposes on them a clear duty to act in concert, and, presumably, enough advantages and power not to need any permanent representation on the proposed National Vocational Assembly.

It could be suggested that the Joint Committee of the three organisations aroused hostility because not only did it include one Protestant, Lucy Kingston, but also because the largest constituent group in it, the Joint Committee of Women's Societies and Social Workers, was composed of a variety of Catholic and Protestant organisations. The Irish Countrywomen's Association, however, was famous for its large number of Protestant patrons, founders and members: Muriel Gahan was from a Church of Ireland background, and Lucy Franks, as already mentioned, was Protestant also.[56] The crucial difference between the ICA session and the Joint Committee session, however, is that the latter laid claim to the title 'feminist' and the ICA did not. This is not to suggest that the ICA or its members were in any way hostile to feminism – as mentioned, they saw it as their role to support women in public life – but that they did not associate themselves directly with it. It was, it can be suggested, the combination of mixed religions and a feminist identity which aroused such suspicion. Furthermore, the Countrywomen focussed mainly on work, while the Joint Committee was addressing issues like infant care and the support of mothers who had to work. It was the spectacle of such activism which not only aroused Browne's inexcusable rudeness, but caused the eventual report to allow representatives of 'home-makers' only a faint, consultative voice in any proposed Assembly. Reading the Report, it is refreshing to note that there is no pedestalisation of the little Irish mother presiding over the little Irish home, and no explicit references to the Article 41.2 in the 1937 Constitution. However, the absence of such idealisation did not guarantee women of the house any additional power.

CONCLUSION

The Report of the Commission on Vocational Organisation must be seen as part of the new way of writing about women of the house from the early 1940s. There is obvious sympathy for the problems that women face in their day to day work, and a belief that they need more support and more help, but a virtual silencing of activists who claim, accurately or otherwise, that they represent such women. It is no accident that the Irish Housewives' Association, which ran with the feminist/'home-maker' baton from 1942, aroused stronger and more vicious opposition than was ever experienced by the older organisations.

The year 1943 was when Eamon de Valera painted his picture of 'the Ireland we desire'. In recent years much ironic and even derisive comment focuses on the comely maidens, athletic youths and fireside matrons who make up this picture, which seems (inexplicably) to some commentators to mark the lowest tide of twentieth-century Irish feminism. What is not as well known is that in 1943 de Valera appointed an interdepartmental committee to look into the possibility of the government subsidising the building of a second dwelling-house on farms.[57] Such a dwelling-house might, he believed, facilitate the earlier marriage of farm sons and daughters who did not want to live with the older couple. The young couple would live in the smaller house initially, and as their family grew, the older couple could retire to it, leaving the bigger house for the bigger family. The committee, chaired by Kerry TD Eamon O Ciosáin, had to be sharply reminded by their chairman more than once that it was not their job to give opinions on the relevance or importance of their brief, but to solicit opinions on it. This they did, from Land Commission inspectors throughout the country. The consensus from the letters sent in by these inspectors was that a second dwelling-house might encourage subdivision, and was not to be recommended. Several inspectors noted, however, that there was a problem with two generations of adults, particularly two women, under one roof. Personal testimony confirms this.[58]

The fact that de Valera set up such a committee in the first place shows that he was aware, well in advance of the flood of sociological and other literature which confirmed the validity of his suggestion, of the problems faced by many rural women of the house in their everyday lives. The fact that not one woman was appointed to this committee, or not one woman asked for her opinion on the proposed dower-houses, is typical of the new approach to social issues involving women in the 1940s. Far more resonant for Irish feminism than the throwaway idealisation of the comely maidens is this new construction of the woman of the house as someone needing sympathy and help, someone whose needs and wants can best be understood by experts but not by women's organisations or advocates who claim to represent her. Neither de Valera nor the committee sought the opinions of the Irish Countrywomen's Association, with 2,000 members, on this issue. Nor were the opinions of any women's organisations, urban or rural, sought by the committee that enquired into the feasibility of introducing family allowances, or children's allowances, as they were also known. It should also be said that no women's organisation seemed to take any interest in this issue either. This will be more fully discussed in the next chapter.

Visible But Silent: Women in the House in Public Discourse in the 1940s and 1950s

I think it will be admitted that in this country at any rate the woman – the *bean a tighe* – is regarded as the head of the household. Now why should we interfere with that practice?

W.T. Cosgrave, 1943, on the proposal to pay children's allowances to mothers rather than fathers

Woman herself is still seeking her real place in the life of the world, and for those of us who belong to an older generation it is difficult to foresee what part she will play in the revolutionised and mechanised world we are entering on. One line of hope lies in a new approach to the home and the domestic sphere, and if the new generation accept home-keeping as a vocation and a social service I believe they will blaze a trail towards a finer civilisation than we have yet known.

Louie Bennett, 1946, writing for the first issue of The Irish Housewife, *annual publication of the Irish Housewives' Association*[1]

The staunchest defenders of the authority of the woman of the house in Ireland in the 1940s came from two very different backgrounds and fought in two entirely different theatres of war. It was a young Fine Gael TD, Liam Cosgrave, who proposed that children's allowances should be payable to mothers in the first instance, and in this he was supported by many from his own party and by the Clann na Talmhan deputies representing the small farmers in the west.[2] Veteran feminist-suffragists and women's trade unionists Louie Bennett and Helen Chenevix were among the well-wishers of the new Irish Housewives' Association, founded in Dublin in 1942 by ex-teacher Hilda Tweedy. This organisation drew attention to a wide range of issues thought to be of particular interest to women generally, and to women of the house, or housewives, in particular.[3] The Dáil deputies who wanted to pay the mother were defeated, and the Irish Housewives' Association remained a small organisation that faced some opposition. A look at references to women in religious and learned journals, two government commissions and one government-subsidised survey in the years 1943–61 seems at first to confuse the issue hopelessly. How could the growing support for women workers and women in public life, which peeks through all of these writings, co-exist with hostility towards these women's representatives and an unwillingness to reward directly with money work that was coming to be recognised as both arduous and valuable – the care of a family?

JUST A LITTLE BIT SCEPTICAL: ATTITUDES TO WOMEN, WORK AND PUBLIC LIFE 1943–61

'The present writer is just a little bit sceptical about modern ideas concerning equality of the sexes, but one can go too far', wrote the Question Box in the *Irish Messenger* in 1944. This was in reply to a question about whether it was a sin for women to whistle and the jocose note[4] in this reference to gender equality suggests that this very popular religious publication was not as gloomily worried as before about the due social consequences of feminism and women's rights. It is true that in the February issue in 1944 the old Irish home was invoked, and the 'calm and holy Irish mother' who 'occupied a pedestal in that old world household'. Home, in 'the world of today' had become a place only 'to keep clothes in and for sleeping'. Amusements outside the home are identified as the great threat to home life, and girls and women of Ireland are addressed directly:

> . . . make your homes happy. It is not necessary to have costly furniture to do so. Little contrivances can transform even the most unpleasant sur-roundings into a haven of rest.

Females are advised to make their homes happy not only with self-abnegation, sacrifice and good cheer, but with handy hints.[5] One almost expects the injunction to conclude with a pattern for a table-cloth or a chair-back. In the *Messenger* in 1951, the ideal home of the Holy Family of Nazareth was invoked, and Mary held up as a pattern for mothers, but no disparaging references were made to feminism or women workers. The word had come down from the top. In this year Pope Pius XII acknowledged that due to 'the marvellous advance of industry', many of the former functions of the home had been taken over and women were needed in the workforce. He hoped that married women would not have to work, but acknowledged that many would, and he addressed them in tones of admiration and sympathy, rather than warning and censure.[6] In the same year, Brigid Stafford, a senior civil servant and a member of the Commission on Youth Unemployment (1951) and a delegate on many occasions to the International Labour Organisation, cited no less an authority than this Pope for her claim that women should receive equal pay for equal work. She firmly reminded readers of the *Irish Monthly* that women were in the workforce to stay.[7] An article by Francis Hanna, BL on the welfare state in Northern Ireland in *Christus Rex*, in 1951 was enthusiastic about day nurseries for children whose mothers needed to work outside the home.[8] Numerous articles in *Christus Rex* in the 1950s addressed the subject of women's role or place in the modern world, concluding that women needed to take full part in public life in keeping with the teaching of Pius XII, but insisted, in common with earlier commentators, that women's 'particular aptitudes' must be recognised in anything they do. This point of view does not seem to have been confined to Catholics. Dr E.J. Wormell from Trinity College, who was presenting prizes at the Bertrand and Rutland High School in Dublin in 1954, said that:

> ... it was a day of opportunity for the growing generation, particularly for girls. He welcomed the changes which created such a wide range of opportunity for girls. There were certain dangers to be considered, however. The change tended to turn young women away from careers in which they had traditionally excelled – teaching and nursing. These professions appealed to one's idealism and were not fairly treated in the economic sense.[9]

Reverend G.J. Shannon CM, writing in *Christus Rex* in 1951, saluted feminism for its 'humanitarian motives, love of justice, a wholly admirable sympathy with the downtrodden and exploited', though he, in common with many of his contemporaries, believed that feminism had been 'tragically vitiated' by application to women of a male standard of achievement.[10] Ita Meehan laid down what she considered to be women's rights and duties in an article in the same journal in 1959.[11] She stated that 'the powers of the intellect cannot be achieved by complete absorption in household tasks' and that husbands were morally bound to foster and encourage women's activities independent of the house, which should be 'woman's primary, but not her exclusive care'. Women needed to take part in public life, not only for their own development, but also to ensure that the state would protect family life. Nowhere did she state that married women should not work for wages outside the house.

Nor did any government consistently and systematically promote an ideology of domesticity to women in Ireland in this period. Fr Shannon believed that a course in 'Catholic Family Science' should be made available in all schools. In parts of America, the recommendations of the notorious 'sex-directed educators' and functionalists, referred to by Betty Friedan,[12] were overlaid with Catholic teaching about woman and the home. Such a scheme was described as operating in California and recommended for Ireland by Sr Annetta McFeely, an Irish-American Presentation sister.[13] While they might not have gone along with this particular scheme with its denominational and psychological characteristics, prominent women like Brigid Redmond, Kathleen Ferguson and Máire MacGeehin had been urging for well over a decade now that a vigorous programme of domestic education be undertaken for the better health and happiness and, MacGeehin suggested, empowerment of women.

They did so to no avail. The very basic *Cookery Notes* first brought out by the Department of Agriculture in 1924, and used in secondary and vocational schools up to the 1950s, was constantly reprinted without being revised. (Popular, accessible cookery and household advice publications will be more thoroughly discussed in the next chapter.) The Leaving Certificate Syllabus C, Domestic

Science, (For Girls Only) had not changed much since the foundation of the state. It offered, in the 1950s as in the 1920s, the general headings of cookery, needlework, hygiene (including scientific items like composition of air, varieties of water, bacteria and a considerable amount of physiology), and household knowledge, although in the 1920s, the latter included 'choice and selection of clothes; good taste in clothing; fitness, colour and fashion'. This had been dropped by the 1950s, but an additional objective had crept into the syllabus:

> Attention should also be given to organising practical work with a view to developing the pupil's appreciation of the importance of household work and of home-making in general.[14]

However, as never more than 9% of females sitting the Leaving Certificate were examined in Domestic Science throughout this period, and never more than 11% of Intermediate female students – and secondary schooling was, in any case, not freely available to all Irish adolescents until 1966 – this appreciation of household work cannot be said to have been widely promoted.[15] Basic cookery and needlework were taught in many primary and post-primary schools up to the 1970s, but this was a far remove from 'Catholic Family Science', or even from the kind of wide-ranging domestic education envisaged by women in public life. Disparaging comments about Irish women's household skills were becoming less common, however, and giving way to sympathy for the conditions under which most Irish women of the house laboured – a sympathy already evident by the early 1940s and growing stronger as time went on. Arland Ussher's uncomplimentary comments about Irish women as cooks in *The Vanishing Irish* in 1954 stand out because they are so unusual at this stage. Almost all the other contributors, Fr John Hayes, Mary Frances Keating, Edmund Murray and the editor himself, John A. O'Brien, lamented the hard working conditions endured by the rural woman in particular.[16] When Patrick McNabb referred to the dark and gloomy interiors of Limerick farmhouses, he was careful not to blame the womenfolk for this and, in common with the other contributors to the *Survey*, accepted that women would not and should not be expected to marry into houses without piped water and electricity.[17] The Commission on Emigration in 1956 considered the provision of such facilities to be a priority.[18]

The conviction that married women should not work outside the house was also being revised in Ireland in the 1950s. The marriage bar against women National School teachers was coming under attack as early as 1953, when a teacher shortage caused the Department of Finance to ask the Department of Education if it were not inconsistent to bar married women from teaching and not from other professions, like medicine and the law.[19] The Commission on Emigration conceded, reluctantly, that removing the marriage bar on women's white-collar work might be necessary to induce men and women to marry and set up house in Ireland. Catholic sociologist Dr Jeremiah Newman, in the *Limerick Rural Survey*, believed that local facilities for the continued employment of married women would be one of the key ways to arrest rural depopulation. The kind of employment was not specified; it was not stipulated that it should be any of the vocations for which women were seen to have an aptitude.[20] Keeping women 'at home' in Ireland was seen at this stage to be more important then keeping them 'at home' in their houses. Paid work for married women was still seen as regrettable, and at best a necessary evil; however, paid work for single women was viewed with approval, even enthusiasm. Fr Shannon suggested that the factory and the office were excellent training grounds for girls and women in the sense of responsibility, cleanliness and order they would need in their own eventual homes.[21] When the *Commission on Youth Unempoyment*, in 1951, made no substantial, detailed recommendations on female employment, Louie Bennett refused to sign the report. She agreed with the commission that the home and family should form the basis of women's interests, but insisted that girls' and women's unemployment was too pressing a social problem to be hidden under vague hopes about girls' natural careers being the home.[22] Five years later, however, when Reverend Thomas Counihan of the *Emigration Commission* wanted to suggest that girls be 'kept out of the strain of industry' and trained for the home, he had to do so in an addendum.[23] At this stage it was considered unusual for a single girl or woman not to be contemplating work. Fr Lucius McClean, OFM, who answered problems in the *Sunday Independent* throughout the 1950s and published some of the most common problems in 1961, strongly advised 'June', a girl in her late teens who, despite having got honours in her Leaving Certificate, wanted to remain at home and help in the house, to get some training or work: 'it seems a great pity that a girl should let her mind lie fallow'.[24]

Fr Lucius McClean also believed that the husband was head of the house. Although in tune with the modern western ideal of the companionate marriage – a wife whose husband would tell her nothing of the prices he got for cows was told to remind her husband that their marriage vows had included one of common ownership – he used as authority for his views on the husband's headship the fact that 'in creation man precedes woman' and the Pauline analogy of husband/wife, Christ/Church. The wife was the husband's helpmate; this caused no difficulty in most marriages. He went on:

> The physical differences between men and women are not the only differences: the psychological are just as important. For the role each has to play within the marriage, each is given by God a psychological aptitude. Where either takes the role of the other in the running of family matters – apart from those circumstances in which a partner is denied the presence and support of the other – things can go wrong.

The invocation of psychology bolsters the traditional Catholic teaching with the secular authorities of the period. He goes on to say that fathers doing mothers' work, and mothers doing fathers' work, can cause boys and girls to 'suffer greatly from this violation of the natural order of things'. And he says in the introduction to this common problem, which he calls 'Who Wears The Apron?':

> Here we have two different problems, one sent in by a man who finds the lack of respect for the 'head of the house' in the modern world most upsetting; the other from a wife who thinks that occasionally her husband should lend a hand with the housework. The man who writes says that feminism has been the ruination of many countries and is making a fair bid to ruin ours. The woman wonders why her husband should have one-and-a-half free days in the week while she must slave from morning to night for seven days a week.

Fr McClean's prediction that he will have 'a real avalanche of mail as a reaction to the present topic and the views I express on it', reminds us just how topical and contentious questions about male and female authority in the house were in Ireland at this stage. Nowhere in his discussion does he agree with the suggestion that there is declining respect for the head of the house, or that feminism is the possible ruination of the country. However, he advises that the husband 'should lend a hand where necessary around the house', but goes on to say that this is not the husband's primary role. He is a breadwinner, and this should be remembered.[25]

As far as Irish social policy was concerned, the place of the husband and father as breadwinner had been consolidated by the introduction of children's allowances in 1943–4, though not without a struggle. It was a struggle in which the feminists of the day played no part whatsoever.

THE INTRODUCTION OF CHILDREN'S ALLOWANCES 1943–4

How to get resources direct to needy children and their mothers was the subject of intense debate in the western world from the late nineteenth century onwards. Governments and voluntary organisations, including women's organisations addressed themselves to this issue as they did to old age pensions, workers' insurance for sickness and compulsory education. Significantly enough, children's or family allowances were the last of these reforms to be settled, in Europe at any rate, not being introduced until after the First World War and then, in widely different forms and for widely different motives. Whether these allowances were means-tested or 'free for all', whether they were seen as supplements to the breadwinner's wages or mothers' wages, all depended upon the kind of state – totalitarian, democratic, social-democratic, fascist, corporatist – and on the level of demand from voluntary organisations and the government's accommodation to these demands.[26]

When support for mothers and children was initially discussed in Ireland in the 1920s and 1930s, it was lone mothers and children who were the focus of discussion. The Commission of Inquiry into the Condition of the Sick and Destitute Poor (1927) recommended that widows with children and deserted wives should be remunerated by the state so as to enable them to look after their children properly.[27] Non-contributory widows' pensions were introduced in

1936, on the recommendation of a committee,[28] but it would take another forty years for payments to deserted wives to be introduced.

James Dillon, a Fine Gael TD, was the first politician to suggest that direct government aid should be made available to two-parent families, in his proprosal in 1939 for a state allowance to be paid for fourth and subsequent children.[29] The previous year, Patrick King CC BD, argued in the *Catholic Bulletin* that because the proprosal of different wage levels for single and for married men was impracticable (employers would hire the cheaper single men), then a father on a low incomes 'must get from some source the means of maintaining his family'. Family allowances were recommended by the Papal enyclicals *Rerum Novarum* (1891) and *Quadragesimo Anno* (1931) as a help to 'fathers of families' and described by a leading Catholic authority as 'a work of the highest charity as well as of social justice.'[30]

Joseph Lee's highly enlightening and entertaining discussion of the inter-departmental correspondence on children's allowances highlights brilliantly the contrasting personalities and ideologies of state intervention involved in it. I therefore do not propose to go over the same ground here, beyond noting that the Taoiseach Eamon de Valera and Minister for Industry and Commerce Seán Lemass were the prime instigators of this measure, and Finance Minister Seán MacEntee, its chief cabinet opponent.[31]

The interdepartmental committee on children's allowances issued its report in 1942, having looked at direct government aid to families in other countries including France, Germany, Italy, Norway, New Zealand and Australia. The British discussion of 'family endowment', as this question was also known, was referred to throughout, and British authorities cited.[32] When Sean Lemass eventually presented his Bill to the Dáil in 1943, he proposed a universal (i.e. payable to all regardless of means), non-contributory system providing two shillings and sixpence per week for every third and subsequent child, payable to the head of the household (the father except in the case of a widow or separated wife) though provisions could be made for the father to nominate someone else, e.g. the mother, to collect it. The timing of the introduction of the Bill and the fact that it was introduced by the Minister for Industry and Commerce links it clearly to government employment policies of the period (1943 was the year of the Wages Standstill Order). The Bill passed both houses of the Oireachtas and became law in 1944.[33]

The interdepartmental committee which advised the government on the allowances was aware that a case could be made for paying these allowances to mothers, and acknowledged the 'feminist and socialist ideas' which motivated some of the support for family endowment in Britain and elsewhere. The arguments of Eleanor Rathbone, the British MP who favoured paying the mothers, were gone into in some detail and it was accepted that they had some merit. However, the older and, to the committee's mind, wiser counsels of a Professor Gray prevailed. Paying the mother, Gray warned, could 'set up a direct and special relationship between the mother and the state to the exclusion of the father'. This could lead in the end to 'the complete nationalisation of women and children'.[34] The idea that children's allowances could be 'mothers' wages' or payments in respect of motherhood was not very strong in Ireland in any case. Unlike many other countries, there was no feminist/women's organisation interested in drawing attention to this aspect of the question. At least two members of the Oireachtas, however, spoke in favour of mothers' wages: Senator Cummins, speaking in favour of a proposed scheme of family allowances for agriculutural labourers (a scheme which was overtaken by Lemass's Bill), urged that it was 'about time, as has been done in many countries . . . to consider the mother as an active worker in the nation's economic life'.[35] Helena Concannon, speaking in the Senate in 1944 on Lemass's Bill, expressed dissatisfaction with the size and the scale of the allowance, making a direct connection between the promises implicit in Article 41.2 of de Valera's Constitution and the introduction of the allowances.[36] Senator Michael Tierney, one of the originators of the Commission on Vocational Organisation and a strong opponent of Lemass's Bill (which he saw, curiously, as completely contrary to Catholic social thinking), reserved his most stinging criticism for the proposal to make payments to mothers, a suggestion he saw as typical of the 'sentimentality' and populism of the scheme:

> One example of this was the proposal that these allowances be given to the mother instead of to the father – an idea which runs contrary to any kind of Christian principle about the family. It was proposed by sentimentalists looking for votes [and it would be] one of the severest blows one could inflict on the most precious institution in this or in any other country.[37]

Senator Tierney was speaking from a position of some security, as Liam Cosgrave's amendment to make the allowances payable to the mothers had been defeated by 60 votes to 34 in the Dáil the previous December.

Sean Lemass stated his views on this amendment with characteristic bluntness:

> There may be some social theory behind that suggestion [to pay the mothers]. If there is, I disagree with it.[38]

It was not for governments, he said, to interfere in 'the domestic arrangements of families' by paying mothers directly.

There were, however, precious few theories of any kind motivating those politicians who spoke in favour of Cosgrave's motion, but simply an alternative view of the balance of power, real or desired, within families. Michael Donnellan (Clann na Talmhan) explained it thus:

> The mother is the chief parent. As a father I do not wish to say anything against fathers, but . . . the mother is the chief guardian of the family. If [payment is made to the mother] I have not the slightest hesitation in saying that the money will be definitely of more value, because this allowance is more or less of help in the provision of clothing and things

like that, and of course the mother has the chief responsibility in that direction.[39]

Colonel Ryan (FG) backed up Donnellan's point, by stating that among the small farmers the woman was the one who paid the bills and incurred the debt while George Bennett (FG) pointed out that 'in rural Ireland' the mother was recognised as the financial and budgetary head of the family.[40] According to Deputy Meighan (CnT), in the west of Ireland and all through rural Ireland 'it is the recognised rule' that mothers did the shopping and provided the food and clothing for the children.[41]

Women's/mother's supposed essential difference from men was also invoked. Patrick Cogan (CnT) said:

> While the father may consider it his duty, and may remind himself frequently that it is his duty, to provide for the welfare of his family . . . the mother without any reflection on the matter, instinctively feels that it is her duty and will make provision for her family without any coercion.[42]

The Interdepartmental Committee had mentioned this supposed greater sense of responsibility of the mother as one of the valid reasons why payment should be made to them in preference to the fathers, only to dismiss it. The other side of the coin from this elevation of mothers was distrust of wage-earning fathers. Captain Giles (FG) was one of those who expressed this:

> We know that there are many good fathers but there are [others] who spend most of their wages in public houses and leave the wife and children in misery. I ask the Minister to see that this little pittance is paid to the mother as head of the family at home, as it would often occur, if paid to the father, that it would never reach the mother or the children at all.[43]

Brigid Redmond (FG) held to the view that the state should bypass the working-class man to reach the working-class woman, a long held principle in 'maternalist' politics, as was the need to educate the working-class woman in such responsibilities:

> If these responsibilities were placed on her, she would be more likely to be careful in expending the money. It is enough for the father to handle his weekly wage.[44]

This suggestion of the working-class man's probable irresponsibility and incapacity was bound to enrage political representatives of the working-class, just as it was bound to reinforce popular stereotypes of women social reformers as upper-class ladies whose ignorance of working-class life was matched only by their tact. And just as assumptions like Redmond's had irritated Ramsay MacDonald in Britain some years earlier,[45] they irritated William Norton (Labour):

One would imagine from some of the speeches here that [the father] was the enemy of the family . . . If modern thought in respect of the family is represented by the speeches made in this House, then I prefer to be old-fashioned and to believe that in Ireland the father displays a loyalty and fidelity to the family which is probably unequalled in any other country. Heavens, do we not know that 10,000 fathers have emigrated and gone to work in Britain, under intolerable conditions in many cases, in order to sustain their wives and children?

If the woman was the budgetary head of the household, Norton argued, it was only because the man allowed her to be:

The position is that the father is the natural breadwinner . . . Deputy Cosgrave stated that the woman was the person who managed the domestic expenditure. That is true, but it is because of the father's loyalty to the family when he says, 'Here, Mary, go and shop; you are the wisest person to shop.' If Mary spends the money it is only because John, being a good husband, provided the necessary means.[46]

Supporting his son's amendment, W.T. Cosgrave (FG) had already made an appeal to tradition to equal William Norton's when he said:

I think it will be admitted that in this country at any rate the woman – the *bean a tighe* – is regarded as the head of the household. Now why should we interfere with that practice?[47]

One reason for interfering with it, according to M. O'Reilly (FF) was that fathers' sense of responsibility to their families could evaporate if they were not paid this money:

The father is recognised by the Church and everybody else as the head of the family and if we, by act of this house, lower his dignity in any way the time may come when he might be inclined to say that as the family is receiving an allowance . . . they might do their best to live on that.[48]

The argument that family allowances paid to mothers might weaken a paternal sense of responsibility had been used by some Labour women in Britain in the 1920s, and was a particular concern of many European feminists in the early decades of the century.[49]

James Larkin Sr was orginally in favour of paying the fathers, though he commented, with a candour that played no gender favourites and paid no homage to essentialism of any kind:

God only knows why some of the fathers are called fathers. They do not accept their responsibilities. That applies to some of the mothers also, who are careless and reckless of their offspring.[50]

Later, however, he changed his mind and supported the idea of paying the allowance to the mothers. Larkin's contribution to the debate showed none of the sentimentality so abhorred by Senator Tierney and which was expressed by Deputy Meighan when he contended, in addition to his other arguments cited above, that paying the mothers 'would be a gesture that is due to the good mothers of the country.'[51] No other Oireachtas member, however, reached the heights of piety of William Francis O'Donnell (CnT):

> Each of us is the son [sic] of a mother machree and the hand that rocks the cradle rules the world. Let us thank our mothers.[52]

Cosgrave's amendment was defeated. The entire Fianna Fáil parliamentary party voted against it, along with most Labour deputies. Clann na Talmhan, some Labour deputies and a number of Independents voted against it. The Fine Gael party was divided more or less evenly on this issue; no party whip was imposed. Turnout for the vote was low. Perhaps some members of the Dáil felt, like historian Joseph Lee, that the question of children's allowances 'was not one of the highest intrinsic importance.'[53]

The deputies who identified the mother as, if not the breadwinner, at least the *provider*, of the family were appealing to tradition and lived, observed experience. The Clann na Talmhan deputies, mainly representing farmers in the west, did not, unlike some Fine Gael deputies, cite potential male irresponsibility as a reason why women should collect this payment, but stuck to the argument of a sex-based division of labour. The suggestion that the woman managed finances only because the man allowed her to do so, was used both as an argument for and against paying the mother. Norton's claim rested on assumptions about a 'natural' marital balance of power, while the FG deputies used this apparent fact of male dominance to argue for some small area of finance to be controlled by the mother.

The successful designation of the father/chief breadwinner as the official recipient of this payment, formulated the problem of the big family as one of financial rather than physical maintenance, the concern of the father/earner rather than the mother. In discussions about ideal family size the figure of the father as provider loomed even larger.

FAMILY SIZE

Initially, children's allowances were paid only for the third and subsequent children, though this was relaxed to the second and subsequent children in 1952. The allowances were conceived of as support for large families, and some of the support for this scheme was rooted in the belief that this would safeguard the practice of large families. Senator Cogan, for example, on his own account born and reared in a one-room Dublin tenement, supported allowances because large families were an Irish tradition that needed to be safeguarded and

3. 'The deputy who brought evidence in support of his allegation . . .'. *Dublin Opinion*, April 1949. The health and welfare of mothers and children was much discussed in Ireland in the late 1940s and 1950s. Kelly's image of the Dáil deputies hiding behind their benches in shock, or shyness, when confronted with the reality of what they were discussing, is a very powerful one.

encouraged 'in these days of artificial birth control, so prevalent throughout the country'.[54] The *Emigration Commission* (1956) saw the downward trend in family size as 'unwelcome, and every effort should be made to arrest it.'[55]

While the *Emigration Commission* believed that smaller families were due to 'the almost universal determination to secure better standards of life' and acknowledged that poverty could be aggravated, 'especially in urban areas', by large families, it also argued that the large family was not incompatible with subsistence or comfort because 'in most cases the burden of a large dependent family lasts for a comparatively short period in a man's whole earning life'. Besides, the argument ran, families with large numbers of dependent children were actually comparatively few in number; only 5% of all couples had seven or more dependent children under 16, and only 18% of all couples had more than four dependent children. (This made 23% of couples with five and more dependent children.) In any case, the problem, the Commission argued, was not large families in themselves:

> It would be unreasonable to assume that our family pattern imposes an undue strain on mothers in general. Moreover, we do not believe that large families in themselves – if questions of poverty and overcrowding which too frequently accompany them could be excluded from consideration – are a direct cause of high rates of infant mortality.

Infant mortality could, the Commissioners argued, be reduced by more systematic instruction of girls and women in child welfare and childcare, and by the promotion of breast-feeding.[56] The Commissioners prioritised infant mortality as one of the preventible problems associated with big families. The turn-of-the-century theory that the bigger the crop of children, the weaker and the more attenuated the health of each had fallen from favour at this stage. Doctors pointed out that it was the effect on child health, due to stretching of household resources and of parental resources of energy, which caused hardship.[57] The Commission went on to say that it still could:

> find no support for the view that, apart from the increased risk associated with child-bearing, large families have a deleterious effect on the general health of mothers.[58]

Bishop Cornelius Lucey went one step further than this in his *Minority Report to the Commission*. Echoing the main Report's claim that the burden of a large family did not last very long in 'a man's earning life', he claimed that big families were actually good for mothers' health:

> Apart from the risk incidental to parturition itself, child-bearing seems to have no effect at all on the health of mothers; as to mental health, the effect seems to be salutary rather than deleterious.

He went on to say that while 'of course' people were not expected to have as many children as they possibly could, 'they are expected to have as many as they can hope to bring up properly'.[59] This focus on the burden of the man of the house is natural enough, given assumptions about the reluctance of men to marry and take on family responsibility, and is also part of the prevailing family ideology that saw the interests of the household as embodied in the father. The parenthetical dismissal of the well-documented mortality risks and chronic health problems associated with what doctors were calling 'grand multiparity' is chilling.[60] It can only indicate that the occasional loss of a mother in childbirth or the chronic illness of a woman weakened by many pregnancies was taken for granted by the Commission. Bishop Lucey's confident claim that large families were good for mothers' mental health might well have been true, but he advanced no evidence whatever for it.

Not everybody agreed. Dr W.R.F. Collis, a member of the Commission, had already referred in his prizewinning essay of 1943 to:

> the large poor family into which numerous children are born doomed to malnutrition and all the ill-health and bodily pain which this means.

He recommended a two-pronged solution; 'wise limitation by natural means as taught by the Church, and family allowances'.[61] Dr Collis expanded a little more confidently on this with Mr Arnold Marsh, in a joint Reservation to the report of the Emigration Commission:

> The good, large, happy, healthy family is an ideal, but the large, unhappy, unhealthy family where the mother is a drudge is that which we would be more likely to arrive at by such a policy [i.e. the Commission's encouragement of large families].

And falling infant mortality would, they argued, if anything increase the demand for family limitation:

> If parents today followed the practices of the past and if both parents and health authorities continued to be as successful as they are now in bringing children to maturity, and if moral duty still seemed to call for another pregnancy every year or two, we should arrive at something very like the conditions of overcrowding and malnutrition and early death from which we seem to be so triumphantly emerging.[62]

Large families, in the views of these Commissioners, lead not only to maternal drudgery and overcrowding of the existing housing stock, but might eventually lead to 'over-population'. The prospect of this was unlikely to be taken very seriously in the 'vanishing' Ireland of the 1950s. Mr Marsh developed this point in his own Reservation where he not only advocated that 'abnormally defective' people should not be allowed to reproduce, but lamented mildly that it was not possible to promote the births of more 'above the average' children. (Dr Collis obviously did not agree with Marsh's eugenicism or these recommendations would have been included in their joint Reservation. Perhaps his work in the former extermination camps of the Nazis immediately after the war had inculcated a distaste for eugenicism). However, Marsh punctures the self-congratulatory tone of the large-family lobby with the common sensical observation that the big family could as easily be the outcome of 'irresponsibility, callousness and selfishness' as of 'self-sacrifice and love'.[63] It is a pity that Collis and Marsh's recognition of the hard work of the woman with a large family was accompanied by the statement that large families in and of themselves led to overpopulation, overcrowding, malnutrition and early death. This point was easily refutable – the advocates of large families could always point to large, happy, healthy families in comfortable circumstances, and to falling Irish population. Those who questioned the policy of encouraging big families would have done better to draw attention to the chronic ill-health and risks to the mother.

Alexis Fitzgerald's Addendum has become notorious for its acceptance of a high rate of emigration as a social safety-valve that 'makes possible a stability of manners and customs which would otherwise be the subject of radical change'. Fitzgerald, a devout Catholic, also believed that smaller families were inevitable: 'If procreation has a purpose it is not just the birth but the proper upbringing of a child.'[64] This recommendation reminds one of Bishop Lucey's phrase about having as many children as one can bring up properly, but one was an advocate of small families, and the other, of large. Reverend A.A. Luce, a Church of Ireland clergyman, was the strongest and most specific advocate of family planning, believing it to be 'a primary duty of responsible Christian parenthood'. He regretted that no information on contraception had been laid before the Commission; the gathering of such information was 'an unpleasant public duty' but it had to be done. Echoing some of those who believed, in the 1920s and 1930s, that outlawing information on contraception and contraception itself would encourage immorality by driving it underground, Reverend Luce believed it was vital for the control of public morality that contraception be acknowledged and controlled, and its use limited to married people. He also believed that, in the absence of any family planning mechanisms or information, people were choosing not to get married, or to delay marriage, so as not to have large families.[65]

The idea that choice exercised by individuals was causing population decline was a particularly worrying one for the Emigration Commission. Its report stated, with pragmatic acceptance, that women were apparently choosing to have fewer children so as to avail themselves of the 'social and cultural amenities' of towns; Bishop Lucey (with less pragmatism and more disapproval) so that they could have more freedom to leave their houses, more entertainment, more material goods.[66] Collis and Marsh, in their joint Reservation, showed that they believed this female choice to be a reality when they said that smaller families were, in any case, inevitable because 'the women themselves have made their views plain by their actions' – by not getting married.[67]

Perhaps Catholics were reluctant to engage with family limitation because of the burden of self-denial which Church-approved birth control practices might place on the man of the house, the overburdened and beleaguered breadwinner who was the converse of the much-criticised 'Single and Selfish'[68] man who would not take on the responsibilities of a family. If single men were cowards, then married men were heroes. When Francis Hanna, writing in 1951 on housing and families, questioned whether kitchen and scullery accommodation was sufficient in modern housing estates, he was certainly thinking of women's working convenience, but in his more detailed descriptions of the family home, he was led into random reflections on drying clothes, low spirits and a room of one's own:

> With climatic conditions as they are in this country it surprises me how little attention is paid to the provision of internal drying space for clothes. Unfortunately the living-room is often used for this purpose. It is not one of the pleasures of life for a father to come home on a wet evening and be obliged to sit and eat in the midst of drying clothes, and this more especially as by a common tradition housewives usually do clothes washing on Monday when a man's spirits are lowest. Finally, as well as outside storage accommodation, the man of the house should have a small outside shed in which to do odd jobs and indulge his favourite hobby without interference from, or annoyance to, the household.[69]

The wife is not seen to need anything other than a comparatively non-toxic and labour-saving working environment. Her load would be lighter, but she would continue to carry it virtually unaided. Her child-bearing was not considered a load which it was socially desirable to lighten.

THE IRISH HOUSEWIVES' ASSOCIATION 1943–56

Lucy Kingston and Rosamond Jacob attended a public debate in January 1944 about whether children's allowances should be paid to the mother or the father, 'and [spoke] up for women having control of the allowance, such as it is'. It was an odd time to have a debate as the question had already been settled at Dáil level. Kingston's shock at the size and scale of the allowance, which she notes in parenthesis in her diary with an exclamation mark, reflects well on her social conscience, but indicates how far removed she was from the realities of working-class and lower-middle class life, where £1 a month for every third and subsequent child could mean a substantial supplement to family income.[70] Indeed, the practical effect of this subsidy can be seen in the improved maternal health which was well under way by 1948. (See Chapter 5.)

Irish feminists in the 1940s and 1950s veered between the very practical and the very philosophical when it came to discussing women's household work. In one way it can be said that Irish feminists were almost completely focussed on the house and women's authority within it, in these decades. Even the veteran trade unionists and champions of women's rights Louie Bennett and Helen Chenevix believed that it was in women's relationship to home and family that the key to her 'advancement' lay. Bennett commented:

> Moreover, woman herself is still seeking her real place in the life of the world, and for those of us who belong to an older generation it is difficult to foresee what part she will play in the revolutionised and mechanised world we are entering on. One line of hope lies in a new approach to the home and the domestic sphere, and if the new generation accept home-keeping as a vocation and a social service I believe they will blaze a trail towards a finer civilisation than we have yet known.[71]

Helen Chenevix insisted that local government should be of interest to all women, whatever their 'special experience and interests may be, whether, domestic, professional and industrial' and she went on to identify the issues of particular interest to women as housing, public health, child welfare and school attendance:

> It may sound platitudinous to say that women are guardians of life and of the home, but if women all over the world would actually rise up and assert their guardianship of life and the home, it would mean our hard, noisy, machine-made civilisation would be revolutionised from within.[72]

The Irish Housewives' Association (IHA) was founded in Dublin in 1942 by Hilda Tweedy, an ex-teacher married to a businessman. The IHA was the immediate successor to the Irish Women's Citizens and Local Government Association, and self-consciously feminist. Many first-wave feminists and veterans of the suffrage movement were among its patrons.[73] Hanna Sheehy Skeffington wished the IHA well, and even had an article published posthumously in the first issue of *The Irish Housewife*, but she was more than a little bemused by this new – to feminists of her generation – preoccupation with the house.[74] The feminism of mid-century Ireland was almost identical to the maternalist feminism of early twentieth-century Europe. Women's interests were defined as those which reflected women's domestic concerns in the wider society. The IHA, while it was made up of mainly middle-class urban women, had a very broad social agenda. It was very concerned about the difficulties faced by what Susan Manning, in the first issue of *The Irish Housewife*, termed 'their [i.e. the housewives'] poorer neighbours'.[75] The wide variety of interests of the IHA comes through not only in Hilda Tweedy's account of it but also in the annual publication – consumer affairs, conditions in National Schools, quality control in foodstuffs, working-class housing, public health, local government, nutrition and diet and adoption. Well in advance of the publication of the National Nutrition Survey, *The Irish Housewife* was pointing out that many labourers' families did not have access to fresh fruit or even to milk.[76] The day-to-day childcare problems of the urban working-class mother of a family were outlined by Sheila Greene in 1946, while nursery schools and school meals

' I believe she's no one in particular. She's just symbolic . . . erected by a committee of grateful husbands.'

4. 'I believe she's nobody . . .' *Dublin Opinion*, September 1951: another obscure comment by Charles E. Kelly on women's household work and public importance. Is he making fun at the idea of housewives in the public sphere (like the Irish Housewives Association), or poking gentle fun at the idea of women of the house in the public sphere at all? Or is the idea that there would ever be a committee of grateful husbands the funniest aspect of this cartoon?

were tentatively recommended by other contributors to this, which can be seen as the association's flagship issue.[77] Helen Campbell was well aware of the argument that nursery schools interfered in home life:

> May we assume that these critics are doing all in their power to challenge and to change a social system which requires so many mothers to leave their children in order to supplement a weekly income which could not provide even the bare necessities of life?

There was no invocation of women's right to earn income regardless of marital status. However, when recommending school meals for children, Olivia Hughes referred to the rushed half-hour for lunch to enable children to be fed 'in the sanctity of the home', a phrase designed to deflate rhetoric about parental obligations and privileges.[78] Neither writer was recommending that mothers work outside the house, or that children be fed communally, but they were advocating some co-operative ventures, some help for the mother in rearing the child and keeping the house. Bishop Browne would probably have accused them of being upper-class ladies of leisure presuming to tell the poor what to do. As if to anticipate, and to mock, such a criticism, Andrée Sheehy Skeffington unlocked the subversive potential of such traditional, philanthropic activism:

'Educate the mothers', we are told. We agree, and we do our best. We tell them first, defend your rights as consumers; never pay more than the fixed price for any commodity; insist on getting the best your money can buy; have nothing to do with the black market; be particular as to the quality and cleanliness of all goods.

She went on to advocate instruction on health and hygiene in school, and school meals.[79]

Apart from specifics like day nurseries and school meals, the IHA's feminism was remarkably like that embraced by 'Eithne', Alice Curtayne, writers in the *Catholic Bulletin* in the 1920s and 1930s and later, Ita Meehan. It was home-centred; it defined women's concerns in the wider society as those which extended their domestic nurturing concerns; it did not question the division of authority and labour within families; it did not argue for educational equality; it did not protest against marriage bars and it never, ever, drew attention to the health risks of large families for mothers. Despite all this, it came in for severe criticism from many social Catholics. Muintir na Tire was quite wary of the IHA in the 1940s and 1950s.[80] Vigilans in *Christus Rex*, a newly-founded journal of sociology, noted sourly in 1948:

> Sometimes I think it would be a good idea if every association had somehow to justify its title before the public, say, by giving membership figures when making public utterances and claims . . . Take for instance a body like the Irish Housewives' Association and the Irish Women's Progressive League and the (just departed) Irish Women's Citizens and Local Government Association, whose joint secretaries write so many letters to the paper. Do they really represent the women and housewives of the country?[81]

The IHA *was*, on its own admission, a small, mostly Dublin-based, largely Protestant, overwhelmingly middle-class organisation. Vigilans' anxiety about representation echoes Bishop Browne's concerns about women's organisations in the session with the Joint Committee in 1940. Vigilans' criticisms of the IHA, however, were not confined to their size or their membership. Going on to reflect on the name-changing of organisations, he referred specifically to the metamorphosis of the Russia To-Day League into the Irish-USSR Society in 1948, thus establishing a link between the IHA and communism. Criticising the IHA for its suggestions about how to carry on without commercial bakeries during a strike, he stated that they were overlooking the obvious:

> namely, that housewives should bake their own bread. The answer to unsatisfactory capitalist bakeries is not communal bakeries but every home its own bakery.[82]

In 1949 Vigilans again criticised the IHA for:

putting over a little propaganda recently in favour of school meals in all the Dublin schools. The occasion, this time, is the report of the National Nutrition Survey . . . the form it takes, the usual one of a letter to the press from the joint Honorary Secretaries.

Vigilans went on to decry the idea that honest parents should be penalised because of the improvidence of bad parents, and to oppose the idea of any kind of universal benefits.[83] Yet Catholic social teaching was generally in favour of universal family allowances, and *Christus Rex* itself published at least one article in the 1950s which warmly supported school meals, infant nurseries for working mothers and universal health care.[84] A handbook of Catholic social thought published in 1949 admitted that 'the feeding of children outside the home is becoming a necessity'.[85] Vigilans' points of disagreement with the IHA are very heavily qualified and not very important in themselves. What is important is that the organisation is being painted as some kind of 'front' organisation. It was not only low-circulation scholarly journals that opposed the IHA: the *Roscommon Herald* suggested in 1952 that the IHA was a communist organisation, which caused consternation among the membership and several resignations; the paper in question published a formal apology a year later, but only after legal action had been taken.[86]

Irish feminists in the 1940s and 1950s were overwhelmingly of the servant-employing classes. Louie Bennett, in her minority *Report to the Commission on Youth Unemployment*, proposed that domestic service should be reorganised, training schools set up and the job given better status.[87] In an article entitled 'The Domestic Problem' in *The Irish Housewife* in 1946, Bennett left the reader in no doubt about what she saw as *the* domestic problem – the difficulty of getting good domestic servants *and* good mistresses, the need to redefine the archaic and mutually unsatisfactory mistress-servant relationship:

> Both [mistress and servant] must approach domestic service as a service to the community just as valuable as the civil service. The woman who sets up a home herself enters upon a form of domestic service and becomes thereby a servant of the community. The domestic help who comes into the home to co-operate in its service must hold an equal professional status with the housewife herself. The fact of the exchange of labour for money cannot affect that status.[88]

Bennett firmly believed that this relationship could be reformulated. She did not touch at all upon the woman of the house who could not afford paid domestic help, or on the question of who would perform the domestic labour of the woman who worked in somebody else's house. As seen in the first chapter, the 1940s and 1950s were the decades when women were leaving domestic service in their thousands. It took some time for the permanence of this departure to register with the servant-employing upper-middle classes. An article in *The Irish Housewife* in 1946 on a group of domestic servants in Northern Ireland who had been properly trained and were insisting on being called 'houseworkers' was determinedly upbeat in tone. It saved until the very end of the article these house-workers' complaints about the aspects of domestic service that were most difficult to change – long hours, unsocial time off, isolation, and, something which was seen by reformers worldwide to boost the professional status of the job but which was loathed by the workers themselves – the uniform.[89] *The Irish Housewife* ran an article in 1950 in which an English woman living in Ireland deplored the bad treatment of their servants by Irish women; this theme was a hundred years old at this stage.[90] It was not until 1956 that *The Irish Housewife* recognised that domestic servants had gone for good, with a bracing article on the psychologically therapeutic powers of housework.[91] The members of the association were obviously quicker learners than the majority of the members of the Commission on Emigration. While this commission acknowledged that lack of amenities was making housework particularly hard for rural women, its greater concern was for people who were suffering from the shortage of domestic servants. The Report's recommendation that families employing a servant should be paid a housekeeper allowance caused one of the commissioners, trade unionist Ruaidhri Roberts, to issue a Reservation to the Report, in which he pointed out that this proposed subsidy to high income married couples at the expense of the community as a whole, would be grossly unfair. He went on to emphasise that the Report's concern was, in any case, misplaced, advising that if money was to be given at all, it should be made available to:

> the mothers of large families in the lower-income group, particularly during periods of illness or childbirth, or other such times when home management is difficult or impossible to the mother.[92]

CONCLUSION

Would it have made any difference to the outcome of the debate about payment of children's allowances if Irish feminists had been involved at any stage of the process? Probably not – the pro-breadwinner scales were too heavily weighted not only by tradition and Catholic social thinking, but also by political expediency. Yet some involvement, even at the level of petitions and protests and resolutions, might have won Irish feminists some unlikely and welcome allies among representatives of small farmers and others. Would such an alliance have worked? The Clann na Talmhan and some of the Fine Gael support for paying the mothers was rooted in a fundamentally conservative view of the household and family, which believed that the sex-based division of labour was natural and that it conferred authority on women even while it limited their field of endeavour. Feminists of this era viewed women's field of endeavour as limited also, but in a different way. By forgoing all discussion of intra-familial authority and division of labour and income, and concentrating on women's domestic responsibilities and rights in the wider society, these feminists were giving up valuable ground without gaining anything in return except the precarious moral authority of the female philanthropist.

This moral authority was more precarious than ever before in the 1940s and 1950s. There was little or no opposition to women workers as such; there was even recognition that some married women's work would have to be countenanced, and there were no attacks on women's citizenship. However, public representatives of women of the house, like the Irish Housewives' Association, were greeted with either derision or suspicion. It was not just the IHA's overwhelmingly Protestant membership that was objected to – the Irish Countrywomen, as pointed out in the last chapter, had quite a large proportion of Protestant members also – nor was it just their advocacy of communal solutions to domestic problems, or the perception of them as belonging to a tradition of middle-class urban female philanthropy. None of these on their own would have been sufficient to arouse hostility, but the combination of all three was potent, and when it was added to an attempt to speak on behalf of the woman of the house, it was deadly. The refusal by those who proposed paying children's allowances to the father and those who advocated large families to acknowledge that different genders had differing experiences of subsistence and reproduction, leaves us in no doubt about how women's representatives who expressed opinions on these topics might have been treated. The pressing social problems of these two decades might have brought women of the house into the foreground, but it was precisely because they were so visible that they were silenced.

CHAPTER FOUR

Being Good To Themselves: Advice in Irish-Produced Popular Publications

Just when I'm all ironed out after a day of the children and I crawl into a chair to turn on the wireless for a half-hour to myself . . . what do I get? A couple of painfully fresh lady broadcasters who sound as if they never did a day's work in their lives telling me how they did in an afternoon what would take me a month. 'I was telling you Lil, last week, about how I mended the hole in the carpet with a piece of old towelling. Guess what I did this morning?' 'I couldn't, Maureen, but I wouldn't be surprised at what you'd do.' 'Well I re-teased and re-covered two settees'

Dublin Opinion 1941[1]

Charles E. Kelly, editor of *Dublin Opinion*, got great mileage out of what he saw as absurd or unrealistic images of women's household work. The piece above was unsigned, but his hand is all over it. Here, he suggests that much of the 'make-do-and-mend' advice to women is absurd, and comments ironically on the levels of energy expected of women of the house. There was nothing new about advice to women, but in this period concern about infant health and public health generally coincided with a belief in the psychological importance of environment, and an ever-growing number of items to be bought for the home not only furniture and fittings, but everything from cleaning agents to processed food. The 'housewife's' skill in producing this environment and managing these resources was seen as crucial. Women's pages, women's magazines, books of household advice and cookery books were full of advice about how to make food go further, items of clothing do twice over and days encompass twice the amount of work – *and* leisure time – as before.

Because Ireland was an anglophone country, most of the household and childcare advice books produced in Britain found their way into the country. Secondhand copies of Amalgamated Press's *The Motherhood Book* (London, n.d. c. 1932), A.C. Marshall's *Every Woman's Enquire Within* (London, n.d. 1930s) Mrs Sydney Frankenberg's *Common Sense in the Nursery* (London, 1922, 1946), Aunt Kaye *The Household Guide* (London, n.d. 1946–7), *Good Housekeeping's Baby Book* (London, 1944, 1952) M. Truby King's, *Mothercraft* (London, 1939), John Gibbens' *The Care of Young Babies* (London, 1940, 1959) have been bought in small bookshops and charity shops in Galway, Cork City, Limerick and Clonakilty. Old cookery books, some of them issued with the first electric cookers, can also be found. British women's magazines like *Woman's Own* and

Woman's Weekly were on sale here. This chapter, however, is concerned with exploring the Irish construction, for popular consumption, of the woman of the house in advice to women, so it will confine itself to advice to women *produced in Ireland* in these years in cookery and household advice books, women's pages of newspapers and journals and women's magazines.

The feminist consensus, up to recently, on women's magazines and advice to women is that they reinforced women's subordinate and secondary social status by putting pressure on them to conform to particular ideals of womanhood. Some writers argue that this advice literally constructed or invented the average woman. More recent discussions of women's magazines, in particular, are careful not to assume that household, beauty and personality advice was taken literally by women, suggesting that we look not only at what women read, but at how and why they read – for discrete (and discreet!) information, for entertainment, as an act of revolt against the values of their immediate environment, or even as an enjoyable act of revolt against what they were reading.[2] This chapter looks at the changing priorities and values in women's pages, household advice books and women's magazines over these forty years and advances some suggestions as to why these changes happened.

HOUSEHOLD ADVICE BOOKS PRODUCED IN IRELAND 1921–61

The books which will be looked at here are the Department of Agriculture's *Cookery Notes* (1923, 1944), Josephine Redington's *Economic Cookery Book* (1927), Roper and Duffin's *Bluebird Cookery Book for Working Women* (1939), Cathal Brugha Street's *All In The Cooking* (1943), Ann Hathaway's *Homecraft Book* (1944) and Maura Laverty's *Kind Cooking* (1946). All were published in Ireland and some incorporate household advice or some thoughts on household work along with the cookery.

'The average cookery book is either too expensive or contains such a bewildering number of recipes that the beginner is unable to make proper use of it', stated the Introduction to *Cookery Notes* (all editions). There is nothing at all bewildering about this very basic book of cookery and household advice. Originally intended for use in classes put on by the Department of Agriculture and Technical Instruction, it was also used in secondary schools in the 1940s. The recipes, realistically, given the living conditions of the majority of Irish people throughout this period, assume that all cooking would be done on the fire; they are comprehensive in range and include general principles for cooking different kinds of food. The book is not as basic as its protestations would suggest. It includes Christmas cake, pastry, mayonnaise and other comparatively 'fancy' items. There is also a section on basic housework – how to clean a stove, clean steel, set a fire, wash kitchen tables, scrub floors, clean saucepans and pots, wash breakfast and dinner ware and clean silver, china and bone-handled knives.[3] These notes, and all cookery and household instruction, had a dual purpose – to train girls for the homes which, it was believed, they would one day manage, and also to provide some basic training for domestic servants. The 1942 edition included the Department of Local Government and Health's pamphlet; 'A Simple Guide to Wholesome Diet'. The latest health information on vitamins, minerals and other food values was included, along with guidelines on accessible ways of getting all the daily requirements. For example, a third of a pint of milk and wholemeal bread and butter with grated carrot or cheese or lettuce was promoted as 'an almost ideal and simple school meal'. Those with the ground to grow vegetables were advised to do so. It was pointed out that tea was not a food as such. These recommendations are very like those provided by the British Ministry of Food, particularly with the stress on raw carrot, cheese and greens. Readers were urged not to 'despise' skimmed milk or separated milk as 'fit only for animals'.[5]

Josephine Redington in the 1929 edition of her cookery book (first published in 1905), recommended that domestic economy instructresses try to dispel 'hurtful prejudices, such as that skim milk is only fit for pigs, that Indian meal is only fit for fowl'. *Cookery Notes* does not mention Indian meal at all, though Maura Laverty's *Never No More* (1942) suggests a familiarity with it in her childhood in Kildare in the 1920s and it was certainly used extensively on the Great Blasket Island in the 1920s.[6] Josephine Redington taught in the Irish Training School for Domestic Economy in Dublin up to 1935, and had been active in itinerant instruction since the early years of the century.[7] Her book is aimed at teachers who would be working in small towns and rural areas. It begins with sample budgets and sample menus for the rural labourer, his wife, and four children under fifteen and vegetables and fruit (potatoes, cabbage, onions and rhubarb) were to be grown in the 'plot of ground attached to the cottage'; hens and chickens were to be kept to provide eggs, the odd table fowl and the wherewithal for a reserve fund. This latter was to be used 'for recreation, or in any emergency, such as in time of sickness or for a wedding or fitting out a boy or girl for domestic service'.[8] For Redington, cookery and home management depended upon a tightly-organised household, with some small resources of its own. She did, however, advise instructors to find out first the average wages in the neighbourhood and its food resources, and to avoid using materials which were too expensive or not easily available. She also made out a 'Practical Application of the Above Table of Weekly Expenditure to the Home', which consisted of day-by-day menus. Monday's menu, for example, went as follows:

Monday:
Breakfast . . . Tea, bread and margarine, 2 eggs for parents – Porridge and skimmed milk and some bread for children.
Dinner . . . Mutton broth (2 lbs boiled mutton), thickened with oatmeal and vegetables, bread (for all).
Supper . . . Cocoa (with milk and sugar), bread and cheese (a quarter lb) (all).

Indian meal, salt ling for Friday and boiled rice as a substitute for potatoes were some of the foodstuffs included. Methods of drawing up weekly accounts were also explained. In these sample menus adults rather than children were given priority in protein intake. This can be seen in the menus given above, and in Saturday's supper menu where the parents were to have tea, bread and butter and an egg each, and the children, 'cocoa and buttermilk pancakes (eggless) alternating with thick oatcake made on griddle'. The faith in the nutritional value of cocoa and the importance of sugar and carbohydrates for children especially was typical of its time, as the children's recipes in *The Motherhood Book*, Truby King's book or even in John Gibbens' later book show.[9] In the sample menus Redington 'allowed' exactly the same amount of food to the mother and the father; this ideal of nutritional equality was also promoted by the British Ministry of Food during the Second World War: '*She* needs as much meat as *he* does. Do heavy workers need more meat? No. Daily wear and tear on the tissues is not materially affected by the kind of work done.'[10]

The Bluebird Cookery Book for Working Women by Margaret Roper (Diplomée in Cookery) and Ruth Duffin (1939), is a very different publication. Like Redington's book, it went beyond cookery with sections on health, but it was far more detailed on the physical and emotional welfare of babies and children. Was the title a recognition of the fact that some women in charge of a house also had to go out to work? In the 1930s, however, 'working' often meant 'working-class', and this seems to be what is meant by the title. The book itself has a rather severe didactic rather than a chatty tone and there is no reference anywhere in it to servants. Granted that most household advice books had some element of didacticism, they did not, by the 1930s, come down as heavily as Roper and Duffin on, for example, the social importance of good feeding and cooking: 'Bad feeding and cooking may make people take to drink as a temporary means of driving away discomfort'. They vilified tea as at best, empty of nutrition, and at worst, poison, in a peroration which would be heartily echoed by today's nutritionists, and was probably even more utopian then than it is now. They go into much more detail than Redington on health, advising fresh air, open exercise and daily moving of the bowels (to be achieved by drinking plenty of water and eating plenty of fresh fruit and vegetables and brown bread). Medicines were to be avoided but if they were necessary then 'a quarter teaspoon of Epsom salts in your breakfast tea will be a help . . . If medicine must be taken, a small dose every night is better than a large one at intervals'. The regular use of laxatives was already being discouraged by health authorities who believed that these 'aperients' would make the bowel lazy and unable to work. Roper and Duffin were also much more detailed on the care of babies, recommending breastfeeding but providing detailed instructions on how to rear babies on bottles, and concurring with the likes of Mrs Sydney Frankenberg that children should be out in the open as much as possible. The last page of the book was a concise guide to childrearing, again, very like that promoted by the childcare authorities of the day:

1. Never threaten a child or shout at it.
2. Never tell a lie to a child.
3. Never frighten a child.
4. Never bribe a child.
5. Be gentle, but firm, with a child from babyhood; give a reason for an order when possible.
6. Regularity and sleep.[11]

Part of the reason for focussing on women of the house in the 1930s in particular was to exhort these women to buy more Irish goods. The Women's Industrial Development Assocation brought out, in 1935, *The Woman At the Wheel: Household Handbook*. This consisted of consumer information about Irish goods, with a small section on household hints. Its hints were taken from *Cookery Notes* and the verse at the end leaves no doubt about the priorities of the association:

> An ideal home has room for no complaints, Tis painted spick and span with Irish paints. From roof to ground no trace of dust is seen, Tis cleansed with Irish goods and therefore clean . . . And those who in this ideal homestead dwell, By Irish food are rendered fit and well, Though hygiene paves the way, they rightly think Good health's maintained on Irish food and drink. Thus hygiene, health and happiness are found, In every home where Irish goods abound.[12]

Maura Laverty's *Flour Economy* (1940) was mainly a collection of recipes based on potatoes and oatmeal in a drive to save wheat. There was a foreword by John Ingram, Chief Inspector of Technical Schools. Saving wheat was women's duty:

> The conscientious housekeeper who prizes her family's health will welcome the opportunity to vary the menu by the introduction of these palatable and health-giving recipes. As a good citizen, she will derive further satisfaction from the knowledge that she is helping to solve the problem of conserving the country's wheat . . . The home-maker who substitutes oatmeal for flour whenever possible is not only helping our national policy, but is also providing health and well-being for her family at low cost.[13]

A number of responsibilities were being referred to, here. The injunction is almost identical in tone to those of the British Ministry of Food, but the emphasis on citizenship is also building on over a decade of advice to Irish women. *All In The Cooking*, so familiar to generations of students, first published in 1946 by the Cathal Brugha St College of Domestic Economy in Dublin, was very technical, quite scientific and detailed, as most of those who attended the college went on to become professional cooks in hotels and other institutions, or domestic science teachers in schools. However, it constantly referred to the 'housewife':

The housewife who studies the market, compares prices and finds out what supplies are available, will be amply repaid by the economical and successful result she will get in running her home. Common sense and discrimination in the choice of food is essential where the amount of money is limited, and the smaller the amount of money the greater is the necessity for spending it to the best advantage.

There followed several tips for economical feeding of a family – food should be bought from hygienic shops where trade was brisk, the shopper should go in person rather than ordering by telephone (obviously aimed at the middle-class house, or the cook working in it), cash payments were best and household accounts should be kept. All this efficiency of administration was to the specific purpose of nutritious and hygienic cookery, and there was no suggestion at all about the mission of the housewife or the social importance of the happy, well-fed household.[14] Nor was there in Ann Hathaway's *Homecraft Book*, published in Dublin two years earlier. This stated boldly as its starting assumption: 'Every housewife should organise her work as a man organises his business'. The insistence on a time-oriented rather than a task-oriented approach to housework, already apparent in the published advice of the earlier period, was ever louder in the years after 1943 and owed something to the time-and-motion studies of those years. Labour-saving devices and strategies were eagerly propagandised. The woman of the house was told to rationalise, reorganise and prioritise, and if she was over-burdened and unable to cope, she had nobody but herself to blame.[15]

The Homecraft Book cost one shilling and sixpence and was printed on emergency paper which has faded to a brittle brown. The book's content is divided into advice on house, health, beauty, and dress. The household advice is relentlessly practical and involves so much recycling that the book deserves to be reissued as a Green classic! The recommended recycling was for economic and time-saving purposes. The book addresses the experience of women doing all their own housework and operating on a tight budget in houses with piped water and electricity and rooms for different purposes, without servants. Readers might like to try some of the hints it contained, if they can find calico, enamel pails, blacking and other staples of fifty-odd years ago: old brown shoes could be made to look like new black ones by rubbing with the cut side of a potato, and then polishing with equal parts blue-black ink and ordinary blacking; pails could be mended by applying enamel paint, a sheet of calico and enamel paint over that again; spectacles could be prevented from fogging up during washday by rubbing the lenses with soap then polishing; matches could be made go farther by being split in two and curtains could be turned upside down when becoming worn and shabby.[16] There are tips on beauty and health, e.g. on how to remove nicotine stains from the fingers (with eau-de-Cologne). A drop of brandy in the palm of the hand, taken up through the nose, would relieve neuralgia. The section on health also involved discussion of a balanced diet – eggs and cheese, fruit and vegetables, calcium-rich buttermilk – and cures for chilblains, indigestion, warts, corns and all the niggling discomforts and chronic complaints suffered by women of child-bearing years on their feet all day in draughty houses. There were hints on how to make one egg go as far as two (beat a smoothly-mashed cold-boiled potato into the raw egg, then fry); recipes for five-minute soup, 'war-malade', and so on – the recipes are similar to the ones put out by the British Ministry of Food, in these years, but they are not copies.[17] The text of the book was interspersed at rare intervals with advertisments for Jessel's Cod Liver Oil, *Question Time* by Joe Linnane (a popular radio programme), Chivers jams and jellies and other Irish products. The author referred in her foreword to her 'long experience as a domestic correspondent'. I have not been able to find her in either the *Irish Press*, the *Irish Independent* or the *Irish Times*, or in any of the women's magazines of the 1930s, 1940s or 1950s. Ann Hathaway could be a pseudonym and a play on words implying resourcefulness (Ann Hath-a-way). She could be Mary Frances Keating, a contributor to *The Vanishing Irish*, whose short biography mentioned that she had published a book of household advice, a book which I have consistently failed to locate under the name of Mary Frances Keating.[18]

Hathaway's time and money-saving hints would have been commonplace enough in the 1920s and 1930s. Her advice to 'go over every inch of your house and remove ornaments or any article you can do without' shows the extent to which aesthetics and sentiment had to be sacrificed to comfort and convenience, a utility-consciousness very popular in the 1940s. Later, in women's pages in the 1950s, there would be more emphasis on buying nice and useful things for the house, though the parallel obligation to convenience would result in some (to my mind) hideous compromises.[19] The inclusion of beauty and dress under the general heading 'Homecraft' was typical of the household advice books of the era – this was a new area of expertise to be mastered by the woman of the house. The introductory remarks on the work of the house display a very business-oriented attitude to the work of the house. A short-term 'capital' outlay of resources – of time and of money – which would save time and money in the long run was recommended. Hathaway sets her face firmly against the woman of the house as a doormat:

> Thoughtless, lazy or untidy members should be made sit up. Adults should at least be able to look after their own clothes and belongings. Any child over 4 years of age can be quickly trained to do the same . . . Offenders should be made to realise how very unfair it is to impose upon the average housewife's willingness to accept the dozen-and-one 'valeting' jobs which no considerate person would consider part of her routine work. It's something worth having a row about![20]

There is no ideal of the self-effacing, self-sacrificing wife and mother here. Assuming this kind of co-operation, the average housewife should get through 'the essential morning programme' of turning back beds, opening windows, collecting dirty clothes, washing up after breakfast and tidying the kitchen,

5. Homecraft book frontispiece. Ann Hathaway, *The Homecraft Book* (Dublin 1944). No open fire, no sprigged pinafore, buckets of water or churns in this popular Irish cookery advice produced in the 1940s; instead, a determinedly modern kitchen presided over by a determinedly modern woman, a feather duster under her arm and an apron being the only 'cut of work' about her. Inside the book however, is a fund of information on making, mending, saving, recycling, in a house with no servant and no hoover.

cleaning and setting firegrates, sweeping and tidying the dining-room and sitting-room, making beds, tidying the bedrooms, cleaning the bathroom, sweeping the hall and stairs and dusting downstairs, in two hours and a half. Then, the midday meal, which had been planned the day before ('It is the only really satisfactory way of ensuring a pleasing variation of meals and their trouble-free preparation') has to be shopped for and prepared. The obligation to provide a pleasant variety of meals has slipped in almost unnoticed. The woman of the house should discourage 'running buffets'; everybody should eat together, so as not to have to keep dinner hot for hours and delay washing up.[21] The afternoon is set aside for special cleaning jobs – turning out of individual rooms, carpet cleaning and so on. The whole point of all these rules, Hathaway points out, is so that 'some little part of the day may be claimed as her own by the efficient housewife'. Work and leisure are put into separate time blocks. Small children and babies could disrupt the routine, in which case all the rules had to be 'considered subject to their special needs . . . Mother must accommodate herself to circumstances'. All was not lost however, because:

> Half the battle is won if the planned routine is adhered to strictly with the children as with every other activity. Fixed times for feeding, bathing, sleeping and their every regular daily need, will be best for the children themselves and will facilitate the readier gauging and rationing of time for other duties.[22]

The importance of regularity of feeding and sleeping and all other needs, for children, was just beginning to fall from favour in the 1940s. Its main benefit for Hathaway was the way it allowed 'Mother' to keep to her time-oriented timetable of work. The reference to its advantages for the children has to be seen as parenthetical, as this is the only mention of children in the book. Indeed, looking after children is referred to only insofar as it is a disruption of the normal routine of the woman of the house.

Writing before the boom in consumer goods and appliances and gadgets for the house, the author does not constantly refer to 'war-time' shortages and, apart from food (even here the war is not mentioned explicitly, except in the case of 'war-malade'), the impression given is that shortages and making-do-and-mending are a normal part of everyday life.

The everyday life that is imagined is that of an urban, lower-middle class family. Hathaway gives as her 'likely average' . . . a house of five or six rooms (excluding kitchen and bathroom) and a family of four or five . . . There is no maidservant. There is no Hoover. It is assumed that there is linoleum on the floor. The cover shows a slim, well-made-up woman sitting in a gleaming, modern kitchen reading. The kitchen has a sink, presses, a cooker and a tiled floor.[23] The house being described is the three or four-bedroomed house of the family of a white-collar worker or artisan who were as far from struggling as they were from ease, with either electricity or gas, and piped water, lino on the floors and the stairs, and frugality the order of the day. The house is bare (all

34 *WASTE NOT—WANT NOT*

RAGS: Always keep a quantity of old rags in the peg basket. When hanging celanese garments they are invaluable : a small piece under each peg protects the garment from laddering.

MACKINTOSH: Cut out best part of old mack as a waterproof apron; very useful to wear under coat to keep front of skirt dry when cycling on wet day·

LINOLEUM: Lino firelighters : Cut old, discarded lino in strips with sharp knife, use these instead of sticks to light fires.

WASTE NOT—WANT NOT

CANDLE ENDS: Here is a way of using up old candle ends : Collect them till you have a good supply and then melt them down. Put the melted wax in a saucer and make tapers from it by drawing short lengths of fairly long string through it. Leave the wax string to set and you will have some tapers all ready to stand in a jar in your fireplace for people to use for lighting cigarettes. Such a saving on matches, too!

CORKS AND TINS (Uses for): Save corks of every size, and condensed milk tins. You can make your own stoppers for holes in enamelware. Slice corks with a razor blade, burn a hole through the centre with an old knitting needle; cut the tin with an old scissors; punch hole through centre with a nail; you can buy the small nuts and bolts to fix in position. You have them for a half-penny each.

STRING (To use pieces of): Save all pieces of string, knot them together and wind in a ball. Get a pair of No. 9 steel needles, cast on 40 stitches and knit plain a piece of twelve or fifteen inches square. These make excellent dish cloths.

EGG WATER (A use for): Don't throw away the water in which eggs are boiled. It can be very useful. Steep the eggspoons in it and the stains which the eggs leave can soon be cleaned off. Or have you weeds in your garden? Well, the water in which eggs have been boiled is a most effective weed-killer·

LABEL ECONOMY: If you have to use a tie-on label for luggage or parcel, write the address across the end, not down the whole length· Next time the label is needed cut this end off and write on the remaining piece.

SOAP SUDS (Use for): Never waste soap suds, no matter how dirty they are; throw them on rose trees and fruit bushes. In these days, when manures and fertilisers are short, they work wonders.

5a. An example of the kind of household advice in *The Homecraft Book*.

ornaments have been removed, remember!), dark (saving on light and on light colours which show the dirt), draughty (no big fire for cooking in the kitchen); groceries are shopped for every day and not delivered weekly – the family is not that well-off. Everything that is bought has to last years. Hathaway's book is not thinly-disguised product advice; she has second and third uses for everything from the water eggs have been boiled in, to apple cores, to old 'hopeless' knitted garments which just cannot be darned. (The tip about making old brown shoes into new black ones can be found in the British-published *Household Guide*, edited by Aunt Kaye and undated, though it seems to have been published a little later;[24] this was obviously a 'hint' which was in the public domain.)

Maura Laverty's *Kind Cooking* (1946) is more properly a cookery book but it contains plenty of prescriptions about the priorities of the woman of the house. Laverty roots her cookery advice firmly in stories and anecdotes about the unspecified past shading into the present, in County Kildare. Her evocation of a rural past of wholesome ingredients and simple way of life is her attempt to establish an indigenous Irish cooking tradition for which she has not been given enough credit. Bríd Mahon tells us that Laverty was a regular visitor to the archives of the Irish Folklore Commission in the 1940s and 1950s for information about food,[25] so we are talking here about a very self-conscious writer who was not only (we can assume) recording what she remembered, but also perhaps encapsulating information collected by folklorists into personal reminiscence. Her enthusiasm for novelty and variety is by no means incompatible with this. She mildly and humourously criticises many 'old ways', making fun of people she sees as wilfully ignorant, best illustrated in the story (in *Full and Plenty* published in 1960) of the prosperous farmer who asked for his hat and left in disgust when presented with a plate of consommé in Lawlor's Hotel in Naas: 'Let them that ate the meat ate the gravy'.[26] The author herself, when she lived in Spain, 'disgraced myself and the country I had come from' when she mistook vegetable marrow for fish.[27] Still, enthusiasm for the new is combined with enduring respect for the old, as is evident from her description of the 'big earthen-floored kitchen at home' and its open fire:

> Maybe the cooking arrangements in our kitchen were primitive. We thought them grand. We had the pot-oven to give our bread and baked meats matchless flavour. There was its young brother, the griddle, for whenever we wanted quick bread, or scones . . .

She goes on to describe the open fire and the various implements that went with it.[28] Writing in 1946, the fireplace on which about half of her countrywomen were still cooking was being identified as 'primitive' and located firmly in the past, but it was not denigrated; its utility, rather than its warmth or tradition, was praised. Elsewhere in *Kind Cooking* she refers to 'our own kitchen at home on the bog'.[29] Rathangan, where Laverty grew up, is certainly on the bog, but she grew up in the town itself. No doubt her mother cooked on the fire, as did most people in country towns and many people in cities too, up to the 1920s but a rural setting is definitely implied in Laverty's description. It is hard to know if the past she is describing in *Kind Cooking* is her own past, or the fictionalised past of *Never No More*: 'Gran' is absent from the former, but several other characters from the latter feature – Moll Slevin and the Reddins of the bog, for example.[30]

Once Laverty has described the open fire with due respect, she goes on to extol the convenience of an electric stove; she praises the idea of a stock-pot, and also welcomes tinned food for handiness, breaking into song:

> When friends come unexpected, do I fuss and tear my hair, Even though there's only meat enough for two? No: I walk into the kitchen with a calm unruffled air, I pick a tin of bully beef that's waiting for me there, I mix it with an onion and a fervent grateful prayer, And for dinner we have savoury ragoût.

There are recipes for French dressing and salads using garlic and hedgerow herbs and garnishes.[31] She is writing for an urban audience – milk comes in bottles, eggs come in boxes – but constantly stresses that she herself has developed this knowledge and expertise in kitchens ranging from the primitive to the modern, thus suggesting its accessibility to everybody.[32] Maura Laverty certainly does not ignore rural life and conditions; in both *Kind Cooking* and *Full and Plenty*, all the stories are set in Ballyderrig, Laverty's fictional homeplace on the bog. Every chapter in *Full and Plenty* is introduced by a well-written story about some characters in Kildare in the 1920s and 1930s. The stories are highly entertaining and atmospheric but, despite attempts to emphasise the best of the old and the new, give the impression that rural life and its characters belong to the colourful past. In any case, cooking is more than putting food on the table, it is lore that should be passed on from mother to daughter: 'Every little girl born into this world loves to help in the kitchen'. The mother was gravely at fault if she hindered her daughter from helping and thus stunted her interest in cooking and food preparation.[33] Another obligation on the mother was to make mealtimes pleasant, not only insofar as the food was concerned – Ann Hathaway's 'pleasing variation' – but in her mood at the meal itself:

> It isn't always easy to be good-humoured at meal times, particularly after a hot and tiring session in the kitchen . . . A cake may fall, a sauce may burn, a custard may curdle, – none of them disasters, but all of them sufficient to make us want to carry our kitchen woes into the dining-room. To do this (and I have been guilty of it many a time), is, I think, the worst kind of culinary crime . . . what is important is to make meal-time the kernel of happy family life, the hour of reunion and relaxation and content.

The mood is as important as the meal, and note that Laverty takes for granted that the woman of the house will be a perfectionist and will be bitterly disappointed when reasonably elaborate cooking techniques fail. The presentation of the meal was also important:

Whether you consider [the serving of the meal] every bit as important as the other two [steps] or merely a detail depends on whether your purpose in feeding your family is just to feed them and get them out of the way, or to give them pleasure of eye and palate and health of mind and body. Naturally it is the latter or you wouldn't be reading this book.[34]

As far as prescription goes, this is a long way from the gloomy but simple prediction that bad feeding might make men turn to drink.

Laverty's emphasis on the moral grammar of cooking is unusual for its time in Ireland and she comes nearest of all the writers to promoting the Happy Housewife Heroine,[35] which is not very near, at that. Her view of the woman's role as sacred is linked to folklore beliefs about food and its power, but there are elements of the modern, too – the woman's duty to experiment with new ways of doing things, her willingness to risk a small daughter spoiling food by trying to cook, and above all the depiction of cooking as fulfilling and rewarding, emotionally as well as physically. Laverty, however, is unusual among advice writers. She is remembered more as a novelist than a journalist, one of her books was banned for its indulgence towards adulterous characters, and in at least three of her other books, her characters – as long as they are not dishonest, mean with money or bullies – regularly get away with breaches of the code of sexual morality. Laverty was also a political activist and a founding member of Clann na Poblachta. An entire study should be devoted to Laverty's vision of Ireland, and her cookery advice was part of this vision.[36] Laverty is very different to Hathaway and to many other advisers of the period. She is not constantly telling the cook to take it easy, to make time for herself; for her, cooking itself is a joy. Even convenience tinned food has to be made into 'savoury ragoût'.

WOMEN'S PAGES AND MAGAZINES

'The modern idea is to get as much pleasure with as little trouble as possible' commented the *Catholic Bulletin* in 1937. This was not, as one might expect, a despairing comment on the depradations of modern youth, but a burst of enthusiasm about picnics. The article went on to extol the advantages of sliced pans and thermos flasks, to wave a cheery goodbye to hampers and gathering sticks to make fires.[37] Bean a'Tighe, who wrote the regular 'For Mothers and Daughters' column in the *Catholic Bulletin*, was always telling mothers not to work too hard, and enjoining daughters to get mothers to take it easy. The only person who never got a holiday, she commented in 1923, was 'the average housewife'.[38] References to holidays, picnics and thermos flasks remind us that the women being addressed are probably middle class. That they were not envisaged as very rich is suggested by the comment in 1923, in the annual spring-cleaning article, that 'nowadays', through 'necessary retrenchment', the housewife 'often combines in her own person the varied duties of cook, housemaid and nursemaid, and the occasional help of a "char-lady" is deemed there wasn't a word that could be said against him for he had a fine farm of land. Having been sounded through a second party, he expressed himself willing to take Miss Mary to his bed, her well-known genius for catering to his board, and her two hundred and fifty pounds to his bank.

On the evening the expected fiancé was invited to drop in for supper and a settlement, Miss Mary went beyond herself in the matter of food. There was a tender brawn with jewels of spicy jelly studding its meaty ruddiness, milky cold roast porksteak that cut into delicate rings enclosing circlets of parsley-specked stuffing, ham as pink as rose petals selvedged with sweet nacre which had been simmered with love and reverence in a nectar of spring water and stout and onions and treacle. There were little cakes and big cakes, fruit cakes and seedy cakes, tarts and treacle scones and scones made of yellow meal. But Miss Mary's chef d'oeuvre was the trifle, a sherry-soaked, cherry-sprinkled glory on which the whipped cream rose in Alpine peaks. All in all, that heavenly trifle should have been enough to make any normal man overlook such mundane trifles as small dowries and middle-age.

Dinny Foran sat down to all this magnificence. He looked from one delight to another. Then he reached for a slice of plain bread. He ate his bread, drank a cup of tea, stood up, broke off the match and walked out of the house. He said afterwards it was the trifle which was mainly responsible. "Three kinds of meat and six sorts of cake were bad enough," he said. "But a woman who would waste good cream on a pudding instead of churning it into butter would have a man in the workhouse inside a month."

Miss Mary had no regrets. She felt that she was well rid of a man who was so lacking in soul as to disrespect her lovely trifle. As things turned out, Mr. Rooney was not displeased to be left with his sister on his hands, for the poultry-instructress suddenly became nostalgic for a boy she knew in Dublin and she went back to him. The people of Ballyderrig were glad to see her go. We had no love for outsiders who came with suggestions as to how we might improve ways that had served us well for centuries.

Page Fifty-Eight

I am sure there are several morals in that story. For me, the most obvious is this: A proper appreciation of the sweet course is of great importance in courtship and marriage. Luckily, there are few Dinny Forans, so you won't be wasting your sweets on the dessert air if you try out some of these recipes.

MILK PUDDINGS

That these are good for the health is no reason for not making them attractive to the eye and thrilling to the palate. Milk puddings were primarily invented for children. These discriminating beings are the true gastronomic experts. The appearance and texture of food mean much to them, which may explain why they so often prefer to be sent from the table in disgrace rather than force themselves to swallow that culinary calamity which is known as plain rice pudding. The artistic instinct is strong in children. It makes them reject chunks of stodgy starch, and value puddings that are light and appealing. The poetic instinct is strong in them, too, making names important. I have noticed that if I beat plumped prunes into a milk pudding and call it Prune Fluff, it is eaten with far more relish than if I serve it as plain cornflour and stewed prunes.

Here are a few suggestions for making milk puddings attractive:

1. Don't cook them over direct heat—it's slow cooking that ensures creaminess and the preservation of food values. Use a double boiler, or, if the pudding is being baked, stand the dish in a pan of hot water when putting it into the oven.

2. In the case of unbaked puddings containing eggs, don't mix in yolk and white together. Take a tip from the cooks of long ago who specialised in flummeries: mix in the egg-yolks before the pudding is taken from the heat, and fold in the beaten whites later on. This will give you a light fluffy pudding which even the most finicky won't be able to resist.

3. When making custards, you need have no fear of eggs curdling if you go easy on the sugar and the heat, and if you . . . .

Page Fifty-Nine

6. 'there wasn't a word to be said against him'. From Maura Laverty, *Kind Cooking* (Tralee 1946): this extract is typical of Maura Laverty's anecdotal way of writing about cookery, and her habit of locating cookery advice firmly in a traditional rural society, while sneaking in modern advice by disparaging unthinking conservatism.

a luxury'. This had its advantages in that it shortened and simplified the cleaning, 'reduces our possessions to the useful and practical, and presses into service the many modern 'labour-savers'.[39] Chronologically this advice precedes Josephine Redington and Ann Hathaway, but it is addressing an entirely different milieu to that of the former, and a more prosperous world to that of the latter. The much more popular *Irish Messenger of the Sacred Heart* which had a 'home page' (under various guises) throughout this period, swung giddily from one social class to another. Madame Marie-Jacques told readers about 'How We Renovated Our Home' in 1927,[40] but the following year she was giving very detailed advice about children's health and well-being, in the form of a story about a nun, Sr Ignatius, who took over the rearing (in a family home rather than an orphanage) of a young family whose parents had died untimely. (Was it felt that a nun would have more authority with readers or was this a preposterous editorial suggestion that only nuns could make proper mothers?) There was a list of things that should never be eaten by children (including fried and tinned food, pork, game, seasonings of any kind except a little salt, all compatible with other books on childcare advice of the period); advice about common childhood illnesses; the need for a separate bed for each child (to prevent cross-infection), and all the other staples of childhood advice of the period including the injunction to fresh air. Regularity was of the utmost importance: 'A child's order of the day should be as carefully planned, and as perfectly kept, as that of a soldier or a nun.' The joyless coercion of much Catholic practice in pre-Vatican II Ireland comes through in some of the recommendations about order and regularity. Dawdling over 'the toilette' was to be discouraged as this would lead 'to much Mass-missing in later life', and children were not to be allowed to drink water 'at odd times' or else they would want to drink water in the middle of the night and would be 'thus incapacitated from going to Communion'.[41] Daily Mass-going was envisaged, a clue that the urban experience was seen as the norm. However, as far as childcare was concerned, the *Messenger* was fairly up-to-date; another article in 1930 insisted that children had to be allowed to make noise and get dirty – overalls could be easily made so that they could spare their clothes.[42] The *Messenger*'s home page changed every year, with new by-lines and emphases (in 1932, for example, there was a series on making 'the family wardrobe' by Eilis).[43] Always there were household hints and advice about health; readers were advised in January 1945 how to get rid of mice, told about how unsafe milk was in 1947, and scolded, Hathaway-fashion, for lack of organisation:

> Many housewives need not complain so bitterly about feeling overworked and overtired if they gave a little thought about how to save themselves unnecessary fatigue . . .

This was to be achieved, not by cutting down on work, but by assembling all the cleaning materials in one place before a job was begun.[44] Again in 1951, 'Fidelma' in 'The Daily Round' suggested that a great deal of labour could be saved in the home 'if regular methodical rules are followed'. Then follows the by-now familiar list of the 'inevitable daily jobs' of bedmaking, firemaking, dusting and washing-up; the weekly jobs of washing and ironing and 'turning out' the various rooms; the monthly jobs of window-cleaning, turning out cupboards and 'odd jobs around the house'. Shopping should be done on only two days in the week, and comfortable shoes should be worn.[45]

Newspaper women's pages differ from those of the periodical-journals in that there is far more preoccupation with appearance in the former rather than the latter, throughout the entire period. The fact that this is often promoted through thinly-disguised advertising copy doesn't make it any less pervasive, possibly even more so. Because few aspects of the life of the woman of the house were left undiscussed, and certainly no material aspects, the question of what she should wear working around the house often came up. But consider the difference between the way this was discussed in the newly founded *Irish Press* in 1931 and the *Irish Independent* in 1943 and 1947. The *Irish Press* never had a woman's page as such, due to the editorial principle that all news should be of interest to women, but Máire Comerford was 'woman's editor' in the 1930s. Comerford had a long record of political activism; she had served on one of the committees of the First Dáil, was an active member of Cumann na mBan, and was for some time secretary to Alice Stopford Green, the historian. In 1969 she was to publish a book on the First Dáil. The *Irish Press* in the early years contains a wide range of features with women as the topic – women in industry, women and poverty and working women's rights, as well as many articles about the household, childcare and appearance.[46] One article complained in 1931 that every other kind of worker had an outfit, 'but nobody seems to suggest a sane, practical outfit for the woman who does her own housework'. The outfit should be warm and durable, with appropriate underclothes for comfort and warmth; the eventual recommendation was for a skirt in a woollen material and a sleeveless knitted pullover. In 1943, a puff for Jane West patterns in the *Irish Independent* showed a sketch of a woman in a pretty dress posing beside a vase of flowers. The copy ran:

> I wonder why it is that some women who are most particular as to how they look when they go out, do not pay a scrap of attention to what they wear while doing daily housework? Probably because they feel that 'anything goes' for the house and, more often than not, no one, except perhaps the children and the unfortunate husband, sees them. This is all wrong, both for you and for them. Here is an idea which should find favour with all housewives – an 'overall frock' that is easily slipped into, yet made up in some gay cotton fabric, is smart and becoming, and at the same time, essentially practical.

In 1947 the case for the gay cotton overall was made again: 'I like to see a woman pretty even when she is busy doing her housework'.[47] In 1931 the emphasis was on comfort and on recognition of the woman of the house as a worker like any other. By the 1940s it was on aesthetics and recognition of the woman of the house as like any other public images of women at the time – pretty, or at least, pleasing to the eye.

Throughout the period women's pages in newspapers (and the same goes for the women's magazines which we will be looking at) were not aimed only at women working in their own houses, they were also directed at 'business girls' or girls and women working outside the home. In a week in 1924 the *Freeman's Journal* carried articles on the following: how not to spoil children; the New Corset; how to stencil wallpaper; how to bake bran bread; how 'business girls' should organise their days; how to trim towels; how to restore a faded, shabby hat; how to decorate a bedsitting room, and also gave several recipes.[48] In a week in 1933 the *Irish Press* had: 'Hints for the Home Laundress'; new necklines; a simple scheme for your bathroom; dry cleaning at home; how to make money at home by making home-made floor coverings (which was intended as a comfort for the 'stay-at-home' girl who did not have a career outside the house); an article on button-hole stitch embroidery and beauty while waiting for the tram ('It is perhaps the business girl – rather than the housewife – that needs definite physical exercise'.[49] On the grounds that housework involved a lot of energy). A week in the *Irish Independent* in 1950 contained: Nuala Costello helps you to make more of your appearance; make slippers as gifts; small talk (pictures of babies sent in and captioned humorously by the paper); a cartoon *Nine to Five* by Jo Fischer (of which more later); learning to embroider (by Frances M. Borroughs); 'Your Baggage Madam' (about packing for that Holy Year trip to Rome); 'Safety First for the Child'; suggestions for tasty stews (by Monica Nevin); 'Put Up Weight'; a fashion photograph and 'Countrywomen Meet in Denmark' (Esther Bishop, an Irish delegate, describes her experiences).[50] In a week in October in 1956 the *Irish Independent's* women's page had: 'Fresh, Demure and Dainty: First Evening Frock' by Marese (Simplicity patterns); 'Make it Yourself, a luxurious stole in Irish Tweed'; 'Charm is Contentment, says Edna Ford'; hygiene for the toddler by a doctor; a batch of scones, with variations (by Monica Nevin); home-made dyes from the wayside (by Maxwell Norris); 'Around the Shops with Mairin'; and several recipes and patterns.[51] *The Irish Times* in a week in 1956 had fashion (by Caroline Mitchell), 'The Classic Suit Goes On Forever'; 'Spoon-Meat' (by Eve Ireland); 'Diary of a Farmer's Wife' (by Ann Kennedy); 'Around the Shops with Caroline Mitchell'; 'Good Food' by Monica Sheridan.[52] A week in the *Irish Press* in 1959 had 'There's Special Magic in a Spring Wedding' ('please remember that pale blue is NOT the only going-away colour'); Mab Hickman's home page; Paris in the spring; hairstyles; 'Potato Who's Who' by Eileen Coghlan; 'Knit This Pretty Jumper'; 'Switzer's New Look'; 'Something New for Easter' by Jill Fisher; Friday's gossip column (by Darina) – about women in the news, writers, artists, sculptors and activists included alongside women famous for looking well.[53]

Consumer advice had certainly become much more prominent by the 1950s. The kind of items to be found 'around the shops' in the *Irish Times* and the *Irish Independent* include dinner services, cruet stands, sandwich dishes, gas fires for picnics, oil heaters, depilatory cream, oven-to-tableware from Holland, shoes and electrical equipment – mostly articles for the house or the self. Clothes and personal appearance feature almost every day by the 1950s; they had not been as prominent as this in the earlier period. Making-do-and-mending was never a very important part of newspaper women's pages, but whatever there was of it had gone by the 1950s. Practical cookery was a staple, but health and childcare featured only occasionally, a lot less often than women's public activity (such as the article about the Countrywomen above). Probably because they are no longer a novelty, the lives and problems of 'business girls' are hardly referred to as such, anymore, but rarely are the articles addressed directly to women of the house either.

The magazine *Woman's Life* referred in 1949 to a 'unique exhibition of particular interest to women in the home' which stressed the need for better-looking and higher-quality household goods. Shops were being flooded by new consumer items after the years of shortage:

> and not all of them are good . . . Since it is women who are mainly the purchasers it is important that you should know something about the durability of what you are buying.[54]

The tone sounds like that of the Irish Housewives' Association, the emphasis on information and decision-making typical of the tone of the magazine. *Woman's Mirror* and *Woman's Life* ran from the 1930s to the 1950s. They were Irish-published and the latter was, according to itself, the largest circulation woman's magazine in Ireland in the 1930s and 1940s. *Woman's Life*, insofar as can be discerned from correspondents and competition entrants, had a wide range of readers from the point of view of social background.

The range of topics covered by the *Woman's Life: the Irish Home Weekly* when it first appeared in 1936, was broader, certainly, than it was to become in the late 1940s, although even then the magazine kept up its practice of having two editorial pages which included comments on current affairs, women's achievements and matters that concerned women. A fascinating and well-produced publication that deserves an entire article to itself, it will be treated briefly here, in a comparison between an issue in 1938 and one in 1951. There will be a general discussion of the editorial content and advertising in both issues, and in some other issues.

The editorial column on the first and second pages in the magazine in 1938 is called 'Mainly for Women' and in the issue of 27 August 1938 there is a photograph of the winner of the Dawn Beauty Contest (a competition sponsored by Dawn Beauty Products) who hoped to become an actress; a snippet on Charles Laughton and his advice about acting; an item about Glasgow Concert Hall ('Europe's most democratic theatre'), and a description of a beautiful garden in Skerries. There are two poems – one about life in general, one about love; two short stories (involving love); a serial *Girl On Her Own* by Deirdre O'Brien about a girl working in Spain; a feature, 'Do You Ever Build Castles In The Air'; two patterns, one of which involved a competition and a news bulletin about An Oige (the Irish Youth Hostels Federation) by Miss E. Ward. Delia Dixon wanted to know, 'How Do You Stand For Beauty? (Posture)' and answered beauty problems; There was also a small sketch of a bolero dress; 'Efficiency Begins in the Kitchen' by Martha Grey, which suggested that the cook's mood is of the utmost importance, and that the kitchen should therefore be properly planned; household hints by the same author on cleaning kid gloves and dyeing properly; two photographs of babies, sent in by their mothers, with details on how the babies were reared – an article accompanied this by Dr Garry Myers, on 'Measuring Baby'; 'A Smile A Minute' (readers' jokes); 'Children's Corner', with a competition; the 'Woman's Life Service Club' (advertisments, situations vacant and wanted, buying and selling) and 'Mrs Wyse Answers Problems'. Other issues the previous year included features on Madame Elizire Dionne (mother of the famous Canadian quintuplets), Mrs Simpson and Maureen O'Sullivan, and an interview with a different working woman each week. This was a feature taken up and left off every few issues; women interviewed up to 1943 included a street-seller, a packer in flour mill, a secretary in a trade union, a commercial traveller, a wife and a mother, a radiographer, a milliner, a hotel receptionist, an oarswoman, a chorus girl and many more.[55] In the August 1938 issue, Mrs Wyse advised a 'problem' who wanted to keep on her work after marriage that, except in cases of economic need, wives should give up work on marriage. However, a variety of opinions were expressed on this topic in the magazine in these years, the editorial writer expressing a strong support for married women working outside the home in a 1937 issue, and also a fear that the Constitution would make this difficult for them.[56] Beauty and appearance were certainly important, as was romance, the theme of nearly all the stories, but work was highlighted. Even advertising copy for that dubious weight-loss product, Kruschen Salts, did its best to make a connection between the effective performance of work and women's weight; '"She Used To Be Slim" – Chance Remark Which Opened Nurse's Eyes' and 'So Fat She Had To Sell Her Business'![57] When women's work inside the house was treated, the emphasis was the usual one on time, labour-saving and recycling, and it was stated more than once that working in one's own house should be like working any where else – with efficiency, a sense of responsibility, time off and co-operation from other family members. Mrs Wyse was very severe on 'problems' who made slaves out of themselves for husbands and children.[58] In the issue of 27 August 1938, there were twenty-four advertisments in thirty-two pages, an average of 1.4 per page; 20% about clothes and beauty products; 37% about household goods, and 37% on health and childcare. (It was, admittedly, difficult to know in which category to place items like Kruschen Salts. In the end, anything that made dubious health claims *for its time*, and which promised to improve appearance, was placed under 'Beauty'.)

The issue of July 14 1951 has many more advertisments, an average of 1.5 per page, which might not seem like many more except that six of its forty-eight pages are given over to advertisments alone. Of these advertisments, 28% are on beauty and clothes, 37% (as in 1938) on household and food and 28% on health and childcare. The increase in the proportion of personal appearance products advertised and the decrease in health and childcare reflects the change in the editorial content of the magazine. The first two or three pages which used to be called 'Mainly For Women' are renamed (since 1949) 'Gossip by Finola'. This 'gossip', however, is informative and wide-ranging, identical in tone to 'Mainly for Women' and it includes, in this issue, an item on the Bourke sisters who were theatrical costumiers (photographed with David Niven); items on writers Kathleen Norris and George Bernard Shaw; a piece on the Eileen Joyce concert the previous month; the story of Malcwzynski, the Polish pianist; a complaint about the length of time it is taking to get Dublin's new concert hall; an item of information about a schoolgirl who won a scholarship to the Holy Faith Secondary School convent in Haddington Road, Dublin, and an interview with Helene Griffin, from Castlebar, of the City School of Deportment in Dublin. Here the variety ends, however. Apart from two serials, *The Heart is on Fire* by Barbara Cartland, and nearer home, a serialisation of Lily McCormack's *I Hear You Calling Me*, (about her famous husband John), and a short story, the rest of the magazine is almost entirely preoccupied with appearances – of houses, of the self and, to a much lesser extent, of children. A lengthy feature on home planning and decoration asks: 'Are you one of those married couples who feel

Mainly for Women

She does not, she told me, pen the rough draft of her novels, preferring, instead, to type directly on to the paper in an abbreviated language of her own. On a neat portable machine, this rough draft is then re-typed in final form.

Generous Authors

*I*RISHWOMEN always had the reputation of being "Flahulac" (generous), and the tradition was proved right in Dublin the other day when the Irish Writers' Guild decided to hold a raffle of autographed books in aid of the Association's benevolent funds: the first four woman authors approached presented right away a copy each of their latest books. And the signatures of Teresa Deevy, Eileen O'Faolain, Annie M.P. Smithson and Kate Forrest will surely add to the volumes.

Mrs. O'Faolain, wife of Sean O'Faolain (founder of the Guild), is of course author of the very successful and very ably illustrated children's tale published at Christmas. Kate Forrest, under her pen-name of "Kit Cavanagh," is also author of juvenile literature, and lives at Moynalty, Kells.

Busy Novelist

*A*FTER thirteen years of work in the interests of Irish nurses, Miss Annie M. P. Smithson has resigned the secretary-ship of the Irish Nurses' Organisation.

During these years she has consistently worked to improve the status of nursing through out the country. Her efforts have not been in vain; she has seen the nurse's salary increase, her hours of working become lighter, and the conditions of that work improve in many respects.

Further proof—if, indeed, more proof were needed—of Miss Smithson's active secretaryship is shown by the organisation's membership, which has risen from 400 in the early days to its present figure of 2,000 or more.

A New Novel

*A*S author of some seventeen books, to say nothing of socials and numerous articles, Miss Smithson's name is known all over Ireland, and when I called on her recently at her home in Rathmines I found her at work on a new novel, to appear later in the year.

Faithful Companion

*B*ESIDE Miss Smithson's table sat Judy, a ninety-nine per cent. thoroughbred spaniel. Judy must be the most famous dog in all Ireland, for not only has she appeared in all her mistresses's books, but she has also taken the stage at the Gaeity, in "Whiteoaks." She has six matinees to her credit and it is not certain at the time of writing but she may have appeared in the gate company production of "The Barretts of white Wimpole Street."

Yet fame has left her modesty untouched, and during my visit this dark haired Judy, so

*WEDDING OF IRISH TENOR'S
DAUGHTER*

*A*SLICE of happiness—an exclusive photograph of Miss Patricia Edith Watt cutting the wedding cake after her marriage to Mr. Philip (Tim) Harvey at Christ Church, Dun Laoghaire.

The bridegroom is second son of the Bishop of Cashel and Mrs. Harvey, Bishopsgrove, Waterford, and the bride is a daughter of Mr. William F. Watt, the well-known Waterford tenor who is so often heard on the air, and of Mrs. Watt, of Cliffe House, Dunmore East, Co. Waterford.

The ceremony was performed by the groom's father, the Most Rev. Dr. Thomas A. Harvey, D.D., Bishop of Cashel and Emly, Waterford and Lismore.

Photo by Poole, Dublin.

often photographed and written about, gazed languidly at the fire, leaving me to admire her glossy coat from my seat near Miss Smithson's well-stocked book shelves.

Meet Red Skelton

*T*HAT very likeable young comedian, Red Skelton, who has risen from a "bit" player in the Kildare films to star status, has his own recipe for success.

"There," he is one reported as having admitted, "sits sixty per cent. of my success. If it weren't for her I'd probably still be picking sawdust from my hair."

He was alluding to his wife, and the reference to sawdust brings us back to Red's early days as a clown in the Hagenback Circus. His talent for comedy was first spotted when he was working in a department store, whose proprietor recommended him to the producer of a local show.

His Nickname

*R*ED'S wife—whom he married when he was only sixteen—is Edna, a one-time page girl in a Kansas theatre. "At first," she says, "I didn't like anything about him," but when he asked her if she'd like to get married —he was promptly accepted!

Between them both the skeltons have so far written all the material used by Red in his film roles. To-day they occupy a fine house in San Fernando Valley, a far cry from those days spent in lodgings—where Edna Skelton once had to fry an egg on the electric iron! Incidentally, Red's official name is Richard— but his vivid red hair gave him his life's nickname.

Charles Lamb, R.H.A.

I NOTE from a contemporary that the well-known Irish artist, Charles Lamb, R.H.A., visited Waterford recently. The purpose of his visit was to open the 7th Annual Exhibition of Modern Irish Art, held at Newtown School.

This Exhibition has always created great interest in artistic circles in Ireland, and many of our most prominent artists have visited it from time to time. The visit of Charles Lamb to Waterford was awaited with great interest, I'm sure.

Kells Badminton Club

A LARGE attendance enjoyed themselves immensely at an At Home held by Kells Bad-

---

7. 'Mainly for Women'. *Woman's Life* April 17th 1943: writers male and female, working conditions of nurses, actors, artists, badminton and a wedding – this is an example of the variety of news items thought to be of interest to women in this very popular magazine in the 1930s, '40s and '50s.

awkward about asking your friends in for the evening . . . because you find your home wanting in some respects?'. This is a far cry from an article in November 1938 in which couples were advised to get married young and struggle together to make a home, rather than saving and waiting to have every material item perfect.[59] The other features are regulars; Delia Dixon advises on beauty problems; 'a new beauty feature' on beauty after forty; 'Woman's Life Service Club', 'What the Stars Foretell', 'Your Personal Problems', by Mrs Wyse, crossword results; 'Children's Corner' and patterns for children's clothes, and one for a woman's dress ('Go Gay With Stripes'). The preoccupation with appearance has extended even to the childcare article; instead of 'Happy Irish Babies' being assessed on their nutritional history and healthy appearance, there is a competition for the best photographs of children. Dr Myers' lengthy, informative and often very practical articles about childcare have been replaced by a small piece, entitled 'Mothercraft'. Steedman's Powders also run a promotional 'Hints for Mothers'.

Woman's Mirror was even more preoccupied by appearances by the 1950s. A sample issue of *Woman's Mirror* in 1955 had 'Mirror of the Month' (an editorial piece on clothes); 'It's Time For A Home Facial'; 'Add Beauty To Your Bath'; home decorating in 'A Dream Come True' (drab, flat, 'modern' bedroom with twin beds, fitted wardrobe, carpet); 'A Bright New Lampshade for Spring, Regency Style'; Be Smart – In Stripes; a story; 'Use Up More Old Pieces of Carpet'; 'Family Fashions for the Home Dressmaker'; 'It's New For Spring – the Mushroom Cut' (hair – you can visualise this yourself); 'An Easy-To-Make Evening Handbag'; '7 Easy Ways To A Better Figure'; 'A Frivolous Hat for February'; 'Some Ideas for Lenten Meals'; 'Get Ready for Pancake Night'; 'Talk for the Young Mother – the Sick Child'; 'Star of the Month: Debbie Reynolds'; story; 'Let Deb Solve Your Beauty Problems'; Facts about Fragrances; news of the films and 'Miranda Reveals Your Fortune In The Stars'.[60] Out of twenty features, twelve are on appearances (personal and house), two on cookery, two on crafts, one (a rather stiff, didactic lecture), on childcare, two on the films and one on astrology. There is nothing about current affairs, nor about people (apart from film stars) in the news there are no resources like the 'Woman's Life Service Club', indeed, hardly any indication at all of reader participation, not even a problem page.

Was the daily, weekly, monthly, annual household round – common in all the household advice of the period, in newspapers also – actually invented by advice books? There are, it is true, certain tasks that have to be done to keep a house habitable and to maintain life from day to day, but do they necessarily have to be done in the order and the manner promoted, or rather, urged, by household advice books and, or rather, by domestic economy texts in use in schools? In these women's pages in journals, and too in newspapers and magazines seasonally appropriate advice was tendered – the Christmas cookery at Christmas, spring cleaning in March, bottling and preserving in September and Lenten meals in February and March. For the months where there was nothing seasonal to be done, jobs suggested ranged from renovating lampshades to decorating hats. There were constant reminders to keep a work diary and, in

Mrs. Wyse Says

TROUBLES MUST BE FACED HONESTLY!

MY DEAR READERS:

Do you remember my letter of a few weeks ago in which I warned "Broken Hearted" about the necessity of facing illness squarely and the imperative need of following doctors' advice? This morning I received a letter from "Mrs. K. O'B.," which she very kindly gives me authority to publish, with the hope that it may bring comfort and help to such as "Broken-Hearted."

About 30 years ago after the birth of my fourth child, I got a bad cold. I coughed day and night, and at last my doctor prevailed on me to go to a sanatorium as my right lung was affected. Like many others, I ignorantly thought that the Sanatorium was the end of all things. However, I went to Newcastle, Co. Wicklow, and spent 56 weeks there in all. I owe my life and good health to the care and treatment I received there. Nothing could exceed the kindness of the doctors, matron and staff. I felt quite lonely when leaving, and always look back with affection and gratitude on the happy months I spent in dear old Newcastle.

The one mistake people make is not to go in time, before the disease has become incurable. People blame the sanatorium if they are not cured, but my advice (from experience) is: if the lung shows the slightest sign of delicacy go at once to a sanatorium, and give the doctors a chance of making a perfect cure. They can't work miracles.

If you care to make use of this letter as an encouragement to sufferers, you are quite welcome to do so.

I wish to thank "Mrs. K. O'B." for permitting me to publish this first-hand confirmation of a truth that cannot too frequently be stressed.

Your sincere friend,

Mrs. Wyse.

IS HE SERIOUS?

A boy who lives about twenty miles away from me has been paying me a lot of attention, taking me out and so on. I have heard he does not go with any other girl.

My trouble, Mrs. Wyse, is that this boy never says anything about love, neither does he write to me. I would be very much obliged if you would tell me if, in your opinion, he likes me or not.—("Sweet eighteen").

Dear "Sweet Eighteen," I think it is perfectly obvious that this boy likes you when he seeks your company. As regards his silence on love matters, you must understand that some boys have a horror of appearing "sloppy", and this is probably why he refrains from putting his feelings into words.

HER AMBITION

I wonder if you could help me. I am a young girl of 17 and my only ambition in life is to be a good singer. Would you please give me the name and address of a good teacher—not too expensive?—("Dance Mad").

Please write to me privately, enclosing a stamped self-addressed envelope, and I shall be very glad to let you have the name and address of an excellent teacher.

NO SOCIAL LIFE

We are three sisters all fairly goodlooking. As we are a large family and not well off, we have very little social life. Could you please advise us how to make some extra money in our spare time and how we might meet some nice boy friends.—("Brown Eyes").

The only way to meet boys of your own ages and tastes is to join your local tennis, dramatic, social or hiking club. To do this, naturally, you will need money for fees, clothes and equipment. I feel that between you you should easily be able to earn a little extra money.

Have you no hobbies,—knitting, jam-making, etc.—you could turn to good account? Or have you ever thought of trying to secure an agency for some line of goods you could dispose of privately or by canvassing?

CAR SICKNESS

I suffer terribly from dizziness when I travel by car. Can you please suggest a remedy? Also, my knee often hurts dreadfully when I walk or cycle? I should be glad if you could tell me the cause.—("Lonely").

Many people suffer from travel sickness, my dear, and I am afraid there is no definite remedy. I can only hope that you will grow out of this annoying tendency as you grow older. With regard to your second complaint, I feel you should have the knee examined by a doctor at once, as there is evidently some abnormality of the joint.

ANSWER TO SEVENTEEN-YEAR-OLD

For my answer to the first part of your letter, please see reply to "Brown Eyes." With regard to your second query, I suggest you read the "Guide to Careers" which is published by Independent Newspapers, Ltd., Middle Abbey St., Dublin, price 1/6d.

CORRECT ADDRESS

When addressing an officer holding the rank of Lieutenant in the Irish Army should one address him as "Lieutenant" or "Mr."—("Tommy Atkins").

An officer below the rank of army captain is styled. "Mr." in social usage, through a letter sent to him in barracks should be addressed "Lieut.–"

ANSWER TO "SHY BEE," "STELLA RUDDY" AND "CORK"

The annoying habit of blushing may be conquered if you think less of yourselves and more of those who are speaking. Become interested in others and you will soon find yourselves more at ease.

PEN FRIENDS

Readers who would be interested in corresponding with pen friends in America are invited to communicate with Mrs. Wyse, who will put them in touch with the secretary of a well-known American Girls' Pen Club.

* * * *

When writing to Mrs. Wyse, please enclose a stamped addressed envelope if private reply is required. All communications in connection with pen-friends must be accompanied by a stamped self-addressed envelope.

Published every Thursday by the Proprietors, Periodical Press Ltd., 8 Pearse Street, Dublin. Telephone 44090. Printed by the Longford Printing & Publishing Co. Ltd., Market Square, Longford. Subscription Rates (Postage included), 13/- per week; 6/6 per half year. In U.S.A. $3.50 per year; $2.00 per half year postage on single copies, one penny, at home or abroad. Registered as a newspaper. Wholesale Agents; Eason and son, Ltd., Dublin, Limerick, Waterford, Belfast, and Londonderry; Dublin Wholesale Newsagency. Ltd., News Bros., Ltd., Cork; C. Porter & Co., Belfast; and all Wholesale Newsagents in England, Scotland and Wales.

8. Mrs Wyse Says: from *Woman's Life: the Irish Woman's Home Weekly* May 28th 1938. Women's media had an important role in encouraging women to look after their health, though access to sanatoria was very limited in the 1930s.

one newspaper in 1947, to keep a notebook with product information and interesting snippets from advertisments.[61] The implication was that women of the house should be always busying themselves so as not to allow the inevitable build-up of work to overburden them. Bean a' Tighe in the *Catholic Bulletin* referred to 'the domestic campaign'[62] as if it were a long war of attrition from which the woman of the house needed regular leave. Articles and advertisments about how to lose 'That Tired Feeling' succeeded or accompanied features on home decoration. Did the sheer volume of advice and information given to women on matters to do with the house and its putative 'routine' contradict or negate the exhortations to her not to make a god out of work, as journalist May Laverty put it in 1935?[63] Certainly there were household hints that saved resources – like beating half a pint of milk into a pound of butter to make the latter go farther, instructions on how to use leftovers, to prevent cream going sour, or to convert and 'turn' clothes – but did it really make dusting quicker and more efficient if the person dusting went about it with a duster in each hand, as Hathaway recommended? Did washing light bulbs in soapy water really 'save electricity' as she claimed?[64] One begins to see why Charles E. Kelly poked fun at 'lady broadcasters' who gave household advice. Why was there no mention, in all this 'make and mend' advice, of those infinitely recyclable objects familiar to most Irish households at this time – flour-bags and sweet cans? Why did advisers not comment on the apparently common habit of recycling the weekly wash water to scrub the floor? Why was there a conspiracy of silence (except in *Cookery Notes*, where the practice was strongly condemned) on the widespread use of paraffin to get a fire to light?[65] One is tempted to the conclusion that many of these writers were not very familiar with the day-to-day short cuts and compromises involved in running a house without piped water and electricity, or even with these facilities, on a tight budget.

Furthermore, placing responsibility on women of the house to organise themselves and their families so as to lighten the load, made no allowances for women whose circumstances might not have allowed them to do this. The assumption was that the houses had a multiplicity of rooms, so as to provide scope for all the cleaning and maintenance that needed to be done, with enough room, and a safe environment, to store food which had been shopped for only once or twice a week as recommended. Shopped for, is the operative phrase; the experience addressed was an urban one.

Rural and farming women were not just left out; when their working lives were addressed at all by women's magazines and women's pages it was with an ignorance that was staggering in a country with such a high proportion of its population engaged in agriculture. (There were women's pages in the specialised farming press, which have been looked at by Carmel Duggan,[66] but because this chapter is concerned with advice to women of the house as such in specialised books and in general publications, the farming press is conceived of as on a level with, say, the *Irish Housewife* or the *Irish Countrywoman* – specialised publications which had nothing like as wide a distribution as the daily papers or the religious periodicals.) The 'Diary of a Farmer's Wife' in *The*

Irish Times (of all newspapers with its limited and largely urban readership) in the 1950s is an honourable exception, as are Redington and Laverty. Redington really belongs to the early twentieth-century tendency in Irish household advice, which concentrated on brightening rural life in particular and generated a number of government initiatives and voluntary organisations to do so. Ann Kennedy, the *Irish Times* farmer's wife, has, it is true, conveniences like a fridge and a bottle-warmer, to say nothing of electricity and running water – in 1956, facilities shared by less than 12% of her counterparts but as a farmer's wife she is on call at all hours of the day and night. For instance, when she is getting up at six to heat the baby's bottle, she notices a fox sneaking around the hen-house and temporarily ignores the baby's loud protestations while she rouses the dog to chase the fox away.[67] As the discussion of women's own experiences of work will show, farm life did not lend itself to a time-oriented system. Women's pages in the *Independent* and the *Press* rarely, if ever, had articles on poultry and butter-making alongside, for example, cookery and fashion (the *Irish Independent* had a regular poultry column in the 1940s and 1950s but it was not on the women's page). Though seasonality was assumed in women's household work (by definition urban), there was no attempt to tackle the far more inevitable seasonality of the farm woman's work; no articles about 'How To Feed Those Hungry Men' at threshing time; no recipes for hot drinks to keep out the cold during the lambing season; no household hints about how to keep drinks cool on the bog or in the fields. *Woman's Life* had a regular 'Letter to a Farmer's Wife' in 1937, but this had disappeared by 1938. It was informed, practical and useful, with advice about poultry, eggs and dairying. The advice to 'go electric' if possible was somewhat utopian in the era in question before government sponsored rural electrification got going in earnest,[68] but it was certainly more realistic than the following advice about personal appearance:

> Compare the average countrywoman of 35 with her city sister and what do you find? The countrywoman looks at best ten years older. The balance should be on the other side, seeing that the woman who lives on the farm gets plenty of God's fresh air, sane, sensible food and regular hours.[69]

This was both insulting and ignorant. In the first place, farming hours were anything but 'regular' – sick animals, bad weather, calving, lambing and a host of other contingencies could have the farm women and men out at all hours. God's fresh air, moreover, was often laceratingly cold and wet. The same level of staggering ignorance can be discerned again and again in the women's pages, and out of them; Marie O'Reilly, in the 'I Sketch Your World' diary column in the *Irish Independent* in 1947 (not the women's page), admitted in surprise that poultry could, indeed, pay its way.[70] She could have learned this from any of the thousands of country women who paid for the weekly groceries with eggs, right up to the 1960s, but what convinced her in the end was a balance-sheet sent in to her by a poultry-rearer in the remote fastnesses of Rathgar. Another article in the *Irish Independent* in 1956 concerned the clothes supposedly worn by women in the country:

You know, of course, the Irish country woman's uniform – the old tweed
suit, the battered felt hat, and the raincoat never too far off. Dull, yes, but
oh so sheltering . . . So next time you are at a local show, if such things are
strange to you, don't just dismiss us as a dowdy lot, even if that is how we
look. We know what we are about.[71]

Refreshing though it is to see some homage paid to utility and comfort in
women's clothes in 1956, the high water-mark of artificiality and discomfort in
women's wear, it has to be said that the 'uniform' described here was not
necessarily what all country women wore *en fête* – it was that which was more
likely to have been worn by 'county women' and the womenfolk of gentlemen
farmers and gentry. Accurate or not, the note of apology is revealing: the
average woman is the town woman or city woman, and the country woman is
explaining herself to her.

Ignorance about change and continuity in rural life is also reflected in In
Frances Enraght Moony's article 'Out of the Wind and the Rain's Way' in the
Irish Independent in 1956. The author confesses that her own ideal is 'one of
those small, crouching, thatched cottages' which would have whitewashed walls,
a paved 'street', a pump in the yard, and it would probably be possible to put in
running water 'with that new and wonderful plastic piping'. The crane would
be left at the open fire in the kitchen, and the grate taken out of the parlour fire
and an open fire put there too. This love of fires is refreshing in the face of all
the 'Around the Shops' emphasis on the convenience of oil fires and gas fires
and electric fires, but Moony's assumptions are essentially modern and urban –
the pump in the yard will be for decoration, obviously, because there will be
piped water in the house, and does she intend to cook on two fires? (Does she
intend to cook on any fire?) If not, why does she want a voracious and hard-to-
light open fire in the parlour? And if she knows that the part outside the front
door of a house in the country is called the 'street', then she must know that one
never refers to a dwelling house in rural Ireland as a cottage, unless one is a
person of higher income wanting to be disparaging, or unless one is referring to
a holiday house.[72] This is the kernel of the piece; in an era when a large
proportion of Irish women were still drawing water and cooking on the fire,
journalism directed at women had this located in the picturesque past. This was
true as early as the 1930s. 'Grandmother Envies the Housekeeper of Today' ran
an article in the *Irish Press* in 1933 where Grandmother envied the shining
stainless steel taps, gas or electric light, mincing and chopping machines,
polishers of all sorts, linoleum and washable paint. This article acknowledges
that not every household has changed, in its reference to 'the drudgery of the
kitchens of even 30 years ago, and the drudgery of Irish country kitchens now',
but assumes a gradual levelling-up to an urban norm.[73]

CONCLUSION

A general guideline to the way the advice changed over time is that the books produced in the 1920s and 1930s, which belonged to the early twentieth-century tradition of advice to women on family health and hygiene, laid much emphasis on survival, basic health, making–do-and-mending, while the books in the later period emphasised sternly the woman's duty both to relax and to make the home pleasant and the meals varied. Women's pages in newspapers and journals and women's magazines also proferred this advice, but laid far more emphasis on clothes and appearance in the 1940s and 1950s. This might have had something to do with the fact that opposition to make-up and fashion had long been a staple criticism of modern women. Stories in the *Irish Messenger* in the 1930s had dealt exile, disgrace and early death as punishments for female vanity or excessive interest in appearance, and recommended Saint Elisabeth of Thuringia (1207–31) as a model for girls to emulate in this regard, but in 1948 the *Messenger* 'Question Box', which gave advice on faith and morals, told a correspondent that the use of 'cosmetics, lipstick, etc.' was not a sin, but a fairly harmless vanity:

> the universality of it is not an encouraging sign. We would be better without it, and maybe better-looking, many of us.[74]

The writer resorts to an aesthetic argument to reinforce a weak moral position. The overall message is that there is nothing wrong with taking an interest in one's appearance. Fr John Hayes was very popular with the women active in Muintir na Tire in the early 1940s because, according to one woman:

> He never scolded about women's fashions and he seemed to like to see women using make-up. We all loved him.

The implication is that many other priests would 'scold' and object to make-up, and that Fr Hayes was ahead of his time.[75] Reading about make-up and fashion might have given young Irish women a sense of rebellion against the older generation. Photographs of young Irish girls and women throughout the country in the 1940s and 1950s show that awareness and adaptation of contemporary fashion was widespread.[76] Returned emigrants or migrants must have been partly responsible for this and newspapers and magazines would have reinforced this influence.

The similarity of woman's page/magazine content in the 1950s to that of very different industrialised societies, and the almost complete lack of engagement with the realities of Irish women's lives (except for recipes for Lenten meals!), is striking, especially when the alternative is seen. The *Woman's Life* issues produced under Emergency conditions give an idea of the rich ore of native material that could have been mined right through the period. A week in January 1946, for example, carried a wide range of articles, despite poor quality paper and small print. There is an interview with broadcaster and playwright Mairéad Ní Ghráda; an article on octogenarian novelist Nora Tynan O'Mahony and an article by John Antrim which suggests that the 'modern girl' is 'chaperoned by her own determination'. The regular 'careers' slot ('What Are You Going To Be?') discusses hotel work, with hard information on rates of pay, working hours and prospects. There is a comic strip in Irish; film news and views; an ABC of cookery; a serial by Kathleen Norris; a short story; a page for children and Mrs Wyse's 'Problem Page'. The 'Mainly For Women' editorial pages carry information on a recent Irish Housewives' Association meeting; a photograph of a military wedding; a snippet on the new airport under construction in Rineanna; Co. Clare, an item on the Wexford Art Committee; George Bernard Shaw getting the freedom of the city of Dublin, and Mrs Eleanor Roosevelt being interviewed at Baldonnel Aerodrome on the subject of women in politics. Appearance is not neglected: there is a pattern for a lady's beret and an item on (significantly enough) 'The Simple Frock'. This is not an isolated issue – the March 30 issue of the same year carries, among other articles, detailed and lengthy advice on careers in the Civil Service; a news item on Connie Pope, administrator/secretary in the National Maternity Hospital in Dublin, who invented a world famous filing system and had taken time off to work with concentration camp survivors; a historical piece about Granuaile; an article on film critic, Dilys Powell; and other highly interesting articles, hugely informative for this researcher at least.[77] But by the end of the 1940s, this kind of information had shrunk to at most two editorial pages of the magazine, the rest – whether *Woman's Mirror* or *Woman's Life* – was concentrated on appearance of the house or of the self.

Childcare featured rarely in the magazines and women's pages, and when it did, there was no indication whatsoever that the conditions of child-rearing in Ireland might be any different to those obtaining elsewhere – no reference good, bad or indifferent, for example, to the particularly large average size of families in Ireland. One is hardly surprised that there was no attempt in women's pages or in magazines, to popularise or to examine, for example, the controversial issues in the Mother and Child Bill in 1950–51, but one might have expected at least an article on the developing health system in the 1940s and how it would affect women. Even staying within the parameters of what was seen to be of interest to women, the absence of any attempt, however light and informal, to place articles within the context and conditions under which actual Irish women of the house – urban and rural – cooked, made/bought clothes, reared families and looked after their appearances (or not) – is striking. The woman hauling water in and out of the house several times a day and boiling feed for calves and pigs might as well have been on another planet, but the townswoman walking to the shops with the baby in the pram, the ex-baby on the pram seat, and the pre-schooler by the hand, buying the makings of dinner for other children coming in at different times from school, and for the husband – the everyday problems of her life were not addressed either.

What we must ask is, would these women have expected women's pages and magazines to address their problems? Perhaps the admonition to 'Go Gay With

Stripes', however unrealistic, was more acceptable reading for hard-pressed mothers with little choice about the number of children they bore, than articles telling them where they were going wrong in child-rearing. The recipes and knitting or sewing patterns that abounded by the 1950s might have tapped into women's creativity in a way that household hints, which told women who were already pushing recycling and economising to its limit how to economise still further, would not. In the same way, magazines and women's pages continued to offer news items on women prominent in the arts, literature, paid work and public life, and women who dressed well, presumably because women were interested in these women's doings, or at least, more interested in them than they would have been in somebody who was held up as the perfect wife and mother. An item in 'Darina's Gossip Column: Women in the News' in the *Irish Press* in 1959 is illuminating. This 'gossip', like that of 'Finola' in *Woman's Life* in this decade, is actually news about women who are, for one reason or another (achievement, political activity, appearance) in the public eye. Women's news was called gossip, but it was still women's news. The item refers to Mrs Charles Coyle, wife of the Master of the National Maternity Hospital, Holles St, Dublin. Mrs Coyle (we are not told her own first name) was pictured at a function in Dublin wearing a wild ranch mink coat and looking very poised and soignée, in the mode of her more famous contemporary Jacqueline Kennedy. Darina noted that Mrs Coyle had eight children under the age of twelve but that 'she never seems to look fussed or worried'. There were plenty of mothers of eight children under twelve in Ireland at this stage, but they would not have attracted Darina's attention. Mrs Coyle's maternity was not in and of itself newsworthy; her appearance was.[78] Perhaps this was how the readers wanted it.

CHAPTER FIVE

Some Aspects of Pregnancy and Childbirth

INTRODUCTION

Up to now this study has been concerned with published opinions about, and advice to, women of the house, and the women themselves and their experiences have remained in the shadow. In this chapter women's own experiences are discussed, alongside medico-social discourses about pregnancy, childbirth and women's reproductive health. This was one area where 'writing about' women had a definite impact on their lives.

These forty years saw major changes – indeed, major strides – in the areas of pregnancy and childbirth. In 1923, 297 women died in childbirth in the twenty-six counties of the Free State in 1923; in 1961, the number was 27.[1] Ireland shared in the worldwide improvement in mothers' health. It might seem logical to infer that this substantial improvement in women's lives was due to the setting-up of a comprehensive health service with its own government department from 1947; to the gradual multiplication of local authority and voluntary maternal and child health services from the mid-1920s, and the inauguration of a free (for all but the very wealthy) comprehensive, countrywide mother and child (up to six weeks) health service from 1953.[2] Some of the evidence presented in this chapter will suggest that there were also other reasons for the decline in maternal deaths.

In recent times the history of childbirth has moved away from a narrative of the triumph of enlightenment and medical science over darkness and superstition towards a timely critique of the impact of the development of medicine on pregnant and parturient women. Some of this writing suggests that medicine, over the past 150 years, has killed at least as many parturient women as it has saved, through infection, unnecessary intervention and experimentation. The great improvements in women's reproductive health, it is argued, owe as much to improvements in nutrition and standards of living as they do to necessary obstetric intervention. Removing the place of birth from the mother's dwelling-house, and replacing the midwife with the doctor 'medicalised' normal childbirth.[3] In the Irish context the heroic medico-historical narrative depicts medicine and hospital care as solely responsible for the decline in maternal mortality, replacing a brutal and barbaric quackery. This is countered by an equally one-dimensional history of Irish obstetrics as a narrative of the oppression and mutilation of Irish women by power-crazy doctors themselves suffering under colonialism.[4] However, even Ruth Barrington's eminently critical history of Irish health care in the twentieth century takes for granted that medical expertise was the decisive factor in the decline in maternal mortality. General practitioner/historian Irvine Loudon's excellent and convincing survey of death in childbirth over the past two centuries in Europe, North America and the Antipodes suggests that there is not necessarily a connection between the extension of midwifery expertise and the overall decline of maternal mortality.[5]

What is perhaps missing from the discussion that follows is women's own descriptions of how they experienced childbirth itself – pain, pain relief, duration and so on. There is plenty of information on the place of birth, the social supports and the attendance, but little on the physical process. Linda May Ballard in her research in Northern Ireland mentions that many of her informants were reluctant to speak to her about this subject until they ascertained she was a married woman.[6] While I did not encounter the same degree of reticence, there was a definite unwillingness to go into detail. Rather than keep asking questions (which would have been intrusive and rude) I respected my informants' silences on this. What is *not* said in personal testimony is as significant, in any case, as what is said, particularly in this kind of broadly defined inquiry which depends upon a self-selected group of contributors. In fact, it is in these omissions that the value of self-selection presents itself; the researcher gets an idea about how people construct their past and the memories they want to present about it. Obviously, pregnancy and childbirth is still, for most people, a subject not to be broached with strangers. Would a medically-qualified researcher – a doctor, or a midwife – be a more appropriate person to elicit this kind of information? I think so, because it is not thought of as a breach of privacy to discuss bodily functions with medical personnel, and also because almost all of my contributors had great respect for midwives, nurses, doctors and hospitals. It could be, of course, that pregnancy and childbirth were taken so much for granted by women that they are not as fixed in the memory as an experience which only happens once, twice or three times in one's lifetime, would be. Child-bearing and child-rearing were constants in the lives of most married women, taking up decades. All those years a house had to be run, meals cooked, clothes washed – even for urban women who had water and electricity laid on, a very busy daily round was the norm. Child-bearing and child-rearing in general, did not loom large in the accounts of the work done by women in the period, although it featured. 'I forgot to mention about children to be minded,' wrote Aggie D., at the close of an exhaustive (and exhausting!) account of her working life on a large Co. Limerick farm in the 1930s and 1940s. Ann C., from a Co. Roscommon farm in the same period, after a long description of the work of the farm woman referred almost parenthetically to the work that was being promoted everywhere in the western world, by the 1950s, as the most important function of womankind:

> Apart from all that [the work of the farm] food had to be cooked, children looked after and sent to school, to say nothing of having babies and as everyone knows there were mostly large families then.

Pregnancy and the care of babies and small children were fitted in around all this work. Only very wealthy women could afford to make an occupation out of pregnancy and paradoxically these people often made child-rearing an occupation for others, nurserymaids, nannies and servants. Women of all classes, conditions and resources had to stop whatever they were doing to actually give birth, but this was not the 'great equaliser'. Women who were badly nourished were less able to withstand infection, trauma or even necessary intervention, while women who could afford to pay doctors risked being subjected to some of the most dangerous midwifery fads of all time.

The first part of this chapter looks at changes in the experience of childbirth over these forty years, and tries to find out something about women's own preferences and how births were conducted at home and in hospital. The second part looks at the decline in maternal mortality and compares maternal mortality statistics in two different areas of the country. Irish midwifery, however, needs its own thorough and detailed historian; what follows is an attempt to chart the changes in the experience of childbirth over these four decades and to suggest avenues for further research. The maternal mortality statistics hide the effort, anguish, worry and often unimaginable pain for the women whose deaths are summarised thus, and not only the irreplaceable loss for the baby, if it survived, and other children if there were any, but also often catastrophe if husbands were dead, absent or incapacitated and the family had to be broken up. The fact that these agonising deaths and bereft families became fewer in number as time went on means that whatever narrative is preferred as an explanation for this improvement, the story has a happy ending.

CHANGES IN THE HEALTH SERVICES

The Midwives Act (1917) made it illegal for an untrained person to assist at childbirth if there were a trained person available; this was strengthened by the Midwives Act (1931). Under legislation predating the setting up of the Free State (Maternity and Child Welfare Act 1918), local authorities were empowered, but not obliged, to set up mother and child welfare schemes of various kinds, and grants were given to these authorities and to voluntary organisations.[7] There were also voluntary organisations of nurses operating in parts of the country – the most well-known of these were the Lady Dudley nurses and the Jubilee nurses. There were also branches of the Women's National Health Association, and District Nurse Associations, often supported by local voluntary groups like the United Irishwomen/Irish Countrywomen's Association, as well as by government grants. The number of these schemes rose in the 1930s, but fell slightly in the early 1940s.[8] The three large maternity hospitals in Dublin – the Coombe, the Rotunda, and the National Maternity Hospital, Holles Street and provided ante-natal clinics and in-hospital and outpatient deliveries for Dublin women and occasionally for women from other parts of Ireland also. There were also a large number of maternity and child welfare organisations in the capital city. By 1935, in addition to the three maternity hospitals in Dublin, Bedford Row maternity hospital in Limerick, the Erinville in Cork, the Curragh Military Hospital and Cork County Home and Hospital were providing ante-natal clinics, in-hospital deliveries and outpatient services.[9]

There were, in addition, trained midwives who worked independently (rather than, or in addition to, being employed by local authorities), but they were not strategically deployed around the country. County hospitals and district infirmaries (former workhouse hospitals) sometimes catered for women in childbirth, but they were not necessarily equipped to do this. The Department of Local Government and Public Health gave a county-by-county commentary on maternity welfare schemes in 1936. In this year there were 140 maternity and child welfare schemes operating throughout the country; 26 run by local authorities and the other 114 by voluntary organisations which were grant-aided by the Department of Local Government and Public Health. The counties Carlow, Cork, Donegal, Galway, Kerry, Kildare, Laois, Longford, Louth, Mayo, Monaghan, Offaly, Sligo, Tipperary South Riding, Roscommon, Waterford, Westmeath, Wexford and Wicklow all had at least one scheme of this kind. County Kildare, for example, had thirteen part-time nurses, and one whole-time public health nurse who had made, in the previous year, a total of 32,891 visits to 'maternity and child welfare cases'. In Westmeath, two district nurses had been responsible for 7,936 visits. Dublin City, as already mentioned, was very well served with maternity and infant welfare services. This left the counties Clare, Limerick, Kilkenny, Tipperary North Riding, Leitrim, Meath and Cavan without any schemes in 1936 and thus dependent upon trained freelance midwives, doctors or handywomen, all of whom had to be paid a fee unless they waived it out of the goodness of their hearts.[10] The first and second reports of the new Department of Health went into great detail on maternity and infant welfare. By the end of March 1949 approved schemes were in operation in the cities of Dublin, Limerick, Cork and Waterford; in fifteen counties – Carlow, Cork West, Donegal, Dublin, Galway, Kildare, Kilkenny, Laois, Limerick, Monaghan, Roscommon, Waterford, Westmeath, Wexford and Wicklow, and in twenty-three urban districts – An Uaimh, Arklow, Athlone, Athy, Bray, Buncrana, Carrickmacross, Cavan, Clones, Clonmel, Dun Laoghaire, Ennis, Midleton, Monaghan, Naas, Nenagh, Sligo, Tralee, Trim, Tullamore, Wexford, Wicklow and Youghal. The schemes in Limerick, Cork and Waterford involved regular clinics, the supply of tonic foods to expectant and nursing mothers, instruction on infant management and feeding, the discretionary provision of tickets for free dinners for expectant and nursing mothers (especially in Dublin City), and home visiting.[11] In the urban districts and counties the schemes provided home nursing services, sometimes by Public Health Nurses. The office of Public Health Nurse was instituted by the Public Health Act of 1945. The PHNs, who were midwives as well as general nurses, were responsible for health education, domiciliary care of old people and people with chronic complaints, and midwifery cases. However, in 1949 the total number of PHNs, whether employed by the Department of Health, local authorities or voluntary organisations, was 200, so the weight of their workload can be imagined. The first report of the Department of Health acknowledged this when it mentioned that comprehensive provision was not made for attendance at childbirth, even in the areas where county schemes were in operation.[12]

In 1953, the Mother and Child legislation finally, after much controversy, introduced a free service for almost all expectant mothers and newborn infants (up to six weeks of age), with GP, hospital and specialist care, free specialist and hospital care of children up to six years and a comprehensive School Medical Service. Mothers could choose doctors from a panel, and no advice was to be given to expectant mothers that would be contrary to their religious beliefs. More or less to placate hierarchical objections (according to Ruth Barrington), women of families with incomes of over £1,000 a year had to pay £1 a year contribution to avail of the scheme, or they could choose to be private patients.[13] The development of this scheme was accompanied by the building of new regional hospitals with maternity units, laboratories, neo-natal, paediatric and other facilities, and co-operation between paediatricians, obstetricians and public health authorities.[14]

Maternal and infant health exploded into a highly charged controversy in 1950–51 between the government on one side (or, more properly speaking, Dr Noel Browne and the Department of Health, the government capitulating rapidly) and the medical profession and the Church on the other. Dr James Deeny, Chief Medical Officer at the Department of Local Government and Public Health (later Department of Health), 1944–51, drew up the scheme in 1945, and Dr Browne, Minister for Health 1948–51, had the job of implementing it. Because this episode is so well-known and so well researched already, and because the high politics of it have little bearing on my work, the briefest of summaries will suffice here.[15] The Catholic hierarchy objected to the Mother and Child Bill because it appeared to be paving the way for state intervention in the family and state control over what were seen to be the most intimate aspects of people's lives. The fear that the proposed 'health education' would involve advice on birth control and abortion was part of this wider apprehension about turning into what Vigilans in *Christus Rex* described as 'the servile state'.[16] The Irish Medical Association objected to the Bill because it looked as if it would make state servants of doctors and interfere in the doctor-patient relationship. They might also have been justifiably piqued because it seemed as if few of the suggestions for maternity schemes which had been made by doctors in the pages of the Irish Medical Association's journal or in the *Dublin Journal of Medical Science*, in 1943–5, had been even considered.[17]

The move to hospital births was not, by and large, a development pushed through by obstetricians, contrary to some suggestions. The proposals of Doctors Quin, Spain and Greene for a comprehensive maternity service in the 1940s, were almost identical to the recommendations of modern home birth advocates. They recommended home births attended by trained midwives and backed up by emergency squads attached to fully equipped maternity hospitals, where women for whom complications were foreseen or whose home circumstances were unfit for home deliveries would be treated. They also recommended thorough ante-natal treatment for all. Dr James Quin was a well-known Dublin doctor and regular contributor to journals on community medicine; in later years he was to contribute to the Irish Housewives' Association Election Fighting Fund. Dr Alex Spain was sometime Master of the National Maternity Hospital, Holles St, Dublin, and Dr P.J. Greene, from Loughrea, Co. Galway, was Connacht representative on the Central Council of the Irish Medical Association. Other obstetricians in the 1940s and 1950s agreed with them. Prospective mothers, said Dr J.K.P. Feeney, Master of Dublin's Coombe hospital in 1954, should come into hospital for their first babies and for every baby after the fifth, (because of the particular risks of complications for mothers on the first and on sixth and subsequent births).[18] Hospitals, said the Master of Holles St, Dr Arthur Barry in 1956, were not the ideal choice for childbirth because of the risks of infection ('death-dealing organisms') and home births or small nursing homes, backed up by fully-equipped flying squads, should be encouraged in pregnancies where all went well and there seemed to be no risk of complications. Another advantage to home births, as far as Dr Barry was concerned, was that there was less likelihood of 'meddlesome midwifery' there – by which he meant unnecessary obstetric intervention. (This phrase crops up regularly in the Irish medical journals around this time.)[19] Dr Ninian Falkiner, Master of the Rotunda hospital, Dublin, in the 1940s, also hoped that domiciliary midwifery would continue to be very important, not only because of overcrowding in the hospital, but also because of the dangers of hospital infection.[20] This confidence in home births was questioned by a visiting London obstetrician in 1956, who believed that hospital births were the ideal for all.[21]

According to Ruth Barrington, it was the scheme put forward by Dr John P. Shanley, president of the Irish Medical Association 1942–44, and specialist in the connection between poverty and children's diseases, that was closest to the system which was eventually adopted. Dr Shanley's scheme recommended maternity hospitals but said nothing at all about midwives or domiciliary care.[22] The fledgling Department of Health tried unsuccessfully in the late 1940s to abolish the Central Midwives Board and to replace the title 'midwife' with 'maternity nurse'. The midwives might not have succeeded in holding on to their autonomous professional status had they not had the vigorous support of Dr Ninian Falkiner. This area needs to be more thoroughly researched, but for the moment it can be noted that it was doctors as civil servants/ministers, and not doctors in general, who posed the greatest threat to midwifery as a profession in the late 1940s and early 1950s.[23] The Department's vision of a maternity service fully integrated into the health service, whose midwives and doctors would be controlled by the Department of Health, eventually became a reality, though obstetricians, unlike most midwives, keep their private practices to the present day.

Women availed of whatever services were on offer, wherever they could, and in the 1930s the numbers of mothers attending clinics increased steadily from one year to the next. In 1935–6, a total of 59,591 mothers were visited by, or visited, maternity and child welfare schemes; in 1943–4, this had risen to 63,276. However, the number of nurses had not risen in proportion to their clients – there were 231 at the earlier date, 237 at the later.[24] When this is taken into account it is easy to credit James Deeny's comments that the voluntary and statutory maternity schemes in Dublin city were catering for only 20% of those they were intended to help.[25] Barrington is on shaky ground, however, when she states that the legislation against untrained attendance at birth 'gave women some protection against untrained handywomen'.[26] Given the scarcity of midwives, skilled medical attention and the unevenness of urban and rural maternity schemes outside the major cities up to 1953, handywomen, grandmothers or neighbours were often the only ones available to deliver babies. These women might have been partially trained by the local doctor or by a midwife, or else they had what Dr James Deeny, Chief Medical Officer in Ireland from 1942, called 'traditional skills'.[27] For example, Méiní Dunlevy, the handywoman on the Great Blasket Island up to the 1930s, had been trained by the doctor on the mainland because she spoke English, having spent some years in America. The doctor wanted her to train and 'get her certificate', but her husband was not enthusiastic about it so she did not train.[28] Though not a trained nurse, Méiní was certainly a good deal better than nothing, and most normal deliveries on the island were carried out by her, as described by Máire Ní Ghuithin:

> When a woman was expecting a child, she used be afraid that the sea wouldn't be calm. Nevertheless someone used go . . . down to call Méiní . . . she was the handy woman. She used come up then, and I don't know if there used to be any other woman with her. There was another woman – Máire Ní Scanláin she was called – and I think she also used to be there, but the thing about Méiní is that she was like a nurse. She used bring the child into the world and then remain on for a while, until evening maybe, and then she'd go home. Other evenings, she used call up again, and one of the other neighbours used come in and wash the child and do every-thing during that week for the woman in bed.[29]

The calm sea was much sought-after in case a doctor was needed; Méiní herself would send some men to get a *naomhóg* ready to go to fetch the doctor if the case was in any way complicated.[30] She knew her limitations, though from what Loudon tells us about the scrappy midwifery training of general practitioners in this period, it is not at all certain that the doctor would have been able to do much more than Méiní herself.[31] In Sligo in the 1910s and 1920s Seán C. tells us that there was:

> a handywoman in about every 3 townlands but they were very old at that time and I think they loved the job. There was always entertainment on an occasion such as that and it wasn't weak tea but they done their job if it was water they got, for poor and rich.

The suggestion of a sense of vocation – 'they loved the job' – is also evident in the account of Méiní, who defied her husband's lack of enthusiasm for her work on the island by saying that if there was anyone in difficulty and she had the means of helping them and did not do it, she would never forgive herself.[32] Handywomen were common in other parts of Ireland also. Tom K. and his siblings were delivered by a 'handywoman' in Mayo in the 1920s and 1930s, a woman who had learned the trade from her mother:

> It was handed down from mother to daughter, in a sense, like, and she'd have told her, don't do this, and you must do that . . . she wasn't trained to be a nurse at all. But she was able to deliver babies it seems, anyway.

Josephine E., in east Mayo, says of the same period that the women in the area were attended by 'a quack in the village . . . very seldom a doctor was there because he had to be paid for'. The doctor would have cost £1 in the 1940s. It was in Mayo that handywomen were slowest to die out.[33] Handywomen were known for not only attending the mother in labour, but for doing basic housework and setting the place to rights. The women who spoke to Nicky Leap and Billie Hunter in Britain described her as 'the woman you called for'.[34] There are many traditions in Ireland about *mná cabhartha* (literally, helping women) which also seem to have been associated with trained midwives once the latter became available. The folklore beliefs surrounding midwives are legion. Richard Denehan in Co. Limerick told the Folklore Commission in 1951 of a belief that the pains of a woman in labour would kill three men, and a popular fear that the midwife could put the pains of labour on anyone who crossed her. The midwife should never be fetched by someone on his or her own (presumably in case of an accident befalling the messenger); the midwife had to be 'treated' with a drop of whiskey before she set out (this could have been a practical way of ensuring her hands did not get too cold during the long walk or drive), and she would take charge of the afterbirth. She would always be 'treated' after the birth, too. The tea and biscuits invariably supplied to medical students 'on the district' in Dublin, (see Solomons' account, below), was a survival of this.[35]

There were a few famous handywomen operating in the Dublin tenements in the 1920s, according to Kevin Kearns' oral history. It is not clear why their clients did not go to one of the hospitals or call for assistance from one of the hospitals, but it must have been out of choice that people like 'Ma Lakey' were called for births.[36] There seems to have been some consciousness of hygiene, because the women were told to save newspapers which they put under them. Older children came to recognise that there was going to be an addition to the family when they saw their mothers saving newspapers. (Newspaper is still recommended as the most sterile underlay for use in an emergency birth.)[37]

> I had 8 children and I had a handywoman called Ma Lakey . . . she'd do everything for you. You'd have the newspapers for the bed and she'd get the hot water and everything, you just had to bring the child into the

world yourself, no painkillers. She'd just stand beside you and hold you down and the baby'd be born . . . She'd look after your baby and do your washing and come in the next morning for the whole nine days. A half a crown [payment].[38]

The reference to being held down suggests that Ma Lakey, unlike the birth attendants mentioned in some anthropological accounts, did not encourage squatting or any other positions the woman might have liked to adopt.[39] Radical midwives Nicky Leap and Billie Hunter, in their study of midwifery in England, were shocked at the handywoman they interviewed. She was a very strong character who had strict ideas about position and progress of labour, who did not believe in breast-feeding and whose idea of pain relief was to say sternly, 'You've 'ad yer sweets now you must 'ave yer sours.'[40] Half a crown was a lot of money to most people living in tenements, but had the tenement-dwelling woman gone to hospital or got a student/midwife from the hospital, she would not have got her washing and other jobs around the place done.

Handywomen were still delivering babies in Dublin tenements up to the end of the 1940s; they would notify the hospital when they had delivered the baby, so that it could cope with 'the third stage of labour' (the expulsion of the afterbirth) and the newborn baby.[41] Possibly they were covering themselves legally and would have argued if arraigned that they had been the only ones available at short notice and that they had notified the hospital as soon as they could. They must also have been aware of the danger of the third stage, from the point of view of infection. They could also have been protecting themselves from being implicated in concealed births. It is likely that for many people, particularly in rural areas, acting 'handywoman' was a neighbourly duty and some people were particularly skilled at it. One example was Kathleen Sheehan's mother, in a 'wild mountainy district of Cavan' in the early decades of this century, who 'could be a doctor or nurse in many emergencies' and was ready to:

> walk miles to deliver a baby, perhaps at night even, when a man would call for her . . . I am well aware of the mothers and babies whose lives she saved. It usually took hours for the doctor to arrive.

Perhaps there would not have been money for a doctor in any case. Later, however, 'the Government appointed a trained Midwife to the District' and Kathleen Sheehan implies that this marked the end of the need for her mother's help.[42] Dr Noel Browne's siblings in Athlone in the late 1910s and 1920s were delivered by a kind widowed neighbour, Mrs Bracken:

> As each of the Brownes came into the world Mrs Bracken would take over our house and our family. So gentle and natural was her presence that we hardly noticed the loss of our mother . . . Mrs Bracken acted as mid-wife; we had no money for a doctor.

Noel Browne's father had a 'good', i.e. a white-collar job, which would have placed him and his family well above the line where they would have been liable for any kind of charitable help, yet with a growing family and high town rents, money was scarce.[43] 'Acting as midwife' involved the house and family being looked after also, in this case. Even after 1933, it was not illegal to attend somebody in childbirth *in extremis*, if trained help was not available, but definitions of what constituted availability varied. The Central Midwives Board and the *Irish Nurses' Union Gazette*, like their counterparts in other countries at this time, constantly inveighed against midwives and doctors who allowed handywomen to assist them, the latter complaining that medical students from Dublin's Coombe hospital were attending births on the district with handywomen. (This is a point that Sandra Ryan does not take into account in her article, which uses 'midwife' to refer to trained midwives and handywomen interchangeably, and does not seem to know about the tremendous hostility of the former towards the latter.)[44] Yet in the absence of a sufficient number of trained medical personnel, this kind of on-the-job training for handywomen was often the safest option. It should not be forgotten either that many medical student attendants at births were very slightly trained, and even some general practitioners were, as Loudon points out, very cursorily trained in midwifery. The doctor who attended Mary Healy, a former domestic servant married to a carpenter in Fethard, Co. Tipperary, on her first baby in 1943, 'had been very careless and had done great damage to me during the delivery' to the extent that she had to have an operation when twelve weeks pregnant with her third child. The birth of her first child had taken place in Mary's mother's house, in the town of Kilkenny. This urban district had, for some unknown reason, a particularly high maternal mortality rate in the 1940s.[45] The trained midwife or the trained obstetrician are the safest birth attendants of all, according to Loudon, but there have, he acknowledges, been some appallingly dangerous fashions in doctors' midwifery over the past century or so. Thus the certificated midwife is the safest of all, generally speaking, and the safest place of birth, the woman's own home.[46] Loudon might be a bit hard, here, on the experienced GPs who had learned skills through years of attending women in labour, or who had actually made a study of midwifery. Irish obstetricians were aware of the lack of training of many GPs in midwifery, which was why they objected to local government county medical officers having responsibility for abnormal deliveries. Alex Spain suggested that, until there could be county obstetricians, a county medical officer with responsibility for abnormal midwifery should be a surgeon, preferably, as surgery was what was most often needed in emergency labours.[47]

The kind of maternity treatment available in ordinary district hospitals (not specialised maternity hospitals) before 1953 depended very much on luck. Mary Healy, mentioned above, who had to have an operation when pregnant with her third child, had had her second baby in St Joseph's hospital in Clonmel. It was probably while she was here that a doctor or midwife noticed that what she refers to as 'a certain portion of my anatomy' (perhaps her perineum or her cervix) needed attention, and booked her in for an operation for when she would have recovered from the birth, by which time she was pregnant again, there being only a year between her second and third children. Luckily no harm came to either Mary or her unborn child, but when she came out she was so weak that she had to sit down to wash nappies.[48]

Even in densely populated, accessible rural areas (i.e. not mountainous or subject to flooding) where there were supposed to be maternity schemes in operation, it was sometimes difficult to get trained attendance at birth. County Laois had maternity schemes in operation in the 1940s, radiating out from Portlaoise and Stradbally, yet when Noreen K. went into labour with her third child during the Emergency years, her husband Larry could not get a midwife. For her first two babies she had gone back to her mother's house in Dublin to go to the Coombe hospital, but on her third she booked the local trained midwife. Her husband told the story:

> [The midwife] sent me word, early that morning, that her own mother was very seriously sick, and that she couldn't, or she wouldn't, leave her, and to get somebody else. And I asked, whom would I get. She didn't know.
> – *Oh God, and there was no other nurse around?*
> She didn't know, and she the nurse herself like
> – *the official, the state [i.e. qualified] nurse like?*
> Ah yes, the official – and a marvellous nurse as well, unfortunately the mother did die, she died that night, so she couldn't be left. But anyway we searched the country, I must have cycled twenty miles in a couple of hours, trying people, no word available for any reason . . . all the good nurses were away in England, with the war effort . . . And I was knocking at their door then, at [laughs] eleven o'clock at night, so I got the doctor then, and he decided, best thing then, into the car and off to the hospital.

The doctor drove Noreen to Portlaoise hospital, some ten miles away, where she had the baby.

If the doctor (possibly, apart from the priest, the only car-owner of their acquaintance) had not been available to drive Noreen to hospital, she would have had to either depend upon a local handywoman – if there were one available, her husband seemed unaware of the existence of any – or have the baby on her own, attended by neighbours she did not know very well. Her husband never felt it necessary to explain why the doctor had not delivered her at home, instead of driving her to hospital; having a doctor at the birth was obviously unthinkably expensive.

The ordinary district hospitals (like Portlaoise) were hardly better fitted for complicated maternity procedures than the woman's home, as Alex Spain pointed out in 1945.[49] Larry and Noreen's story illustrates how subject to chance it could be for a family on a steady wage, in a well-populated and relatively well serviced part of the country, to get help at childbirth. District midwives had a very heavy workload. Teresa Murphy, a Jubilee nurse in Co. Kerry throughout this period, could be called out in the middle of the night in all weathers, and because Jubilee nurses only got six weeks' maternity leave, was often heavily pregnant when she did her deliveries:

> I remember one of the women I delivered telling me that seeing the size of me when I arrived she didn't know if it was me or herself would be having the baby first![50]

Mary Quain, a Lady Dudley nurse in Carraroe, 1937–43, often passed a week or more without getting a night's sleep, napping in patients' homes while she waited for labour to progress. She was ten years in the service before she managed to get a break for Christmas.[51] The midwife in Larry K.'s story understandably did not want to leave her dying mother; there was no cover for her, so her patient had to be abandoned. Stories like this put Mary Healy's complaints about being left overnight in early labour (see below) into perspective.

In town and in country, trained midwives were called upon for the births of people of all classes. T.J. McD. and his four brothers, born on a seventy-acre farm in Cavan between 1935 and 1940, were delivered by a midwife who travelled by bicycle. Maureen O'R.'s mother, in a working-class family in a Cork town, had a midwife who came for the birth and came in every day for a week. Nora Healy, who trained as a midwife in the USA in the 1910s, served the area around Charlestown Co. Mayo, in the 1920s, 1930s and 1940s. According to her son, certain families of Travellers would come all the way from Fermanagh and Tyrone in late pregnancy on horse-drawn transport (which cannot have been comfortable, but might have hastened labour!) to be delivered by her. They respected her cleanliness and her 'lucky hands.'[52] Some middle-class women had both the local doctor and a midwife, like Ethel R.'s mother, a bank official's wife in the 1940s, Delia R.'s mother, whose husband had a small business, and who had twelve children in Limerick City between 1918 and 1935, had a midwife who came in every day for a fortnight. Eamon B.'s mother, a shop-keeper married to a schoolteacher in a North Tipperary town, had both a doctor and a midwife in the 1930s. Sometimes a doctor was only called in for difficult cases; Joan K. and her brothers and sisters were all delivered by a trained midwife in rural Wexford in the 1920s, but a doctor was called for one of the births because it was a breech. Standards of care varied. Mary Healy was unimpressed when the midwife attending her on her sixth and last child left her alone all night when she was in early labour, with her elderly mother and a number of her children, none of whom was over the age of eight at that time. A neighbour came in and sat and prayed through the night with her, and the midwife came back next morning as planned and delivered the baby. What is surprising to the modern reader is that Mary, a working-class woman, was accustomed to a high standard of midwifery care, one which would have been unknown to many private, wealthy hospital patients in the 1930s, 1940s and 1950s who were 'left to get on with it', as the saying went, alone, during the very difficult late first stage of labour.[53] A trained midwife who was loved and revered on Tory Island in the 1930s and 1940s, did little during labour except sit with the woman and pray the Rosary, and was considered very good at cutting the cord and skilful at delivering the afterbirth. This was the most important midwifery skill before ergometrine became widely used; the number of women who died from retained placentas and consequent infection can be seen in the morbidity reports. Her less revered successor lacked this skill: 'Isn't it funny how the Tory people . . . keep the afterbirth' she said once.[54] Saying the Rosary and concentrating on the mysteries might have been good distraction therapy, an equivalent of the modern breathing and relaxing, as Mary Healy's account (above) of the saintly neighbour who prayed with her through labour, suggests. Mary Healy used to meditate on the Joyful Mystery of the Visitation, where Mary visits Elizabeth when both are pregnant.[55]

Some midwives could be extremely skilled and make discoveries of their own; Mary Kelly mentions Sister 'Biddy' Hayes, a senior labour ward sister in the Rotunda (retired in 1956), who developed skills in listening to foetal hearts that would not be discovered until the introduction of electronic foetal monitors some decades later. This would come as no surprise to Leap and Hunter, whose pre-NHS trained midwives' 'tricks of the trade' involved skills the two midwife authors had never heard of – estimating the progress of labour without internal examinations, and delivering breech babies without the presence of a doctor.[56] Women themselves had skills to speed up labour; such as castor oil, and feet in a basin of hot water, according to Josephine E.

Up to the 1950s, birth in a hospital other than a specialised maternity one, seems to have been a last resort for women. Even in an area serviced by three renowned maternity hospitals not all women, as mentioned earlier, availed of the free service provided. 'Joan Dunn', the artisan's wife interviewed by Humphreys, gave birth to all her five children at home in Dublin in the 1920s and 1930s, and confessed to having had 'a dread of hospitals.'[57] Mary Healy only went to hospital ('not the lovely modern hospital it is today, but a bleak stone building') for her second child, because, as she states tersely in her memoirs, 'my late sister-in-law stated clearly that she or her mother would not have time to give any help'. The maternity ward consisted of 'a long room with a timber floor that had to be scrubbed, and a small fire lighting at one end.' Her main worry was 'How will I tell Catherine when she grows up that she was born here'.[68] Lily G. was more pragmatic; when her first child was born in 1951 she went into Castlebar hospital because her mother was dead, her sister lived some miles distant with her own young family, and even though her older neighbour was very good, Lily did not want to impose upon her. However, she gives to understand that hospital births were fairly unusual at this stage in Mayo: 'There certainly wasn't a big mad rush on it [the hospital], because it was only a six-or nine-bedded ward, and that was it.' Mayo, as will be discussed below, was poorly served by maternity and child welfare services up to the late 1940s. Local authority hospitals were traditionally associated with the Union, or workhouse, and seen as places of disease and death. This might be why five mothers in Co. Kildare in 1930–31 who had been advised to enter hospital refused to do so, and had neither doctor nor midwife at the births of their stillborn babies. It could also be that these women could not leave young families, as was the case with mothers in Dublin who employed handywomen, or who refused to go into one of the free convalescent homes on the outskirts of the city 'but would gladly

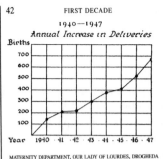

42 FIRST DECADE
1940—1947
Annual Increase in Deliveries

MATERNITY DEPARTMENT, OUR LADY OF LOURDES, DROGHEDA

Along with this increase in admissions there has been a marked expansion in the area served by the Maternity Department. A large percentage of the cases come from Drogheda and Dundalk areas, but an increasing number are now coming from the counties of Monaghan, Cavan and Armagh. About 80 per cent. of the cases are booked. The remaining 20 per cent. are emergencies referred by their own doctors.

It is worthy of note that 89.6 per cent. of the patients either attended the Ante-Natal Clinic or were under the care of their own doctor prior to admission to Hospital. This is gratifying, as it is most essential that every expectant mother should be seen by a doctor; not because she expects a spell of ill-health, on the contrary most mothers feel well, but because it is a period allotted during which she must be instructed in Maternal Hygiene with regard to diet, exercise, rest and emotional control. Furthermore she must be reassured and all unnecessary fears allayed. Should complications occur, as they sometimes do, they can be treated; many of them can be prevented, as X-ray facilities are to-day an invaluable aid to early diagnosis.

This marked increase in the number of Maternity cases has given us considerable cause for anxiety owing to the danger of over-crowding. To prevent this we might be impelled to shorten the time of the mother in hospital. At present the mothers are kept from ten to twelve days after the birth of the baby. In the case of a first child this enables the mother to gain confidence in taking care of her baby, and for the other mothers, it gives them rest and freedom from domestic duties. It also enables the Physio-Therapist to complete her course of exercises and treatments so necessary for the well-being of the mother.

Our thanks are due to those who have made possible the increased facilities in every Department of the Hospital and to those who have generously co-operated by sending us patients. The desire of the Medical Missionaries of Mary is that through those facilities they may be enabled to be of greater service to those in need and whom it is their privilege to serve.

G. CONNOLLY,
Resident Obstetrical Officer.

THE WAND OF HERMES (MESSENGER OF THE GODS) A MEDICAL SYMBOL ESPECIALLY CONNECTED WITH

ALCHEMY, THE FORERUNNER OF CHEMISTRY. — *The Medical Missionary of Mary, Jan-Feb., 1947.*

9. Graph and text on Lourdes hospital, Drogheda taken from the Medical Missionaries of Mary, *The First Decade 1937–1947*, extract from the annual report, 1947, illustrating the rise in the number of hospital deliveries in one area of the country; the text shows the increasing medicalization of pregnancy and childbirth in this period.

avail of the treatment offered by these institutions if accommodation for one or two young children could be provided'.[59] A survey of natality in Dublin in 1945 noted that the more children a mother already had, the more likely she was to have a home birth, even though grand multiparas – defined in the 1940s and 1950s as women on their seventh or subsequent full-term deliveries – were the very ones urged by obstetricians to have their babies in hospital.[60]

The shift to hospital births seems to have happened quite rapidly in the 1950s. Home births showed a steady decline in the second half of the 1950s, from just over a third of all births in 1955 to just over a fifth (20.3%) by 1961. The others were either in hospitals or in registered private maternity homes.[61] After 1953, and before the building and equipping of major maternity hospitals and regional hospitals with maternity units, nursing homes could be used by public patients and were less exclusive than before. Many were very homely and non-institutional.[62] Having babies away from home was considered a modern thing to do, and a necessary rest for the woman. 'I wouldn't dream of it!' said Olive A. emphatically when I asked her if she had had any of her children at home, in the 1950s and 1960s, and she added that she had always had 'the best gynaecologist in Cork – those things I always had.' The almoner in Dublin's Rotunda hospital noted with some regret in 1955 that the women whose houses were ideal for home births – new local authority or privately-owned dwellings with water and electricity – were the very ones who came into hospital to have their babies, because they had nobody to help them 'out there' in the suburbs.[63] Artisans' wives in Dublin in the 1940s were less likely than labourers' wives to rely on the help of neighbours at times of childbirth and illness, relying instead on relatives who often travelled long distances for this purpose, according to Humphreys.[64] Delia R. remembers how she began to associate a certain room in the house being prepared for her unmarried aunt with the imminent arrival of a new sibling. Her aunt came to help out with the other children and keep house, a reminder to us, incidentally, that single women often had inescapable family responsibilities. This was in the 1920s and 1930s. Joan K., who lived in one of the new Dublin suburbs and had her first baby in hospital and her four subsequent children at home, 'with the local nurse' (1948–56) was a dying breed; she preferred to be at home. Mary Ellen D., the wife of a fairly large farmer in the midlands, who married in 1952, believed that home births had 'more or less gone out at that stage' and seemed embarrassed by the suggestion that she might have had her babies at home.

Home births in the period are described below in different ways by different doctors, giving us an insight into the advantages and disadvantages of domiciliary midwifery in the period in question. Dr Michael Solomons, a student 'on the district' of Dublin's Rotunda hospital in the 1940s, emphasises the warmth and neighbourliness of childbirth in the tenements:

> Female family and friends were often around and they gave us a warm welcome, calling us 'doctor' even though they knew we were not qualified. We would arrive to find newspapers covering the mattress for protection and kettles and saucepans somehow full of boiling water ready for our instruments. We would often be working in a confined space . . . Although the environment in which many women found themselves giving birth was far from satisfactory and the medical treatment they received was patchy, Mother Nature took care of her charges pretty well. Provided that the baby seemed to be lying in the normal position, its heart sounded normal and the mother was reasonably at ease, each of us would take turns sitting on the bed encouraging, reassuring and rubbing her back during contractions. Someone would be given the job of watching for the appearance of the baby's head and many an unsuspecting student received a splash in the face when a mother's waters broke. While in our amateurish way we would try to assess how a birth was progressing, the opinion of an experienced mother, or of her friends, would often prove far more dependable than our own . . . Aware of the potential for complications, we felt a terrific sense of relief once a baby was born and crying. When a delivery was completed, friends and neighbours would take over. A fresh nightdress and a cup of tea would be produced for the exhausted mother. The chamber-pot, often borrowed from a neighbour as not every family possessed one, would be gratefully returned and the bedclothes would be straightened . . . whatever their circumstances [the women] always provided us with tea and biscuits after a birth.[65]

Dr Solomons' respect for 'Mother Nature' and for the experientially-based skill of formally untrained people, seems genuine and is shared by Dr John O'Connell in his memoirs:

> We were worked so hard we were constantly exhausted. For that reason it is fortunate that nature herself takes care of so many births. She would not have wanted to have depended on us all the time.[66]

The inexperience of students could also be dangerous, hence the huge relief described by Dr Solomons. Dr Noel Browne tells a heartbreaking story of a perfectly formed and otherwise healthy newborn baby who died because neither Browne, then a student, nor his colleague knew how to unblock his air passages of mucus, a skill which anybody trained in midwifery would have had.[67] However, because of the lack of antenatal care (see figures below in the section on maternal mortality), midwives or doctors called to a birth never knew what they were facing into, as Dr James Deeny graphically illustrates with an account of a birth he attended in rural Armagh in the 1930s. Armagh is, properly speaking, outside the scope of this study, but because Deeny went on to become the most important figure in the public health of independent Ireland in the 1940s, all of his stories and perspectives are of central importance. Besides, there were remote parts of the twenty-six counties where women were equally vulnerable:

> One night I received a call to a case in the Montiaghs. [Armagh] The people were very poor and lived in a little cottage on a bit of cut-out bog. To get to it I had to wade through a flood from the Lough. When I arrived I found that the patient was having a severe haemorrhage because the placenta was blocking the birth passage . . . I had two options. I could send the husband back through the flood to ride on his bicycle the few miles to the police barracks to ring for the hospital ambulance. She could well be dead by the time she got there [i.e. to hospital], but everyone would say that 'Dr Jim, the moment he saw her, sent her to hospital and did his best.' I would be in the clear and would not be blamed. On the other hand, I could 'do a version', turn the baby and stop the haemorrhage. This was a serious procedure, and with a poor half-fed woman, she could well die. So I said a prayer, did the version and saved her. If it had gone wrong, all the water in Lough Neagh would not have washed me clean and for the next generation I would be haunted by that poor man and his six motherless children every time I saw them on the road. No woman's life should be at the mercy of such circumstances.[68]

This account illustrates the difficult decisions that doctors and midwives working on emergency maternity cases often had to make. Deeny implies that all were lucky, or blessed, that the procedure succeeded; the matter-of-fact reference to his appeal for divine help before he attempted the version, and the plausibility of the grim alternative scenario he paints, make it a story of quiet courage rather

than a flamboyant tale of modern science and medicine going through flood and
fire to save the day. He readily acknowledges that the woman's poor nutritional
state was one of the greatest risk factors in the whole affair. Moving a woman
who was haemorrhaging over bumpy roads could have killed her, if she hadn't
bled to death waiting for the ambulance in the meantime, but he would have been
'covered', acting entirely properly, had he sent her the long journey to hospital
and almost certain death. Had the procedure failed, would he have been one of
the general practitioners vilified by obstetricians of the time as 'incompetent' and
'inexperienced'?

The long lying-in period seems to have been a universal ideal in private
homes, nursing homes and hospitals, in births attended by doctors, midwives
and handywomen, and in places as far apart as the Great Blasket Island, where
women lay in for a week, and Dublin city.[69] Joan K.'s mother, in rural Wexford
in the 1920s, stayed in bed for ten days; Delia R.'s mother lay in for a fortnight;
in Youghal cottage hospital in the 1950s women were kept in for a week to ten
days, and in Castlebar hospital, according to Lily G., 'you wouldn't put a foot
on the floor . . . until the seventh day' and went home on the ninth. Mary Ellen
D. tells us that Portiuncula hospital in Ballinasloe in the 1940s kept women in
for twelve days. Dr G. Connolly, the Resident Obstetrician of Lourdes Hospital
in Drogheda, noted in the annual report of 1947 that mothers were kept in from
ten to twelve days, but acknowledged with regret that this might have to be
shortened due to overcrowding. For him, the most important aspect of the
lying-in period was the 'rest and freedom from domestic duties'.[70] Handywomen,
as already mentioned, were just as insistent on, and authoritative about, lying-
in; 'And dare you get out of bed – she would NOT let you.' was said of Ma
Lakey, the renowned Dublin handywoman.[71] However Dr John O'Connell
believed that many women who had babies at home in Dublin tenements at any
rate, were up and about after two or three days.[72] This was not considered
proper practice, even at a popular level. Joan K. described with horror to me
about how some of the poor women in the country in the 1920s and 1930s
would go out working in the fields not long after giving birth. Many women
who talked to me looked with pity at modern women who are expected to be up,
dressed and more or less back to the routine two or three days after the baby is
born. It is now known that lying still for a long period after childbirth can cause
anything from constipation to blood clots, but in the period in question it was
believed, according to one authority, that getting up too soon:

> puts a strain on the pelvic floor, the various internal organs are likely to
> drop; while the contractions of the uterus may cease and it may thus
> remain permanently enlarged.[73]

The long lying-in period was colluded in by women themselves. It was the only
rest most of them ever got in their lives.

MATERNAL MORTALITY AND MATERNAL HEALTH

Dr Alex Spain claimed in 1947 that maternal mortality in Ireland had been reduced 'almost to vanishing point'. Although he was being a little premature, there were grounds for optimism; there were 130 maternal deaths in Ireland in 1947, the lowest since 1923. Numbers continued to fall (though not always steadily from year to year) until they reached 27 in 1961.[74] See Table 5.1.

Table 5.1: *Maternal Mortality (Ireland) 1923–1961: Rate and Numbers. Nations, all-inclusive rate taken from statistical abstracts: breakdown and numbers taken from reports of registrar-general, 1923–49*

Year	Total	Puerp. Sep.	Other
1923	5.32 (297)	2.19 (135)	2.63 (162)
1924	5.21 (303)	1.94 (123)	2.84 (180)
1926	5.38 (299)	1.88 (115)	3.01 (184)
1927	4.80 (271)	1.28 (77)	3.23 (194)
1928	5.37 (292)	1.74 (103)	3.19 (189)
1929	4.85 (239)	1.37 (80)	2.73 (159)
1930	5.04 (278)	1.39 (81)	3.38 (197)
1931	4.76 (246)	1.16 (66)	3.15 (180)
1932	4.98 (256)	1.39 (78)	3.16 (178)
1933	5.16 (255)	1.39 (80)	3.05 (175)
1934	5.25 (271)	1.80 (104)	2.88 (167)
1935	5.10 (272)	1.53 (89)	3.14 (183)
1936	5.14 (273)	1.79 (104)	2.91 (169)
1937	4.19 (203)	0.90 (51)	2.71 (153)
1938	4.69 (234)	0.81 (46)	3.30 (188)
1939	3.89 (190)	0.68 (38)	2.71 (152)
1940	4.01 (208)	0.97 (55)	2.70 (153)
1941	3.68 (182)	0.76 (43)	2.45 (139)
1942	2.86 (163)	0.65 (43)	1.82 (120)
1943	2.51 (144)	0.56 (36)	1.69 (108)
1944	2.69 (156)	0.50 (32)	1.90 (124)
1945	2.63 (159)	0.50 (35)	1.90 (124)
1946	2.39 (137)	0.30 (20)	1.70 (117)
1947	2.15 (130)	0.40 (31)	1.40 (99)
1948	1.88 (104)	0.30 (18)	1.30 (86)
1949	2.01 (116)	0.30 (18)	1.50 (98)

Overall Maternal Mortality Only

Year	Total	Year	Total
1950	99	1956	52
1951	103	1957	81
1952	92	1958	61
1953	83	1959	39
1954	69	1960	35
1955	70	1961	27

Explanatory note: After 1949 annual maternal mortality figures were computed in a different way, so numbers only are given for 1950–61. Numbers taken from Department of Health, Vital Statistics from 1953.

Two years earlier, Dr Spain had attributed what he called this 'most remarkable decline' in maternal mortality from 1934–43 to two factors; the introduction of sulphonamide drugs to treat puerperal sepsis, and 'the more frequent resort to institutional midwifery for the abnormal case'. The phrase 'institutional midwifery' highlights the fact that obstetricians themselves thought of hospital births as unusual. In 1945, Dr Spain set out the priorities of an improved maternity service:

> Survival of the mother is, and always will be, the most important criterion of a good midwifery service, but it is not the only criterion . . . we must endeavour to deal with the great problems of toxaemia and maternal ill-health following childbearing, and we must endeavour to give to the newborn baby, be it mature or premature, the best possible chance of survival.[75]

The mother's priority is taken so much for granted that the reader has almost to be reminded that there is a baby in the picture too. (Dr Deeny's account of the Montiaghs delivery, above, does not even mention whether the baby survived or not.) Good maternity care, according to Dr James Quin, also in 1945:

> should bring the mother safely through her pregnancy, labour and puerperium. It should secure the birth of a healthy infant with tissue endowed to protect it against the diseases of childhood. It should leave the mother at the end of her puerperium at least as well as when she became pregnant . . . maternal and infant deaths are too frequent, to say the very least, and this is the only factual method we have of estimating our present efficiency. What cannot possibly be estimated or guessed at is the impaired health and chronic illness which are the result of a badly-conducted or infected delivery.[76]

The mother of Dr John O'Connell, for example, had a permanently swollen leg as the result of a puerperal infection: 'Even as a child I was conscious of her embarrassment over that leg'.[77] Puerperal sepsis was in retreat throughout Europe from 1938 due to the introduction of sulphonamide drugs, and also, Loudon believes, perhaps because the bacterium exhausted itself, or played itself out.[78] The decline was certainly dramatic in Ireland where the average ninety-five deaths per year from this cause in 1923–36, fell to an average of thirty-five per year 1937–49. However, as maternal deaths from all causes declined definitively towards the end of the 1940s, puerperal sepsis, or infection as it was also called, still accounted for between one-fifth and a quarter – sometimes slightly more – of all maternal deaths up to 1961.

Deaths from 'other accidents/diseases of pregnancy and childbirth' began to fall definitively from 1942. From 1923–41, the average number of 'other' maternal deaths per year (as we shall call them, for convenience) was 172. This fell to an average of 107 per year from 1942–51, and to 62 from 1952–61. (This last average might mask the fact that from 1959, numbers of maternal deaths

Table 5.2: *Major Causes of Maternal Mortality in Ireland 1938–1950 for*
1938–1950, from Table xxxi, Annual Report of the Registrar-General 1950
(1953), p. xliii), and 1953, 1954 and 1958 (from tables in selected
years, Vital Statistics 1953–58:) as percentage total deaths.

Year	Deaths	Tox	Puer	Haem	Other
1938	(234)	4.6%	39%	26%	11%
1939	(190)	4.6%	45%	23%	11%
1940	(208)	13%	34%	31%	10%
1941	(182)	17%	32%	23%	10%
1942	(163)	11.7%	31%	23%	17%
1943	(145)	11.6%	24%	33%	14%
1944	(156)	9.5%	34%	27%	17%
1945	(159)	16%	31%	28%	15%
1946	(137)	20%	11%	36%	16%
1947	(130)	24%	29%	23%	11%
1948	(104)	19%	20%	37%	13%
1949	(116)	16%	19%	32%	13%
1950	(99)	14%	20%	34%	5%
1953	(83)	19%	21%	19%	20%
1954	(69)	24%	26%	7%	11%
1958	(61)	26%	26%	14%	21%

Note: Tox = Toxaemia of pregnancy; Puer = puerperal sepsis/infection; Haem = haemorrhage of pregnancy/childbirth; Oother = other accidents of pregnancy and childbirth. Other
minor causes of death included ectopic gestation, septic abortion, other or unspecified
puerperal conditions, other diseases of pregnancy.

dropped significantly to something like half of what they had been throughout
most of the decade.) 'Other' maternal mortality was caused by toxaemia of
pregnancy, haemorrhage, conditions that could have required Caeserean section
(placenta blocking the neck of the womb, a baby too large for the mother's pelvis
and similar tragedies) and embolisms (strokes brought on by blood clots).

In 1936 most of the 'other puerperal conditions' which caused maternal
death were toxaemia or albuminuria, heavy bleeding and blood clots. 'Other
accidents of childbirth' accounted for 16% of all maternal deaths from causes
other than puerperal sepsis, in comparison with toxaemia which accounted for
over a third (36.8%); haemorrhage, particularly dangerous in women who were
already anaemic, for 29.6%, and blood clots and strokes for 17.6%. (It was
decided not to tabulate these deaths along with those from 1938 in Table 5.2 as
there seems to have been a slightly different classification of causes from 1938.)

There were, in addition, deaths from conditions which were exacerbated, but
not caused, by childbirth such as heart disease, anaemia and tuberculosis. In 1936,
for example, a year when the maternal mortality rate was 5.14% (representing 273
deaths overall) there were an additional twenty-six maternal deaths in Ireland
due to heart disease, nephritis, influenza, pneumonia and tuberculosis, which

the *Report of the Department of Local Government and Public Health* described as 'diseases or causes associated with but not chargeable against pregnancy and childbirth'.[79] This 'dark figure' of fatalities given the final blow, but not caused, by pregnancy and childbirth must be kept in mind when we are trying to assess the comparative safety of childbearing for Irish women in this period, as they do not feature in the maternal mortality figures. Haemorrhage, toxaemia of pregnancy and 'other accidents of childbirth' accounted for most of the total maternal deaths throughout the period, not forgetting that puerperal sepsis was still killing, for example, over a quarter of the women who died in childbirth in 1958 (Table 5.2). At this stage, however, toxaemia of pregnancy was seen as the principal cause of avoidable maternal deaths in Ireland.[80] Medical opinion was divided on a phenomenon called 'obstetric shock' – unexplained maternal death some hours after a normal, if particularly protracted and traumatic delivery. Alex Spain in particular believed this to be a convenient scapegoat for medical carelessness and negligence.[81] Other doctors, however, believed it to be the only explanation for some maternal deaths, and from what is now known about shock, it might well have been true of women whose systems were already weakened.[82] The dangers of haemorrhage are apparent when it is borne in mind that two Dublin doctors, W.R. Fearon and W. Dockeray, in a survey of the eating habits of a number of pregnant wives of unemployed men in Dublin in 1939, concluded that almost all were anaemic.[83] Toxaemia can be closely monitored with ante-natal care, but the remedies, or preventive measures, blood pressure drugs, good diet and most importantly of all, what we would nowadays call a low stress level, were beyond the reach of many women. The *National Nutrition Survey* found that lower-middle class and working-class women had a progressively lower intake of nutrients as family size expanded.[84]

It is difficult to put an exact date on the development of an awareness by women themselves of the need for ante-natal care. It has already been mentioned in the first part of this chapter that women, in ever increasing numbers, availed of such care when it was available to them. In county Kildare in 1931, 60% of mothers whose babies had died in the first year of life had had no ante-natal supervision of any kind. This, however, implies that 40% of this group had had some kind of ante-natal care, which indicates such awareness by two-fifths of a sample weighted in favour of people in moderate to indigent circumstances.[85] In Lourdes hospital in Drogheda in 1947, 89% of the patients 'either attended the Ante-Natal Clinic or were under the care of their own doctor prior to admission to Hospital'. The hospital had a catchment area of Louth, Meath and parts of Monaghan and Cavan. As late as 1956, however, between a quarter and a third of the women who had babies in the National Maternity Hospital, Holles St, Dublin (28.9%) were 'unbooked', that is, they had had no ante-natal care at all, so the potential for danger can be understood.[86] This was 1956, when there was a comprehensive maternity service in place, and Dublin, where ante-natal care and skilled attendance at delivery in hospital or outside it had been available for many years at this stage. If this was the case in Dublin, then the difficulties, practical and otherwise, of pregnant women in small towns and rural areas getting some kind of ante-natal care can only be imagined. There was sometimes cultural resistance to ante-natal supervision. Dr Deeny states that this was the case in Lurgan in the 1930s, when the mothers of young pregnant women did not appreciate their daughters being advised to have intervention in potentially dangerous conditions, due to reticence and a belief that interference with the natural order of things was wrong. Dr P.J. O'Farrell commented in 1956 in a discussion on the need for greater awareness of ante-natal care:

> How is it going to be carried out? How are you going to get the patients to report? The doctors cannot go out themselves. You know that in the country parts people keep pregnancy very much to themselves because they regard it as a natural phenomenon.[87]

However, the alacrity with which women availed of whatever services they could, and particularly the speed of the changeover from domiciliary to hospital confinements once the new health service got underway, would seem to imply that practical difficulties like transport, child-minding, and pressure of work were more likely to discourage women from availing of services than 'tradition' and shyness.

None of this answers the key question, however: why did 'other' maternal mortality begin to decline in Ireland from 1942? A county-by-county examination of the services which existed, and the maternal mortality rates in each county, would, be beyond the scope of this work. It would, moreover, involve a multi-dimensional inquiry into the local economies and employment patterns of each area, along with variables like accessibility of towns, general health and class balance. However, to test the supposition – which would seem to be a logical one – that improved midwifery expertise and facilities of themselves reduce maternal mortality, we will look at the maternal mortality figures in a largely rural county which had an abundance of such services throughout this period, and a very different, largely rural county which was lacking in them.

MATERNAL MORTALITY IN KILDARE AND MAYO 1923-49: A BRIEF COMPARISON

Kildare and Mayo were both predominantly rural counties (1926–46, 11% of Kildare's population and 7–9% of Mayo's were urban-dwellers), yet they were very different. Mayo, with its high proportion of small-holders and subsistence farmers and its high rates of emigration and seasonal migration which persisted into the twentieth century, encapsulated all that was considered precarious and 'backward' about the economy of the west of Ireland. Kildare, though not considered as 'backward' or as economically problematic as Mayo, had pockets of serious economic vulnerability, rural unrest in the early twentieth century and chronic underemployment of agricultural labourers. A very high proportion of

Table 5.3: *Number of Midwives and Doctors per head of Population,*
Kildare and Mayo, 1926, 1936 and 1946

Year	Kildare		Mayo	
	Doctors	Midwives	Doctors	Midwives
1926	1/1,160	1/3,627	1/3,257	1/19,184
1936	1/1,603	1/1,862	1/2,870	1/2,876
1946	1/1,507	1/2,701	1/5,110	1/3,900

its population was on public assistance in the 1920s and 1930s. Even though Kildare's level of urbanisation was, like that of Mayo, comparatively low, there is a huge difference between the closely situated villages and small towns of rural Kildare and the vast rural stretches of Mayo. Mayo has, moreover, a larger surface area and had a much larger population than Kildare, even though the population of the western county fell significantly while that of the eastern county rose slightly between 1936 and 1946.[88]

Irvine Loudon concludes in his exhaustive survey that the safest birth attendant over the past two centuries has been the well-trained, patient midwife.[89] Given this, the ratio of midwives to the population in a particular area is a more reliable indicator of midwifery expertise than the ratio of doctors. Also, midwives were more accessible and cheaper and therefore more likely to be called. In this case, however, we will give doctors the benefit of the doubt and consider their ratio to the total population to have significance for midwifery expertise also. In any case, general medical students trained in Dublin often had considerable experience of midwifery on the Dublin district.[90]

Table 5.3 shows that Kildare was far better equipped than Mayo with both doctors and midwives throughout the period.

There was a striking improvement in the number of midwives practising in Mayo between 1926 and 1936, but the situation deteriorated again (though not to anything like 1926 levels) by 1946. Kildare showed a similar pattern, though the improvement 1926–36 was nothing like as dramatic as it was in Mayo. Doctors showed a different pattern in Kildare from Mayo, where their decline 1926–36 probably had something to do with the departure of personnel associated with the British army. However, while the ratio of doctors improved slightly in Kildare 1936–46, it disimproved significantly in Mayo. The apparent fall in the number of midwives in both counties, 1936–46, can be accounted for by the emigration patterns of the early 1940s. The counter-attractions of work in Britain were too strong and would continue to be so until the 1950s when the Department of Health made an effort to attract Irish nurses back from Britain.[91] More important than the actual numbers of midwives and doctors, however, was their deployment in these counties. Again, Kildare had a clear advantage over Mayo. The eastern county had at least seven voluntary and local authority nursing assocations and clinics as early as 1932, spread throughout the county from Maynooth to Athy. In 1949 it had a county scheme funded by the local authority, and one in the urban district of Naas. While Mayo could boast 49,599 visits by Lady Dudley and Jubilee nurses in nineteen health districts in 1936, this must have represented seriously overworked nurses; there were only three district nursing associations in Mayo receiving grants from the Department of Local Government and Public Health in the 1930s – in Ballina, Kilkelly and Westport. By 1943 Westport was not receiving any grant, which implies that it had faded away. Mayo, furthermore, was one of the handful of counties which had no local authority maternity and child welfare schemes in 1949.[92] Furthermore, the western county was considered notorious for its handywomen continuing to practise long after they had been outlawed; Barrington mentions this, and two of my contributors from Mayo referred to 'handywomen' or 'quacks' delivering babies up to the 1940s.[93] Not only was Kildare better supplied than Mayo with trained birth attendants, it was also more evenly spread with schemes and associations catering to pregnant and parturient women and their infants. If the spread of midwifery expertise made a significant difference to maternal health in Ireland in this period, then one would expect higher rates of maternal mortality in an area which was lacking in such expertise and indeed, threatened with its opposite – supposed ignorance and 'quackery'.

A comparison of the maternal mortality rates in these counties, 1923–49, does not, however, give the clear advantage to Kildare as far as maternal survival was concerned. The numbers of maternal deaths are higher in Mayo than in Kildare throughout the period, yet, as Mayo had between two and three times the population of Kildare, this is to be expected (See Table 5.4).

In this case, the maternal mortality rate – the rate per 1,000 births – is the most reliable indicator of the level of maternal mortality in both places. Looking at the rates, it can be seen immediately that Mayo had a higher rate of deaths from puerperal sepsis than had Kildare, 1923–36 – an average 1.94 per year in Mayo, compared with 1.34 in Kildare, and, unlike Kildare, no years without maternal deaths from this cause. This comes as a surprise because puerperal sepsis in the twentieth century is associated with hospitalisation, over-worked, careless or just unlucky birth attendants (trained more so than untrained, hurrying from one case to another) and urbanisation. Almost all of these deaths in Mayo took place 'elsewhere' than a hospital, nursing home or infirmary, i.e. at home, and most in rural areas. The epidemiology of puerperal sepsis baffles even the specialist medical historian, Loudon noting that it spread like wildfire in some areas and spared others completely, and that it dogged the footsteps of the best trained and cleanest birth attendants.[94] The annual reports of the Department of Local Government and Public Health show that some parts of Ireland in particular years were completely free of this infection, while others were bedevilled by it.[95] Contemporaries would no doubt have attributed Mayo's comparatively high mortality from this cause in these years to ignorant and dirty handywomen, but until we know more about the practices of Mayo handywomen, we cannot make such suppositions. The insistence of Mayo (trained) midwife Nora Healy's Traveller clients on having her clean and 'lucky' hands to deliver their babies in the 1930s and 1940s, and the Dublin

Table 5.4: *Maternal Mortality in Counties Kildare and Mayo, 1923–49, Rates and Numbers, divided into deaths from Puerperal Sepsis and 'Other Accidents/Diseases of Childbirth'*

Year	Puerp. Sepsis		Other Accid/Diseases	
	Kildare	Mayo	Kildare	Mayo
1923	1.67 (2)	2.06 (7)	3.34 (4)	2.65 (9)
1924	0.82 (1)	1.09 (4)	2.46 (3)	2.73 (10)
1926	3.33 (4)	3.36 (11)	3.33 (4)	1.53 (5)
1927	–	0.98 (3)	2.53 (3)	3.93 (12)
1928	0.80 (1)	2.53 (8)	3.20 (4)	2.21 (7)
1929	0.81 (1)	1.63 (5)	2.44 (3)	4.25 (13)
1930	–	0.99 (3)	4.40 (5)	2.63 (8)
1931	–	0.34 (1)	5.09 (6)	4.82 (14)
1932	0.82 (1)	2.05 (6)	2.46 (3)	1.71 (5)
1933	1.69 (2)	1.34 (4)	1.69 (2)	3.68 (8)
1934	1.58 (2)	2.05 (6)	4.74 (6)	4.09 (12)
1935	2.27 (3)	1.40 (4)	0.76 (1)	3.14 (9)
1936	2.35 (3)	2.11 (6)	2.35 (3)	2.11 (6)
1937	0.84 (1)	0.75 (2)	4.19 (5)	2.25 (6)
1938	2.27 (3)	1.12 (3)	5.30 (7)	5.21 (4)
1939	1.56 (2)	0.77 (2)	3.13 (4)	2.68 (7)
1940	0.79 (1)	0.73 (2)	3.93 (5)	2.19 (6)
1941	0.82 (1)	0.72 (2)	2.46 (3)	1.79 (5)
1942	–	0.32 (1)	–	0.95 (3)
1943	–	0.34 (1)	2.46 (4)	3.35 (10)
1944	–	0.03 (1)	0.60 (1)	0.30 (1)
1945	0.6 (1)	0.30 (1)	2.30 (4)	0.30 (1)
1946	0.60 (1)	–	0.60 (1)	2.50 (8)
1947	–	0.90 (3)	1.1 (2)	1.60 (5)
1948	–	–	0.60 (1)	1.75 (5)
1949	–	0.30 (1)	2.40 (4)	1.40 (4)

(For national figures see Table 6.1)
Note: From 1950 the annual maternal mortality figures were computed in a different way.

handywomen's emphasis on boiling water and newspaper, referred to above, would suggest some insistence on cleanliness in childbirth among 'uneducated' and poor people, in this period, and a popular unwillingness to tolerate dirty birth attendants, for whatever reason.

Looking at 'other' maternal mortality gives us more of a chance to evaluate the importance of midwifery expertise in attendance at childbirth. If 1942 is taken as the cut-off point – the year when 'other' maternal deaths began to fall – then average mortality rates from 'other diseases/accidents of pregnancy and childbirth' can be worked out for both counties for 1923–41, and 1942–49. In 1923–41, the average 'other' maternal mortality rate was slightly higher in Kildare than it was in Mayo, admittedly not by much – 3.20 to 2.90. There was a turn-around in the 1940s, however, when Kildare had a 0.4 percentage point advantage over Mayo. Such differences are too small to shape into any conclusions about one county or the other but what can be tentatively suggested is that improvement, when it happened, came slightly more rapidly to the county which was already well-equipped with maternity services. The fact that Kildare's 'other' maternal mortality was not lower, and was in fact, slightly higher – than that of Mayo in 1923–41, makes us think twice about equating rurality and remoteness with inevitable danger to mothers in childbirth. Similarly, the greater vulnerability of Mayo women to puerperal sepsis throughout the danger period for this infection shows that remoteness, rurality and domiciliary confinements did not necessarily afford protection against it. It should also be mentioned that, in this period, hospital births formed a minority of all births in both counties. A much more in-depth study of maternal mortality in each of these areas would have to be undertaken before any more conclusions could be drawn.

Bearing in mind that midwifery expertise was not always available, even when it was local (as Noreen K.'s story, above, illustrates so graphically), and that it might not always have been adequate even when it was available (James Deeny's, above, very nearly was not, through no fault of his), its unavailability in a particular region does not seem to have been reflected in strikingly higher rates of maternal mortality. Factors such as standard of living, levels of stress, quality of diet and availability of other resources must be taken into account. For example, while the diet of small farmers in the so-called 'congested districts' (Mayo, for example) was considered inadequate according to the standards of the National Nutrition Survey carried out in the 1940s, it was nonetheless more nutritious than that enjoyed by rural and town-dwelling labourers in other parts of the country (Kildare, for example).[96] Poor diet made women very vulnerable to toxaemia and less able to withstand any kind of childbirth trauma as Deeny's comment about the risky version he performed on the 'poor half-fed' Armagh woman indicates. It is also notable that Connacht had the lowest rate of infant mortality in the country throughout this period, which suggests a certain level of good nutrition (and perhaps, comparatively high standards of cleanliness?). (See Chapter 6.)

The slow but reassuringly steady decline in maternal mortality from 1942 certainly owed something to stepped-up government action on public health in general and maternal health in particular. The same factors that led to the decrease in deaths from puerperal infection throughout the western world operated in Ireland also, but this small-scale comparison of two regions suggests that other factors such as a rise in the standard of living could have played an important part in improving women's chances of surviving pregnancy and childbirth.

HIGH FERTILITY AND GRAND MULTIPARITY

The maternal mortality rate in Ireland in the 1950s, while it was comparatively high, was lower than it could have been, given the number of times individual women experienced childbirth. Cormac O Gráda suggests that some Irish people in predominantly Catholic parts of the country might have been limiting family size as early as the 1930s. Brendan Walsh, in a survey carried out in the 1960s, concluded that more than one-third of women who married between the ages of 20 and 24 in the period 1932–6, had at least seven live births. Kennedy's exhaustive and detailed analysis of Irish fertility shows that a fertility or 'desired family size' that was significantly higher than that of other Catholic countries – (or of Irish Catholic immigrants to America, for example) persisted up to 1961.[97] Translated into terms of pregnancy and childbirth, 32% of mothers giving birth in 1959 had given birth to four or more children already, and almost a third – 30.9% – of births were to women over 35.[98] Dr Michael Solomons comments that 11.9%, or 93 of the 785 home deliveries he attended while he was Clinical Clerk of Dublin's Rotunda in 1943, were of babies born to women pregnant for at least the tenth time.[99] Dr John O'Connell in the Coombe hospital in the early 1950s was 'dealing as a matter of routine with mothers of ten children'.[100] A 'grand multipara' was defined by Dr J.K. Feeney in 1953 as a woman who had had seven or more vaginal deliveries of a foetus of more than 28 weeks. This term was coined by Dublin obstetricians who became world experts on this medical phenomenon.[101]

Without wanting to intrude as a layperson upon the historical problem of medical phenomena which I am not qualified to assess, I would like to look at some medical opinions on grand multiparity because of the positive and negative – mostly positive – comments, cited earlier in the text, about the large Irish family. Dr Feeney's clinical study of 518 cases of grand multiparity in 1953 concluded that these mothers were at high risk and more than twice as likely to miscarry and to suffer from hypertension particularly as:

> social and domestic deficiencies and disadvantages are more frequent in the lives of poor women with many children; and large families are more common in the homes of poor mothers.

Varicose veins, dental caries and haemorrhoids (piles) were some of the minor (i.e. not life-threatening) chronic ailments; high blood pressure and its possible culmination in eclampsia was a real danger, and there were also problems with the womb. The later in birth order, the larger the baby (usually), so rehabilitation of the abdominal wall was vital to restore muscle tone. Slack muscles could encourage falling of the uterus and dangerous positioning of the baby, as well as making it difficult to bear down efficiently when giving birth. There was also more of a risk of pre-eclampsia and eclampsia among grand multiparas than among other multiparas. (First-time mothers were always at risk.) The doctor was advised to check everything and to take nothing for granted:

> Improvement of nutrition and hygiene with careful supervision of pregnancy and management of labour should reduce their [problems'] incidence.

The Commission on Emigration and Dr Lucey were right about one thing, however; grand multiparity had no impact on the health of the child being borne, and there was no causal connection between it and infant mortality.[102]

Three years later Drs A.P. Barry, D. Meagher and E. O'Dwyer published an article on heart disease in pregnancy, which contained detailed instructions about pregnancy and management of labour and rest during the puerperium:

> At the end of the puerperium the patient must not be abandoned until the next pregnancy, but should continue in the care of her family doctor. Advice as to the spacing of pregnancies and the use of the safe period should be tendered if thought necessary, but no matter how severe the lesion or disastrous the pregnancy, no woman should ever be told that if she has another baby it will kill her. With proper care between and during pregnancies even the worst of cases will, if not improve, at least fail to deteriorate further.[103]

These doctors obviously believed that the psychological danger of being told that another pregnancy might kill her outweighed the health risks of that pregnancy, should it happen. The medical articles cited take for granted that the 'next' pregnancy will happen. The grand multipara is not to be discouraged from having another baby; the woman suffering from heart disease, however severe, is to be given advice on 'natural spacing' (not birth control, though 'natural spacing' could well have been a euphemism), if the *doctor* deems it to be necessary. Loudon states that heart disease was never one of the major maternal killers as such, and that its role in maternal deaths has been overstated in literature and popular memory. However, as we have seen, every year a small number of women in Ireland died of heart disease exacerbated by pregnancy. Michael Solomons mentions a woman dying of heart disease in the sixth month of her fourth pregnancy in the Rotunda in the 1940s.[104] These articles show us not only the risks associated with the bearing of many children, the risks which the *Emigration Report* and Dr Lucey dismissed so airily (not to mention the chronic complaints and discomforts which they did not notice at all), but the acceptance by many people, including doctors (and mothers themselves) of the inevitability of these risks.

There was a minority view among some Irish doctors, as we have seen in some of the reservations and addenda to the *Emigration Report*, that because multiparity was dangerous, it should also be avoided. Dr Bethel Solomons called grand multiparas 'dangerous multiparas' in an article in *The Lancet* in 1933, and his son mentions that doctors advised women with a history of eclampsia or other diseases to be careful about starting another baby.[105] The four doctors who wrote the two articles above might also have done this without advertising it, though this is unlikely, if they were Catholics; John O'Connell tells us that he, as a medical student and young doctor from a very religious working-class Dublin background, was 'not immune to this prejudice [against family planning] myself'.[106]

Irish obstetricians can, in one sense, be considered models of non-intervention in that they did not attempt to prevent the problem of grand multiparity from occuring. However, this initial non-intervention invariably led to greater, and necessary, intervention later on.

CONCLUSION

'. . . there's no use in saying they didn't . . .'

Was Dr Spain right when he claimed confidently in 1945 that the fall in maternal mortality was due to drugs to control puerperal sepsis and recourse to hospitals for the worst cases? It is difficult to pinpoint, with confidence, the safest place of birth for Irish women, particularly before 1953. A simple comparison of the maternal mortality figures in 1936 and in 1950 shows us that an almost identical proportion of maternal deaths at both dates were 'elsewhere', i.e. at home (36%, or 36 out of 99, in 1950; 98 out of 273, or 35%, in 1936).[107] The advantages of hospital births were often offset by the risks of puerperal infection, up to the 1940s, yet home births did not escape infection either. Proximity to maternity and child welfare services – domiciliary or institutional – does not seem to have guaranteed their use, or their safety if used (though this area needs more specialised treatment than can be given here) any more than reliance on 'untrained' attendants guaranteed a high maternal mortality rate. It was quite obviously unsafe for a woman who needed emergency skilled intervention to be in an inaccessible rural area some distance from expertise, but distance could be notional, too, and determined as much by the family's economic standing and ability or inability to pay a midwife or doctor. When it is borne in mind that average family size was largest among the lower income levels,[108] the dangers of a combination of risky high multiparity, low income, low levels of nutrition and, perhaps, high levels of stress, can be understood. Even the most conscientious attendance at clinics and the most skilled help at birth could be defeated by these factors.

In town and in country, many women before 1953 fell between the cracks of the piecemeal system of district nursing associations, local authority schemes and freelance midwives and general practitioners, but maternal mortality was already falling quite significantly. This must have been due to improvements in the standard of living. The Children's Allowance, available from 1944, might have made a significant difference, and the large-scale exodus of single people to England in this decade might have relieved some of the pressure on resources at home. Women's own heightened awareness about maternal health is obvious from the rising numbers of women attending clinics, seeking help and eventually, in the 1950s, deciding, for one reason or another, to have babies in hospitals or nursing-homes. The definitive fall in the numbers dying in childbirth from 1958 would indicate that they made the safest choice available to them. To a Mayo woman like Josephine E who grew up in the 1930s and

1940s, the fact that Mayo's maternal mortality was not significantly higher than that of Kildare meant nothing. In response to a general question about who attended mothers in childbirth, she replied:

> Yes, oh yes, there was always the woman in the village that knew, and very seldom a doctor had to be there because he had to be paid for.
> – *Anyway the woman would know?*
> She did, yeah, she'd be an older person, now, and she'd have been going to houses with her mother, maybe, or some friend of hers, and – if there was any difficulty, the doctor had to be sent for, a lot of babies died, and a lot of mothers died, there's no use in saying they didn't . . .

The emphasis in the last sentence quoted gives the impression that Josephine believes that modern medical care is on the whole a great boon. As far as she is concerned, one mother dying per year was one mother too many.

CHAPTER SIX

The Decline of Breastfeeding in Ireland: Coercion or Choice?

INTRODUCTION

Throughout the world, and at every period in history, the infant mortality rate is one of the surest indicators of hard times and of pockets of chronic poverty and malnutrition in 'good times', as the weakest and smallest members of society give up the impossible struggle for life. One indication of the improvement in Irish life in general in these four decades is the decline of the infant mortality rate, from 66 per 1000 births in 1923 to 30.5 in 1961. In Ireland the deaths of babies reached their peak in both urban and rural areas in 1943, a year when university professor and senator Michael Tierney, making a case against children's allowances, claimed to see no evidence of any great hardship in the country.[1] Table 6.1 shows that the infant mortality rate did not start to fall definitively until the early 1950s.[2]

The death of babies under one year old was always highest in cities and towns and lowest in rural areas.

In 1931–2 the Department of Local Government and Public Health carried out an inquiry into infant mortality in Cork City and Co. Kildare. It found that gastro-enteritis was the chief cause of death in Cork, 'debility and marasmus' in Kildare, with gastro-enteritis coming second. In Cork city it was found that 75% of gastro-enteritis deaths were of infants in families of moderate to indigent circumstances.[3] In Dublin in the 1940s, according to James Deeny, the poorer the family, the greater the risk of infant mortality.[4] Deeny also noted that hospitals and clinics were also breeding grounds for the enteritis virus, and that the Coombe Lying-In Hospital, where the newborn babies were put into the same beds as the mothers, never had enteritis.[5] Sleeping with the mother seems to have been common among the poorest people at any rate; 'Our arms was our cradle; I reared mine in a shawl', a woman born and married in the tenements of Dublin's northside in the early 1920s, told Kevin Kearns. Breastfeeding, which was more likely when the baby slept with the mother, also offered strong protection against infection.[6]

The strong commitment on the part of the Department of Local Government and Public Health, later the Department of Health, to reduce infant mortality bore some fruit in the 1940s and 1950s, along with the benefits of improved nutrition and, in the 1950s, housing. Gastro-enteritis was no longer the major killer of Irish babies at the end of this decade. Infant mortality

Table 6.1: *Infant Mortality in Ireland 1923–61*

Year	Number	Rate per 1,000 Births	Year	Number	Rate per 1,000 Births
1923	4,098	66	1942	4,591	69
1924	4,543	72	1943	5,319	83
1925	4,067	68	1944	5,198	79
1926	4,552	74	1945	4,739	71
1927	4,254	71	1946	4,390	65
1928	4,016	68	1947	4,687	68
1929	4,012	70	1948	3,313	50
1930	3,965	68	1949	3,415	53
1931	3,935	69	1950	2,922	46
1932	4,060	72	1951	2,876	46
1933	3,742	65	1952	2,674	41
1934	3,664	63	1953	2,463	39.4
1935	3,988	68	1954	2,364	37.8
1936	4,309	74	1955	2,264	36.7
1937	4,121	73	1956	2,162	35.6
1938	3,794	67	1957	2,027	33.1
1939	3,691	66	1958	2,109	35.4
1940	3,759	66	1959	1,927	32
1941	4,175	74	1960	1,777	29.3
			1961	1,827	30.5

1923–52 F figures taken from the Annual Report of the Registrar-General: 1953–61, from Department of Health, Vital Statistics, published annually.

declined most markedly in 1945–7 in the four cities and in the counties of Dublin, Kilkenny, Louth and Tipperary SR, where there were vigorous and well-established infant health schemes at this stage.[7] Rapid response machinery was put in place in Dublin city where the disease was worst, and the Public Health Nurses, employed all over the country by local authorities from 1945, had a longer-term positive impact upon infant and, no doubt, maternal health.[8] Gastro-enteritis had moved off centre stage by 1950, when the major killers of Irish babies in 1950 were unspecified 'other diseases peculiar to first year of life' (25%); pneumonia (14.5%), and premature birth (16%). Congenital malformations accounted for 10.8% of deaths, while diarrhoea and gastro-enteritis made up 8.4%, the rates in the cities of Cork, Limerick and Waterford, although they had fallen, being higher than elsewhere. Convulsions, which is properly speaking a symptom rather than a disease, accounted for 4% of deaths, and injury at birth for 5.4%.[9] High parity did not in itself lead to a greater risk of congenital malformations, but poor nutrition of the mother and lack of ante-natal care, was all too common among poorer women with large families, were contributory factors in infant mortality. Healthier mothers had more energy; if breastfeeding they had more milk, if bottlefeeding, more energy and perhaps more money to buy good milk or formula. In rural areas and on farms, bottlefeeding seems to have been comparatively safe as the milk came straight from the family's herd and was fresh and safe to drink. Not all people living in the country had access to a good milk supply, as the IHA and the National Nutrition Survey noted,[10] but the significantly lower infant mortality rates in rural Ireland speak for themselves.

Proposals for improved maternity services invariably included suggestions about how to improve infant health. Infant mortality was not an issue on which the fortunes of politicians rose or fell. 'The slaughter of uneconomic calves arouses the ire of politicians more than this slaughter of the innocents' remarked James Quin in 1945.[11] James Deeny suggests with his usual candour that there was no great fuss about infant mortality among 'the ordinary people in the Dublin slums':

> A baby dying here or another there was to be expected. Very few could appreciate that six hundred little Dublin souls going to heaven every year, though perhaps well out of this cruel world, was from a public health point of view something preventible, something terrible and something to be avoided at all costs.[12]

Were the parents and siblings of these children as phlegmatic, or as fatalistic, as Deeny suggests? Several of Kevin Kearns' informants recalled with sadness the deaths of their babies forty, fifty, seventy-five years ago.[13] The frequency with which thanksgivings for infants' survival crop up in the widely-read *Messenger* in the 1940s compared to the 1930s, suggests high anxiety about infant survival, from higher expectations due to a long-term fall in infant mortality:

> Thanks for wife being brought safely through a most trying confinement, and secondly our little baby who was brought to hospital when only 10 hours old, recovered. She was in hospital eight weeks and there was little hope of her living, but on the way to hospital we promised to publish it in the *Messenger* if she was spared to us.[14]

or the shorter but no less heartfelt:

> Thanks to the Sacred Heart for the safe confinement of my wife and the blessing of a fine, healthy baby girl.[15]

The *Messenger* Question Box assured a correspondent in 1951 that baptised babies and children who died before the age of reason could be prayed to in Heaven, because they had never offended God and were therefore 'saints though not canonised'. Some years earlier a *Messenger* authority had answered the most common questions in a Question Box compendium, and there it assured readers that unbaptised babies 'according to the opinion universally held' went to Limbo, and 'do not undergo suffering of any kind in the next life'. Limbo was presented very specifically here as a matter of opinion, not dogma.[16] Babies' deaths were not as a rule announced in death columns in newspapers, and were rarely commemorated in 'In Memoriams'. This does not mean that they were not experienced as sad. Stillbirths and sometimes neonatal deaths, were often treated as a private matter, too closely linked to pregnancy and the birth process to be discussed openly. Maureen O'R. describes the way a stillbirth was dealt with in her very warm and otherwise open family, around 1950:

> Anyway I was kind of expecting this, she was going to have it, up to the hospital she went, never said, a day or two afterwards my father came along, my aunt was there, she was saying, we must get this box. I said, 'What's wrong, why,' and she said, 'You're big enough to know now.' [crossly] And that's what – my mother came back, there was never a word said. And that baby's buried, obviously where they're all buried, now, but there was never a word said.
> – *I think that was, a lot of families were like that, the baby went to Heaven and that was it, or maybe the baby went to Limbo.*
> We never were told where it went! We weren't even told we had this one.

The aunt had told Maureen she was 'big enough' in an impatient rather than a confiding way, and there was literally no more information offered. I found that women were quite reticent about talking about babies they had lost, either as stillbirths, neonatally or in infancy. Josephine E. was talking to me for over three hours about her life before she mentioned that she had lost a baby girl, and Olive A., who, like Josephine, was very forthcoming, did not go into detail about her second stillborn child.

None of my contributors ever complained, other than parenthetically, about the 'work' of child-rearing. Rarely if ever was information volunteered about, for example, the age at which children were 'dry' and 'clean' – considerations which must have been central to women's work because of the amount of sheer effort involved in dealing with nappies, especially when every drop of water had to be brought into the house and heated on the open fire. It took some questioning to find out about methods of infant feeding. As in the case of childbirth, I encountered reticence about breastfeeding, a reticence that made it difficult to find out as much about it as I would have wished. This reinforces, for me, the opinion that for any research to do with the body, a sympathetic and sensitive midwife-historian would be the most effective person.[17] The scarcity and inadequacy of hard data about breastfeeding rates over this period means that what follows are some suggestions and lines of inquiry that the historian might like to pursue.

DECLINE OF BREASTFEEDING

If breastfeeding almost died out as the primary method of infant feeding in this period, it certainly was not for want of awareness of its benefits by health authorities. The connection between breastfeeding and the lesser likelihood of infant illness or death and the consequent need to promote it was stated almost annually by the Department of Local Government and Public Health in the 1930s and 1940s.[18] Promotion of breastfeeding was to be an important part of Public Health Nurses' work from 1945; the decline of infant mortality was seen to hinge partly on it and the *Commission on Emigration* advised it in 1956.[19] Magazines and newspaper articles promoted it. The *Woman's Life* 'Happy Irish Babies' column solicited photographs and dietary details of babies throughout the country and about half of the babies whose photos were sent in 1936–9 had been or were being breastfed for anything from three months to a year.[20] Was this a reflection of the situation in the general population, or was it that *Woman's Life* readers were either more inclined to worry about babies' health and therefore more inclined to breastfeed or more inclined to bottlefeed for the exact same reasons? We have no hard information – yet – on rates of breastfeeding in Ireland in this period, though three surveys will be referred to below. Meanwhile it should be noted that all the medical and household 'experts' noted the importance of breastfeeding or 'natural feeding' of infants. 'A Trained Children's Nurse' writing in the *Irish Press* in 1934, gave the usual line when she stated: 'Right feeding is natural feeding but failing that, if the baby has to be artificially fed, a proper modified milk mixture approximating the natural food as closely as possible should be given.' Then she went on to give detailed instruction about bottlefeeding.[21] This was the common pattern. Redington and Roper and Duffin also recommended natural feeding, but hurried quickly on to describe how to make up bottle feeds.[22] Bottlefeeding of its very nature demands detailed instructions as to composition and cleanliness while there was little published advice on breastfeeding.

It has been suggested that the decline in breastfeeding in the western world is linked to the rise in the power of medical personnel, whose expertise depends upon scientific observation and proof. It is quite difficult to 'prove' in terms acceptable to science the intake of a breastfed baby from one day to the next, or to measure its wellbeing in the same way as that of a bottlefed baby. Medical 'experts' did try to control and monitor breastfeeding by insisting on strict regularity of feeding, on the regular washing and drying of the breasts and on test-weighing.[23] Modern opinion on 'regularity' is more in tune with *what we believe to have been* traditional practice; babies kept within reach of their mothers at all times and fed on demand.[24] Medical opinion in the 1930s also held that overfeeding was more dangerous than underfeeding, with breast or with bottle, and as the breasts need the stimulation of the baby's sucking to produce more milk, it is easy to see how adherence to strict timetables would have reduced the supply and led, in the end, to a hungry baby who did not appear to be thriving on the breast.[25] When Máire Mullarney was breastfeeding her first baby in the late 1940s, she was constantly warned by a female friend, a doctor, of the dangers of overfeeding. She was also guided by the advice of the influential Dr Truby King, who advised strict regularity, though she had abandoned this and was feeding round the clock by the time the baby was six weeks. By this stage her little daughter had not gained on her birth weight, so a bottle supplement was introduced thereafter and Máire's subsequent babies were fed with breast and bottle.[26]

Is it as true for Ireland – as breastfeeding advocates suggest for the western world in general – that breastfeeding declined not only because of the rise of a milk surplus worldwide and changes in lifestyle, but also because childbirth and mothercraft were 'taken over' by medical personnel who knew very little about how it worked in practice, and who gave advice that was so difficult to follow that mothers gave up in confusion?[27] It certainly did not help that doctors and midwives were setting themselves up in opposition to the general health advice dispensed by older females. As the *Irish Nurses' Union Gazette* put it in 1927:

> Our teaching should fit the mother to manage her affairs alone, and not be obliged to turn to her neighbours and to kind-hearted old women who are learned in all the old superstitions, who are sure to find the doctor's treatment too difficult to carry out and who will replace it with those old women's remedies which can be so dangerous.[28]

Thus was dismissed an entire generation's lore and expertise about breastfeeding, a loss that was keenly felt by women some generations later who wanted to return to breastfeeding. We have to ask, however, why women who might have followed their mothers' example in other aspects of childcare, such as traditional remedies for coughs and colds and traditional disciplinary practices, discarded their mothers' expertise and advice when it came to feeding babies. Furthermore, medical advice is often disregarded in practice, or adapted to the needs of the consumer, and it is unlikely that most Irish mothers were blind and timorous followers of 'expert' advice. Besides, many women in Ireland gave birth without recourse to doctors or even midwives right up to the 1950s. While the advice given by medical experts might have made successful breastfeeding impossible for some women, it cannot be held wholly responsible for the virtual disappearance of this method of infant feeding in Ireland. After all, doctors and midwives all over the western world dispensed identical advice – they certainly did so in Britain, where, as Curtin's research shows, rates of breastfeeding were far higher than in Ireland in the late 1940s.[29]

Doctors and midwives had their own theories about why breastfeeding did not always work. Dr Spain blamed a short lying-in period for failure to establish a good milk supply.[30] Dr Deeny, as mentioned earlier, blamed the practice of putting babies into cots rather than into bed with their mothers. This shows his practicality, perceptiveness and courage; most doctors and medical authorities campaigned against mothers and babies being in the same bed because of the perceived dangers of overlying.[31] Low nutrition was also seen as a cause of a poor milk supply. Nursing mothers in the Rotunda hospital in Dublin in the 1930s were given a bottle of Guinness a day,[32] and several charitable organisations in Dublin and in other cities provided free meals for expectant and nursing mothers.[33] Indeed, the ante-natal clinic in the Rotunda in Dublin 'respectfully' drew its clients' attention to the availability of these dinners in the 1950s.[34] However, problems of malnutrition and weakness were evident in many other countries where breastfeeding rates remained buoyant.

An obstetric tutor in the National Maternity Hospital, Holles St, Dublin, in 1945 published an article on breastfeeding which gives us some idea of how a hospital that promoted and actively supported breastfeeding went about this task. It was, according to one source, against hospital rules in Holles St in the 1940s for a baby to get a feed from a bottle,[35] barring, one imagines, exceptional circumstances. Dr Coyle, the obstetric tutor, and later Master of the hospital, did not believe in Truby King-style physical preparation: 'The use of a nail-brush, hard or soft, on the nipples, we absolutely condemn.' This was still being advocated in some advice to mothers at this time.[36] Nor did he believe in disinfecting the nipples before and after every feed, as was sometimes recommended(!); washing in soap and water once a day, and the washing of hands before feeding, was all that was required. Mothers should not worry about 'emptying the breast'; those who advocated it were influenced by agricultural practice and the milking of a cow, Dr Coyle reminded readers was 'a wholly unnatural and artificial process'. Sessions of feeding in the days after birth should be 'comfortable and undisturbed'. However, he did believe in regularity; a baby over 6 lb should be fed four-hourly, a baby under 6 lb, three-hourly. Information and encouragement were considered vital for the ante-natal and nursing period.

While there can be no doubt that breastfeeding underwent a serious decline in Ireland in this period, it is not clear exactly when it started to decline to the very low levels of the 1970s. A survey in Cork City in 1930–1 revealed that of a sample of births, just over 61% of babies received some breast milk; 25.4% were 'breastfed only' and 35.6% were 'breast and artificially fed' by six months. The rest, 39%, were artificially fed only. In Co. Kildare in the same year 40.9% of babies were 'breastfed only', 36.84% were 'breast and artificially fed', and 22.37% were 'artificially fed only'.[37] These are only two regions, admittedly, but in the absence of any other information whatsoever for this period we can note that in the more rural area over three-quarters of the babies had some breastmilk, compared to three-fifths in Cork City. Unfortunately there is no breakdown by urban and rural residence in the Kildare survey, and because there are several towns in Kildare and a long tradition of non-agricultural employment (in the army, equestrian pursuits and all their ancillary supports), we do not know whether these mothers and babies were on or off farms. Chris Curtin and Tony Varley, reviewing the anthropological literature, suggest that breastfeeding had died out in some rural areas by the 1930s.[38] When Méiní Dunlevy, the Blasket Island handywoman, brought her new baby back to the island from her mother's house on the mainland in 1897, she brought a new teat and milk bottle with her which suggests that the baby was not breastfed, or that it was partly bottlefed at least. The fact that the bottle is remembered in the lore of the island suggests that it was unusual. Méiní had spent time in America; did this have anything to do with her infant feeding practices? She was also a very authoritative and respected figure in the island.[39] Nancy Scheper-Hughes interprets the failure to breastfeed in the Kerry community that she anthropologised in the 1960s as part of the Irish pathology of cold and unfeeling child-rearing. John Russell in the Gaeltacht community he studied in the 1970s noted that breastfeeding was uncommon – 'Breastfeeding isn't good for the little ones, you know', a 65-year-old female informant told him – and was inclined to the same conclusion as Scheper-Hughes. However, neither Russell nor Scheper-Hughes are able to explain, to their satisfaction or to anybody else's, why this physical distancing of mother from child did not extend to an aggressive and proactive 'management' of the child into early toilet-training. Children, they noted with some bewilderment, were often left in nappies until they were ready to go to school.[40]

What is also noticeable about the Cork-Kildare survey is the proportion of babies who were, like Máire Mullarney's babies mentioned above, both breast *and* bottlefed. Though not immediately relevant to this study, referring as it does to Belfast, Dr James Deeny's survey of infant mortality in that city in 1940 explained that the designation 'breastfeeding' covered even mothers who gave a bottle as well as the breast, 'as nowadays so many receive supplements'.[41] There are, however, other indications from some rural areas that bottlefeeding had definitely come to stay by the 1930s. 'When I was a boy there was no talk of bottles to rear children,' John McAuliffe from north Cork told the Irish Folklore Commission in 1933, going on to tell an archetypal story about a mother, dead in childbirth, who came back to nurse her child.[42] Liam O Caoimh, a pensioner from Dungarvan in Co. Waterford opined that:

> Na leanaí atá siad ag tógaint anois níl phioc den dúchas na máthar ná an t-athar ionta mar níl siad ag ól bainne na máthar. 'Sé bainne na bó atháid ag ól agus dá chomhartha sin go bé béic an laoigh atá ag a bhformhór.
>
> [The babies that are being reared now they haven't a scrap of their mother or father's heritage [dúchas] because they're not drinking their mother's milk, they're drinking cow's milk, and signs on, it's the cry of the calf that most of them have.][43]

Arensberg and Kimball quote the remarks of an old farmer in Clare comparing his son's wife with his own wife, when both were present:

> Here is a woman that has no more milk of her own. They shouldn't allow a woman like that to breed because a man should always keep his wife in the milk. The old woman, God bless her, raised every child on the didi [breast].[44]

The anthropologists are surprised at the old man's frank references (in mixed company) to fecundity and bodily functions. For our purposes it can be noted that such insensitivity, if indulged in by many older people (male or female), cannot but have inculcated in younger women a negative attitude towards breastfeeding. The sentiment that 'a man should always keep his wife in the milk' would have been anathema to most of my contributors, urban and rural, who deplored this kind of crude patriarchy.

A survey in Cork City and suburbs in 1952–3 by Michael Curtin gives us some more information about the extent of breastfeeding.[45] Curtin, in a survey of 1,007 infants born in this period, found that over a third of infants received no breastmilk at all, and that less than half (46.6%) of two-week-old babies were being breastfed, and just over a quarter at two months. The comparable figure for British eight-week-old babies in 1946 was 57%. In Cork, only 9% of babies were still being breastfed at six months. Curtin found that babies born at home were slightly less likely to be breastfed than babies born in nursing homes or hospitals, which would appear to contradict some modern breastfeeding advocates' beliefs about a link between institutionalisation and artifical feeding. A survey in Holles St Dublin, in 1951 found that 51% were still relying on breastfeeding alone 'a few weeks' after leaving hospital, and a further 20% were breastfeeding with a supplement, figures that compare very favourably with Curtin's for Cork, two years or so later. Hospitals like Holles St and Portiuncula in Ballinasloe often virtually coerced women into breastfeeding. 'The nuns in Ballinasloe [hospital] made us all breastfeed,' commented Mary Ellen D. of the 1950s; she approved of this, but she did not keep it up afterwards. The same seems to have been true of the Lourdes hospital in Drogheda in this period. Michael Curtin also found that while first-born babies were more likely than second or third babies to be taken off the breast before the end of three months, 83.6% of babies with more than three siblings were artificially fed by the end of the third month. Artificial feeding, he noted, allowed older children to take over the baby. When Mary Ellen D. brought her ninth and last baby (born when she was in her late forties) home from the hospital, she never had to give him more than one feed a day, because his brothers and sisters were competing with each other to look after him, and his father used to get up in the middle of the night. Curtin found that as far as class was concerned, a higher proportion of working-class mothers succeeded in establishing breastfeeding, but by the time the baby was three months old the incidence was more or less the same across class lines. Alexander Humphreys found that breastfeeding, or nursing as he calls it, had been 'universal' among artisan mothers in the 1920s and 1930s and that it was still 'common practice' in the late 1940s early 1950s.[46] It was, however, starting to become less common at the latter date. Betty S. did not know anyone else in middle-class Dublin in the late 1950s and 1960s who breast-fed: 'I think they all thought I was extremely odd!'

Reasons that mothers gave or give for not having breastfed varied. A startlingly large proportion in Curtin's survey – over a fifth – 'did not believe in breastfeeding'; 17.5% had 'abnormal breasts and nipples', and there were a number of other almost equally weighted reasons – mother in poor health, insufficient breast milk, debility or illness of the child, prospect of paid work, or heavy domestic commitments and prematurity. The smaller the baby, the more it needs the protection of its mother's milk, but perhaps because of incubators and the greater trend towards in-hospital care of premature babies, there was less chance of establishing breastfeeding; premature babies cannot suck very well and are often fed by tube. However, even here and with hospital-isation in general, expressed milk could be used, given the right amount of encouragement. When Joan K.'s first baby suffered an injury at birth and was kept in hospital for some time, Joan expressed milk and brought it into Holles St. hospital to him. As far as weaning was concerned, nearly 70% of those who weaned early did so because of insufficient breast milk 'but only in a few cases was failure of lactation confirmed by test-weighing'. Curtin concluded that a negative attitude to breastfeeding was probably the single most important factor predisposing women to bottlefeed. He advised the provision of education and information, and cautioned against imbuing mothers with a sense of failure for not breastfeeding, or overstressing the supposed psychological benefits of breastfeeding.

All of the women who answered my appeal and who had had children throughout the period had at least considered breastfeeding, and most had tried it. Was this because women who answered an appeal like mine – or their menfolk – would have been more likely to have had a positive attitude to breastfeeding? Not necessarily; among those who married from the late 1940s, the general attitude was that breastfeeding was a very difficult task which demanded a lot of time and energy, and which did not always work out. For the reasons outlined above, I did not cross-examine women about the exact reasons why they stopped, or did not start, breastfeeding. Lily G., a teacher turned small farmer married to a man who was employed locally, in Mayo, told of her experience:

> I breastfed the first one for quite a while, the second one then, was a lad, and of course he wasn't as easy. I had to start giving him a bottle as well as breastfeeding, I did mix, then. I fed them all for nearly a month.

Lily had three children in three years, then another three children subsequently; she had to work inside and outside. (Her view that a boy is harder to keep satisfied than a girl was, and is, a common one.) Another reason for Lily's switching to bottlefeeding was that her husband, or the neighbour who helped her out a lot, could give feeds when she was busy. Josephine E., another Mayo woman in a similar situation to Lily G., though she married eight years later, fed her eldest child also, but:

> my doctor at home said I wouldn't be able to do it, because I had to be inside and outside and I had my mother, I couldn't.

Her mother could also give bottlefeeds, and she was a semi-invalid and had to be looked after. For breastfeeding to succeed the woman needs to be able to sit down with the baby several times a day, sometimes every hour. If she is on her feet all day feeding family and farmyard animals, drawing water from a well and so on, she is not likely to have this time, unless she has plenty of able-bodied help. In certain societies described – one might say idealised – by breastfeeding advocates, mothers working in the fields tie on their babies and let them feed at will. The kind of work that the Irish farm women of the house were doing in the 1940s and 1950s did not lend itself to this kind of solution – hauling buckets of water and feed, looking after livestock large and small. And besides, I doubt if such an arrangement would have been aesthetically or culturally acceptable to many Irish women in this rapidly modernising period. The coming of running water and electricity to dwellings, a golden opportunity to save time and devote some of it to breastfeeding, seems if anything to have made bottlefeeding easier. Ann Kennedy, the hardworking, very modern farmer's wife with electricity who wrote a column in *The Irish Times* in the 1950s, described bottlefeeding her month-old baby at 6 a.m., taking the bottle from the fridge and heating it in an electric bottle-warmer.[47]

It is significant that Michael Curtin found that the larger the family, the less chance there was of the new baby being breastfed.[48] If one baby is succeeding another rapidly, a toddler has to be seen to as well as a baby, and older children have also to be looked after and controlled. Why was the extended family/ neighbour structure not utilised to take over the jobs of childcare, housework and farm work to let the mother feed her baby? Probably because giving a baby a bottle is an easy and pleasant job which can be done by a feeble grandparent or a quite young child, someone who might not be physically able or trustworthy enough to do the vital everyday jobs, especially on the farm. John D. Sheridan and Croistóir O'Flynn both remember being relied upon to feed the baby once it was weaned off the breast.[49] Fathers could, and did, give bottles while mothers were busy tidying and cleaning, cooking and seeing to other children, but sometimes also, while they were sleeping or resting, as in the case of Mary Ellen D.'s last child, above. Babies could feed themselves bottles from around six or seven months, rather than tying down the services of a worker many times a day. The dying-out of the horizontally extended family in rural Ireland that is, the tendency for single women to leave their brothers' or sisters' houses to get work elsewhere from the mid-1940s, contributed to the decline in breastfeeding, as it removed able-bodied people who could have taken over some of the *women*'s work around the place. The departure of this extra 'womanpower' was, by all accounts, heartily applauded by women of the house, who often refused to 'go in with a sister' or to have their own sisters living with them once they married.[50]

It is difficult to come to a clear conclusion on the geographical or class situation vis-à-vis breastfeeding. Both Michael Curtin and Humphreys note that in the cities of Cork and Dublin respectively, in the late 1940s and early 1950s, working class mothers were more likely to breastfeed, (Joan K.'s experience bears this out); Delia R.'s mother, lower-middle class, breastfed all her children for at least three months in the 1920s and1930s. Croistóir O'Flynn refers almost parenthetically to his working-class mother in Limerick city in the 1920s and 30s 'breastfeeding the latest arrival', a task she fitted in around all her other work.[51] However, it also seems to have been common in a variety of rural areas in the 1920s and 1930s. Tom and Joan K., born in Mayo and Wexford, respectively, in the 1920s, were breastfed as were all their siblings (they did not know for how long). T.J. McD. and his three brothers, born on a seventy-acre Cavan farm in the late 1930s, were breastfed for 'a few months' then put on milk 'straight from the cow'. Jane S., a farmer's wife in Cavan, breastfed all her children, born in the 1930s, for a few months. Anna A. from a small holding in Sligo, and all her brothers and sisters born in the 1940s, she believes were breastfed – the two youngest she knows, definitely were. Ethel R.'s mother, a bank official's wife, bottlefed her four girls, born in the 1940s, and Olive A., who got married in 1951 to a man with his own small business in Cork City, gave breastfeeding a try:

> I tried breastfeeding with one, and she had lovely rosy cheeks, – she was a beautiful baby, with lovely rosy cheeks, and in six weeks she had hollow cheeks, skin like a sheet. And she was screaming her head off. And I wasn't too well myself with it all. And the next one then, I gave it 12 days, and she was screaming too, so, bottles after that.

She resented one of the midwives – a nun – in the hospital who said that cow's milk was only fit for calves, linking this sentiment with what she saw to be a very severe and austere attitude to childbirth:

> But then, it may have been she or some other one who said that she hated midwifery because mothers don't need nursing. I mean, did you ever in all your life!

Propaganda in favour of breastfeeding, which emphasised it as a maternal duty, might (like the prescriptions of elders, above) have deterred mothers completely, and it seems that women sometimes wanted to have some choices. However, Olive also said, 'if you can breastfeed, it's marvellous', suggesting that it was a worthwhile feat, but a feat, nonetheless.

Nobody who gave evidence denied the value of breastfeeding, and it seems that some who breastfed their babies did so because they believed it to be good, and not necessarily because it was convenient. Betty S. heard about breastfeeding from a League of Health lecturer on natural childbirth in Dublin in the 1950s, before her second baby was born, and wrote:

> I look back on my various stints of breastfeeding as having been quite lonely times – but something that I felt was the right thing to do.

This suggests that there are two kinds of breastfeeding mothers covered by this study – those, mainly working-class and farming women from the 1920s to the 1940s , who did so because it was the natural and expected way to feed babies, and those like Betty S., Madge C. and Maureen O'R. who took up breastfeeding because they had been told it was good for the baby.

Other ways of encouraging the milk supply are: plenty of rest and good food; fresh air; freedom from worry.

Any other ways of bringing about a greater flow of milk, such as hot-and-cold bathing of the breasts, or the taking of special medicines, which used to be believed in, have been found to be useless.

HOW TO BREAST-FEED

For the first few weeks of a baby's life he is either asleep or feeding; the times, therefore, that he is lying in his mother's arms taking food are also his first glimpse of his new world, and are very important to him apart from the food he takes. Feeding times should, naturally, be times of happiness for mother and child and, taking place at least as often as five times a day, they can be a source of much appreciated rest and peace for the new mother as well.

Both mother and baby should be comfortable. The nursing chair should be a low one for greater comfort; it is often an old chair with its legs sawn off to make them shorter. But a footstool used with an ordinary chair is just as good.

The baby's head is cradled on his mother's arm and his hands are left free to wave in the air or to caress his mother's breasts. You will, of course, arrange to be in a room by yourselves if possible so that there will be no distracting noise or interruptions.

HOW LONG IS A FEED?

For the first few days, baby is put to the breast for a few minutes only at each feed. The period is gradually extended until, at the end of the first week, baby is expected to take about ten minutes at each breast. This varies a lot, however, with individual babies. Some get all they want in three or four minutes and, if they do, this is quite all right. A mother can soon tell if her baby

31

10. 'How to Breast-Feed'. Taken from the very popular *Glaxo Mother and Baby Book* (Dublin 1964), this breastfeeding advice is on the whole practical and positive. However, at this stage, breastfeeding had almost died out. Note, in this advice, the emphasis on solitude for the breastfeeding mother.

Did the decline in breastfeeding delay the decline in family size? Some tentative research indicates that birth intervals (i.e. gaps between babies) were shorter in the 1950s than they had been previously.[52] Breastfeeding can delay ovulation, so full breastfeeding for even six months could have put off the next baby for fifteen months. Some evidence, however, suggests that there is a link between low nutrition and lack of ovulation; the better-fed the mother, the more likely she is to conceive even if breastfeeding.[53] Irish women's nutrition improved in the 1940s and 1950s, so this could have worked against the contraceptive power of lactation. There was a popular belief that breastfeeding offered some protection against pregnancy, at least according to Josephine E. who says that this is one reason why many of her neighbours in Mayo went on with breastfeeding:

> They used to have a [belief], that when you were feeding a baby you couldn't get pregnant, and twas more or less a safety thing, and there were a lot trying it . . . Some of them the creatureens they used be feeding a baby and they wouldn't even get to feel the [new] baby [kicking], do you know what I mean?

If this popular belief was proved false then it could have proved a disincentive to breastfeeding.

Did the small, intimate, patient-centred and female-run nursing homes of the 1940s and 1950s also discourage women from breastfeeding? Betty S. had her first baby in a Dublin nursing home in 1955:

> She was bottlefed and there was no suggestion other wise either on my own part, or my mother or the nurses, or the doctor (Dr Coyle, as a matter or fact.)

Dr Coyle was the keen promoter of breastfeeding in the National Maternity Hospital in Holles St in the 1940s, as mentioned above, and later Master of that hospital. Politician Mary O'Rourke told Una Claffey that after she gave birth to her first son in a nursing home in the midlands in the early 1960s, she wanted to breastfeed him but was told briskly by the nurse: 'Nonsense, I have your bottles all made up'.[54] Two other women who had nursing-home births in the 1950s emphasised the rest they had had while lying-in, part of this being that the baby was taken off them and everything done for them, including the feeding of the baby.[55] One can imagine how much easier this would have been for staff also.

One last point needs to be addressed; was there a belief that breastfeeding was somehow immodest? None of my contributors seemed to think it was; however, because of the conversational way the interviews were conducted, most of them would have been aware that I breastfed my own babies, and might have tailored their responses with this in mind. (See Appendix 1 on methodology.) As far as religion was concerned, nuns as nurses seem to have been among the most fervent advocates of breastfeeding, the religious figures – Catholic and

Protestant – on government commissions always seemed to support it, and the *Messenger*, which can lay claim to having been the most widely-read Catholic publication of the period, also supported it – it carried a highly technical article about care of the nipples in 1947, for example.[56] Maura Laverty, however, suggests that a kind of false modesty could ruin healthy and happy breast-feeding. In her novel *Lift Up Your Gates* (1946), young middle-class mother Eileen Harte delights in breastfeeding her little boy, contrasting it to her own mother's furtive and over-modest way of feeding Eileen's little brother under a voluminous shawl.[57] Laverty's autobiographical account of governessing in Spain, *No More Than Human* (1944), also mentions breastfeeding, and there is a key difference between the original edition and the 'Irish edition' of this book. In the original (and recently reprinted) edition, a wet-nurse in the Spanish house in which Delia Scully (the first-person narrator) is a governess, squirts her milk up in the air to amuse the children. When another Irish governess, depicted by Laverty as joyless and repressed, objects to this, the wet-nurse squirts milk at her, hitting the front of her blouse. In the 'Irish edition', the wet-nurse's only offence is to feed the baby opposite the other children, and her insult to the joyless Irish governess is a hissed 'Mierda!'. It is significant that Laverty toned the incident down for the Irish market, but did not change a word in an admittedly oblique and understated reference to an abortion, an abortion moreover, carried out by a character who was an exemplar of the Christian virtues of kindness and generosity.[58] The book was banned in any case,[59] probably because of the abortion, but the joyfully crude or foul-mouthed (depending on the edition) wet-nurse probably did not help matters.

In the 1940s and 1950s many Irish people were desperately ashamed of the earthiness, frankness about bodily functions and general closeness to animal life which were seen as characteristic of rurality. The furore over *The Tailor and Ansty*, an extremely conservative and even religious book, in the early 1940s is one example of this shame.[60] Breastfeeding might have been a casualty of this hankering after urbanity because of its close association with animals feeding their young. The oft-used equation of the nursing mother with a cow was, one woman suggested to me, partly the reason for the decline of breastfeeding in dairying parts of the country.[61]

CONCLUSION

In a book which attempts to defend the makers of artificial baby milk from their critics, the editors and authors, while acknowledging that 'breast is best', point out that the decline in infant mortality and the decline in breastfeeding have gone hand in hand in the western world.[62] This is certainly true of Ireland, at least at first glance, but the historian must ask if infant mortality would have fallen even more rapidly in the 1950s had improvements in living standards, maternal nutrition and public health, which were the main causes of the decline, been accompanied by higher levels of breastfeeding.

Up to the 1930s and 1940s, and the evidence does not allow us to be more specific than that, it seems that most babies born in Ireland received at least some breastmilk, and that this was considered the normal method of infant feeding. Bottles were already being remarked on, in rural areas in the 1930s, but it is impossible to say whether these were bottles from birth, or bottles introduced after a month or two. The change seems to have happened in the late 1940s and early 1950s. What the abandonment of breastfeeding meant in practice was, that in the first months following birth, mothers often did not have even the rest of sitting down with their babies at intervals during the day. The British mothers investigated by the British Women's Health Inquiry Committee in the 1930s mentioned that sitting down to breastfeed babies was the only rest they got. The Committee also noted, however, that breastfeeding meant that mothers' night's sleep was interrupted on average two or three times.[63] The rise of bottlefeeding could have been connected with an increasing tendency of fathers and other family members to take responsibility for certain aspects of infant care, sharing night feeds and letting the mother sleep, for example. In Ireland from about the mid-1940s, women of the house, urban and rural, seem to have started insisting on certain comforts in their lives of unceasing hard work. Water and electricity (or the aspiration to these services), a good spouse (the next few chapters will clarify what women were coming to mean by this in the 1940s and 1950s), a domestic environment in which there was no competition from sisters, sisters-in-law or, if possible, parents/parents-in-law, and a chance to get 'out', if only once a month, or even a year, were all mentioned as things that made life easier. Cutting down on family size was not a widely available option, but choice in methods of infant feeding was. Breastfeeding was seen as something which tied the person of the mother to the baby, day and night (which it undoubtedly does). With families of seven, eight, nine and ten children, this could have meant not less than fourteen and up to twenty years of virtual isolation as social life and social events (weddings, 'functions', dances) became more formal, official and confined to adults. Mary Ellen D. weaned her second child at six weeks because she wanted to go to a wedding in Dublin. She was a very hardworking woman who got out to a social event at most once a year; she would go on to have seven more children. Betty S. breastfed her second, third and fourth children (she had five altogether) but:

> the real drawback was the amount of time I had to spend alone up in the bedroom while feeding the baby. It was most certainly not socially accept-able [to middle-class Dublin] to be seen even by close family members.

She wrote that she will always remember the summer of 1959 'because I seemed to spend the whole of it up in the bedroom feeding the infant. Never saw the sun at all!'

Gabrielle Palmer mentions that in parts of southern Germany in the nineteenth century, and in a particular region in Finland, breastfeeding was seen not only as a 'filthy' practice, but as lazy and self-indulgent also.[64] These were regions where the women's contribution to the family economy was vital. I did not come across this attitude at all in the course of my research, though it might well have existed. It seems, however, that there was a belief that breastfeeding was a 'drain' on women's health, and that giving it up was an indulgence which they allowed themselves. Bottlefeeding is often depicted by breastfeeding advocates as a sign of modern women's pitiful lack of self-confidence and self-worth, and this might well be true,[65] but I suggest that the virtual abandonment of breastfeeding in the particular context of Ireland from the 1940s is, on the contrary, a sign of mothers' immense confidence in themselves and their choices, a confidence that enabled them to go against the counsels, not only of some doctors and midwives (especially when the authority of the latter was reinforced by a religious habit), but probably of older relatives also. This whole area needs more thorough research but for the moment it can be tentatively suggested that breastfeeding declined in twentieth-century Ireland because of mothers' own choices about their health and comfort.

CHAPTER SEVEN

The Day's Work: Change and Continuity

Clotty Malotty she lived in the lane
She was every day washing and ne'er a day clane
Traditional

WATER

John Healy's mother, Nora Healy (née O'Donnell), kept house in Charlestown, Co. Mayo for her insurance-salesman husband and their five children in the 1930s, 1940s and 1950s. This woman might not have been counted in the census as 'engaged in home duties' because she was a district midwife, certified and trained, but she was a very houseproud and fanatically hygienic woman, calling her hapless sister-in-law a 'slawmeen Saturday' because she was washing and drying clothes from Monday to Saturday.[1] (A slawmeen, according to Maura Laverty, was somebody who 'only quarter-did anything.')[2] As early as the 1900s, Joanna Bourke tells us, advice books were advising women to do just this – a little washing every day so as not to have an overwhelming load on Monday; but can they have intended their advice for the woman who had to draw water from a source outside the house?[3] This makes no sense at all from a time and motion point of view, and is simply another example of the way household advice books took certain facilities for granted. Ann Hathaway, for instance, recommended this in 1944 when 48% of all dwellings in Ireland, and 91% of rural dwellings, were without an indoor water supply. In 1960, despite the vigorous onward march of rural electrification and aquafication (the two often went together, as electricity was sometimes used for the water pump), only 12% of rural households had a piped water supply, though improvement accelerated from then on.[4] In the majority of the working lives encompassed by this study, water had to be carried into the house several times a day, and disposed of, once used.

Water for drinking, for cooking and for making tea, was acquired from a well, a spring, a pump or a stand-pipe. Water for washing was often rainwater collected in barrels or, less commonly, river water. Rainwater was soft and needed little soap to work up to a lather. Barrels could be put up under the eaves of the house, one running into another, as in the case of Delia R.'s grandmother in a Kilkenny village in the 1920s, or under the corrugated roof of a shed. The rain barrel used by Larry and Noreen K. in their house in a Laois-Offaly village in the 1940s was five feet or so in height – a wine barrel was how Larry described it.

Going for the drinking water was a job that had to be done at least once a day, sometimes twice, three times or four times a day. Who went for the water? It varied: boys in rural Limerick in the 1950s according to the *Limerick Rural Survey*,[5] children generally in many other accounts, e.g. in a rural area of Louth in the 1930s. This was a job where a number of children were a definite advantage, as Joan K., remembering growing up in Wexford in the 1920s and 1930s, put it: 'It was, go to the well for a bucket of water, two would go and bring home two buckets . . .' and three, three buckets and so on. However, children are unable to lift heavy objects for at least the first four years of their lives, and probably would not be trusted not to spill filled vessels for another two, so in the early years, when she was perhaps busiest and needed water most (probably supplementing the rainwater with some spring water for the everyday task of washing nappies), the woman of the house would have to go for it herself, or to get someone else to go for her. Going for water wasn't a man's job normally, according to Larry K., although he always did it:

> There was men [locally] I have them in mind two particular men, and I never yet saw them going for water. I don't know would they know where the pump was, but they always had water to drink at home, and if they didn't, the kid was sent running for it, the wife would put a shawl on her shoulder and go out.

Water could often be at a distance: a quarter of a mile away, at the local creamery for a lodgekeeper and his wife and their twelve children near Fethard, Co. Tipperary, in the 1930s and 1940s;[6] 500 metres distant, as in the case of the farm on which T.J. McD. grew up in Cavan in the 1940s, or it could have had to be carried up flights of stairs, as in the case of Dublin tenement dwellers or flat-dwellers. In towns without a water scheme distances were also travelled. For instance, a couple who married into a flat on the top floor of a house in Rathangan, Co. Kildare in the 1940s had to bring the bucket of drinking water up from the pump 'at the top of the town' and had barrels out the back to collect rainwater.[7] Talking of Rathangan, Maura Laverty has her fictional mother in *Never No More* taking sheets down to the river to wash them.[8] None of my respondents mentioned river washing, except for Anne D. in Sligo, a blacksmith's daughter and later a farmer's wife, who mentioned that nappies could not be washed in river water as it turned them brown, so they had to be washed in spring water, which meant six or eight trips to the well every day. This suggests that some other items could have been washed in river water. However, the water would still have to be hauled up to the house and boiled. I did not come across washing being actually done in rivers as it still is in parts of the world.

Before toilets, people managed as best they could. In Hannah C.'s homeplace in rural Sligo in the 1920s and 1930s:

> Our loo was a crude affair set up in a section of the horse's house and our Granny used a commode. A potty was under each bed!

A dungheap, some distance from the house, would be the final destination of the contents of pots and commodes in rural areas. There was never a smell off the dungheap until the day it was moved, to be spread. Then all the windows would have to be shut.

Washday was usually Monday: 'The clothes would be all over the place . . . it was gone, the whole day Monday!' Maureen O'R. comments. Washing, if it is not always remembered as the heaviest of the woman's tasks – and on farms, there were heavier – is remembered as sheer drudgery, 'that awful job' as Aggie D. called it. The zinc bath, usually the same bath that was used for washing the person on Saturday night, put up on two chairs was a common feature; the washboard or scrubbing board also featured prominently:

> The washing was done in a galvanised iron bath, the water having been heated on the fire in a big round pot, sheets, towels, and such like were boiled first before being put in the 'tub'. A washboard was sometimes used for the heavy scrubbing; this being the nearest she ever came to a washing machine!

Memories of washing long ago cannot but be influenced and to a certain extent determined by awareness of the comparative ease of today's automatic washing machines. Still, people remember dreading washday which disrupted the whole house, and children in particular hated it because it made mothers crosser than usual.

Sometimes, as in Annie R.'s parents' house on a seventy-acre farm in west Limerick, clothes were actually boiled over the fire. Christine Zrmoczek, writing about washday in Britain in the same period, notes that many old women today do not believe clothes are washed properly unless they are boiled.[9] Sometimes the washday work started on Sunday night, as in the case of Delia R.'s grandmother, when clothes were steeped. On washday itself, cottons and linens were often boiled, then wrung, then rinsed (once, it seems) then wrung again, and hung out to dry. Eamon B. with his usual precision remembers the scrubbing part of the washing as having taken 'a good hour or two'; every item had to be wrung out individually. Wringing required great energy. There were smaller basins for rinsing individual articles one by one; seldom was the washtub emptied at one go and filled again with rinsing water. In houses as far apart (geographically and socially) as those of big farmers in Limerick, tenement dwellers in Dublin, railway workers in the midlands and big farmers in the midlands, the washing water was reused:

> It [the washing] was a full day's work and all the water was re-used to wash floors, cement, and boards and kitchen furniture.
> *A.D., Limerick 1930s and 1940s*

> After washing the clothes the kitchen table and chairs got a scrub and the kitchen flagged floor was washed out.
> *M.C., Laois*

You kept that [water] while ever it was useful!
L.K., Laois

Kevin Kearns, in his vivid history of the Dublin tenements, tells of how vats of water were passed from one neighbour to another, sometimes more than one family's washing being done in one lot of water, and how the water was used then to scrub the stairs 'and the floors would be like milk [i.e. very clean]' one woman remarks.[10] Given the uncertainty of the quality of the milk supply in Dublin City up to the 1950s, her analogy is (albeit unwittingly) an apt one; this practice of reusing warm water in which clothes had been washed to 'clean' surfaces on which food would be prepared or off which food would be eaten (e.g. the kitchen table), must have been very unhealthy. Drying in the open air would have sanitised clothes washed in second-hand water, as sunlight has a germicidal effect, but sunlight rarely penetrated the dark, poky kitchens characteristic of many urban dwellings or tenement houses. In none of the advice literature, or the health literature, however, was there condemnation of this practice, as there was, for example, condemnation of drying urine-soaked nappies without washing them, or throwing paraffin on a fire. It was obviously a practice of which the public health authorities were unaware.

The washing, although it took all day, was only part of the work. Drying often took days, depending on the weather; a breezy, sunny day was a godsend, but wet weather saw clothes being dried around the fire or on lines along the top of the room, for days, or on clothes-horses – some kitchens had pulleys along the ceiling for this purpose. People who did this were not like some of Zrmoczek's informants in Britain, who removed every trace of washing and drying clothes from the living space before their menfolk returned from work.[11] Indeed, none of the contributors to the project mentioned that they did this. Máire Ní Ghuithín's account of washday on the Blasket Island in the earlier part of the period is valuable for its detail:

> . . . we used have to draw the water from the well with a bucket, put that water in a big pot-oven to heat at the fire. When that big pot-oven of water was fine and hot you'd throw it into a big keeler, and throw more cold water in afterwards. Then you'd make a lather of soap on the water. We used put the white garments in to steep first, and knead them under the water with our hands. Then you'd take them out on the table one by one. You'd spread each garment out on the table, rub soap into the cloth, knead it again for a while, on the table with the hands, put it down into the lather in the keeler and knead it again until all the dirt would be taken out of it. Then you'd wring it out of the keeler onto the table, put it down into a vessel of lukewarm water that had 'blue' dissolved in it, and rinse them and wring that water out of them. After that you spread them out on a clean stone bank until they were dry.

Stubborn stains were removed by being put out under the air to bleach for a week. In persistent wet weather, the clothes would dry very quickly in a room above and behind the fire, in the 'new' Blasket houses which were constructed in the early 20th century: 'there never was a hotpress to better this room'.[12]

Washing-machines not only required electricity, but were expensive into the bargain. Not every serviced house had one. The *Household Budget Inquiry* found that it was only the two highest income groups which spent money on large labour-saving electrical items.[13] Washing-machines were prohibitively expensive. A Hoover washing-machine cost £25 to buy in 1951, about a month's wages for a working man[14] so it is not surprising that many middle-class families did not have them. Ethel R.'s mother, a former secretary married to a bank official in an electrified town dwelling in the 1940s and 1950s, is remembered by her daughter as hand-washing clothes with Sunlight soap; Eileen K.'s mother, married to a Garda in a town dwelling with all modern conveniences in the same period, did her washing in a big zinc bath. Small wonder that Delia R.'s father's purchase of a Thor washing machine in 1937 (after they had moved into a house with electricity) is remembered as the high-water mark of his generosity: 'It was a great boon to Mammy, oh it was wonderful,' Delia remembers. The machine had a big tub with an agitator and a mangle on the top. When Olive A. got married in 1952, she was delighted that her husband was buying her a washing machine as a present. ('And the girls in the office said, "How romantic". But how romantic is washing?') Washing machines saved mainly on the scrubbing and wringing. The tub still had to be filled, manually, with a pipe from the tap at the sink or, in houses with electricity and no running water, with a bucket. It also had to be emptied, when washing was finished. Washing was still done only once a week, as setting up the machine was a big job; large and unwieldy, it was not a permanent fixture in the kitchen and was usually kept in a scullery or a shed. Clothes still had to be sorted, steeped and dried. The kitchen/living room or scullery, if there was one, would still be steamed up, clothes unwashed, washed but unrinsed, rinsed and ready to go out (or to go up on lines around the room) would still be all over the place. The pre-automatic washing-machine emphatically did not create 'more work for mother', in the sense of encouraging women to wash every day, and it certainly saved on arm muscle strain, but washing was still a big disruptive job which required almost a full day's attention.

There are two aspects to people's memories of washday; one, which has already been mentioned, is the complete absence of nostalgia – the washboard does not rank with the pot-oven or the flour-bag sheet in fond and loving memory. The other is the pride taken in the cleanliness of the wash. One of Kevin Kearns' informants supplies memories of his mother, in a one-room tenement in Dublin's Liberties, in the 1920s:

> There was a washboard and she stood over the big vat of washing and bring the water to a boil [over the fire] and she'd beat the clothes down and they were SNOW WHITE . . . On Monday she'd be in terrible form she'd be so *tired* and so weary.[15]

Kearns notes that among his informants a good clean wash was prized and that the woman hanging out dirty (i.e. badly-washed) clothes was looked down on. Margaret Q., the mother of a growing (in every sense) family in a town in the south-east in the 1950s and 1960s, tells with gleeful horror the story of an acquaintance she met in a shop who advised her not to buy white cotton underpants and vests for the boys: 'Who wants them? Only to be washing them!' Another woman, to whom Mary remarked one day that it was a great day for drying, said: 'Washing? Who wants to be washing?' She laughed loudly telling this, finding this devil-may-care attitude to washing outrageously amusing. Washing had to be done, and these women were less than respectable because they were shirking it. Olive A.'s mother and aunt, in Cork City and in a small town in Co. Cork, with eight and nine children respectively in the 1920s and 1930s, washed by hand – her mother from a solitary tap in the kitchen, her aunt with water from a pump which was at a distance of seven minutes' walk:

> And her washing was as white as that [snowwhite table napkin]. All done by hand. And the washboard. But my mother used the washboard. But I never did, thank God.

Dorothy Macardle concluded a sympathetic portrait of a hard-pressed wife of an unemployed man, and mother of six children, in Dublin in 1932, with the observation that the woman's face was 'as white as her sheets'.[16] By stressing whiteness and cleanliness she established the woman's respectability. When advertisers sold detergents on the boast that they washed 'whiter than white' they were appealing to a traditional respect for the spotlessness produced by the hard work of the woman of the house.

At its most extreme – a pregnant woman carrying a toddler in her arms as she went down three flights of stairs to get a bucket of water to rinse the wash (a common sight in the tenements, according to Kevin Kearns' study; a toddler could not be left in the room alone with a tub of hot water unless padded tea-chests or cots were available to confine him or her)[17] – washday was horrifically hard physical work. It was slightly less hard for people with a pump or a water supply on a level or not too far away. Margaret Q. considered herself in heaven when she married in 1954 to have a tap in the yard, while a blacksmith's family in another south-eastern town in the 1930s to the 1950s considered themselves well set-up to have the town pump outside their door. Croistóir O'Flynn, who spent the first part of his childhood in a two-roomed ground-floor flat in Limerick, comments about how lucky his family was not to have to carry water up several flights of stairs, but mentions the terrible difficulty of drying clothes.[18] The drawing and disposing of water were time-consuming tasks for the tenement women, and for those with water on a level, as a lot of water was needed not just to wash, but to rinse the clothes. It is significant, however, that in a survey of farm women in the 1950s, mentioned by Michael Shiel, in which they were asked to rank in order of importance the advantages of a piped water supply in the house, easing washday came half-way down the list.[19] Was it that the elbow-grease and sheer strength involved in actually washing, rinsing, wringing and drying were so hard that the drawing of the water was considered the least onerous part of the whole enterprise, at least for those who did not have to carry water up steps?

Next in order of hardship came people with running water and built-in drains in their houses – a tap and a sink in the kitchen or scullery, perhaps – who had to wash by hand, but at least, did not have to carry heavy buckets from a distance. A step up in comfort from this were people who could afford washing-machines, or who could afford to pay somebody to do the wash for them, though this still left the considerable work of sorting, soaking, drying and ironing to the woman of the house. Those for whom washday meant nothing but sorting out the clothes to send to a laundry fall, in general, outside the scope of this work, but Madge C. who grew up in old suburban Dublin in a terraced three-bedroomed house in the 1930s (her father an insurance salesman), gave as the main (and plausible) reason in support of her belief that women 'had life much easier then' the fact that her mother never had to concern herself with the washing:

> Someone came in to do the heavy work in the house [up to 1940] and did the washing. The things like Father's shirts, and bed-linen, and I think, towels, I can't remember, went to the laundry, a person called for the laundry once a week, and that was from the convent in Drumcondra who had a house for, as they called them, wayward girls . . . And this nun knocked at the same time, the same day, every week, you gave her a bag, you had a cloth laundry bag and the shirts, collars – can't remember now what else went into that – these were left to the laundry, came back beautifully starched, last week's laundry would be delivered when this week's was picked up, and she just had to open her bag and put them away in drawers.

This sounds like bliss even to the modern owner of an automatic washing-machine who still has to dry and iron and fold. A contributor to *No Shoes In Summer*, Billy French, who grew up in Crumlin village, Dublin in the 1930s, remembers that his mother 'allowed herself the luxury of a bag wash' (i.e. a laundry wash) the week leading up to Christmas, as she was so busy.[20]

Water was also needed for washing the butter, which had to be done with cool spring water: 'the butter took three buckets and more to wash', according to Aggie D. Churning had to be done two or three times a week, as milk could not be left too long. Milk pans and churns had to be 'scoured, rinsed and scalded' then left to dry. (John Healy's grandmother scalded everything with 'iron kettles of hot water'; he remembers making several trips to the well on those days.)[21] When separators arrived in the 1940s and 1950s, they were very difficult to wash as they had so many component parts. This might explain why they were not universally used, even by substantial farmers. Mary Ellen D., who made her own butter up to 1970, always used milk pans.

Women of the house were also in charge of keeping the children clean. Children were usually given a hands and face wash once or twice a day, and bathed in front of the fire on Saturday nights in the same tub that was used for washing clothes. It is unlikely that the water was changed between children; as in the case of washing dishes, the dirtiest was probably washed last. Clean underclothes were put on for the week: 'In those days we were not as clean in our persons as people are today,' Mary Healy reminds us with her usual candour.[22] Larry K. remarked that the day-to-day washing of face and hands was always done in cold water, taken from the rain barrel: 'There was never – you wouldn't dream of it – hot water to wash yourself. Oh no way. It was too scarce.' Dublin people without bathrooms, if they had a few pence to spend, went to Tara Street or the Iveagh baths once a week, but more often they washed with Sunlight soap and water heated on the fire and poured into a vat. Some of the women, in summer, washed 'down at the tap' (the common source of water for the building), getting somebody to stand guard while they washed their bodies and their hair with cold water and Sunlight soap.[23] In Nora Healy's house in Co. Mayo, washing took place two or three times a week; family members took the tub of water into their bedrooms and washed there. In smaller houses, the parlour or another room was set aside for washing.[24]

Not all women of the house in Ireland in this period were as preoccupied with cleanliness as the women or their relatives who responded to my appeal, or who wrote accounts of the period. Ruth Barrington's history of the evolving health service suggests that typhus-carrying body lice were a real public health problem in Ireland in the 1930s and 1940s, and James Deeny, leading public health figure of the period, confirms this.[25] There is an account in John Healy's *No-one Shouted Stop* of the humiliating fumigation endured by all Irish people emigrating to wartime Britain, regardless of their health and state of cleanliness; James Deeny describes this also.[26] There are a few indications, however, that cleanliness had become an almost universal preoccupation by the 1950s. Firstly, the *Household Budget Inquiry* shows that the lower-income groups spent proportionately more money than the higher-income group on soap, probably because they had more dirt to battle with. But they were actually doing battle.[27] Secondly, in the survey already mentioned, cited by Michael Shiel, of Irish farm wives which was carried out in 1954 in which they rated in order of importance the advantages of piped water, personal cleanliness came first on the list of concrete uses. The first advantage mentioned was that this would save the labour of carrying buckets from the well; the second, that it would ensure water at all times; the third, that it would enable a bathroom and toilet to be installed; the fourth, that it would improve personal cleanliness; the fifth, that it would be a safeguard in case of fire; the sixth, that it would make washday easier; the seventh, that it would ease the preparation of food and eighth, that it would enable the installation of a hot water system. Points nine to twelve had to do with watering stock, cleaning dairy utensils and cleaning out stock houses. Shiel's conclusion from this is:

It is worthy of note that the first eight placings referred to the standard of living in the home. The advantages out on the farm were relegated to the lower positions. This result left no doubt about the women's priorities, but it also carried a suggestion that farming was still regarded more as a way of life than as a competitive business.[28]

This is debatable; the first two advantages after all, are mechanical ones, and could as easily refer to water being on hand to boil food for stock and to water stock. It could also be argued that as farming involves a lot of muck and dirt, the availability of water to clean this off is part of the work. Farm dweller Kathleen Donnelly described in 1954 the comfort of 'us[ing] all the water you like without anyone saying, "Don't waste the water please"'.[29] John Healy's mother 'availed herself hungrily' of the piped water after years of privation when it was brought to the house in the 1950s.[30]

The appearance of clothes was also a high priority in the 1950s, judging from (again using Shiel's evidence) the survey of the most popular electrical household goods in the period. The electric iron vied with the electric kettle for first place throughout the 1950s, sometimes displacing it.[31] Electric irons rank with immersion heaters, incubators and churns in one west of Ireland farm woman's dream of how electricity will change her life, in 1949.[32] Small electrical items like irons were popular in the first instance because they were a lot cheaper than washing-machines and electric cookers, it is true, and therefore more likely to be bought, but the fact that irons were sometimes more popular than electric kettles indicates that the appearance of clothes was considered of paramount importance – more important, sometimes, than the late-night cup of tea when the fire had gone down, or the rapid heating of the baby's bottle, particularly with the rise of bottlefeeding. One of the reasons for the popularity of the iron was that the pre-electric iron was another item for which there is no nostalgia. The box-iron had a little vent into which was placed a block which had become red-hot on the fire. The flat-iron was heated down in the fire itself, and a cover put on it to do the ironing, but it was apparently very difficult to prevent smuts of ash from getting on the clothes, and it was a constant race against time to get as much as possible ironed before the iron cooled and had to be heated again. Madge C.'s mother had two irons, both of which were heated at the gas flame in the 1930s; you used one while the other was heating up. This itself was a laborious system and, in any event, not everyone had two irons.

The preparation of meals was another constant in the daily work of the servantless woman of the house, but it differed from washing in that it varied much more according to income, location and household facilities.

FOOD

Maura Laverty's location of the open fire in the distant past as early as 1946 has already been referred to in Chapter Four. At this stage, a good half of Laverty's fellow citizens were still cooking on the open fire. While electrification was to advance rapidly from the early 1950s, there was still a significant minority of people cooking on the open fire at the end of our period in unserviced houses in the country, in older houses in small towns and in tenement houses in city slums. Hannah C. describes the open fire:

> A big open fire, with a raised hearth and two hobs was our Aga. A crane, with two crooks swung over the fire where the kettles were hung; all the big pots of potatoes for human and animal use were boiled, little pots were used on the hearth to cook porridge or boil milk, and an oven in which the bread was baked also on the hearth with coals under and over it. For roasting the same oven was used.

The kitchen, she points out:

> was our dining-room and sitting-room as well. We had what was called a scullery outside the back door . . . The kitchen table under the window was where we prepared food, made our bread etc. It was scrubbed white but was covered with an oil-cloth in many colours for our meals.

Such a setting would be familiar to many people who grew up in rural Ireland before the 1960s. It is significant that Hannah sees the Aga as something very modern, when it is widely considered today to be part of a designer-traditional lifestyle. Houses built in cities and towns from the 1920s often had electricity and gas laid on, or some kind of stove. Houses with electricity did not always have electric cookers; Eileen K.'s mother cooked with a range, an oil stove and a primus for boiling the kettle quickly. The primus was also used by Delia R.'s mother in an old, non-electric house in Limerick City in the 1930s; the range was for baking bread, the primus for boiling pots and kettles. The primus had pipes that had to be heated before the paraffin would be pumped up through them and lit in a flat flame. Part of Michael Hartnett's *Maiden Street Ballad*, which is about the shift from his eponymous first home in Newcastle West to the new local authority houses on the hill, mentions how people 'pumped up the primus for the kettle to boil'.[33] Some people, like Maureen O'R.'s mother in a Cork town in the 1940s and 1950s, had electricity for light, and an electric ring for boiling quickly, but did slower cooking on the range, or even the fire. Whatever about an electric ring, a primus was an awkward and dangerous thing to have about the house where there were young children. Ranges, however, were slow to light, slow to heat up and often smoky – the difficulty in lighting the range was the first thing mentioned about her mother's life by Maureen O'R. in her written testimony:

> My earliest memories in a working-class family was the lack of turf during the war years – we had a range and could only get wet turf which was impossible to light and it had no heat so it was hard to cook on it.

Timber was very hard to get and pricey too – I can remember my mother crying with frustration over that range.

Particular designs of range could be awkward to clean, awkward to light and awkward to cook on. Larry K., born in 1914, recalls the range in the house where he grew up, in a midlands, non-farming village family:

the oven was a torture . . . to get it lighting, there was a little small hole, it was down on the very floor, now twasn't even upon a pedestal of any description, the fire for the oven was down on the very floor, the fire for the hob was farther up all right . . . Well I often saw my mother down on her hands and knees and she trying to get that fire working.

The open fire was usually right down on the floor, but it was open; this kind of range seems to have incorporated all the disadvantages of the open fire without any of its advantages of size and exposure. Alice Taylor describes how the fire in her home-place in county Cork in the 1940s and 1950s had a funnel under it through which air could be fanned by the bellows.[34] Lighting the fire was the first task of the day for most women and some men of the house: Anne D., who married on a small farm in Co. Sligo in 1942, gives the following description in her written testimony:

Get up in the morning, rake the ashes, a few small dry sods and a few cippings [or kippens, *cipíní* – small sticks] the kettle would be boiling in ten minutes.

In Alice Taylor's home the fire comprised little balls of hay, *cíoráns*, (small bits of turf) and cipíns also, and it was fanned into life by the bellows.[35] When fire was needed for cooking, it was usual to have some 'seed' left over from the night before, or hot embers under the ashes, to speed the process. A fire good enough to boil a kettle or eggs or heat up porridge could not be started from scratch with just small sticks and firewood. In houses where the family retired early, other strategies had to be used. *Cookery Notes'* spare and sparse instructions about household work includes a fairly detailed section on lighting the fire, and it assumes that embers will be available from the previous night:

To Set A Fire
Take some cinders and place them at the bottom of the grate, next, some pieces of loosely crumpled paper, over these arrange the firewood crosswise, and on top, a few pieces of coal.
NOTE 1: Unless the fire is set so as to allow a free current of air through, it will not light.
NOTE 2: The practice of throwing paraffin on the fire in order to light it cannot be too strongly condemned. It is not only extravagant and dirty, but very dangerous.[36]

Make that kitchen range earn its keep

NOW that the winter is here many more fires are lighted. Even people who all summer cooked with gas or electricity have now lighted their kitchen ranges, uneconomic as most of them seem to be.

The truth is that we cannot get on in the winter without some sort of permanent heat in the kitchen, and the old fashioned coal range has to fulfil that need for the present, anyway. I am glad to see in many of the new houses a small combustion turner which burns very little coal, together with all the household rubbish, and gives the necessary heat. But all of us haven't got modern houses.

Kitchen Range

So it is up to us all to get the best value we can out of that old kitchen range. In towns now we seldom use it for baking or roasting. So that its principal job is boiling. This gets me to the stockpot. With a casserole for the slow oven and a stockpot for the top you really do have the satisfaction of knowing that the range is at least doing some of the work. I won't go so far as to say that it earns its keep.

The household stockpot was one of the features of the comfortable household of our grandmother's time. It was never off the range. It provided the basis of all the soups, sauces and gravies used in the kitchen and saved a lot of money.

Unwanted Saucepan

Let us start a stockpot for ourselves. You need to devote one saucepan utterly to the job and pension it off when it is worn out. In every household there is one large saucepan that is too cumbersome for the gas and generally too heavy for much handling. Turn it into a stockpot. It must have a well-fitting lid and it must be fairly strong.

All you need for a foundation are a few penny-worth of bones. Marrow bones are cheap and very nourishing. Break them . . . . strain off the water and use it as stock.

In most . . . . are going simultaneously

Long Boiling

The stock pot can be kept going with odd scraps added to it as they accumulate. do not discard rasher rinds and everything like that. Fat should never be added and do not add too many vegetables especially turnips, or the stock is apt to turn sour.

If the range is going all day do not transfer the old stock going all day at the back. Strain it off each night and turn out the meat and stuff into a bowl. Start the pot off again next day but do not transfer the old stock into the new stock for more than two days in succession, because old stock is most dangerous.

Vegetable Soups

You can make all sorts of vegetables soups, using this stock as a foundation. You do not need good meat at all. There are plenty of carrots, celery, tomatoes, artichokes, onions, not to mention the potato, which we have always with us.

Artichokes are only 2d. a pound. You need a pound of artichokes, 1 pint of stock, 1 oz. butter, a little milk, pepper, salt and flour.

Change the artichokes to celery and you have a celery soup.

Potato Soup

Potato soup is great stuff for this cold weather, and what could be cheaper? You need a few pounds or one pound of potatoes, a pint of stock, a stick of celery, an onion, milk, flour and seasoning.

And don't forget green pea soup. Which is very nice indeed. With this you could use some mint.

Spinach is still flourishing away in many gardens. If the family are tired of it as a vegetable do not forget its possibilities as a soup.

Method of Making

All the soups are made along exactly the same lines. First you prepare the vege-tables and chop them small.

Then you melt butter or some nice dripping in a saucepan and toss the vegetables in it until they have absorbed all the fat.

Next add the stock, flavouring and seasoning. Boil up and then keep at a simmering point until tender. I'd give them a few hours, but don't let the good boil away.

Fine Sieve

When well cooked rub to vegetables through a fine sieve. You will get one for about 2s. Add some thickening agent, either flour or cornflour. I prefer plain flour myself. Return to the saucepan.

Keep your eye on it now for you have to stir carefully until it thickens. If you stir carefully it will not lump.

If you are using packet soup squares, add them to stock, never to plain hot water, for the result is terrible.

Soup is one of the best resistants to disease, colds and chills. It costs scarcely anything but a little trouble and forethought to give a hungry family a bowl of it every day.

N. M.

---

11. 'Make that Kitchen Range . . . ' *Irish Press*, November 7, 1934. At this stage the majority of Irish women of the house were still cooking on the fire, and ranges were still considered novelties in the 1950s. Women's pages in newspapers obviously played their part in making women of the house aware of developments in household technology.

It seems, nonetheless, to have been common practice. Delia R.'s first task of the day from the age of eight, was to bring breakfast to her grandmother in bed. Lighting the fire to boil the water for the tea and to boil the egg was the bane of her life:

> And I had a job lighting the fire! [laughs] I used more paraffin than she ever dreamed I used! Throwing it on and standing well back! That was very dangerous.

The reference to 'more paraffin' implies that there was an acceptable level of paraffin to use, in that house at least. The fact that *Cookery Notes* warned against it is itself a sign that it was common practice. The firelighters we use today are, after all, a safe form of paraffin, and anyone who has tried to light a fire without either embers from a previous lighting or firelighters will know how difficult it is.

Baking bread was an inevitable part of the day's work for most of the women who are the subjects of this research. This was invariably soda bread or 'cake bread'. Shop-bread, or loaf bread, as yeast-risen bread was called (usually white, except during the war years) was a treat for country people. It was bought from the travelling shop in Mayo in the 1930s by an occasionally indulgent mother and spread with butter and shop jam for a treat for her children, or made into 'goody' (bread, warm milk and sugar all mixed together) for the baby or, as Alice Taylor points out and Larry K. remembers, for many who were considerably older.[37] The local shop in South Roscommon where Mary Ellen D. grew up in the 1940s did not even stock bread on a regular basis. The *National Nutrition Survey* worried that too many people, (especially children) urban and rural, from all backgrounds, were having 'bread and spread' at every meal. If this bread was home-baked cake bread, brown or white, and the 'spread' home-churned butter, as it would often have been in rural households, the nutritional content was moderately high and the food itself by no means a lazy option for the woman of the house, having taken at least as much, if not more, effort to make than, say, potatoes and cabbage. Journalist Olive Ashmore describes the process:

> I see the beauty of it – its crustiness, with a deep slash down its centre and another across its width, making a cross; its look of wholeness; its smell, with my mother in the background dusting the flour from the tin in which she had baked it. Indeed, she had done more than that – there was the churn in which she had made the butter that now too has its place beside the loaf of bread . . . And that wasn't all, for the buttermilk that was left behind in the churn after the butter had been formed had been used to mix the flour for the bread-making.[38]

In big families, several cakes of bread were baked a day. Tom K.'s mother on a Mayo farm baked two or three cakes daily for her large family; Anna A.'s mother on a twelve-acre farm in Sligo in the 1940s and 1950s made 'a few sodacakes' every day; Brendan McN.'s mother on a seventy-acre Clare farm in the 1920s and 1930s baked up to seven or eight loaves a day, according to her son. Noel Browne remembers the 'cartwheels of bread' baked by his mother, a countrywoman living in Athlone in the 1910s and 1920s.[39] Francis MacManus gives an evocative description of a Kilkenny thrashing supper in the 1940s:

> Bustle and fuss, bacon sizzling and spitting on the gigantic pan, strong brown tea swirling in mugs, wheels of wholemeal bread vanishing from the slicing knife . . . and a cairn of scones whipped away by thrusting, grabbing hands.[40]

Bread was baked on the fire, or in the range; if on the fire, in the pot-oven, a vessel which (or its like) was also used for roasting meat. Some townswomen baked their own bread also. The *Household Budget Inquiry* found that the larger the town, the more bread was bought, and that purchases of flour increased appreciably in inverse proportion to the size of the town. Lower income groups in towns spent proportionately more on flour than higher, regardless of town size – the lowest income group spent 1.7% of all its weekly food expenditure on flour, while the highest income group spent 1.1%, and actually less money than the lowest income group, on flour.[41] It was necessity that produced those large brown and white cakes of bread; for farmers, regardless of wealth, and country people generally, distance from the nearest shop and availability of ingredients were crucial factors, while in towns a comfortable level of income seems to have turned people away from the bakery. An attachment to tradition, and an awareness of the high nutritional value attaching to home-baked soda bread, might have been partly what motivated some middle-class people to bake their own bread; Ethel R.'s mother baked her own bread, as did Eileen K,'s mother, a Garda's wife with a certain level of frugal comfort. Delia R.'s country-bred mother stepped up the baking when a confinement was imminent so that her family would have plenty of it when she was laid up. It is likely that some loaf bread was also consumed in these houses, as it was to hand.

Another reason why cakes of bread were baked so often in country dwellings was because they were a convenient way of using up buttermilk left over from churning, though buttermilk was also a very popular drink; only the very old and the very young drank whole milk, according to one authority.[42] Townswomen used sour milk, or acquired buttermilk from a source. However, even in the country buttermilk or sour milk were unavailable when cows were dry in the winter. A simple substitute was the water in which potatoes had been boiled, and in places as far apart as Meath, Kilkenny and the Blasket Island, a kind of mock buttermilk or 'sour flour' was made. Maura Laverty's recipe for winter buttermilk is given here – it is broadly similar to that of Máire Ní Ghuithín:

> Mix a quarter pound of flour to a smooth paste with 1 cup cold water. Put this in the bottom of a large jug or crock. Add 2 grated raw potatoes and 2 mashed cooked potatoes. Now mix in 7 cups cold water. Cover and leave it on the kitchen mantelpiece or some such warm place for 2 days. When you are baking, pour off carefully, and without disturbing the sediment . . . Add fresh water to make up for what you have used.[43]

These were ingredients readily available in every household.

The *National Nutrition Survey* established that fruit and vegetables were eaten more in Dublin than in large towns and more in large towns than in small. While fruit and vegetable consumption was higher on farms than in towns and cities, fruit consumption in particular was lower than expected in rural areas, and the surveyors were surprised to find less fruit eaten in the 'congested districts' than in urban areas, especially in autumn.[44] There is no natural unbroken link between rurality and healthy diet, as Irish Countrywoman Olivia Hughes noted in 1946.[45] Many labourers' families, for example, did not have ready access to milk, though many people who were not farmers but had another source of income, Lucy O'S.'s parents in rural Cork, for example, and the cook

Darina Allen's parents who were publicans in a village in Laois – kept hens and a cow in the period stretching from the 1930s to the 1950s.[46]

While there are undoubtedly traditional ways of cooking a variety of vegetables, this does not mean that every household had this variety. 'Often in the country they have not the vegetables to cook', one of the ICA delegates told the Commission on Vocational Organisation. The Countrywomen saw the promotion of a variety of fruits and vegetables as part of their mission.[47] Kate Rohan, an 'ex-exile' and contributor to the 'Can Irish Girls Cook?' debate in the *Independent* in 1938, believed that a variety of vegetables was a recent phenomenon:

> Our country gardens now boast peas, beans, celery, cauliflower, brussels sprouts, carrots, parsnips, beets and the modest but very important onion. Lettuce queens the lot, and it is not a surprise today to find a nice lettuce and tomato salad (with dressing) and delicious home-cured ham in a country cottage at tea-time.[48]

Maura Laverty made a joke about it: there were only six kinds of vegetables in her home place when she was growing up (1910s and 1920s) – turnips, onions and cabbage, boiled potatoes, mashed potatoes and potatoes steamed in the baker. It was only Protestants, she said, who diversified.[49] Delia R. had her first taste of mayonnaise in the house of Protestant farming friends, where the mother was very good at salads, and Myrtle Allen, a member of the Society of Friends in east Cork, who started her family in the late 1940s, had learned, and kept alive, traditional ways of using natural, locally available ingredients from field and hedgerow.[50] The possible causes of 'Protestant' ease and familiarity with old and new ingredients, however humble, are too complex to explore here, but could well have something to do with long-term comfort, self-confidence and access to resources.

On a large farm in west Limerick in the 1920s, the vegetables eaten, according to Annie R., were:

> cabbage, a lot of cabbage. And turnip. In those days you didn't have any carrots or those fancy – that's only in the last 10 or 15 years since you were born. Sure ye [to town-bred husband] never had carrots either. Turnips and cabbage. And parsnips I think we would have.

On a small farm in Sligo, according to Anna A., in the 1940s and 1950s it was the same story; onions were grown mainly for flavouring (a lot of people I spoke to forgot to mention onions, not thinking of them as a vegetable but more as a flavouring), but potatoes and cabbage were eaten every day. There was a definite difference between what was eaten out in the country and what was eaten in towns. Eamon B. noticed this difference when he went from his home in a north Tipperary town, where they had red meat most days, potatoes and a variety of vegetables, to his paternal uncle and aunt's home in Co. Clare:

From one end of the week to the other, the meal was the same, they killed
a pig every winter and hung it up and salted it and we ate that nearly every
day. On Sunday a bit of meat might be bought just because I was on
holidays, but generally I would say their basic meals would be potatoes,
and cabbage, and bacon, and of course, of course, plenty of eggs for
breakfast.

Note that bacon is not thought of as meat. Townspeople had more variety;
lettuce and salads were eaten by Delia R. at home in her parents' house in
Limerick City in the 1930s, but they were unknown to her grandmother in
Kilkenny, who subsisted on a diet of potatoes, milk, butter, salt, occasionally
bacon and cabbage, a stew on Sunday that would do for Monday and eggs on
days of abstinence. Stew was a ready option in cities, towns and villages because
cheap cuts of meat could be bought from the butcher; one of Kevin Kearns's
informants reminisced about how you could get leg beef or a sheep's head or an
ox-tail which you would then put into a three-legged pot over the fire.[51] There
were local specialities that depended on the availability of ingredients. Coddle,
a potato, rasher and sausage stew, is still eaten in Dublin and was also popular in
the city in the past. Cork City is noted for the imaginative use of pig offal in the
cuisine of its inhabitants.[52] Ita O'C. whose widowed mother was hard-pressed
to feed her family in Athlone in the 1920s and 1930s, described a very varied
diet indeed, by any standards:

> Our food consisted mainly [of] bacon and cabbage, mutton or beef stew
> with dumplings, steak and onions, pig's head and cabbage, the odd roast
> chicken, some people eat roast kid goat, fish only on Friday. For dessert
> stewed apple, rhubarb and custard, stewed gooseberry, boiled rice. For tea,
> home-made bread and butter and jam or boiled egg with celery or
> watercress. Sunday morning after Mass there was usually a big fry, eggs,
> rashers, black or white pudding or sausages. Stuffed beef's heart was
> another favourite Sunday dinner.

A woman who wrote in defiant response to the 'Can Irish Girls Cook?'
controversy and who identified herself as 'one of the bad ones' described in
detail the weekly menu she provided for her two apprentice sons, on a budget of
£1 a week; she did not grow her own vegetables, or keep fowl, or bake bread. If
her sons were apprentices she was most likely living in the town, but not
necessarily; she was definitely not a farmer or a farmer's wife. On Monday, for
example, she would have:

> Breakfast: porridge, egg, brown bread, butter, tea or ovaltine. Dinner:
> meat, 4 vegetables, soup, pudding of stewed fruit of some kind. Tea:
> Good (bought) soda bread and brown bread, butter, honey or jam.
> Supper: oaten meal porridge, milk.

On fast days there would be eggs, vegetable soup, cheese, spinach, leeks, tomatoes, potatoes, pudding and prunes. This woman confessed to spending most of her morning reading the paper, and then preparing dinner between 11 and 1, so maybe this was where she got some of her ideas for ingredients which were unusual for their time.[53] In town and in country, a lot depended on the individual cook. Anne D., on a medium-sized farm in Sligo, for example, described a stew which I did not come across anywhere else:

> every vegetable under the sun would be chopped into it. My favourite dish is still a stew or a casserole, liver and bacon one had a great flavour, the bit of garlic you pulled at the garden somewhere, then the vegetables we grew ourselves.

Ruth Schwarz Cowan suggests that in the USA before the advent of ranges and stoves, 'one-pot' cooking on the fire was the norm, with stews and casseroles offering optimum value nutritionally and logistically.[54] Yet this does not seem to have been the case in rural Ireland, perhaps because the meat used was usually bacon, which does not stew as satisfactorily as red meats. One reason why stews might not have been an everyday dish might have been because stews take a long time to cook and pots would have been needed for boiling or parboiling food for animals. Was it because a brisk fire was needed for breadmaking and boiling feed for livestock, and this might not have suited the cooking of a stew? (But the stew could always have been cooked slowly on the side of the fire.) It could have also been because the skins of cooked potatoes were valuable food for pigs and poultry; it did not therefore make sense to chop peeled raw potatoes into a stew, and the pot was needed for the potatoes for the livestock in any case, so it made sense to cater for the family as well. Stews must have been made, but few people mentioned them to me. Maura Laverty gives her usual mouth-watering description of all kinds of stews and one-pot dishes her fictional 'Gran' used to make in *Never No More*, but she comments that ' Gran' was unusual among women of the locality in her interest in cooking.[55] Was it that Irish 'girls' simply could not cook anything out of the ordinary? Boiling, frying and roasting, which were the most common methods of food preparation in rural households, are fairly uncomplicated methods of cooking, though they are arguably more labour-intensive than, say, the preparation of a stew, needing more lifting, turning and vigilance. Cooking over the fire took skills of manual dexterity which have been lost; nobody but Máire Ní Ghuithín, who went into detail on everything, describes how careful one had to be lifting lids off pots and so on. Like many of the other skills of the women of the house, this was taken for granted so much that it was not mentioned:

> This is what we used to do to look at it [the cake of bread, to see if it was baked]: we used catch hold of the tongs, we used put one point in under the ear of the handle of the lid, and the other point inside the lid. You'd

lift the lid dexterously lest any peck of ash from the fire fell into it. And it used not, for we were well-skilled in this business.[56]

A joint or a pudding had to be turned with two plates, and there is a detailed description of this also. Cooking on the fire required great dexterity and coordination. Yet beautiful meals could be produced, as Jane Spence, via Theodora Fitzgibbon, tells us:

> I remember a farmhouse meal which I had about seventy years ago [c. 1910]. Every item we had was produced on their own farm. We had vegetable soup, roast chicken and boiled ham, fresh peas, broad beans and new potatoes, followed by carageen moss as light as a sponge. Then for tea we had carageen moss as light as a feather, and all was cooked in a pot oven. Turf on the lid and underneath, vegetables cooked in a saucepan at the sides of the pot, but on the floor of the fire.[57]

Ní Ghuithín's account of the food that was eaten on an island populated mainly by subsistence farmers who also fished, indicates that variety in diet was not linked to income; the Blasket people ate stuffed rabbit, mutton pie, Indian meal bread, Indian meal porridge, puddings (made out of sheep's intestines), lots of mackerel, puffins, cormorants, pollock, several kinds of shellfish, and those who kept fowl had great peace of mind as there were no foxes or weasels on the island. The Blasket people did not shy away from food that was scorned by some people on the mainland – yellow meal, rabbit and coarse fish like pollock and even mackerel, believed by some mainlanders to be 'the rats of the sea'. There were also countless ways of cooking potatoes. However, even with this variety and health, as far as vegetables were concerned it was only potatoes and turnips and mushrooms, in season as a delicacy, which were eaten by the islanders:

> They used to keep the potatoes and turnips in the corner of an outhouse. Those on the island that kept strangers [i.e. visitors] used sow carrots, parsnips, beet, lettuce, cauliflower, radishes, turnips, onions, cabbage and potatoes.[58]

The Blasket Islands were attracting 'strangers' from as early as the 1880s and 1890s; by the 1920s and 1930s such vegetables would have crept into the diet of the families keeping the 'strangers' also. This reminds us of the way in which tourism could change significantly the material culture of an area, while other parts of the country, even if more prosperous, could remain unchanged. On a large farm in the midlands in the 1940s, with two grown-up daughters who, though both worked at home full-time, went to evening classes in dressmaking and churning and often went dancing – who were, in other words, by no means remote or in a cut-off part of the country – the diet was very plain; an egg for breakfast, bacon and cabbage or bacon and turnip for dinner, tea and bread and butter for tea, porridge going to bed. Occasionally beef would be bought in the town.When one of the daughters of the house married onto another big farm in the early 1950s, she and her husband and their growing family consciously and deliberately set out to grow a wide variety of vegetables and herbs; membership of the local ICA was crucial in disseminating this kind of knowledge.

The 'bad cook', mentioned above, remarked that she did not have her own vegetable garden as if this were something for which she was resolutely refusing to be ashamed. Local authority houses were built throughout the period with allotments of land, and during the Emergency allotments were made available to town-dwellers. Nearly all the non-farming people who responded to my appeal for information had grown vegetables themselves, or their parents had. This is not surprising, as people who responded to such an appeal in the first place would, it could be argued, be particularly interested in provisioning and perhaps, proud of their skills in the past. The *Household Budget Inquiry* shows that town-dwellers certainly spent money on vegetables. The average weekly expenditure on vegetables per household was 7.4% of the average weekly expenditure on food, 4% of this was on potatoes alone. To give some idea of scale, bread purchases made up 7.5% of the total expenditure, just slightly more than what was spent on vegetables. Expenditure was, in order of magnitude, on potatoes, cabbage, tomatoes, onions, carrots and turnips, which could imply that people were growing turnips (they are very easy to grow and need very little care) and onions and carrots themselves, but that tomatoes, cabbage and potatoes were more difficult. The popularity of the tomato, incidentally, suggests that salads were coming into their heyday; outside the upper classes, people who ate tomatoes were considered eccentric in the 1930s and 1940s. Breaking it into income groups, it is striking that the lower the income group, the greater the proportion spent on vegetables (8.1% for the lowest income group, in contrast to 6.2% for the highest). However, the second lowest income group had an expenditure on vegetables that was only slightly higher than the highest income group, 6.9%. This suggests that the lowest income group were less able or willing to grow vegetables than those slightly better off.[59] Among the people who responded to me, what struck me was the variety of non-farmer vegetable-growers. For example, the family of a railway worker in the midlands, a part-time factory and agricultural labourer in a Cork town, a male teacher married to a female shopkeeper in a north Tipperary town, a teacher and his wife in rural Cork, an ex-British Navy man turned refinery worker in a Cork town, a small-town-dwelling dressmaker in Kilkenny and a British army pensioner from the First World War with a large family on the east coast. In most of these cases it was the men who did the gardening; on farms, the garden with vegetables for the house was the woman's responsibility. In rural Mayo and Sligo in the 1930s and 1940s, the only people who did not cultivate vegetables were the small sheep farmers on the mountains, and Hannah C. remembers how strange it was to see men with bags of potatoes and carrots on the handlebars and carriers of their bicycles.

Food is, of course, an emotionally loaded topic and people remember fondly the food their mothers used to make. Into this category come the apple tarts on 'Dunville's trays' that a *No Shoes In Summer* contributor, Dersie Leonard's mother, used to make on the open fire, the butterscotch Josephine E.'s mother made on the pan on the fire for herself and her brother,[60] and Alice Taylor's lyrical descriptions of the psychological benefits conferred by comfort foods like 'goody' (bread and milk) and 'pandy' (creamy mashed potatoes) which she describes as a tranquilliser and an antibiotic. (Its American-Jewish equivalent would be chicken soup.)[61] Jimmy O'M. remembers the 'decent, fully risen cakes' of apple and rhubarb which his mother made in the bastible. (The bastible was a shallow fireproof cooking dish with a lid: it was usually used for cooking bread and cakes, with hot sods on the lid and under it.) Mary Ellen D. associated what she saw as the unappreciative emotional atmosphere of her home of origin with the fact that they had a boring and monotonous diet, and made some changes when she was boss of her own house:

> And as I said, I cooked a bit of dessert every single day for years and years although we never got dessert at home! Because I loved a nice dinner, and oh, I love a nice sweet and I love to be appreciated. And when I think back on it now, I often feel I wasn't appreciated. I used to get lots of giving out to.

PRIORITIES AND PROGRESS

A thirty-five year-old mother of four 'lovely boys' with a 'devoted husband' and a 'nice home', wrote in despair to Mrs Wyse in *Woman's Life* in 1949 that there were times lately when she wanted to 'kick and scream';

> and where I used to be able to romp through the day's work I find myself worrying over meals, jumping out of my skin when the phone rings and generally cross and irritable. I bark at the children and hate myself afterwards for it. In short life is getting me down. What can I do?[62]

This situation and these symptoms would have been described by Betty Friedan fourteen years later as 'the problem that has no name',[63] the alienation and boredom felt by 'happy housewives' in white middle-class America, but Mrs Wyse had a much brisker and simpler diagnosis, concluding it with the commonsensical advice:

> You're tired out, that's all, and the cure is a couple of days in bed.[64]

Ghostly, hollow laughter echoes from the mothers of six, eight and ten children whose husbands were *not* devoted and whose houses lacked running water, not to mind telephones. Yet Mrs Wyse might have been right, and her thirty-five year-old correspondent might have been simply exhausted. Facilities such as running water and electricity cut down dramatically on physical work, and non-farm households had a lot less work for the woman of the house, yet urban women of the house seem to have worked very hard too. This is not to suggest simply that 'housewifery expands to fill the time available'. Amenities like water and electricity certainly did cut down on the hard physical work of hauling, lifting and carrying water and fuel, to say nothing of the time they saved. Still, urban women of the house had different, and almost equally time-consuming priorities, and progress brought its own new jobs with it. Ranges, considered novel in some rural areas as late as the 1950s, were difficult to light and often difficult to clean; electric and gas cookers had been in cities and electrified towns since the 1920s. The physical advantages of a waist-level cooking space over a floor-level one can be immediately appreciated; easier on the back (Lucy O'S.'s very style-conscious mother had a 'dree' as her daughter put it, from constantly bending over the fire), safer from children or old people and easier to manipulate pots and pans. Did meals simply become more elaborate, putting more work on the woman of the house? Several people expressed nostalgia for pot-oven bread, remarking that bread cooked in the electric oven or range was never as good, but no woman gave me a version of the 'more work for mother' theory, and thirty years is a sizeable cooling-off period. People took for granted that the new ways *were* easier. For Joan K., married onto a Dublin housing estate in 1951, these new ways were the first thing she mentioned when I asked her how she believed her work in the house to have differed from that of her mother:

> Well of course when we got married here we got an electric cooker, electric kettle, electric iron, electric light and we had no central heating but we had a fire, like . . . and water, just turn on a tap.

After a long account of farm work, cooking over the fire and all the other jobs of 'long ago', Ann C., a Roscommon farmer's wife, concluded:

> I've shown this to another woman and she said I didn't put in the half of it. When Rural Electrification came it all became much easier.

Anne D. remarked:

> later years of course we got running water and electricity came, begod . . . we didn't know what end of us was up.[65]

'No modern conveniences' was mentioned by Aine Uí Gh. as a discomfort on a par with living with in-laws and constant child-bearing with hard work. But the women of the house who had electricity and running water from the 1920s and 1930s seem to have worked very hard also, because the work of the farm woman and the non-farming woman were almost completely different, electrification or no electrification. Comparison of the accounts that women themselves *sat down and wrote*, in response to my appeal for information about the work of the

```
┌─────────────────────────────────────────────────────────────┐
│  What a Unit can do                                          │
│                            IN THE HOME                       │
│        ● GENERAL                                             │
│          LIGHTING    ...    ... Light a 100 watt lamp 10 hrs.│
│                                 or a 60 watt lamp 16 hrs.    │
│                                 or a 40 watt lamp 25 hrs.    │
│          IRON        ...    ... Iron for 3 hrs. (one week's  │
│                                 average ironing).            │
│          KETTLE      ...    ... Boil 18 pints of water.      │
│          RADIO       ...    ... Give 12 to 25 hours use.     │
│          BOILING RING       ... Give 1 to 2 hours use for one│
│                                 unit.                        │
│          WARMING PLATE  ... Give 2 to 10 hrs. warming.       │
│          TOASTER     ...    ... Give 2 hrs. use.             │
│          COFFEE PERCOLATOR  Give 2 to 3 hrs. use.            │
│          DISH WASHER ...    ... Give 3 to 5 hrs. use.        │
│          TOWEL RAIL  ...    ... Give 2 to 20 hrs. warming.   │
│          HAIR DRIER  ...    ... Give 1½ hrs. drying.         │
│          FAN         ...    ... Give 10 to 50 hrs. use.      │
│          COOKING     ...    ... Cook for one person for one day.│
│          WASHING MACHINE    Give 4 hours use (four weeks'    │
│                                 average washing).            │
│          REFRIGERATOR   ... Give 1 day's running.            │
│          VACUUM CLEANER ... Give 6-8 hrs. use.               │
│                                                              │
│        ● WATER PUMPING                                       │
│          PRESSURE SUPPLY OR Provide 3 days' supply in an     │
│             TAP IN HOME     average size household.          │
│          FARMYARD......     ... Pump 400 gallons, i.e. require-│
│                                 ments for 1 horse for 40 days,│
│                                 or 1 cow for 26 days.        │
└─────────────────────────────────────────────────────────────┘
```

12. 'What a Unit Can Do in the Home' From *Muintir na Tire Official Handbook*, 1947. Muintir na Tire and the Irish Countrywomen's Association were enthusiastic promoters of rural electrification for the home and the farm. Note the emphasis on the water pump, here, as aquafication often went hand in hand with electrification in rural areas. Of the electrical appliances mentioned in this list, only the iron, the kettle, the radio and perhaps a cooker would have been in common household use by the end of the period – dishwashers, hairdryers, toasters, coffee percolators and even washing machines, were distant dreams in most Irish households in 1961.

woman of the house, yields some insights. My appeal (see Appendix 1) was worded very generally, so people wrote their own interpretation of what I meant by 'work'. Ann C. wrote this account:

> Usually first thing in the morning she prepared breakfast for all in the house. Milking came next and that most likely had to be done by hand. Then hens, pigs, and calves had to be fed. Most women churned their own butter so cream had to be skimmed off and the fresh milk set in crocks for skimming next morning. Some households were lucky enough to have a dairy but mostly the milk was stored on a large table in the corner of the kitchen. After 3 or 4 days the cream had to be churned or it would go rancid and make very ugly butter. So great care had to be taken. Most women baked their own bread, tarts, buns etc. Apart from that the washing had to be done by hand and ironed with an iron which had to be put into the fire to heat up. Most men then wore white collars and fronts that had to be starched. So it was some feat to get it all done perfectly. Also the house had to be cleaned. If one was very well-organised and

nothing went wrong, everything would be done to a timetable but things didn't always work out like that. A cow might be calving or sheep lambing, so the woman was always expected to be on hand. If hay saving or potato picking or lots of other things was on she had to help out. Apart from all that food had to be cooked, children to be looked after and sent to school, to say nothing of having children, and as everyone knows there were mostly large 'families then. After 6 o'clock each evening the chores had to be done all over again. She also had to boil large pots full of potatoes to feed pigs and calves and hens, and pots of gruel for calves. All cooked over an open hearth fire.

This is the woman whose friend told her she hadn't 'put in the half of it', but what she did put in is significant in its own way. The emphasis is on the skills needed for butter-making and the preparation of clothes, and the wide variey of farm tasks. Cleaning the house and feeding the family are disposed of in four sentences. This does not mean that houses were not cleaned or maintained – information in the folk tradition, and some contributors, especially from the west, mention that it was the woman's job to whitewash the house three times a year and paint the doors with red oxide. Anne D. and Josephine E. went into detail on the extremely labour-intensive uses of flour-bags which provided free and hardwearing fabric for a variety of uses only when they had been soaked, boiled and bleached. Ann C. probably did all this too but it is the above tasks that stand out in her mind as most important. Kathleen B., a Co. Laois woman, describing the work done by her mother who married in 1927, gives more attention than Ann C. to the housework, but slightly more priority to the farm work than the housework. Compare this with Olive A.'s written account of her early married life in Cork City in the early 1950s. She began by telling me her maiden name and the years of birth of her six children, then went straight into the work:

> When I married I could not make a handkerchief or put up stitches for knitting. Through practice and prayer I mastered both, but it did not come easy. I was a really good cook, and absolutely loved baking. I made lovely meals, made jam, bottled fruit, and was forever making cakes and entertaining. Anyone who gave me even the tiniest wedding present was invited to tea . . . I had never done any gardening, but became quite expert at it. I had done a small bit of decorating at home, and eventually ended up doing practically all the decorating here.

No domestic help was employed. Knowing about sewing and knitting was not just make-work, it was an important resource in a household living off a small business where there could often be shortages of cash. Gardening – growing their own vegetables – was another resource which Olive managed.

It could be argued that it is not clear if Ann C., above, is talking about her mother's work (1920s, 1930s), or her own (1940s, 1950s), but before electrification and aquafication her work would not have differed significantly from that of her mother. Look, for example, at Josephine E.'s written account of the first decades of her married life in east Mayo up to the end of our period, and after:

> I got married in 1957 in England and my father died in '59 and I returned to my mother as she couldn't be left alone she had a heart condition. My husband got a job with a contractor building houses £6.0.0 per week, and we had 4 children after and during the '60s, things got very hard. We did everything to make a £. We had a few cattle. Sowed our potatoes and vegetables, cut and saved turf. I had my mother from the bed to the fire for 14 years (no carer's allowance then). 4 young children, carry the water, cook and bake on the turf fire. Wash clothes in a tub, milk the cows, feed hens and a few calves, dig potatoes, churn the milk for the butter.

Not a word here about decorating, preserving or baking, even if she did it. Jim D.'s recollections of his mother's work 'on a small Mayo farm (10–20 acres) in the 1950s was typical, he said, 'of at least 50% of the women of my area, some working even harder, and some doing less'. At this stage there were only three children at home, Jim included, of a family of nine:

> Rise 7.30. Make fire and get breakfast for family.
> 9.00 hand-milk one cow.
> 10.00 Fetch (or dig) potatoes and veg for dinner Cook dinner for 1 p.m. During this time hand-churning, washing of clothes, drawing water in bucket from surface well – no electricity, no running water. Feed calves.
> 1 p.m. Get dinner for family and wash up. Feed pigs, hens.
> 3 p.m. Work in fields at relevant activity – hay, oats, turf etc.
> 4.30 Leave field to get tea at 5.
> 6–8 Darn socks, knit, sew on buttons, clean house. Draw more water.
> 9.30–10.30 Read. 10.30 bed-time.

This was the bare minimum of work, Jim stressed in his letter; in addition, about thirty turkeys were reared for Christmas, and in season potatoes had to be 'cut', 'turned', 'dibbled', 'quenched', moulded, dug and picked. Turf had to be footed and clamped. Two pigs and forty hens were kept. 'As you can see life wasn't a bunch of roses in those times but this work was taken as a matter of course,' he commented. Mowing hay with a scythe and cutting turf were considered jobs too heavy for women, but women without men did these jobs too.

What is striking is that as far as work and material conditions are concerned, Josephine and Jim's mother had more in common with Jack R.'s mother who married onto a medium-sized Tipperary farm in 1916, than they had with Olive A. Here, just to compare, is Jack's written account of his mother's working life:

> Her first son born 1917, one in '18, one in '19, myself in '22, a girl in '23, died at 4 months, a girl in '25. Six cows were kept. She got up before 7

o'clock every morn, 6 on Sunday, milk 3 cows before getting breakfast and getting us out to school, feed calves, 3 pigs, hens, and ducks. Bake a cake [of bread] in the oven on the open fire on the hearth of timber, get dinner on, potatoes, bacon, cabbage, white sauce or fresh meat, soup with pearl barley. After dinner a pot of small potatoes was boiled for pigs or fowl, buns or something for the tea . . . When we were saving hay she would bring the tea at 3 o'clock to the meadow about half a mile from the house, she'd bind the sheaves of corn during the harvest for a couple of hours each day.

Compare this with two other written accounts of non-farm or town-dwelling women's work. Lucy O'S.'s father was a National teacher, and her mother kept a cow and some hens. Here is her written account of her mother's work:

I was born in 1932, my father was a primary teacher in a rural area of our county – 2 in family, I have one sister. Mother worked herself to the bone for us and her standards of cleanliness in the home were really beyond belief. The pots and pans were literally shined after use, the lino (we had no carpets in the early years of our childhood) in each room was scrupulously washed each day and I never remember mother eating a proper meal even though she always made sure we had nice and substantial repasts. To supplement my father's income she kept a cow to supply us with milk, and there was the surplus which a neighbour collected and took to the local creamery. She kept hens, day-old chickens and turkeys, and she was always the one who cleaned the houses which the fowl occupied and also the stall for the cow, each May she would set to and wash all the blankets in a large iron bath and squeeze the water from them. Then the clothes line was in the haggart which was approx. 25 yards from the house . . .

Even though it emerged in an interview that her mother did a lot of what could be called farming work, to the extent of selling her eggs in the market in Cork City, it is her household work to which her daughter gives priority. There is a similar prioritisation in Eileen K.'s account of her mother's work, as the wife of a Garda in the 1930s and 1940s:

My recollections of Mother were she was always at home cooking, baking, washing and sewing etc. Cooking was done on a range, oil stove and a primus lamp for boiling the kettle quickly. We had electricity always but no cooker in those days. Washing was done in a big zinc bath, washboard for scrubbing clothes, Sunlight soap, Rinso and Persil were used. We had lino on floors, stairs and this was washed and polished with Mansion polish regularly. Mother sewed on her sewing machine and made skirts, pinafores for us. A safe was kept in a cool place to store milk and butter. Fresh vegetables were always used, home cooking and baking were what we were reared on. Wages were paid monthly, so we had a notebook where a record was kept of groceries bought in a certain shop and Mother paid the account at the end of each month.

SCULLERY WORK.

To Clean a Stove:

If very greasy wash with strong soda and water, and apply a coat of blacklead, and when dry polish well off with a soft brush. Where the stove or grate is very rusty and neglected, use a little turpentine to moisten the blacklead for a day or two until it is a better colour, when water may be again used.

To Clean Steel.

Remove grease with a piece of soft paper, polish with a little monkey brand soap, or powdered bath-brick moistened with a little paraffin oil, or, if very rusty, use emery paper.

When a stove or range has steel fittings, much labour will be saved if a little vaseline or suet (free from any trace of salt) is rubbed over before cooking begins. Where this is done the only cleaning necessary will be to polish off with a soft paper, followed by a cloth.

To Set a Fire.

Take some cinders and place them at the bottom of the grate, next some pieces of loosely crumpled paper, over these arrange the firewood crosswise, and on top of a few pieces of coal.

Note 1.—Unless the fire is set so as to allow a free current of air through, it will not light.

Note 2.—The practice of throwing paraffin oil on a fire in order to light it cannot be too strongly condemned. It is not only extravagant and dirty, but very dangerous.

To Scrub a Boarded Floor.

Take a bucketful of hot water and a little soap. Wet the floor, a small piece at a time, scrub along the grain of the wood, and dry as quickly as possible with a flannel cloth wrung out of hot water. Change the water frequently, use very little soap or soda, as they make the boards a bad colour, and finish off each piece as quickly as possible, as allowing the water to lie on the boards will ruin any floor.

To Wash Kitchen Tables.

For every-day cleaning use hot water and *very little* soap, scrubbing along the grain of the wood. The edges of the table must not be forgotten. If scrubbed with fine sand, once a week, all unpainted wood can be kept a good colour.

To Clean Saucepans and Pots.

Greasy Saucepans.—Wash with strong soda and hot water, rinse thoroughly in hot water, place to drain and dry.

Where *milk or cereals* or both have been used, steep in water for half an hour or longer, then wash with a brush, rinse well in hot water, drain and dry.

Note 1.—If very hard and burnt boil for half an hour, using soda in the water.

13. 'Scullery Work'. From the very basic *Cookery Notes* published by the Department of Agriculture (1924, reprinted constantly; this is from the 1944 edition). This gives some idea of the kind of everyday housework in a house where cooking was done on the fire, and there was no piped water.

When there was no farm, then more work went into the house and into cooking for the family and for friends. When butter did not have to be made, there was more time to make jam. But new facilities created new work. Electrification showed up the dust and the need for interior decorating – though it should be remembered that oil lamps, electric light's immediate predecessor, took a lot of cleaning and maintenance also.[65] If there was lino, it had to be polished. The sheer labour of hauling water from a source some distance from the house (in all weathers), lighting a fire first thing in the morning and bending over that fire a hundred times a day – to say nothing of the relentlessly regular cleaning and disposal demanded before toilets – cannot be underestimated. However, even where there was running water and electricity, among all but the wealthy, the feeding and clothing demands of what were often large families had to be met, money saved and spared, corners cut wherever possible.

CONCLUSION

Mary Ellen D. was particularly proud of the fact that she knew as much about farming as her husband. She had had a small (by her standards) dowry getting married, but:

> John said, 'Well lookit, I'll take her without anything', which was great, well you see, John knew, listening to me, he knew I understood farming because years later when he had a neighbour here, down the road, he said to him, 'Well whatever about the money she had, she helped me to make a lot of money.' Now that was a nice compliment, do you understand, because like, I'd always be here, and I would know, when he'd go to the mart, now, I'd know exactly what to do with an animal, if it was anything, that I'd be able to treat it, what I'd need to give it, and my judgment was never questioned, you know. And that made a shocking difference.

To Mary Ellen, the farm was what gave her satisfaction, that and making good meals for her family – orchards, vegetable gardens, flower gardens, fruit bushes were all testimonies to her industry. The house did not get that much attention, except for necessary modifications and extensions over the years. Decorating, entertaining and making good meals for her family were what gave Olive A. satisfaction. Both women were in comparatively comfortable circumstances, the first depending on good land, the second on a thriving, if small, business though neither had domestic help. It was different for Josephine E. in Mayo, struggling on poor facilities and a small wage, with nurturing responsibilities on both ends of the age spectrum; she derived satisfaction from keeping her family going, but was conscious of the fact that there were women of the house whose burdens were not as heavy as hers. Her pride, and that of Olive A. and Mary Ellen D. and all the other contributors, was probably what motivated them to get in touch with me in the first place.

Women who would not have had as much much pride in their position in charge of the house would not have bothered responding to my letter. This is accepted: what is significant is that such pride exists, in a variety of geographical and occupational settings. Whatever their opinions about change and their priorities in the work of the house, these women believed – rightly – that their work was of crucial importance. The fact that some men responded, referring to their mothers' or wives' work, indicates that this sense of the importance of women's work was shared by some men, at least. The next chapter will look more closely at women's relationships with others in the house and outside it.

The most obvious conclusion, however, is that the provision of water and electricity on the whole made women's working lives physically easier, but that these services did not necessarily give women a lot of leisure time. In that sense work expanded to fill the time available, but it was work which was less physically demanding and not as dirty.

CHAPTER EIGHT

Relationships, Money and Authority

When you are married
And your husband gets cross
Pick up the poker
And say, I AM THE BOSS
Popular girls' autograph-book rhyme, c. 1930s–1960s

Personal relationships are notoriously difficult to research and to generalise about. It is very difficult to find any kind of 'hard' statistical information on the distribution of power within a relationship, or a cluster of relationships. In the case of research on women and women's lives we are in grave danger of extrapolating from our own experiences of life and our own opinions. There are also the manifold dangers associated with soliciting and interpreting personal testimony, and then selecting what to use from it. To what extent is the interviewer 'shaping' the testimony by her questions? Perhaps some of the women and men who responded to me would never have thought about these questions had I not asked them.

However, the fairly simple and open-ended questions I asked (see Appendix 1 and questionnaire) to find out about relationships, power and authority were set by the assumptions, implicit and explicit, in the current narrative about women's work and status in Ireland since independence. These assumptions are as follows: firstly, that unpaid household work is disempowering work of low status; secondly, that women carried a heavy burden alone without any help from men; thirdly, that the men of the house had most of the power.[1] First of all, however, an attempt will be made to place women's household work in the context of the wider family/household and community, by looking at women's relationships with other women in the house and its vicinity.

'YOU CANNOT PLEASE YOURSELF AT ALL NEARLY': TWO (OR MORE) WOMEN UNDER ONE ROOF

The kind of family model promoted by social commentators, advertisers, government commissions, churchmen and advice books in this period was, as we have seen in previous chapters, the nuclear family with a breadwinner father and a home-making mother. So natural and right did the nuclear family ideal appear in the 1940s that a committee was established in 1943 to look into the

CAFÉ is the family favourite. Its pure, nourishing and wholesome qualities are proved and recognised by all. By mothers for their children, by the wife for her husband and by the entire family. This delicious beverage is one that has been wanted in the home—a drink for every meal with flavour and nourishment. From grocers in ¹/₂ lb. and 1 lb. packets. If your grocer has not got Café write to **J. C. Reynolds, 13 Dame Street, Dublin.**
                                    Phone: 51384.

14. Café is so delicious – Here are two conflicting advertising images of women of the house from the 1940s; the modern, pretty woman serving her small family including white-collar worker husband, and the rolling-pin-brandishing stout woman whose stilleto heels are her only concession to modernity. The second woman, though very crudely caricatured, was probably closer to the reality of everyday life.

possibility of making available a second dwelling house on farms, so as to encourage younger marriage. This was founded on a belief that farming people were delaying marriage because of not wanting to bring wives or less commonly, husbands, in on top of the existing family. This smaller house would be occupied by the young couple for the early years of their married life, but as the older couple retired more and more from the business of the farm and the younger couple's family grew, they would exchange houses. The committee solicited evidence from District Inspectors of the Department of Agriculture all over the country and reported in 1944 that such an idea would be impractical, mainly because of the danger that it would lead to subdivision of already small holdings.[2] Some of the comments of the District Inspectors will be considered again, in the light of the discussion about power and resources within the household, but the fact that it was set up in the first place indicates an official acceptance of the ideal of one couple, one family home. This belief seems to have become widespread from the middle of the period.

The household made up of an ageing couple/father/mother, one of their offspring and his, or less commonly her, spouse and children, is termed the 'stem' family by sociologists and some historians. In the late nineteenth and first half of the twentieth centuries, it was more common in Ireland than elsewhere. Arensberg and Kimball's classic anthropological account of a Clare rural community in the 1930s noted the prevalence of this family type; while co-residence of three generations was by no means an inevitable feature of rural or of urban life in Ireland even as early as 1911, it did exist, two sociologists remind us, as a norm 'among a very substantial proportion of the rural population.'[3] The decline of the stem family began after the Famine, but really accelerated from the mid-1940s. Anthropological accounts of rural communities in the 1960s and 1970s – by Brody, Kane, Scheper-Hughes and Russell – note that the nuclear family had become more common, and among Humphreys' 'New Dubliners' in 1949–51, the nuclear family was the norm in all classes. By 1973 living with parents or in-laws was associated with poverty: 'Unless they come from very deprived homes, they will mean to set up a separate home', said Dr Peter Birch, Bishop of Ossory, referring to young married couples.[4]

Several contributors to this project, particularly those who married in the late 1940s, expressed, with varying degrees of vehemence, the belief that married couples should live on their own and not with other relatives. The frequency with which this sentiment was expressed and its apparent universality in rural and urban settings was almost on a par with the vehemence about not going into debt. And indeed, moving in with the parents (or parent) of either spouse was sometimes represented as a price that would be never paid:

> Frank's mother was a terrible *extremist*, [i.e. very strong character and very black and white in her views] you know, and then she wanted us to move down, and I said to my father, 'But Mrs Q . . .' and he said, 'Stay in your own house.' She had a big house down the street . . .

Frank and Margaret (Q.) were living in a small house with a tap in the yard and a growing family. Here, the advice not to move came from Margaret's father, a member of the older generation, who was living on his own himself.

It was not only parents or in-laws who were considered problematic. *The Limerick Rural Survey* reported that women would not 'go in' where there was a sister (i.e live with their husband's sister) and that a sister-in-law in residence was a greater obstacle than a mother-in-law[5] presumably because of the cruel logic that she was younger, stronger and would be around longer. A short story in *The Irish Countrywoman* (the ICA annual publication) in 1963–4 explores the difficulty of the sister-in-law relationship and ends with the unmarried, schoolteacher daughter of the house who is living with her brother and his wife, deciding to stop worrying about the misuse of her dead mother's tablecloths and tableware and to take a loyal, loving but comparatively unlettered boyfriend up on his long-standing offer of marriage. The implication is that by doing so she is making a choice for the better, but not without regrets.[6] The one–couple, one–house arrangement was thus being promoted as the natural one by the ICA. Annie R. thought that 'going in with' a sister-in-law was a very bad idea, citing the example of the tensions experienced by her sister who married a strong farmer and lived with him and his sister.

Tensions could also spring from a mother-in-law's idea of the unsuitability of her son's choice. Frank and Margaret Q. had to get married without his mother's blessing, and a maternal uncle had to sneak out to be at the wedding: Frank's mother, who still had a large house though they had lost their business years previously, did not like Margaret as a prospective bride because she worked in a factory. However, there was no money coming to Frank so he could do as he liked. The older people had no veto (apart from an emotional one) if their offspring were living independently of farm or business. With the decline in the number of assisting relatives on farms and the rise in the availability of subsistence in towns, cities or Britain in the 1930s and 1940s, many young people were in a position to ignore parental rulings. Although Tom K., a Mayo-born Dublin transport employee, loved his mother and had nothing but the strongest admiration for her struggle to rear them all single-handed in the 1920s and 1930s, he was still amused (as was his wife) nearly fifty years later, at her comment when he first brought home his wife-to-be, Joan:

> Mam was there that evening, Joan wasn't there, and I said, 'Well now Mam' – she [Joan] was out somewhere – 'that's the girl,' said I, 'that I intend to marry'. 'Hmm' said she, 'she can't have much money.' 'Well now Mam,' said I, 'I haven't a whole lot myself either.' [laughs]

It is significant that Tom's older brother, who inherited the farm, never married. Tom and Joan were both against made matches, Tom more strongly than Joan, and mainly because he believed that they were emotionally hard on the woman. But significantly it was Joan who stressed what she saw as the advantage of independence in the modern marriage. Their dialogue as they explained this to me ran as follows:

> T. But I'll tell you this much, Joan and I had none of that [match-making]. I put my eye on her, apparently she put her eye on me, and from there we took it and nobody was any way influential in telling us what to do.
> J. And to go into a house on your own was the proper thing to do with a young couple I think, because the mother-in-law and the father-in-law there, like you know you're trying to please them and you're trying to please your husband and you cannot please yourself at all nearly, that's the way it is.

Mary Ellen D., left the farm which she was due to inherit and on which she had worked as her sole occupation since her mid-teens and married onto her husband's farm in the early 1950s she remembered the 'words of wisdom' an aunt had given her:

> 'Wait now *a ghráidhín* till I tell you, if you get a chance, you get a man that'll take you out of here, because you'll only have him to please', she says, ' whereas if you bring a man in, you'll have to please your father and your mother.'

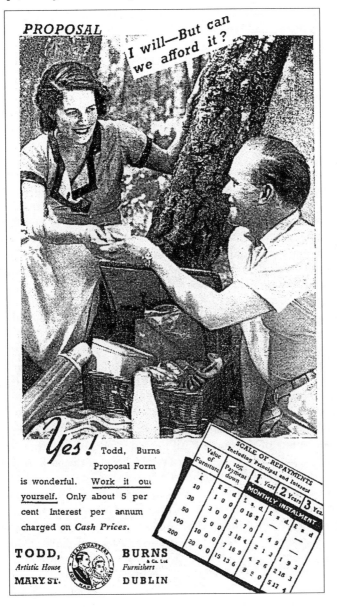

15. Advertisement: 'I Will – but can we afford it?' Advertisements like this one were common in the 1940s, depicting an ultra-modern companionate, freely-chosen engagement, complete with picnic hamper, flask and leisure wear. The proud boast of never owing a penny was under siege from the pressure to buy furniture on the hire purchase, as is advertised here; the emphasis is on the new home for the couple for which they will buy their own furniture. Whatever about the Hire Purchase, a home of their own was coming to be considered the norm for new couples starting out from the mid-1940s.

However, on farms, particularly small farms where money was not available to build a new house, married couples often had to start life with the older couple; the unmarried sister was becoming less common from the mid-1940s. In any case, as some Land Commission inspectors commented, somebody had to look after the old people:

> It is doubtful if the existing owner and his wife would cheerfully look forward to being isolated at the tail-end of the farm during their declining years.

Another Inspector argued that while there was undoubtedly friction between two women under one roof – this seemed to be taken for granted – this could be modified by delineating responsibilities and by 'the elder woman taking charge of some special sideline such as the poultry'.[7] What seems to have happened in many such households was that the younger woman worked inside and outside while the older woman minded the younger woman's children. This is what happened in the case of Anna A.'s parents in Sligo; her father's elderly aunt (whose farm it was) looked after herself and her brothers and sisters while her mother, who died at the age of 40, worked outside on the holding and worked locally also. When Carmel C. married in the 1940s in east Galway, according to her written account:

> I went in with a mother-in-law, she ran the house for years after I going in. I just worked as one of the family. She minded my kids while I was out on the farm working.

In this case the younger woman was an assisting relative, and probably had little say in the running of the house until the older woman died. In assessing the multi-generational experience we must remember that the position of the older woman is equally worthy of evaluation. She was also a woman of the house and she is represented here as still working hard but also having a lot of power in her declining years. That this power and authority was taken very much for granted is evidenced by the incredulity expressed by Bishop Michael Browne in 1940 when the ICA told him that women of all ages were of equal standing in the organisation: 'Surely a grandmother would not permit a girl of 16 to talk up to her?'[8] A number of women living under one roof could take some of the pressure off each other: '*Bíodh cuid des na mná agus deiridis go mb'fhearr an tseanbhean ag an tine ná an plúr sa mhála.*' according to one folklore source. This translates as: 'Some of the women used to say that the old woman at the fire was better than flour in the bag.[9] Larry K. certainly believed that his mother, who stayed with them for months at a time, was a great help to his wife and got on very well with her. However, the way he describes this gives rise to doubt:

> Noreen had an awful lot to learn, and she knew that, she hadn't done much housekeeping in her time, and she could do it, but in a tear of a way

and it was gone again . . . and she was delighted with Mamma there, and she [mother] told her what to do, and how to do it, and left it at that then, she didn't keep harping on at her. No. I remember one occasion Noreen washed shirts, one of my shirts, and Mamma came in, she looked out, and 'Oh Christ', says she, they weren't washed at all. Out she went and brought them in off the line and washed them again. And Noreen said, 'Well I thought it was as good as I could do', but this could be better. But there was no problem, no trouble.

– and she didn't mind?

Oh she didn't mind, she corrected her there, and told her what she thought was wrong, you know, and she was quite happy to accept that. Then there was times she was right, and Mamma might have thought she was wrong, there was complications. But no trouble, they sorted everything out.

The modern writer/reader is sceptical and inclined to ask, 'Did they really?' and to surmise, in view of the numerous pieces of evidence about younger women in the 1940s and 1950s resenting the advice of older women, that Larry had a rosy view of a very tense and fraught relationship. On the other hand, maybe the two women got on very well, the older, who had never had any daughters, taking to the younger and genuinely helping her out with the intricacies of housekeeping in a small village. Two of the contributors to Patricia O'Hara's study, referring to the 1950s and 1960s, mention how helpful co-resident older relatives were, even though they still believed that couples should live on their own. Did old people themselves feel that they were sometimes in the way? In south Connemara there was a little proverb (quoted by one of the respondents to the Dower-house committee of inquiry) that looks as if it was composed by a grimly realistic old person (it can hardly have been offered as a precept for youth!):

> *An tseanbhean ag an teallach, tá sí sa mbealach, An seanfhear ag an doras, tá sé sa solas.*

> [The old woman on the hearth, she's in the way, The old man at the door, he's blocking the light.][10]

It seems to have been on smaller farms and in cases of necessity that the tensions were most apparent. Josephine E. came home with her husband from England to look after her mother; her mother, while she liked Josephine's husband, would have preferred her daughter to marry someone local – 'an old fellow now, that never left the ashes, he'd do for me,' Josephine said. While she loved her mother, she also felt that she interfered a bit too much in her relationship with her husband:

> She was a great help, but at the same time I would never expect – or want – young people to live with older people. She *was* the best in the world, she *meant* the best in the world, but at the same time, she can make a

terrible change in your life. You can't even sit down with your husband to
have a row! . . . And she was a bossy kind, my mother, with the children.

Mothers could also expect a lot of help from daughters (and vice versa), even if
they were not living with them. Again, we must remember that the power and
resources at the disposal of one woman of the house could mean the disempowerment and exhaustion of another woman of the house. The Rotunda
almoner, giving an example in 1953 of the kind of social conditions that could
lead to women being run-down, referred to the case of a Mrs K, 21-year-old
married woman who had been seriously ill in her early teenage years. Living on
a top-floor tenement, she was up and down all day helping her mother on the
bottom floor. Mrs K's mother had nine sons and a heart condition, so her only
daughter was 'very good' to her, making meals and cleaning and helping her:
'We will visit her family and point out gently, but firmly, that they must not
make too heavy demands on her services,' the almoner commented, after Mrs
K had been delivered, against the odds, of a healthy baby boy.[11]
   In any kind of household, relationships depended upon personality. Brendan
McN. described his paternal uncle, who lived with them on their Clare farm, as
'tight-fisted and supercilious', always arguing with Brendan's quieter, though
more authoritative, father. His mother's life he sees in retrospect comprised
'Keeping the peace and praying'. Relatives, and not just female ones, could be
causes of tension. Looked at from the point of view of older women of the house,
we can see that their power and control began to be seriously questioned in the
1940s and 1950s in rural Ireland, and possibly earlier in urban areas. In Arensberg
and Kimball's Clare, the husband was expected to side with his wife if a serious
disagreement arose between the latter and his mother, but it was believed that a
certain amount of deference and deception vis-à-vis the wishes of the old people
as to how things should be done, would go a long way. Much depended upon
individual personality. Mary Ellen D. referred to an aunt by marriage (who had
died young), who lived with her husband's mother and his uncle:

> because it wasn't easy . . . She married a man that was 25 years older than
> her, my grand-mother was all that much older again, and still she got on
> like a house on fire with her, she had six children, she used to love to chat
> to the uncle . . .

However, the fact that she mentions it in the first place gives the impression that
it is unusual.

NEIGHBOURS

Mary Healy's mother had a saying: 'You can do without your own but you can't
do without your neighbour'.[12] Neighbours were extremely important for most
women of the house throughout this period, but this does not mean that they

were universally loved, respected and appreciated. Historians and anthropologists have noted that men in rural areas regularly shared labour, machinery and resources at busy times of the year.[13] For women, all year round was busy, and the exchange of goods and services was even more important. However, because of the physical and psychical closeness of women's work to the living space and to the family relationships, such exchanges were more likely to be fraught with tension. In rural areas neighbours were needed for provisioning and basic amenities – sometimes milk was bought from them and springs or wells were often situated on rights of way through their property. Baby-clothes, cups of sugar, eggcupfuls of tea and unusual items like curling tongs were passed around. In Lily G.'s homeplace 'the neighbour was a great person. Surely to God.' Older women especially, when she was a young woman, were a great support, sitting up nights with her dying mother, taking over the chores when Lily was in hospital with her babies, coming in 'like the [public health] nurses nowadays' after Lily came home to check on her and the new baby, and later, on hand sometimes to give a bottle if Lily was busy. Hannah C. describes the woman of the house thus: 'The mother was manager, mother, nurse and neighbour-helper all in one.' Helping the neighbour is included matter-of-factly along with the other functions. Brendan McN. says there was an 'immense closeness' between his mother and the women in the locality, in rural Clare in the 1920s.

This kind of closeness was not confined to rural areas. Olive A., in a very different, urban setting, also depended upon her neighbour during her early married life:

> I had a neighbour who moved to Dublin [after that] and she was great, she taught me how to feed my child, like, what to do, when to introduce egg and all the rest of it, and if I couldn't make curtains, like, she would make them for me.

There seem to have been three levels of neighbourly intimacy. The first, that experienced mainly by urban working-class people living at close quarters to one another, was dictated by proximity and mutual dependence. Humphreys noted that among the labourer and tenement-dwelling Dubliners in the 1940s:

> ordinary daily exchanges of service, as well as co-operation in times of crisis, is even more marked than among the artisans.[14]

Mary Healy has much the same to say about the working-class neighborhood where she grew up in Kilkenny city in the 1920s.[15] Kevin Kearns's oral history of the Dublin tenements is full of examples of similar neighbourliness; one woman, born in 1915, said:

> When they started tearing the old tenements down it was like tearing *us* apart. It tore *me* apart . . . If I had a tenement house now I'd go back and live in it . . . yes I would.[16]

16. Photograph, children minding children. From *The Irish Press*, September 26, 1931. Mothers used their considerable authority to get older children to mind younger ones and keep them from harm. It is unlikely that mothers without domestic help – that is, the majority – in small and cramped accommodation would ever have got through the day's work otherwise.

However, even apart from the obvious tensions and discomforts associated with living at close quarters with one another, neighbours even in the poorest working-class areas did not invariably help one another. Sometimes they simply could not risk the loss of health or of reputation that this might have entailed. Another of Kevin Kearns's informants tells of her mother being paid half-a-crown by a nun some time in the 1930s to do a load of washing for a mother dying of TB, and her mother did it because her own husband was very sick. Kevin Kearns tells us that it was only the most strong-willed and big-hearted older women of the area, or those who needed the money, who would risk contagion in this way, but does not draw what I would consider to be the natural conclusion from this that neighbourliness had its limits, even in the tenements.[17] Still, the help that working-class neighbours rendered each other could be extra-ordinary. Maureen O'R., who remembers money being scarce and occasional crises but never actual hunger, tells of a time in the 1940s when her father was sick, and therefore not working:

> . . . and one of my sisters was getting Communion, and all the neighbours they all brought different things, and my mother kept – all that Communion gear was kept for everyone.

This level of interdependence does not mean that privacy was unknown. In fact, keeping a certain amount of one's business to oneself was all the more important.

People rarely if ever ate in each other's dwellings; some households fed hungry neighbouring children out of charity, but for any child to accept food in another house was like saying their parents could not feed them. Another custom that seems to have been stronger in working-class areas and lower-middle-class areas in cities and towns, than it was among people of equivalent income out the country, was the use of the title 'Mrs.' Mary Healy tells us that:

> none of our neighbours ever called each other by their Christian names, but always Mrs, but it was different with the men, they were Pat, Jim and John, which were the names of most of our neighbours.

The only female of her own age with whom Mary's very sociable and neighbourly mother was on first name terms was a friend from school days.[18] Hugh Leonard, in his autobiography, also notes this about his mother and her neighbours in working-class Dalkey; he speculates that this might have been a way of holding on to dignity and status in the face of daily, grinding poverty.[19] It could also have been an attempt to keep neighbours at what was at least a symbolic distance – the same neighbours who might know about the most intimate aspects of one's life, having assisted at childbirth and lent and borrowed all kinds of things. There could also have been the practical reason, mentioned by Marilyn Silverman, that more married women than men would be newcomers to the area, or 'blow-ins',[20] so they would not have been as well-known and would therefore be kept at a certain distance.

The second level of neighbourly relationships was the one which obtained mainly in rural areas, where there wasn't as much propinquity but there was just as much, if not more, interdependence, not just material and economical, but social and cultural. Neighbours in the country were, paradoxically, harder to keep at a distance than neighbours in the urban community, however overcrowded. With even the smallest farms or gardens, the opportunities for disputes over land and straying livestock were legion. These kind of disputes were mentioned a lot, according to Josephine E:

> There was a lot of bad blood between neighbours not great with one another, the hen used sneak over the fence and root up the bit of oats, and that could cause a row, you know, that time.

Anna A. explains the sociability, the need and the conflict:

> Both women in our house [mother and grand-aunt] did a lot of visiting friends, not really close neighbours. Some weren't on good terms from years back. Possibly they didn't know why they weren't friendly. They had long forgotten. But we did have a lot of friends. Some of these people had Apple or Rhubarb or maybe they would give my mother clothes from their own grown-up children.

Joan K. remarks of her native Wexford in the 1920s and 1930s: 'You mightn't
be speaking to your next-door neighbour over a blow-up'. She also describes in
vivid detail the amount of talk that used to go on. Josephine E. has a very
negative view of this kind of talk:

> They visited one another, and they talked to each other, talked about
> young people, chit-chat talk, they weren't nice people, now, they were
> very ugly to the youngsters.

Seán C. and Delia R. claim that women who did not join in the local gossip were
considered odd and were unpopular. Whether they were gossips or not, they
needed their neighbours. Josephine E. admits that neighbours always helped
each other out:

> Well if a woman was sick, the women would go, and they'd go splitting
> the potatoes, now, that was a very big job, do you know, cutting the
> potatoes up for seed. Or say now if the woman had a baby or had very
> young children, a few women in the village that was maybe, older women,
> or that had more time, they'd go and they'd do that, they'd go and do a
> wash for her, do you know, and they might make a cake [of bread] and
> bring it to them, yes they would.

As Joan K. tells it, talking and speculating about the doings of others was a way
of passing the time and of finding out vital information about neighbours:

> and Mammy would say then, 'I heard a car going down last night about
> two o'clock', and that'd be the doctor, no-one had a car but the doctor and
> the teacher . . . Jimmy [neighbour] then would say, 'Well I heard So-and-
> so wasn't well all right, and if I hear any news I'll let you know' . . .

Neighbours visited each other at night to pull up to the fire and talk; this was
known as 'miching' in Kildare/Offaly; 'cuardaíocht' [visiting] in Laois, 'céilidhe-
ing' [getting together] in Westmeath and 'rambling', scoruíocht, walking or
cabin-hunting in many other parts of the country. A house which was much
visited and where there was a lot of music and amusement was sometimes called
a 'rambling house'. When battery wirelesses came in, people came in to each
other's houses to listen to 'Question Time' by Joe Linnane, or 'Hospitals
Requests', two very popular programmes, or to the All-Ireland finals.

In rural Ireland it was men as much as women, if not more so, who were
retailers of news and what we might call 'gossips', because most often it was
men who had the free time to do the 'rambling'. Certainly in Clare in the 1930s
the men went 'ar chuaird' far more than the women.[21] Women rearing young
families had to depend on whoever came to them for news and entertainment.
When Mary Ellen D. moved into a completely new area on her marriage, she
found the men who worked on the farm a great source of news and information

about the neighbours when she'd be giving them their dinner. Old women whose work was over were also great visitors, though they could sometimes be a nuisance, according to Annie R.:

> ... there was this woman next door [i.e. in the nearest house] ... and she'd come in, there. Sometimes my mother might be a bit annoyed, she might come in when she'd be very busy, like, you know in the evening when she'd have lots of things to do. Ah she [her mother] was always very nice, and she'd chat, like. She was going blind at the end, and they'd have to convey her up, [i.e. walk with her] ...

The third level of neighbourly relationships was where neighbours could be ignored altogether, and were not needed. This was the case in some urban middle-class areas, but a lot depended upon personality, and as we have seen, Olive A.'s neighbour meant a lot to her. Ethel R.'s mother had friends rather than neighbours, an important distinction:

> Mam had a lot of friends, [the town] was small. Through ICA country markets, card playing, she met women from all social classes. I would say she preferred to keep a distance from neighbours and friends with regard to coming in and out of the house, as she met most of them in clubs.

In one way, Ethel's mother was very like her neighbour-dependent counterparts in that she did not consciously entertain friends; however, she met them outside the house. She did not need neighbours either for economic or for social purposes. Madge C. can never remember neighbours in her house in middle-class northside Dublin, but believes that this was because all her mother's relations lived nearby so she did not need her neighbours for company and because she was a very independent-minded woman, a sort of loner. Nor did Humphreys' Dublin artisans depend upon their neighbours, calling on relatives for help at times of crisis, but not going in and out of one another's houses a lot.[22] Aquafication and electrification, and eventually (though later than our period) nationwide television; as a form of in-house entertainment, lessened the opportunities for contact with neighbours. Exchanges of goods and services still went on and still goes on, but the need for these exchanges would have been reduced with rising standards of living.

With the decline of the multi-generational household and the increasing tendency for single girls and women to go to school or work away from the house, the woman of the house became more and more isolated, if this word can be used neutrally. Nobody mentioned that this was a problem. If the woman of the house was more isolated, her authority was also less likely to be challenged. And all the indications are that in a nuclear family this authority was often considerable.

POWER AND RESPONSIBILITY

In research for this study, the simple question 'Who controlled the money?' yielded anything but simple answers. It was not that people were evasive. They were clearer and more definite on this question than on any of the others. Nobody talking of their own experience had forgotten this, and if talking of their parents' experience, they did not have to dig deep into their memories – it was family knowledge. Exploring the question a little further, however, it became clear that controlling the money (for the house) and controlling the family income were sometimes two separate things. Also, this was one area where power brought with it a high degree of responsibility.

Josephine E.'s comments on the respect due to the man of the house provides a useful starting-point to discuss the power relationships between men and women:

> Men like you to respect them and appreciate them. They do. They don't like to be taken for granted. They're middling pettish, they are now, they like to see a little bit of appreciation. They don't like a woman to get any bit above them with earnings and things . . . they like to be the chief. I suppose it's in them to be like that.

Appreciation and respect, in Josephine's own marriage, involved having the meal on the table when the husband came in from work, reserving the head of the table for him, and not nagging him about having an occasional pint, despite her mother's disapproval of this habit of his. However, she believed that the woman should make the decisions about money. In answer to a question about who would make the big decisions that had to be made, she said:

> The man was supposed to be, the woman was the most – unless it was a man they used to call them more of a fighting man, now, the one that'd – he was more or less a bully, that done the shopping, no the women mostly, the women yes.

– so she'd have the say?

> She would really, yes. That's now, if it was any kind of a middling happy home, it was the woman. And they always said, the woman was best at it, much better than the man . . . In most houses it was the woman, what she'd say, it'd be done. She'd talk it over with him, you know that way . . .

The woman was the real head, but she had to indulge her man's comparative powerlessness by giving him certain privileges and freedoms. The similarity of the tone of her initial description of the respect and appreciation due to men is very similar to the way newspapers and magazines and popular psychology talked about the way the man should treat the woman – rule her with a firm hand, but give her plenty of respect and some freedom. Lily G., in a household economy that was almost identical to that of Josephine E., but a decade or so earlier, was less definite, but still identified the woman as the authority:

> Yes I often look back and think to myself that on this women's lib and all this . . . Yes there was no such thing as anyone putting their foot down and 'I'm the boss' or 'You're the boss'. I really think deep down the woman was making, maybe in her own quiet way, the [decisions] – that's now, unless, you know yourself, you can be up against an individual, or marry an individual –

– a bully or something?

> Yes, yes, he wouldn't take that, or have that, twould be what he'd say and he'd say alone. But I think men were gone about their business so much, they'd be on the farm, they'd be doing their thing, now down in Mayo a lot of them would be working as well, my husband often did, you know . . . They'd be gone , they'd make no decisions. You know there was never [laughs] big hassle about it. No, no.

Although Lily's husband was working locally, in Mayo and Donegal there was a tradition of the men going on seasonal migration for several months a year, and the women taking complete authority in their absence – and probably, like Lily and Josephine, being recorded in the census as 'farmers', rather than as 'engaged in home duties'. It must have been partly this tradition which prompted the Clann na Talmhan deputies (see Chapter Three) to make so much of the role of the woman of the house on small farms in the west. There was also, simply, the tradition of the woman being the boss, as explained in Carmel C.'s written account of the twelve-acre holding she grew up on in east Galway in the 1920s and 1930s. The fact that she brings this up indicates how central she feels it to be to any account of women's work in Ireland in this period, as this is what she wrote in response to my initial appeal (see Appendix 2) in the paper, which had not referred at all to money or to the balance of power in houses:

> In those days the woman was the boss well what I mean is. It was she that kept the money. If the man got work for a week or two he'd give his pay packet over to the woman of the house, likewise if any of the sons got work the pay packet was turned over to the mother. She gave them pocket money if they were going anywhere, like to a sports or funeral. When the man went to the fair to sell cattle or pigs she'd give him a few bob in case he wouldn't sell. She was running the house.

Jack R.'s mother, who married in 1914 on a medium-sized Tipperary farm, also controlled the money, handing over money to the father if he was going to a GAA match or a funeral, two kinds of social event which could be relied upon to crop up regularly. However, there would have been little cash in that house, unlike the three other households into which wages were often brought. In two wage-earning families, one in the midlands and one in a Cork town, in the 1940s, 1950s and 1960s, the husbands handed over unopened pay packets. Larry K.'s wife Noreen controlled the money:

> Oh she would. Not always it worked but Noreen and myself – because I didn't want money. No way. I never got the money. When I got my wages, my pay, whatever they were, I handed them over, and if I wanted a newspaper afterwards she'd make sure I got that, or any other thing I might want but I kept out of the shops, nothing to do with them.

Frank Q. explained it as a general practice:

> And when you got the wage packet you gave it to her, that was kind of automatic . . . What I used to have out of the wage-packet was three small bottles of stout a week. And she used to give me them you know.

There followed a story about how Margaret once gave her father, when he was visiting, a bottle of stout and he asked if Frank was going to get one, and Margaret told him, 'He got one yesterday'. Margaret's father was shocked at such treatment being meted out to a man in his own house. Humphreys suggests that in the older generation of artisans in Dublin – those of an age with Margaret's father, married in the 1910s and early 1920s – the men had much more control over family finances than in the succeeding generation where there was more equality between husband and wife.[23] Larry K. never drank, so he claimed not to need any money – drink, newspapers and cigarettes being the main male indulgences. However, many men who 'liked a pint', like Maureen O'R.'s father, depended on their wives for money. When I asked Maureen who controlled the money in her house, she replied:

> Oh my mother. Very much so. And I can remember him asking for a shilling to go out for a pint, but I suppose a pint was only sixpence, but like that, she mightn't have it, I can remember her saying, 'I haven't got it', going mad, you know.

Drink had a bad effect on Anna A.'s normally hard-working and good-tempered father, making him cross. But he didn't often get drunk, because here, too, the wife controlled the money:

> My mother made most of the decisions in our house. She had to manage the money so that we could get what was needed when we needed it. My father worked hard but handed every penny to my mother, because if he got to a pub he would spend it on drink. I don't say he drank every day, or even every week. But if he went to a fair or market she'd go with him so she'd get the money when he sold something.

Among larger farmers also, the women sometimes made the decisions: on Annie R.'s parents seventy-acre farm in west Limerick, for example, it was her mother who made the decisions and controlled the money, because 'she was a stronger person'. Her father was some years older than her mother, and a very quiet man:

> But she managed the money and all that, because he was the type, like, he'd work away . . . he didn't mind, like, because she was very capable, very economical with money.

Did it all come down, simply, to personality then? Eamon B.'s shopkeeper mother made all the decisions about money:

> my father freely gave it to her, in a way he avoided the responsibilities of it because he had a very ordinary lifestyle and she provided him with cigarettes and tobacco from the shop . . . and she probably left him a certain amount of the money for pocket money, we'll call it, and if he was going anywhere, he would say he wanted a tenner to go here, there, or everywhere, and she'd give it to him freely, there was no trouble about it, but she controlled the money.

It was the same story down on his paternal uncle's farm in Clare, where an uncle lived with two aunts. Here, it was one of the aunts who controlled the money:

> the senior aunt controlled all the money here. She made all the decisions . . . and he really had to take whatever money was given to him. If he sold cattle, the money was put into a central fund, and she controlled that, and doled it out to him for his pints on Sunday, according as his requirements were.

No general conclusions about women's power in the household can be drawn from such far-flung and self-selected evidence, and none are being made. However, it is notable that in a variety of locations and household economies – on big and small farms, in working-class households and a middle-class household where the wife had an income of her own – the woman was seen as the person who controlled vital resources. Josephine E.'s belief that the woman was boss in 'middling happy' households suggests a view of woman of the house as benevolent despot. The 'good' or 'quiet' husband gave up his money and was indulged a little in return. Men's right to these indulgences were never questioned (though some men chose to limit or to forgo them). Charles Clancy-Gore in his study of the family economies of working-class households in a Dublin local authority housing estate in 1943 took for granted that no man should be expected to forgo these little luxuries.[24] Women did not as a rule have indulgences like pints and newspapers – did those who had the power to grant such privileges have something far more precious than this in their control of the household finances? Perhaps, but Eamon B.'s comment about his father avoiding the responsibility of allocating resources should make us stop short of equating responsibility with power in every case. The *Limerick Rural Survey*'s discussion of the family balance of power among farmers stated that, in general, the husband exercised little authority over certain aspects of household and family management, including children's destinies: 'the father limits his field of rule by his own choice'.[25] How much power did her administration of the family finances give 'Joan Dunn', the wife and mother of one of the artisan families researched by Humphreys in 1949–51?:

> I not only pay the bills for the food and the clothes, I also pay the rent, coal and light bills. In fact, all the bills for everything. John pays only his fees in the organisations he belongs to, and I should have said he keeps enough money to pay for his own clothes. Even if it is a question of buying extra-ordinary things like furniture, I am the one who decides that. And I am also the one who has to provide the money. If I were thinking of buying a dining-room table, I would not have to consult John about it though most of the time I would mention something like that to him . . . all he would say would be, 'Well, all right if *you have* the money'. [italics mine]

In this partnership John gave Joan 'all but a little spending money he keeps for himself' and he never questioned Joan's spending of the money; 'How she made ends meet kept me guessing.'[26] Here, the woman certainly controls the household finances, but the man does not turn over his paypacket to her; he gives her a certain amount – one hopes, most of it – keeping back not only enough for clothes and for clubs, but to have a few pints every night (though not a heavy drinker, John went to the pub almost every evening). In this arrangement the woman had the lion's share of responsibility without power; she had to manage on what he gave her, in contrast to the women who got a full pay packet and handed back pocket money.

In Clancy-Gore's survey also, the women controlled the household spending but none of them knew how much their husbands earned.[27] Jim Larkin Snr commented in the debate on whether to pay family allowances to the mother or the father, that he knew tradesmen earning £5 a week who gave their wives only £1 to run the house and pay all the bills.[28] Looking at it from a purely mechanical point of view, it was easier to hand over a regular pay packet *in toto* than to hand over money received for a job, which would be how many artisans working for themselves would have been paid. The artisans in Humphreys' sample, however, were all working in Guinness's brewery, so they got wage-packets at regular intervals. However, it seems that the more men earned, the more likely they were to hold the reins themselves. Humphreys noted that among general labourers the tendency for the men to give their wives control of the finances was 'even greater',[29] but here again it is not clear if these finances constitute the total family income or what the man deems to be necessary for the family's subsistence. Handing over the pay packet seems to have been common practice among Dublin dockers, according to one of Kevin Kearns' informants, who said revealingly: '. . . there was a percentage of them that wouldn't dream of *handing over* the wages'. According to Joan K., it was the norm in wage-earning families:

> The husband had a pay packet coming home and he handed it to the wife and it unopened, and out of that she gave him back so-much for a couple of pints, and then she worked a miracle with that pay packet.

Her husband added: 'Even Gay Byrne had it, he said it once.'

The *Limerick Rural Survey* observed – took it for granted, indeed – that among the smaller farmers there was more consultation between husband and wife about how to spend the money. Patricia O'Hara found that women on smaller western farms were almost invariably on a level of equal authority with their menfolk as far as money was concerned, compared to women in the east of the country. This ties in with the impression of female financial headship given by the Clann na Talmhan deputies in the debate on children's allowances.[30] (See Chapter Three)

Eamonn B., having described the balance of power in his own family of origin growing up, went on to discuss his wife's family of origin:

> her father was a sergeant in the Guards [Garda Síochána] there was no question of that, her father controlled his money and cashed his cheque at the end of the month, and when the bills came in he would be tut-tutting over them if he thought some of them were too high, and give the money to pay for them and that was it . . .

In four urban middle-class households described to me, where the man was the chief or the only earner – Madge C.'s. Lucy O'S.'s, Ethel R.'s, and Olive A.'s – the man of the house controlled the money. Olive A.'s husband had a business; Ethel R.'s father worked in a bank; Lucy O'S.'s was a teacher, and Madge C.'s sold insurance. Delia R.'s father had a business and he kept a very tight rein on the money. Only one of the wives (Lucy O'S.'s mother) actually performed any kind of extra-household, remunerative work in the period in question, but she saw the house as her main work. Certainly the women were consulted but the perception was that the father was the head of the house:[31]

> Mm. Who controlled the house [sic]. It's a sore point. My husband. And he still does. Still makes the decisions . . . Without consultation mostly. The odd time there is a bit, but mostly, no.   [Olive A.]

> I never remember any discussion about money as Dad provided enough for all requirements.   [Ethel R.]

> It would be my father. Now he would probably consult her, or she would say to him, look, Madge wants piano lessons, I think she should have them, but he, being the keeper of the purse, would have been the ultimate authority on things like that.

– so he would have controlled the money?

Oh yeah, and he would have given her extra housekeeping money, and I can remember when the sales would come up, January, I suppose, he used to give her extra money . . . she'd do all the buying, except for his clothes, he'd buy his own clothes.   [Madge C.]

– he controlled the money?

Oh he did, and he was tight with it, you know. Twas always a bone of contention with me, that he had a large dowry for each of us, there was just the two of us, my sister and myself, a thousand pounds each he gave us . . . He could have given it to my mother, like, over the years.   [Lucy O's][31]

In all of these cases the man was actually bringing in the money, but the same could be said of Larry K. and Frank Q., who handed over wage packets. Even on farms, the fact of the farm actually being the woman's by inheritance did not always guarantee that she would control the money. Mary Ellen D.'s mother, even though she often threw it back at Mary Ellen's father that it was her 'place', allowed him to handle the money:

Married into the farm, and she owned the farm, and was very much the boss, my father was a great worker, after some years debts were paid back, and they had money in the bank, but he went straight to the bank with the money! . . . He didn't believe in spending it.

It was to their father that Mary Ellen and her sister had to go to beg, borrow or steal (literally, according to Mary Ellen, lift the money out of his trousers after he had gone to bed) money for a dance. According to Aine Uí Gh:

in the case of a man marrying into a farm as a *cliamhan isteach*, the holding was completely signed over to him. More often than not the dowry paid by this gentleman was borrowed money which meant the poor wife slaving for the remainder of her working life to pay debt.

The word 'gentleman' is not used in any complimentary sense here! There were married women farmers, as seen in Chapter one, but mainly on poorer land. This was true of women farmers in general, married, single or widowed.

     Even the women who controlled the family finances, however – even those who had inherited holdings and worked them while their husbands earned wages elsewhere – do not seem to have thought that this entitled them to the same kind of privileges which earning wages conferred on men, or on other single or married women. When I asked Josephine E. if she had found it a big change coming home to Ireland from England the first thing she mentioned, unbidden, was having had to give up the possibility of part-time earning:

I did [find it a big change] and I often regretted it. I always said, as I said to you, even though if you had children, what I used do in England, you could work in the evenings. Crying out for them . . . But I could always do that, when my husband would come from work, if I was in England, which I couldn't stir here. It was like a black mark, if your wife had a position, we'll call it, to go out now minding children, or cleaning like they do now, oh it was terrible, you'd be –

– 'twas like saying your husband –

Oh they wouldn't let you do it! That's what it was yes. Pride . . . And then you'd have no way of getting into the town, or of getting out. Yes. But I missed that very very much that's why I'm all out for women when they get married having jobs. It keeps you young also . . . and if you buy a few things for yourself, even a bit of cream for your face, it gives you those little bits of perks, do you know what I mean? It gives you that bit of a lift. Well you see I couldn't afford any of those things in my time. Couldn't.

Were 'they' husbands, or just society in general? Josephine's other remarks about men not liking to see women get any bit above them with earnings would lead us to believe that she was talking about husbands in general, and not necessarily her own; her husband had obviously not objected to her working part-time in England. Nor did she believe that she was as entitled, by her work on the farm, to luxuries like face-cream as her husband was to his occasional pint. In the farm households under discussion, even where the woman controlled the household money, she doled it out to the man for recreation, for a fair 'in case he wouldn't sell' (i.e. so that he would not be empty-handed if he met up with friends on a fair day, even if he did not succeed in selling). His drink or two was not thought of as a reward for selling, but something to which he was entitled on a day out in any case, or if he was going to a funeral or a match or some other social event. The woman of the house might have controlled the egg money, and might even have controlled all the money that came into the house and made the major spending decisions, but that does not mean that she spent money on herself. It should also be remembered that in many cases the 'egg-money' was notional, seeing as the tea, sugar, flour and other groceries were often paid for by the eggs in a barter system. Nor was there any guarantee that the woman who opened her husband's pay packet would slip a few shillings into her pocket for her personal use. The kind of things that women in the past were seen to lack – the equivalent of men's pints, matches and funerals or meetings – were usually defined in terms of appearance and the wherewithal to get outside the house, such as clothes, cosmetics and transport of some sort. The worst thing about the made match and what was seen as the old style marriage, was, according to Tom K.:

if she was only buying a shift for herself she had to consult him, he had to be brought along . . . and the woman couldn't buy a coat or a hat for herself without his command, and if he didn't think well of it, 'ah couldn't you get another while out of it, there's a couple of calves I want to buy now instead.'

What is taken for granted here, by Tom, is that the woman's and the man's interests would be at variance with one another, and that the woman would prefer a hat or a coat to a couple of calves. What is also suggested is that even if the woman were in charge of the household finances, she still had to ask 'himself' when large expense was incurred – items of clothing, nice things for the house. But the urban wage-earning, salary-earning or self-employed husband who kept back some of his earnings and gave housekeeping money had even more actual control over the household expenditure than the farmer. This was because there was no widespread urban equivalent of egg-money, and since most of the household requirements had to be bought rather than reared or grown, the provisioning of the urban woman of the house was a lot more prone to headaches, and indeed, if he were so inclined, to interference from the man of the house than was that of her farm-dwelling counterpart. However, for farm women who had been 'assisting relatives' before marriage and had no actual money in their own possession, the iniquities of the dowry system have not been exaggerated by critics. Mary Ellen D.'s story of her penurious wedding day ended happily because she got a man who was not mean with money, but it could have gone the other way, as she explained to me:

> [the dowry] was only handed over after the wedding. It was the week before, we [her father and herself] went into the bank. Now if he [husband] was a mean man, I would have got nothing, do you understand?

She went on to describe her wedding day and her predicament when she was getting ready to go away:

> But my uncle's wife came up to help me change, and that, and I said to her, 'Go down and tell my father I want him now.' I hadn't THAT much change [holds up thumb and finger], now generally I might have a few shillings, but it worked out whatever shopping we did, the last day, the day or two before that, I spent the last penny, and I said, 'Go down and tell my father,' and . . . that's what I got, a pound, now. Now that is difficult for you to understand, but that was the truth.

She felt it humiliating to go away with her husband without a penny in her pocket, and to have to ask her father for money on her wedding day. It must be remembered that this was 1953, comparatively late in the period; that it was not a 'made match'; that Mary Ellen herself had had plenty of friends and a good social life before she got married; that she was not on bad terms with her parents, and that she had worked day in, day out on the farm for several years at this stage. Her repeated insistence that I understand what she was saying shows that she believes that somebody born less than ten years after the events she describes would have trouble believing her story. This is an example of the way contributors portrayed the past as a dim, distant country, a theme I will return to in the last chapter.

DOING THEIR SHARE: MEN ABOUT THE HOUSE

Many women of the house in Ireland in these years had, it has been suggested, some strategic resources in running the house – the recycling of goods, the help of children, neighbours and female relatives, and often, some control over household finances. The help of menfolk around the house was a resource also, and like the others (except perhaps the recycling), it was by no means guaranteed. The work had to be done anyway.

Men, towards the end of this period, were somewhat more inclined to associate themselves with housework and childcare than at the beginning. Damian Hannan found in a survey of four hundred couples in ten western counties in the early 1970s that over a quarter of all families interviewed had 'considerable breaching of the sex-role divison of tasks in household and child-rearing'.[32] Even in the period 1921–61 there were men who were not afraid to cross this boundary. It should be emphasised strongly that the kind of man who answered an appeal like mine would have been more likely to have taken an interest in household work, so their responses cannot be taken as representative. Most of the men who responded to my appeal came from either all-boy families, or families where all the older children were boys and/or families where the mother was widowed while the family was still young. It seems that some women of the house in these circumstances depended a lot on boys for help around the house, instilling in them a lifelong interest in the work and a sense of responsibility towards it, and possibly creating, in the process, 'good catches' for discerning women.

The non-involvement of men in the intimacies of childcare in the past is almost universally seen now, by women and men alike, as having been a bad thing. The men who responded were anxious to prove their own proficiency at it at a time when it was 'neither profitable nor popular'. Frank Q. and Larry K. both said that they had pushed out prams in the 1940s and 1950s. At least two respondents expressed approval at modern young fathers carrying babies and toddlers 'in to Mass' – Mass being singled out as an arena where people are on display.

'Not at all, they would not be let, and they would be regarded as sissies,' wrote Seán C. in reply to my question 'Did the men ever help out with the housework/childcare?' He did not say who would regard them as sissies – their womenfolk who would not 'let' them? Their peers? Arensberg and Kimball note the strict division of labour between the sexes in Clare in the 1930s. Russell comments of the Gaeltacht community he studied in the late 1960s that a man changing nappies was regarded as 'a sissy or worse', presumably by his peers.[33]

Eileen Kane comments that masculinity was in general defined in a negative way, by what men would not do.[34] Dublin artisans who helped around the house or shopped in the late 1940s early 1950s would be called 'traitors' by their fellow-artisans.[35] A man who looked after poultry in some rural areas would be called *'Síle na gCearc'* [Síle of the Hens].[36] This was the traditional attitude, but it seems to have been changing, in urban households at least, from the 1940s. Still, some other men from a variety of backgrounds also helped out in the house. Larry K., when he was doing shiftwork on the railway, was able to come home in the morning and mind his two small children to let his wife off to do the shopping:

> Then again there was other work that had to be done as well. You see that was where the husband could help and did help. A lot of them, then, wouldn't do that. Too selfish. But they were really – the black crows like you know.

> *– would they be thought of as –*

> Oh yeah everybody would say, they weren't right, they weren't right at all, no, no . . . They should help out, do their share.

But what was their share and who defined it? To Larry K. it meant going for the water, tending a vegetable garden, fixing things around the house, looking after the children, cleaning up after them, cleaning them if they got dirty and not being afraid to bring them out on walks, even pushing the pram. He was a good plain cook – his mother had made sure of that – so he was able to run the house and let his wife up to Dublin for a few days every so often. He expressed disdain on more than one occasion for men who left everything to their wives:

> They couldn't take a cup – they'd get a young girl, or a kid, Here Mary, take this cup and put it on the table for me . . . now not many, fortunately, there weren't many would do that, – in general a man would tip in, take up his duty where the woman would not always be in humour to keep going.

A similar disdain for irresponsible and selfish men was expressed by Frank Q., who recalled a conversation he had with a drunken neighbour, a father of nine children, who advised him on the way he should go:

> And he came out with the most selfish phrase I ever heard, he said, 'Leave the women to do the effing [sic] worrying, and you do the effing drinking.' That's what he said to me you know!

Frank had a vegetable garden also, and looked after the children as much as he could. Richard O'Flynn, a coalman and part-time bandsman in Limerick in the 1920s and 1930s:

like every man of the house in those times, had his own family chores to attend to after his daily grind as breadwinner; he was cobbler and barber and general handyman, so that on a typical night in winter he might be cutting our hair or repairing shoes.[37]

'Men were very handy that time' commented Larry K. A good man, according to him, could cut the boys' hair and many mended shoes. A last was a basic item of household equipment in the 1920s and 1930s.

Were these men unusual? Larry K. and Frank Q. had also ceded control of the money. So had Eamon B.'s father, mentioned earlier: he did not lift a finger around the house, did not even chop and carry in wood, but he kept a vegetable garden, played with his children and went on walks with them. Lucy O'S.'s father (also a National teacher) remembered as the controller of the money and the head of the house, bathed and dressed the children when they were small, took them for walks and was very close to them: 'But he never lifted a plate off the table, never, never.' There was a maid in each of the last two houses, yet the mothers still had plenty of housework and other work to do, particularly Lucy's mother. The two Mayo women, Lily G. and Josephine E., described their husbands' contribution to the housework in similar ways:

> Oh he did [help out], he was good, my husband was good. He wouldn't, now, wash nappies, but he'd change the baby, if I wasn't around. [Lily G.]

Josephine E.'s husband would 'do a little bit if I wasn't there', even undertaking the rather specialised job of washing the eldest girl's long hair. These women, like Mary Ellen D., implied that their husbands were particularly good, and not like most men at the time. Mary Ellen D. said:

> They didn't do much. In fact, most of them would never even take a child in their hand – 'Here Mammy the child is crying' – John [husband] would mind a child, change nappies or anything, he would . . . even someone down the road, now, he made out if he ever took the child in his hand the child knew him and start crying. [laughs] No as a general rule they didn't. But my father now, would . . . if he came in and dinner wasn't ready, he'd say 'Hurry up where's the dinner' and he might start setting the table . . . he would wash the spuds if the need arose, but he shouldn't have to do it if there was three women, do you understand. He would now. And he was able to bake a cake, my mother always went to Galway for a week . . .

Annie R.'s father was able to bake a cake (of bread) also, when her mother took off to Ballybunion for her annual holiday with the smallest child. She and Seamus expressed disdain for a brother-in-law of Annie's in the 1950s who wouldn't 'take up' i.e. carry and look after his child, town-bred Seamus in particular believing that this was 'unnatural'.

What men did inside the house and what they were seen to do were often two different things. Madge C.'s father would wash up and help out in the house, but he:

> wouldn't be seen to – wouldn't be seen to walk down the street with a loaf of bread in his hand . . . And I mean no man at that stage would put a hand on the handle of a pram.

Larry K. referred to men who would not be seen carrying sweet-cans, because of their domestic associations (the sweet-can was one of those infinitely recyclable household objects like the flour-bag), and he went on to tell a story about how he and his colleagues once tried to trick one of these men who shunned all domestic objects into carrying a 'po' on the handlebars of a bike. Prams, sweet-cans, pos and even children were disorderly items associated with the house and the body, and it was seen to be below the dignity of some men at least, to invite such associations. The fact that this male aloofness was being ridiculed by some men at this stage implies that it was coming to be seen to be somewhat ludicrous in some circles. They would probably have laughed at Humphreys' artisans who saw shopping as beneath their dignity:

> I certainly would not know anything about shopping for food. The only time I go into a store [sic] except the tobacconists, is when I am buying clothes for myself. The men here leave that sort of thing to the women.[38]

Yet some contributors believed that men's involvement in shopping could make a miserable life for the women. Josephine E. mentioned this, and Tom K. gave a description of:

> the fellow that'd come into the town, and she'd say to him [whispers] 'Sugar', and he'd say, [loudly] 'We want a halfstone of sugar'; 'we want tea' [whispers] she'd say, God help her, and she hadn't any – he'd root down then and he'd take up a *sparán* and he'd be rooting through it –

If the woman was solely responsible for shopping not only would she have more freedom and power of attorney, but she would also have the external appearance of being in charge of the house and its spending and therefore higher status. Josephine E.'s definition of a 'bullying' man was one who did the shopping, as we saw earlier. Delia R's artisan father, as said earlier, kept a very tight rein on the household spending, but he was not afraid to help out in the house, especially on Sunday evening:

> after tea he'd put on the apron and send Mammy and the girls away to devotions for a break, you know – and I'll tell you twas he who gave the kitchen a good clean and a good sweeping! . . . I'll tell you, he was one

person – he showed me how to dry a cup [laughs], going around the handle [demonstrates].

Did he also impart this knowledge to Delia's mother, and was she duly appreciative? Did men's taking an interest in household work always mean an easier life for their womenfolk?

Women seem to have appreciated men's involvement in childcare and their other efforts to lighten women's workload, rather than what might have been either ineffectual or domineering intervention in shopping and household work:

> he ripped [the rock] up with his hands, and when we did get water eventually we were one of the first in the village to have it . . . he discovered that the water would come on gravity, from the well.   [Lily G.]

Lily's husband had already built on an extension to the house:

> Yes well he had built on the kitchen himself, with the neighbours helping him, and he helping the neighbours again, if they wanted it. They were fine men. They were fine men.

The men were doing this work in addition to a heavy working week. Mary Healy's husband, Ned, who worked very hard for the County Council for most of this married life (and died comparatively young, as did Lily G.'s husband), also carried out extensive work to make their house more comfortable:

> In time we got running water and a bathroom, but it was through hard labour on my husband's side. He hacked through earth and rock to bring the water to our house . . .

He also designed and built a new kitchen. Ned Healy was a carpenter but not all the men who did this kind of work were qualified to do it, many had to teach themselves or get help from friends.[39] Frank Q. also built an extension. Myles na Gopaleen (Brian O'Nolan) could poke all the fun he liked at 'The Man Who Does His Own Carpentry', but Myles na Gopaleen was a well-paid senior civil servant who spent most of his spare time writing and drinking so it is unlikely that he ever had to lift bradawl, chisel or paint-brush.[40] One can imagine Myles's reaction to Ethel R.'s father who:

> washed dishes in the evenings. He stayed home when Mam was at ICA, Tech Class etc. He also cooked from time to time especially if visitors were coming or when Mam made jams and jellies. Dad would help pick the crab-apples for jelly. He also helped with cutting the marmalade oranges in January. Dad also helped with bath-time when we were very young. He chopped wood. He cut the lawn – push mower. One winter he made a rug with Mam.

These contributions were all co-operating and helping and enabling, rather than taking the initiative, but Ethel's father was working full-time outside the house, and her mother was working full-time in it. The reference to his agreeing to stay at home to let the mother off to her classes and other activities implies, however, that looking after young children, even outside working hours, was seen as the mother's primary responsibility. Joan K. explained that there would be criticism sometimes of mothers who would go to the ICA. When she was young and single in the late 1930s and 1940s she used to go to meetings:

> But farmers' wives now, what we'll call a girl that'd be 35 or 40, or even 45, she might join, and you'd hear now, even my own mother saying, 'Wouldn't you think now, it would fit her better to be at home and not have Pat trying to look after the family and he has enough to do.' You know. And that was the idea.

Obviously more men were content to hold the fort while their wives went to meetings, as membership of the ICA rose in the 1950s. Certainly the idea that a man should be responsible for some aspects of his own maintenance at least was gaining currency at this stage, particularly among urban people. Eamon B., who never had to polish his shoes when he was young, got a shock when he got married in the mid-1950s:

> Well we didn't polish our own shoes, which, to my wife's chagrin, I told her that I expected her to do them and she certainly threw them at me! . . . but anyway, that was the first awakening I had . . .

Eamon's wife came from a house where the father kept a tight hold of the purse, but he might very well have helped in the house. Whether he did or not, it is significant that his daughter was determined not to do certain jobs.

Madge C., who married in 1960 in Dublin City, however, sees huge changes between her own early married life and that of her son who married in the 1980s. Even though men were helping out more than they had in the previous generation when she married:

> the difference in attitude between the young marrieds now and what I would have have been, as regards men helping in the house, is just astounding. I mean they just take it for granted that they'll do their share and there's no question about it. It wouldn't have been the scene in the 60s when I married. You would expect help but not to the degree they do now.

Again, the words 'share' and 'help'. Discussing whether men nowadays actually and measurably perform equal amounts of housework, even in two-income households, is beyond the scope of this work, but there are indications that they do not.[41] However, contributors to this project believe that they do. In the period in question men could 'help' in very important ways, not only by ceding control of all the household *income* (and not just the household *finances*, though this seems to have been preferable to no control at all) to their womenfolk, but by making sure that their own exercise of breadwinner privileges – drinking (even moderately), smoking and other entertainment – was either forgone or kept to a minimum, and by looking after the children when necessary.

Damian Hannan found in his research, which, although it took place in the 1970s, is the closest we have to the period, that there were several different patterns of spousal relationships in the couples he studied. Where there were strictly separate spheres of activity and day-to-day work, spouses were not wholly dependent upon each other for 'emotional sustenance', and conflict was often managed by being avoided. The highest level of emotional integration between spouses occurred when there was agreement on the priority of spousal/parental goals *or* when wives prioritised spousal/parental goals and men the status/consumption goals. If both spouses prioritised spousal/parental goals, then this implied that the man 'helped' the woman with her work and with the children.[42] The second 'model' seems hard to understand, at first. If such a model were proposed today, it would suggest women pouring forth love and understanding while men fret about the make of car they are driving. However, if this is applied to the early 1970s, and by implication – as many of the couples had been married over a decade – to the tail-end of our period, it could be interpreted as a workable complementarity of roles where the man and woman agreed on her devoting herself to the house, the children and him, while he worked extremely hard to earn money to buy things for the house, to install services and facilities, and to enable the children to stay at school.

CONCLUSION

Because this chapter is based largely upon self-selected personal testimonies there must be a bias in the evidence towards people who had strong feelings about the subject of men, women, money and relationships. Most of my respondents had had experiences of dealing with interfering elders or in-laws, good or bad neighbours, men either ceding control to women or ruling benevolently themselves, or giving control to the woman in some areas (e.g. helping in the house) while holding it back in others (e.g. keeping back some money, or scrutinising the accounts). The man who considered his wife and the work she did beneath his contempt would not even have finished reading my newspaper appeal; his wife, after a lifetime of this attitude, might not have had the self-confidence or the energy to respond. Interpreted at its most fundamental, the personal testimony for this particular section of the thesis (both in the way it was selected and the way the responses were made), suggests that women and men who had experience of some kind of co-operation or negotiation in spousal (or adult sibling) relationships, were more likely to want to talk or to write about it. These contributors strongly condemned relationships where their chosen level of co-operation did not exist.

Some tentative conclusions can be suggested, based on the sheer variety of responses. In the first place, the smaller the family income, the more likely the woman was to control it. Secondly, this control could be a great advantage to her if she were handed an unopened pay packet, or knew how much her husband earned or was paid for livestock, but it could be a nightmare if she was kept to a restricted housekeeping allowance, working in ignorance. Noreen L., whose own father was definitely the boss, writes: 'Women were mostly dependent on the husband's income', and a few lines later: 'The mother was the financial controller of the home'. There was no contradiction here. Being financial controller of the home meant finding and allocating money for everything that was needed, out of whatever the man of the house allowed her. At the end of the day, men could choose whether or not to support their families. Frank Q. commented:

> Somebody asked me one time how much was the Children's Allowance. 'I couldn't tell you', says I, 'I never saw it.' [laughs]

Frank made the decision that this money belonged to his wife, and signed over payment to her, but the choice was his to make. And he was well aware of the absurdity of the money being payable to him.

Thirdly, the man was no less the man of the house or the boss because he helped out in the house; such a role, because he chose it, could even extend his arena of power, as in the case of Delia R.'s father. Similarly, the man who did not lift a finger in the house might also be the kind of man who never lifted his voice, or his hand, either, like Eamon B.'s father. From the 1940s, however, this, or any, kind of aloof father was becoming less acceptable. Both Larry K.'s and Frank Q.'s disapproval of the men who distanced themselves from family concerns prefigure to a certain extent the 'ridicule' which Hugh Brody mentions as pertaining to the father of the family in a small rural community by the 1960s. The *Limerick Rural Survey* had already expressed concern about this phenomenon.[43] Predictably enough, Hannan found that most conflict between spouses was caused by men's insistence on 'traditional patterns of dominance'.[44] There were many ways a man could forgo dominance – keeping his exercise of breadwinner privileges to a minimum and allowing the wife to manage the money were the ways most appreciated by women; helping out in the house or with the children was also good, provided it did not involve a perpetuation of dominance by intrusion into the woman's area of authority.

Nuala O'Faoláin, in her recent autobiography, mentions that her mother always wanted her to get married and have children:

> 'I don't really care if you get a degree or not.' she wrote to me, 'I'd far rather see you with a husband and a few kids.' This – when her burning resentment showed that she felt as trapped as a slave, kept out in a suburb with children! But she blamed the person, my father, for that. Women did blame their husbands.[44]

Most of my contributors would have believed that O'Faoláin's mother was perfectly right to blame her unfaithful, tight-fisted and sometimes violent husband for the state her marriage was in. They would have contended that the life of a married woman who stayed at home was potentially satisfying, though never by any means easy, if the husband was hard-working, faithful, good-tempered, good with the children, and – very importantly – not mean with money. The fact that this 'generosity' came from a position of superior power was more or less accepted, though it was sometimes resented. Josephine E. explained single women's unwillingness to marry with a story about a good friend:

> she was in the Civil Service in Dublin, now she was getting on about 35 or 36 and she wasn't married, and her parents . . . would have liked if she was married. And she said, she'd go to a girl who had worked with her, going back five or six years, of an evening, and this girl would be maybe living in a flat, two or three children with her, and maybe waiting for her husband to come in with two or three pounds wages to get something to eat. She said, I couldn't do that. She said, if I don't get married to somebody that . . . we'd have a better life, she couldn't do it . . . And she'd rather stay the way she was.

Another friend of hers, a teacher born in 1939, never married because:

> she said, 'I'm too fond of *going*'. Now she's into the Legion [of Mary] work, and she's into a lot of these things, she smokes and she plays cards, she plays Bingo . . .

Marriage and motherhood certainly put an end to financial independence and to 'going' (independent movement and activity). In the years covered by this study, even the most favourable scenario – where the woman got an unopened pay packet into her hand, or controlled all the money on a small farm – while it gave the woman some power, also gave her a lot of responsibility and did not give her much comfort or independence of movement. The woman who was totally financially dependent could have a comfortable life if her husband allowed her plenty of money and dealt with all the bills uncomplainingly. At lower-middle class/working-class/medium-to-small farming level, however, few had this kind of leeway, and careful management of money was very important no matter what the arrangement was. Some level of physical and material comfort in the daily round, rather than power or responsibility, seems to have been what the women who set up house in the 1940s and 1950s, craved, though they saw personal financial power as a necessary prerequisite of this comfort. The next chapter will look at how this generation of women and of men, saw itself as one which was emerging into comfort, from the harsh domestic conditions (material and emotional) of 'the past'.

Conclusion

'ONE OF THE REAL *MNÁ NA hEIREANN'*: EXPERIENCE, MEMORY AND DISCOURSE

Did life get better or worse for Irish women of the house in the first four decades of independence? It got better, though a first glance at women in 1961 might not show this immediately. Family size remained large, which meant that the woman worn out with constant child-bearing (suffering a variety of chronic discomforts and disabilities, or just exhausted) was still on the scene at the end of the period. However, mothers' general health was improving from the early 1940s. The benefits of this development for mothers, potential mothers, fathers and children cannot be overestimated; its benefits for young and middle-aged single women, who would not be called upon as often to rear motherless families should not be ignored either. Infant mortality fell, which made motherhood less traumatic. The standard of housing, and therefore hygiene and comfort, improved in town and in country. The woman embarking on a life of keeping house in the late 1950s was more likely than ever before to be married rather than single, and moving into a house that she did not have to share with females her own age or even with older relatives. Whether her husband helped out in the house or not, allowed her to control the money or not, or was generous or mean with what he earned, seems to have depended upon personality and the dynamics of the relationship. However, many women at this stage seem to have been turning their faces against the kind of old-fashioned patriarchy that ruled with incontrovertible authority and kept aloof from house and children. Influential opinion was dismayed at this kind of paternal aloofness, although its ongoing support for the father as head of the household might well have legitimated such authoritarianism.

Rural electrification and aquafication were slow and only 12% of rural dwellings had an indoor water supply by 1960. Changes came about rapidly thereafter, but by the end of our period, the aspiration towards water and electricity was firmly established. These services vastly improved women's lives by cutting down on work, and certainly anybody whose pipes have frozen and whose electricity is cut off temporarily will appreciate how much work is saved by the turn of a tap, the flick of a switch and the insertion of a plug. Yet women without servants who lived in dwellings with one or both of these facilities still seem to have worked very hard, indeed ceaselessly, from morning to night, particularly if they had children. Serviced houses in towns and cities were often hard to heat, draughty and awkwardly designed. Flawed though they were, however, they were better than the one-room dwellings of the courts and tenements. Anybody who believes that moving to a two or three-bedroomed house with a garden 'elaborates' housework is not taking into account the amount of time and trouble saved by not having to stow away bedding or work around beds every day (the British working-class wives investigated by Margery Spring Rice in the 1930s mentioned a living-space 'full of beds' as a huge handicap in the daily round[1];) having a garden and a washing line, and by simply having room to turn around in, to say nothing of taps, sinks and toilets, even if there was only one tap and the toilet was in the yard. Moving away from familiar neighbours was a wrench, but what is less often appreciated is that in smaller cities and towns like Michael Hartnett's Newcastle West or Croistóir O'Flynn's Limerick, the neighbours would often be housed near each other so the separation would have been a lot less.[2] Besides, neighbourly proximity had its disadvantages as well as its advantages; women of the house in particular knew this.

As far as farming life was concerned, we know that the nuclear family without resident relatives was easier on the young woman of the house starting out. We do not know how hard it might have been on the older ex-woman of the house now gradually being exiled from the hub of family life – a woman who had knuckled under an older despot (however benevolent!) in her day and who was now deprived of that power in the latter part of her life. Government commissions and other influential authorities were proposing, by the 1950s, that farmers will their farms directly to their sons instead of their widows, so as to facilitate earlier marriage. This outright attack on women's economic power was welcomed by younger women, which reminds us that one woman's empowerment was another woman's disempowerment. The emigration of females her own age from the 1940s meant that the young woman of the house was left without able-bodied help in the women's work. This was not experienced as a deprivation by her – although we should not be surprised that 'isolation' came to be seen as a problem for rural women in the 1970s. It has become an article of historical faith that the single women who left the land were better off wherever they ended up, single or married, than they would have been 'at home', unpaid and apparently unappreciated. Migration and emigration, however, were often lonely and confusing, and marriage was not always a happy ending. Joseph Lee uses William Trevor's *Ballroom of Romance* to illustrate the lack of choices facing Irish women in Ireland, but there were plenty of lonely Bridies in Dublin, London, Huddersfield and Leeds, and no shortage of Bowser Egans to take lifelong advantage of that loneliness. John McGahern's hard-working Maggie Moran, whose loneliness in London causes her to make a disastrous marriage with the first shiftless charmer who pays her any attention, is as realistic a character as Trevor's Bridie.[3] And like Maggie, many emigrants remained prisoners of the values and expectations of their families in Ireland, without the everyday support and companionship that normally goes with such bonds.

In the 1920s and 1930s the working lives of urban women of the house differed a lot from those of farming women of the house, but by the 1950s the gap between them, as far as aspirations were concerned in any case, was closing.

These aspirations were water and electricity, a companionate marriage where the husband, if he did not help in the house would not, at least, be domineering or mean with money, and some small comforts like the occasional outing to a wedding, a 'social', a meeting, face-cream or an occasional visit to the hairdresser. There were twenty times more female hairdressers in Ireland in 1961 than there had been in 1926, despite falling population, and the major growth happened between 1946 and 1961.[4] By the 1950s, there was a huge increase in the number of advertisments for cosmetics and items of clothing (even small items like stockings, gloves and scarves) in daily and provincial newspapers, while editorial copy insisted on women's right (rather than duty) to pay constant attention to their appearance.

Self-selected personal testimony of the kind used in this study shows us how those who respond construct the past. No universal, general conclusions can be drawn from such evidence, which comes from people who not only have opinions on the subject, but go to the trouble of writing, stamping and sending an envelope, and often giving an interview. Such effort indicates a high level of commitment to the subject. Yet, themes recur in contributions from very different geographical, social and occupational backgrounds. Most of the contributors to this project came to adulthood from the late 1940s to the early 1960s and, with two exceptions, they all believed that their working lives were easier than those of women of the house in the previous generation. If some of them lamented the passing of pot-oven bread and flour-bag sheets, this was as far as their nostalgia went. These women who set up house from the late 1940s also worked ceaselessly and endured many hardships, but hardship was something they located in the lives of the women of the previous generation, rather than in their own lives. If they did see their own lives as particularly hard, as Josephine E. did, they saw this as atypical – something that should not have happened at that time. The following quotations are taken from letters that people *sat down and wrote*, in response to the very generally worded newspaper appeal (see Appendix 1, and Bibliography for details about contributors):

> My recollections of Mother were she was always at home cooking . . . Mother's life revolved around her home . . . She never went to a hairdresser despite living in town as she had nice hair and her own style to it.
>
> [Eileen K.]

> I was born in 1937 and my memories of the housewife is my mother and I was the eldest of eight . . . and my mother always said that a big family made for a lot of work and little leisure and as a lot of big families existed then all women had to work hard . . . I can't ever remember my mother going out at night as there was always a baby around.   [Maureen O'R.]

> At night she'd sit knitting or sewing, darning socks . . . She worked all her life . . . she died in 1966 a saint if ever there was one.   [Jack R.]

The Art Of Looking Lovely • • • • • • *By Delia Dixon*

BEAUTY for MOTHERS

Bathing babies, cooking meals and keeping house need not make you relinquish your claims to the loveliness that is your right.

THE fact that you have a house to look after and a family to cook and care for are no reasons why you should not make the most of yourself and look as young as your years.

WATCH YOUR HANDS

The chief characteristic of the well-groomed woman is a pair of smooth, soft hands and nicely manicured nails. Rough, red chapped hands betray, unsuitable cleansing methods, lack of general care and exposure to cold weather.

Of course, everybody sees your hands. Whether you are in the business world, lunching, playing cards or entertaining friends in your own home, hands are very much in evidence. The home woman and the busy business woman's are under constant observation. Therefore, it behoves all womankind to pay regular attention to the home care of the hands and nails, and to have a professional manicure when possible. But not all women can run to the beauty parlour when her hands and nails are in need of special

treatment. It is the daily home care of them that counts in the long run.

PROTECT NAILS

One of the most important things about hand culture is protecting the hands from dirt, cold exposure, and too much water which coarsens the skin and makes them old looking. Rubber gloves and cotton gloves may always be kept on hand, the rubber gloves to protect from too hot water, scouring soaps and powders, and the cotton gloves to keep the hands clean while dusting and putting the house in order.

It is not difficult for the busy housewife who does all her own housework and cooks for her family to wear gloves of some sort when preparing vegetables such as peeling potatoes, scraping carrots, paring fruit and dish-washing. This simple precaution will prevent staining the fingers and will protect the hands and nails from the harsh soaps, washing powders and the vegetable minerals which are hard to remove from fingers and nails.

Hard nails, brittle nails and soft finger nails need warm oil baths for several minutes at bedtime. A good nail oil, cream and hand lotion should find a place in every woman's bathroom and should be used regularly. A few manicure tools and a little time each day devoted to the home beauty care of the hands and nails will keep them well groomed, smooth and youthful looking, and will prevent that "hard-worked" look which so many mothers seem to accept as unavoidable.

IMPORTANCE OF COIFFURE

In any group, some types stand out among the rest. Why? Because they have achieved the "Art" of making the most of themselves.

For example, if your dress is not up-to-the-minute and you are not a walking fashion plate, there are several ways by which you can achieve that distinction which will make people exclaim "how charming and chic is Mrs. Blank, or what a striking looking woman is Mrs. So-and-So!"

Your coiffure, at least can be smart. If you are used to a simple coiffure for everyday wear or for business, a new arrangement of soft waves and curls will make you feel like a new woman.

The problem of how to make a thin, worn face seem fuller and more youthful, evidently troubles many people, so here are a few pointers

on solving this problem:

In the first place, a long face should not be allowed to become too thin, especially if the cheek bones are high.

Very often the first step towards improving such a face and neck is to build one's weight. Remember that one's face shows the loss of weight sooner than the figure. The health and lustre of the hair and the condition of the finger nails also register when one's system is not receiving proper nourishment.

The coiffure for a slender face should be rather flat on the crown of the head though it may be slightly waved with ringlets about the brow and on the cheeks.

Pimples, Rashes, Blotches Vanish before the Healing Action of this Skin Lotion

YOU can give such care to your skin and complexion and yet perhaps there are pimples, spots and blotches which resist all your efforts to remove them. Now get from your chemist a bottle of D.D.D. Prescription and apply a few drops of this amazing liquid healer to the blemishes.

D.D.D. penetrates to the deepest layers of the skin and its healing action begins at once. In a few hours the eruption has faded visibly and after a few applications of D.D.D. it disappears completely and permanently. A dab of D.D.D. on heat blotches and irritation spots will prevent pimples and keep your skin spotless. Get a bottle 1/6 and try it today.

17. 'Beauty for Mothers: the art of looking lovely by Delia Dixon.' From *Woman's Life: the Irish Home Weekly*, May 21, 1938. Many women seem to have read advice like this as entertainment rather than pressure, though it was not until after 1946 that the huge growth in the number of hairdressers took place throughout the country, and the ideal (not necessarily the reality) of the coiffed and cosmeticised woman of the house took almost universal hold.

My mother was never a night out of the house till she had to go into hospital. She never had a holiday and very few days at the seaside. I never knew her to go to a hairdresser and she never used make-up.

[Jimmy O'M.]

In spite of all this [three pages detailing work] my mother and those of her generation had a great attitude to life and were very good-humoured . . . She was one of the real 'Mná na hEireann.'   [Kathleen B.]

Mother worked herself to the bone for us . . . when I compare my lifestyle with Mamma's I'm afraid comparisons are odious!   [Lucy O.S.]

My mother was a widow from 1927 with eight children . . . and a mortgage payable to the then Congested Districts Board . . . She was a gutsy, capable woman – she needed to be . . . the nightmare of feeding and cleaning eight kids faced her . . . A huge difference between our life now and our mother's time.   [Tom K.]

It seems to me that the housewives of the period in question [from 1932] were very worthy ladies indeed, and were doing a very good job in 'keeping things rolling' without any trace of self-interest or introspection. Their sole interest was centred in the home and family, and my memories of them are ones of happiness and stability.   [Marian B.]

I was born in 1939. Only girl with two younger brothers. Life was hard . . . My parents were victims of an arranged marriage, as was the custom of the time . . . Looking back over the years I feel that women on the whole have a better deal now . . . Education is the key to everything and it teaches people to think for themselves.   [Noreen L.]

The amount of work involved in the running of the house was truly immense, despite the help of a nanny for the young children and of a maid in the early years [1920s]. The children were trained to help in the ordinary way . . . But the brunt of the work fell on my mother; thinking out ways of providing for food and clothing, schooling and medical expenses for 9 children was daunting.   [Michael E.]

[Detailing all the work of the farm women 1920s–50s.] So the women in the house in those days were super women.   [Carmel C.]

Only two dissenting notes were struck; one by Madge C. who (in an interview) envied her urban middle-class mother in 1930s Dublin for her leisured life compared with Madge's own life. The other was conveyed by Gretta M., a solicitor's daughter from Cork born in 1952, who wrote of her mother's generation:

I honestly think that these women [wives of professionals with families of at least five children each] had a privileged existence, without any pressure, and did not know what the word meant!

She summarises in her letter the kind of work her mother would do; 'gardening, cooking with plenty of help as well to mind the children'. She is referring, it is true, to a later generation than the contributions cited above, but upper-middle class women in the 1930s would have had if anything a more leisured life than those twenty years later, contending with a servant shortage. Yet Michael E. remembers his mother's life, in the 1920s and 1930s, as very hard despite the fact that she had a nanny and a maid. Michael entered the priesthood; would he remember his mother's work as having been easier had he married and reared a family on a low white-collar income, without servants, in the 1950s? Gretta M. is a busy professional; is she lamenting the more leisured life of women in the 1950s who did not feel obliged to juggle motherhood and career? To say that her letter sounds like the plaint of the overworked modern mother-with-career is not to dismiss it as untrue. It is every bit as true as the narratives of heroism and hardship of which a flavour is given in the quotations, above; like them, it tells us as much about the storyteller as it does about the story. Those who grew up in the servantless farming/lower-middle class and working class in the 1920s and 1930s and experienced the 'modernised' domestic working environment (and the modernised, more co-operative marriage?) of the 1950s and 1960s, obviously felt it to be so dramatically easier than what had gone before, that they looked back to their mothers' time with more than piety – with something between a shudder of revulsion and a sigh of pity. Yet Kathleen B.'s description of her mother as 'one of the real *Mná na hEireann*', in its use of a phrase common in the early 1990s implying a sense of triumph and celebration in the wake of Mary Robinson's election as president conveys admiration and sympathy for the women of 'the past' and a certain gentle rebuke of those who have appropriated, as she sees it, the title '*Mná na hEireann*'/women of Ireland, today.

'VERY SELDOM THAT TIME I WASN'T THERE': GETTING OUT OF THE HOUSE

A remembered characteristic of the life of women of the house from the start of the period to its end is their confinement to the house and its environs. What do people mean when they say that they or their mothers 'never went out'? Assuming a good husband or other relative who minded the children or did what needed to be done to let the woman out, where would she have gone? Institutionalised entertainment was not as common then as it has since become; much social life, particularly in the country, centred around the house in any case, with house dances, rambling houses, stations and wakes. Married women might not have gone to these occasions in other peoples' houses, but they would occasionally have hosted them. Women did not usually go to the public house (if they occasionally did, like Mary Ellen D.'s mother, they were careful to go into the snug); going to the pictures involved a trip to town, and organisations like the Gaelic League or the Irish Countrywomen's Association or Muintir na Tire were not organised in every parish or townland. Being, as a rule, outside the paid workforce, women of the house did not have trade union meetings, for example.

Yet even women who were, by the standards of the day, involved in 'public life' were described by their offspring as totally identified with the house. Eamonn B.'s mother, for example, ran a grocery shop and depended for her business upon dealings not only with local people, but with commercial travellers and suppliers. She would go out occasionally to a concert or a play, particularly one on an Irish theme as she was passionately devoted to nationalism, cultural and political, and she also went to Gaelic League meetings and céilís with Eamonn's father:

> She was attracted to all things Gaelic and Irish, the Gaelic games, the culture, ceilidhe music and everything that pertained to Ireland as a nation. So if I told you that she was getting the odd postcard from fellows who were interned in Tintown internment camp during the war, and I still have some of the post-cards, handmade, that some of the lads sent her, you'll know the kind of woman she was.

He went on to say:

> And really her life revolved – we discussed here, my wife and myself – mostly around her own family; her total horizon ended once she went outside her family group . . . she WAS the house really.

This was quite a high level of political and cultural commitment, for a man or a woman, yet this woman's son sees her as having been synonymous with the house. Other respondents had a view of the lives of their mothers as particularly narrow and circumscribed. However, inquiry on apparently unrelated topics such as relationships with neighbours/relatives, and strategies for getting work done reveals that daily working life often brought women outside the actual house and into contact with others. T.J. McD. writes about his mother, for example:

- – Entertainment by modern thinking, nil.
- – No radio, no TV.
- – Gramophone, wind-up type, played now and again all 78 records. It was kept in the parlour.
- – She used to visit relatives, one visit to 3 or 4 houses each year, in winter or spring – no time in summer or autumn – walk there and back two miles . . . Usually on a moonlit night. Visits would be returned on a somewhat similar scale.

So if this woman visited three or four times in the winter and spring, and was visited three or four times in that period, then she had between six and eight

"Oh Joe, me nylons!"

18. Cartoon: 'Oh Joe, me nylons!'. *Dublin Opinion*, May 1950. Charles E. Kelly is, as usual, getting enjoyment out of the disjuncture between image and reality in the lives of women of the house. Is there also a certain element of derision here, of countrywomen and women generally, for presuming to like nice clothes? Or is the criticism levelled at the hard farm work women had to do, which prevented their looking nice? Many women, on and off farms, would have concurred heartily.

'social occasions' every winter and spring. It wasn't 'going out' in the sense of getting dressed up and going to a public place like a hotel, a restaurant or even a parish hall for a 'social', but it was still contact and diversion. In the summer and autumn this particular woman would be working hard herself and supervising workmen (she was a young widow), and in daily contact with as great a number of people as if she were working for wages outside the house, with the difference that she was the one paying the wages and setting the pace of work. This was not true of all rural or farm women; Jane S., on a big farm in Cavan, for example, only 'got out' once in the first twenty years of her marriage – her husband took her to a football match in Cavan when they hadn't been married very long. Her contemporary, Madge C.'s mother, might as well have been on another planet; she dressed up and went out regularly with her husband, to the theatre, cinema or dances and had regular breaks away in London. It is tempting to see the Dublin middle-class scene in the 1930s as representing the values and aspirations that would extend to all classes all over the country twenty or thirty years later, and certainly, as far as household services and appliances were concerned, this was true. But women keeping house in town or in country as late as the 1960s could be quite restricted and confined, through no fault of their husbands or their own. 'Very seldom that time I wasn't there', as Josephine E. said with a laugh, when I asked her if her husband would undertake household tasks in her absence. Margaret Q., whose very cooperative husband worked long hours, remembers her brother-in-law asking her in 1966, when she had last been out of the house: 'I said, "I was at Mass Sunday". This was Friday.' However, what is as significant as the fact that she had not got out for five days, is the fact that her brother-in-law, a priest, asked her this question in the first place, and was so shocked by her answer that he enouraged her to join the Irish Countrywomen's Association. A generation later, 'we only got out to the ICA' would be a complaint about a restricted and circumscribed social life,[5] but as late as the 1960s ICA membership represented a significant level of activity outside the house.

Two historians who use oral evidence and personal testimony to discuss women, paid work and/or household work in Britain in this period remark that their contributors seemed often not to have thought, until asked in the project, about themselves in relation to the past.[6] What struck me about the contributions to this project was the assured and well-rehearsed note in all of the written and oral testimonies, the flow of the narrative, the certainty about the meaning of change and the confident historical voice. The stories were packed and ready to go. This does not make them any more or less valuable or 'true' than the stories recovered by Summerfield or Giles, but it does indicate that stories of women's work in the past are a tremendously important component of identity for some people. As well as this, nearly 90% of the people who answered my appeal came from struggling backgrounds, urban and rural, where there was no regular paid domestic help, where money was always short and eked out by a hundred strategies. The pride and the desire to make such work known must not exist to the same extent among people in more comfortable circumstances, or more of them would have responded to my appeal. It seems that the actual performance of work, even when it is unpaid and formally unrecognised, can give people a strong sense of identity and pride, and that this can be transmitted to those observing and helping them – children, for example. Joanna Bourke concludes that women's movement into full-time housework in the years 1890 to 1914 was 'a sensible strategy for reducing the risk of poverty and for maximising possible control over their own lives and the lives of their families'. However, her suggestion elsewhere that employment opportunities were narrowing in any case, implies that women had little choice about their increased devotion to housework and makes her use of the word 'strategy' problematic.[7] But did a later generation have that choice, and can the significant movement of adult females away from gainful employment and into 'home duties' between 1926 and 1961 be described as a strategy? I do not think it can. If the first stage in the rising importance of housework happened between 1890 and 1914, then the second stage must have been from the 1940s, with the coming of electricity and water to dwellings, or the growing aspiration to these facilities. Demographically, what happened was not a clear-cut process whereby domestic service and familial (though formally gainful) agricultural work were rejected by women in favour of the job of woman of the house – those who might have become domestic servants found service work in towns and cities, or emigrated; those who might have been assisting relatives stayed on at school and

The Fire on the Hearth

By E. Estyn Evans, M.A., D.Sc., F.S.A., M.R.I.A.
Professor of Geography, Queen's University, Belfast

Author of : *France, A Geographical Introduction ; Irish Heritage,*
etc.

THE fuel difficulties of recent years have brought home to Irish people the practical importance of the fire that burns on the hearth. But always the fire has been something more than a means of cooking and warming the house. Man's oldest ally in the subjugation of his environment, it has been, through countless ages, the very centre and focus of his home, the place around which the work, thought and tradition of the family revolve. In other cultures the fire has now lost its visual and spiritual significance and has been relegated to a position of less importance in the fittings of the house. Not so in Ireland. It is partly no doubt a response to climate, a defence against rain and constant high humidity,

Centre and focus of the home

19. The Fire on the Hearth. From *Muintir na Tire Official Handbook* 1947. For Dr. Estyn Evans, the open fire was distinctive to Ireland and interesting from a socio–cultural point of view. About half of all Irish households were still cooking on the fire at the time this article was written, but it was already being located firmly in the past in women's media, and would come rapidly to be associated with the back-breaking toil and self-sacrifice of an older generation.

qualified for the Civil Service or got into teacher training and migrated or emigrated. Some ended up as women of the house, at home or abroad; some did not. However, the proportionate increase in the numbers of women engaged in home duties need not necessarily represent a step backwards for Irish women in general as far as power and control over their lives are concerned. The job of woman of the house offered, increasingly over this period, more power and crucially, more comfort than the life of a domestic servant or assisting relative would have. These women were still embarking on relentlessly hard working lives (whether houses were electrified and supplied with piped water or not), constant child-bearing, and a child-rearing period that could last thirty years. Given these facts, the relative unavailability of paid work for married women and ongoing change in agriculture which reduced the demand for labour on farms, we cannot say that control of the house was a 'strategy' women adopted to maximise their power. However, because the alternatives to marriage were clearly marked out from, roughly, the 1940s – emigration, migration, comparatively well-paid jobs for single women – we can suggest that women who embarked on a life of keeping house for husbands and having children from this time onward had more bargaining power than ever before.

MISSED OPPORTUNITIES OR DISASTERS AVERTED? WOMEN OF THE HOUSE AND THE STATE

As far as the public dimension of the lives of women of the house was concerned, the forty years in question can be seen as a series of missed opportunities for the state to make life easier for them and to recognise them in any meaningful manner. The well documented attacks on women's citizenship and employment in the 1920s and 1930s need not be gone into again, though it should be noted that the census occupational tables show clearly that outside the big cities, marriage bars had a definite effect on married women's white-collar work after the 1920s. There were other, smaller marginalisations of women – the failure of Eamon de Valera, for example, to appoint even one woman to his very commendable dower-house committee in 1943, and the failure of that committee to solicit information from female rural dwellers or even an organisation like the ICA. There was also the outright unwillingness of the voice of progressive Catholic thought of the 1940s the Commission on Vocational Organisation – to engage with the idea of permanent public representation for women of the house, an unwillingness so great that it led to hostility and obstruction in the evidence session, and confusion and contradiction in the published report. Then there were the two feminist/quasi-feminist ships that passed each other in the night – the Dáil deputies who supported paying children's allowances to mothers, and the feminists of the day who had no effective opinion on this crucial issue. In fact, Irish feminists' failure to organise on the children's allowance question underlines their upper-middle class base and shows how sadly out of touch they were with the concerns of the majority of women. The

Fianna Fáil government which introduced children's allowances could have presented this benefit, payable to mothers, as fulfilment of the promise implicit in the 1937 Constitution. They did not do so, because it was considered more important to placate the working man (and to get the support of the Labour parties and labour movement) by supplementing his wages and supporting his authority than it was to recognise mothers' work.

Neither the ill-fated Mother and Child Bill of 1950–51 nor its luckier successor were drawn up with any cooperation from women, either as mothers, doctors or midwives. Furthermore, many women seem to have been unaware of this controversy, and its application to them, while it was going on. Even Máire Mullarney, who was very socially aware and who was, moreover, a nurse before she married in the late 1940s and well-read in theology, confesses that the Mother and Child debate passed her by at a time when she was expecting her third child. Mothers' health was not a matter for public debate. As late as 1956, majority opinion refused to engage with the overwhelming difficulties associated with the bearing and rearing of large numbers of children by mothers in poor circumstances. It is this dismissal of clear evidence of mothers' preventible ill-health and hardship which is the most shameful aspect of attitudes to women in these years, arguably worse than marriage bars, Constitutional recommendations about motherhood or even payment of children's allowances to fathers.

As far as women's household work was concerned, policy-makers and official opinion inhabited a different world from the one inhabited by the majority of Irish people, male and female. Two government commissions in the 1950s failed completely to understand that the two-tier system of household organisation long familiar to the upper-middle classes – the mistress/maid relationship – was lost and gone forever. It is true that the print media of the day in its working and recreational 'advice' to women never addressed the experience of rural, farming women and understood little about the day-to-day working life of women of the house without servants, urban or rural. But if this media is 'read' as primarily escapist and recreational in function, rather than advisory – as I think it must be – then such omissions are not very serious.

But if we notice missed opportunities, we must also acknowledge the many disasters averted. These are harder to enumerate because, like women's household work, they are invisible. Not only did women manage to hold onto political equality and the right to earn income, but they retained equality in education at all levels, equal access to the learned professions and equal freedom of movement, in a Europe where such rights were by no means universal or taken for granted where they existed. There were no compulsory domestic science courses; there were no bars on female emigration or migration. And, very importantly for the future development of feminist activism in Ireland, Protestant and Catholic women got together and stayed together in women's organisations throughout the period. The fastest growing and most widely distributed women's organisation of all, the Irish Countrywomen's Association, had always had a mixture of Catholic and Protestant women. Women of all persuasions came together in the Joint Committee of Women's Societies and

Social Workers and the Irish Housewives Association. Louie Bennett was a high-profile Protestant and feminist convert to vocationalism, but vocationalism as exemplified by the Commission on Vocational Organisation did not manage to get women's movements as allies – the ICA was quite wary, despite having one of its members on the Commission. No strong Catholic women's organisation developed. Such an organisation might have posed formidable opposition to the IHA, for example, and eventually to the feminist organisations of the early 1970s. The years from 1939 might have encompassed several missed opportunities for Irish women and Irish feminism, but these were also the years when the state – exemplified by the government of the day – and the Catholic church – exemplified by its most modern and progressive tendency, vocationalism – failed to get representatives of women of the house on their side.

What would have happened had the government paid children's allowances to the mother, in explicit fulfilment of the Constitution, and intervened in farm family relationships with the full cooperation of farm women? What would have happened had the Commission on Vocational Organisation acquiesced fully in the demands of the ICA and the Joint Committee and given 'countrywomen' and 'home-makers' full representation on the National Vocational Assembly, a body that was in turn – to extend the fantasy further – actually set up? A golden age for women in general, and women of the house in particular, would probably not have ensued. Certainly, having children's allowances paid directly to them would have been a good thing for mothers, but would it have been beneficial for Irish women's citizenship in the long run, had this very important benefit been linked with the synonymity of women and motherhood in the 1937 Constitution? Such a link would undoubtedly have been made to satisfy those who objected to this bypassing of paternal authority. Some of the demands put forward by representatives of 'home-makers' and 'countrywomen' – crèches for mothers who worked outside the house, consumer information, training in public life – would have been good, but what about some of their other suggestions? Compulsory domestic education for all females? An identification of women in the public sphere with matters to do with the house and family and little else? Supervision of poor mothers by rich mothers acting on a voluntary basis? Universal domestic service for women of the working and small-farming and labouring class so as to facilitate the professional and philanthropic activities of upper-middle-class women?[8] Governments and influential public opinion might have been wary of representatives of women of the house for anti-feminist and anti-socialist reasons, but their shying away from institutionalised idealisation and all its dangers cannot be lamented. Irish women in the years 1923–61 had several lucky escapes from coercive, state-imposed domesticity. The fact that the women's media of the day, concerned as it was with appearance and consumerism, was out of touch with the realities of women's lives, also worked to women's long-term advantage by not propagandising anything like Betty Friedan's 'feminine mystique' in the 1940s and 1950s. In Irish-produced media at least, Irish women were not subjected to psychological and pseudo-scientific reinforcement of the idealisation of motherhood.

LAST WORD

There are many published images of women of the house in Ireland from the 1920s to the 1950s – in Dáil debates; government commissions; articles in learned journals; advertisments; newspapers and magazines; the few advice books that existed; in the fiction of Maura Laverty, Mary Lavin, Francis MacManus and many others; the journalism of John D. Sheridan and the cartoons of Charles E. Kelly. Research into actual experiences shows how important it is not to take any one of these images as representative of all; there is no single prototype of the woman of the house at any point in this period. All through these forty years, in every kind of household economy, there was not just the farming/non-farming difference, there were also the variations according to occupation, income level, marital status, size of family and personality. As well as this, the relationship of paid workers, male and female, to this world of maintenance and nurturing influenced their experience of (paid) work. The difference between the artisans who kept four-fifths of their wages for themselves, handing over only a fifth to their wives for housekeeping, and others like Larry K. or Frank Q. who handed over pay packets intact to their wives, is as great as the difference between aristocracy and labour. The man who came home from a long day's work to help with the dishes and put the children to bed had a working day which continued long after that of the man who went to the pub for the evening. Nor must we forget women in the paid workforce. The factory or office worker living at home whose mother's cooking, washing and ironing facilitated her daughter's working day, was privileged compared to, say, the unmarried shop assistant supporting an elderly parent who had to do housework and shopping on top of long and exhausting hours, the married hotel worker who had to fit in all of this and make childcare arrangements as well or the dressmaker or shopkeeper fitting her work around the dinner or the child or the clothes drying on the line.

Maintaining the house and its inhabitants was a job that impinged on and related to the paid work of everybody who lived outside of an institution; those in charge of it seem, moreover, to have made a long-lasting and indelible impression on their in-house audiences. Their sphere of influence was wider than this; what we now believe to have been the experience of women of the house in post-independence Ireland still influences our hopes, fears and aspirations for women's lives as we approach the millenium, just as the narratives of hardship and heroism drove many of the social and demographic changes and reforms up to the 1980s. The historian can never find out what life was 'really like', particularly for a group like this who were by definition diverse, but can try to move the discussion beyond simplification and myth. The women whose 'duties' made and re-made daily life over several generations deserve to be seen in all their complexity. Few groups have ever been in such thrall to what E.P. Thompson called 'the enormous condescension of posterity'.[9]

Personal Testimony and Oral Evidence: A Note on Methodology

Personal testimony must, like all historical sources, be treated with care. Testimony from a self-selected group must be treated with additional caution. My reasons for opting for a self-selected group, i.e. people who responded to an appeal in national and provincial newspapers countrywide[1] were mainly practical. On limited resources of time and money, I had not the wherewithal to select a random sample from the population. Besides, had I done so, I would have then have had to approach people and perhaps force questions on reluctant interviewees. This I would not have liked to do. In the end, there was an unforeseen advantage in sending out an appeal – seeing who responded was in itself a valuable piece of research.[2] Though I responded to each and every letter, I did not interview everybody: some people were quite happy to provide written testimony and to leave it at that, others filled in questionnaires that I devised and sent them back in stamped addressed envelopes. Because I was using the personal testimony in a corroborative rather than originative way, i.e. because the questions I was asking were set for me by other primary and secondary sources, this was sufficient for my purpose. My only regret is a personal one, that I did not get to meet all the very interesting people who contacted me.

Interviews, except in one case, were always taped with a small cassette recorder and transcribed as soon as possible afterwards. The average length of interview was an hour and a half, as I did not want to overstay my welcome or overextend the endurance of the contributors. I approached the interviews, with some very broad and some very specific questions. In my 'conduct' of the interviews, I was heavily influenced by Luisa Passerini in that I asked the pre-set questions, but also some open–ended ones.[3] I never stopped anyone from talking and found silences and elisions as significant as what was said. Nor did I usually stop people from apparently digressing or going 'off track' since we were having a conversation, usually a very enjoyable one, and it was interesting to see where a conversation about women's household work could lead – in effect, anywhere! Besides, because quantification of the personal testimony responses would make little sense in a self-selected group, it did not matter whether everyone answered the same questions or not. For most contributors it was an opportunity to tell their life stories.

This is not to say that such life stories were called into being for the first time by my newspaper appeal, or by my questions in the interview or questionnaire. Some historians mention the problem of 'composure' in the taking of personal testimony, by which they mean both the contributor's composition of a 'self' for the interviewer, and the contributor's demeanour throughout the encounter.[4] Not only were all my contributors entirely at ease in conversation with me and/or with the process of writing (judging by the flow of their accounts), but I also had the strong impression that I was gaining access to a narrative that was in existence for a long time – that the discussion of women's household and farm work, particularly in relation to the two issues of comfort and male domination, were of long standing. Several contributors used fictional examples or quoted journalists, writers and broadcasters to emphasise points they made – John B. Keane, John D. Sheridan, Gay Byrne, the TV adaptation of William Trevor's short story 'The Ballroom of Romance' and Alice Taylor.[5] While Alice Taylor's books are quite recent, Gay Byrne's comments choric and ongoing, and Trevor's short story adapted for TV comparatively recently (sixteen years ago at the time of writing), John D. Sheridan's very funny weekly column for the *Irish Independent*, mainly a man's eye on the ups and downs of urban domestic life with some forays into rural life, was appearing since the 1940s, and John B. Keane's first play, 'Sive', was first staged to wide acclaim in Athlone in 1959. To ask if 'ordinary people' like my contributors got their opinions and perceptions from the print media, stage and wireless or vice versa, is to miss the point. The conversation about women's relationship to house, family and work has been going on for a long time, with many participants. What I was getting from the personal testimony was what Penny Summerfield calls 'the endless feedback loop between personal accounts and discourse'.[6]

This was not all I was getting, however. Quantification of the information from the contributors would not have made any sense in a self-selected sample, as people with strong personal opinions (or conversely, a consciously objective outlook due to an interest in history) are likely to have answered my appeal in the first place. So if all contributors were fulfilled by, or loathed, housework, for example, I would not and could not have extrapolated from this to all women of the house. The personal testimony was invaluable in other ways, however; first of all for the detail that it provided on material aspects of life in the past – house design, work methods, lighting fires, washing clothes (and reusing the water afterwards!), cooking and baking, infant feeding, recycling and resources. Secondly, it was useful for information about how people managed particular situations and relationships; general conclusions cannot be drawn from this, of course, but suggestions about strategies and resources can be made.[7] Thirdly, if a similar theme or opinion popped up, unsought by me, in testimony from people of widely different backgrounds, then I would, if possible, look for corroboration of this in published or other sources.[8] Personal testimony was also very useful for the insight it provided into people's ideas of what constituted the past. For many Irish people now in their sixties, seventies and eighties, the contemporary era was inaugurated not with television and the youth culture of the 1960s, but with running water, electricity, hospital births and hairdressers, and it happened any time from the mid-1940s. For this book, the historical past is any time up to 1961, but frustratingly, I was unable to get people to recreate as vividly or in as much detail the modernised farm or the urban serviced house before 1961, even though I had several contributors who had lived most of their lives in this setting.

In conclusion, I believe that oral evidence and personal testimony are extremely informative about Irish economic, social and cultural history, and that, as Raphael Samuel said, 'The sense of the past, at any given time, is quite as much a matter of history as what happened in it'.[9] This is all the more true when we are looking at a subject like women's relationship to household work, which has been in the public domain for all of this century, and still is today.

Original letter which solicited testimony and sample questionnaire

Department of History,
University College Galway
20 April 1995

LETTERS PAGE

Dear Editor,

I wonder if I could use the letters column of your newspaper to make a request. Right up to 1961, half, rising to two-thirds, of the Irish adult female population was listed in the census as 'engaged in home duties'. I am currently engaged in research towards a PhD thesis on women's work in household and family in independent Ireland 1922–61. It would be great to hear from anybody, married or single, in any walk of life and from any background, urban and rural, who either ran a house or was closely connected with somebody who ran a house – and that includes almost the entire population! (Men who have memories of wives/mothers/sisters running the house would be a great source of information too.) Your everyday memories of home life in the first four decades of independence are of crucial importance in hauling up this submerged 75% of our social history. No detail is insignificant, no experience unimportant. Old newspapers and magazines, government records and learned journals are vital sources of evidence but they cannot tell the full story – the living, breathing archive of human memory must round it out.

If you would like to participate in this project, I would be delighted to hear from you. I need hardly add that I will answer all letters.

Yours sincerely,

Caitriona Clear.

Sent to the *Irish Independent, Irish Press, Examiner, Clare Champion, Western People, Roscommon Herald, Connacht Tribune, Limerick Leader, Sligo Champion, Farmer's Journal, Kerryman, Leinster Leader, Anglo-Celt.*

RESEARCH QUESTIONNAIRE

In Original, 1 A4 Blank PP were provided per question, and larger print used. These were also more or less the questions asked in interviews.

Wording of the Questionnaire
First of all, could I have an idea of your date of birth and your occupation/ former occupation/the occupation of the 'head of the household' of the woman/women you are talking about (e.g. rough idea of size of farm, if applicable). Also size of family, boys, girls, etc.

(These and other details will all be treated with the utmost confidentiality, i.e. no identifying details about any informant will be included in the thesis and eventual publication.)

What was the work of the woman of the house, in your experience? (Mother, and/or wife/sister, between 1921 and 1961? Her daily routine, tasks she would have to carry out from time to time etc.)

Who made the decisions in the family, about e.g. spending of money, children's destinies e.g. work, education, etc? Who controlled the money in the house?

Did the men ever do any of the housework and/or childcare i.e. would they ever have washed dishes, cooked, looked after babies etc?

When the babies were born, was there a midwife, a local handywoman, a doctor or, as in some parts of the country, the woman's female relatives to help out? Or did the women go in to the local hospital? Can you remember if the babies were breastfed?

What did the woman of the house, do for entertainment and relaxation (if anything)?

Were the other women in the locality important as friends, to help out, share work etc? Were they in and out of one another's houses all the time, or did they keep a distance from one another, or was it somewhere in between?

Did the woman of the house read newspapers, listen to the wireless (if any), take an interest in politics, local or national? Would there have been magazines coming into the house, if so, what sort e.g. the *Messenger*, the *Far East*, or any other magazines.

Can you remember if the introduction of Childrens' Allowances in 1944 made any great difference to the family economy?

Table 1: *Married Women in Main Occupations expressed as percentage of Total Females in that Category, County by County and Major Cities, Saorstat Éireann/Ireland 1926, 1946 and 1961*

	Saorstat Éireann/Ireland				Carlow		
	1926	1946	1961		1926	1946	1961
FGO	6	6	5		7	4	8
FRS	8.4	6.5	9		4	5	7
IND	5.4	6.5	7.6		11	9	12
WC	12	3.5	3.6		9	3	2
PROF	12.6	12.5	12.3		13	13	11.5
SERV	4	5	5.4		4.7	5	4.5
SA	3.2	–	4		4.7	3	6
SK	24.7	–	29		30.8	17	26

	Dublin/Dunlaoghaire				Co. Dublin		
	1926	1946	1961		1926	1946	1961
FGO	4	4	8		5	4	9.7
FRS	–	–	–		6	6	8.2
IND	5	7	7.7		6	6.5	8.9
WC	2	1.9	5.1		13	2.8	7.7
PROF	5	3	8.7		5	7	13.3
SERV	3	6	19		4	2	8.6
SA	2.2	3	5.6		2.6	3.5	6.7
SK	27	13	27		27	17	33.8

	Dublin City				Kildare		
	1926	1946	1961		1926	1946	1961
FGO	5	4	5		7	3.6	8
FRS	–	–	–		6	7	8
IND	5	4.6	7		8	4	6.6
WC	2.9	1.9	3		17	5	1.7
PROF	4	5.6	8		10	9	11.7
SERV	6	5.5	12.5		4.6	5	8.4
SA	2	7.9	4.5		5.2	2	3
SK	26	22	27		24	22	27.5

fgo = females gainfully occupied: frs = agricultural occupations: Ind = industrial incl. textile/making-up: wc = white-collar/office/clerk/telephonists etc: Prof = professional, incl. teachers: serv = domestic and in 1961, hotel/institutional service: sa = shop assistant/barmaid: sk = shopkeeper, hotel/restaurant keeper, publican

	Kilkenny				Laois		
	1926	*1946*	*1961*		*1926*	*1946*	*1961*
FGO	6	4.6	8.4		6	4	7.8
FRS	3	4	7.6		3	5	8.5
IND	15	13	7.4		14	6	2.3
WC	20	4	2		19	4	2
PROF	14	15	13		17	13	10
SERV	3.9	5.5	5.3		4.4	5	5.5
SA	5.3	6	3.3		5.7	3	3.2
SK	19	17	30.7		22.7	15	33.4

	Longford				Louth		
	1926	*1946*	*1961*		*1926*	*1946*	*1961*
FGO	7	4.8	8.7		6	4.8	9.8
FRS	7	6	8.5		7	6	4.5
IND	18	16	6.3		9	8	12
WC	12	6	3.5		19	4	4
PROF	11	21	14.8		9	8	8
SERV	4	3.5	5.3		2.4	4	12
SA	4.2	2	5.6		3	1	4.4
SK	25	13	25		22.6	20	27

	Meath				Offaly		
	1926	*1946*	*1961*		*1926*	*1946*	*1961*
FGO	5.5	4.5	8.6		7.6	5.4	10.6
FRS	5	6	9.5		5.5	4	6.6
IND	10.9	9	9		19	8	14
WC	16	6	5		13	8	3
PROF	16	22	17.5		14	14	17.5
SERV	2.6	3	5.7		4	5	7.7
SA	1.5	2	1.8		6.8	4	4.7
SK	17.5	24	27.6		20	20	32.5

	Westmeath				Wexford		
	1926	*1946*	*1961*		*1926*	*1946*	*1961*
FGO	6	4	7.6		6.9	4.7	7.9
FRS	4	4	5.8		4.8	5.5	8.2
IND	10	7	6.5		12	11.5	5.7
WC	15	2	2		18	9	2.6
PROF	15	15	14		11	12	11
SERV	2.6	3	4.6		5	4	5.7
SA	2	2	3		5	3.8	4.5
SK	16	23	29		25	25	30.8

	Wicklow				Clare		
	1926	1946	1961		1926	1946	1961
FGO	7	5.5	9.3		7	4.7	9
FRS	6	8	8		2	4	9
IND	9	5	5.2		19	12	6.8
WC	17	4	5.3		20	8	3.6
PROF	14	15	15.8		19	24	16
SERV	4.8	7	9.5		5	5	8.6
SA	2	3	4.3		4.5	8	2.6
SK	21	23	30		28	35	22

	Cork City				County Cork		
	1926	1946	1961		1926	1946	1961
FGO	7.9	5.8	7.3		6	4.7	8.4
FRS	–	–	–		6	5	6.7
IND	6	5	4.4		13	12	7.2
WC	9	1	2		18	4	3
PROF	7	5	5		12	15	12.3
SERV	4	7.5	13.3		9	4.5	5.4
SA	2	0.1	2.4		2.3	3	3
SK	29	14	37.7		22	24.5	30

	Kerry				Limerick City		
	1926	1946	1961		1926	1946	1961
FGO	7	4.7	9.7		9	5.2	7.6
FRS	7.5	5	5.5		–	–	–
IND	10	8	6.3		12	6	5.7
WC	16	9	6		11	3	3
PROF	23.5	20.5	16.3		3	6	9.6
SERV	2.5	5	6.5		4.8	6	8.4
SA	6	8	6		2	2	3
SK	23	23	30.8		33	28	33.6

	County Limerick				Tipperary North		
	1926	1946	1961		1926	1946	1961
FGO	6	4.5	8.9		6	4.9	8.4
FRS	5	6	6.6		4.5	3.5	6.4
IND	12	8	5.7		15	14	6.7
WC	23	7	3.2		15	3	2.5
PROF	17	19	16.7		14	16	13.5
SERV	3	4	4.7		3.5	5	7
SA	5	6	4.5		3	7	2.6
SK	21	23	29.8		28	29	29.8

	Tipperary South				Waterford City		
	1926	*1946*	*1961*		*1926*	*1946*	*1961*
FGO	7	5.5	10		8	4.8	7.8
FRS	4	4	8.6		–	–	–
IND	18	15	11.4		12	4	7.6
WC	22	5.5	3.7		4	9	3.6
PROF	13	14.5	10.8		4	14	7.1
SERV	4.7	6	8.2		3.4	5	10.4
SA	5.5	8	6		3.4	3	3.4
SK	19.4	26	30.5		19.4	24.5	26.8

	County Waterford				Galway		
	1926	*1946*	*1961*		*1926*	*1946*	*1961*
FGO	7	4.8	8.8		7	5	9
FRS	5.5	7.5	8		6	8	8.5
IND	10	9	2		11	9	5.2
WC	16	9	5.4		15	6	3.1
PROF	13	14	13		11	14.5	12.3
SERV	4.2	5	5.7		4.2	5	8.3
SA	4.5	3	6.2		4.3	2	3.2
SK	22.7	21	27.4		24	25	26

	Leitrim				Mayo		
	1926	*1946*	*1961*		*1926*	*1946*	*1961*
FGO	7	4.3	11		9	8	10.8
FRS	9.8	4	8.4		9.8	19	11
IND	6.8	16	7.3		9	10.5	6.7
WC	26	4	0.5		18	7	4
PROF	23	23	20		22	23	17
SERV	4	3.5	8		4.4	7	7.5
SA	2.2	2	3.6		8	3.5	2.6
SK	25.6	26.5	40		25.8	23	27

	Roscommon				Sligo		
	1926	*1946*	*1961*		*1926*	*1946*	*1961*
FGO	8.7	5	10.7		3.3	5	9.5
FRS	12	9	10.4		10	7	9.2
IND	9.8	10	7.3		6	8	3.5
WC	10.8	9	3.8		15	7	2.8
PROF	25.6	24	18.3		16	18	15.2
SERV	4	4	5.5		3.3	4	7.4
SA	2.7	3	1.7		3	3	3
SK	24.4	18	30		25.5	19	32

	Cavan				Donegal		
	1926	1946	1961		1926	1946	1961
FGO	6.4	4.6	9		1.6	7.4	10
FRS	6.2	4	6.7		8.5	10	8
IND	8	8	6		7	10	9.8
WC	13	4	4.2		18	9	3.7
PROF	28	26	23		16	24	21
SERV	2.5	3	3.8		1.8	5	5.3
SA	3.4	8	2		6.5	4	4
SK	18	26	28.5		22	24	31

	Monaghan		
	1926	1946	1961
FGO	6.7	5	10.7
FRS	9	5	9.6
IND	7	4	12.3
WC	18	7	4.5
PROF	12.6	17	15
SERV	2.8	4	7.3
SA	2.7	3	2.6
SK	27	22	35

Table 2: *Percentage of Adult Females who are Gainfully Occupied in Counties and Major Cities of Ireland, 1926, 1946 and 1961*

	1926	1946	1961		1926	1946	1961
Saorstat Éireann/				Cork City	33	34.8	36
Ireland	30.5	30.9	28.6	Co. Cork	29.6	28	24.9
Carlow	28.8	27.6	24.3	Kerry	28.7	26	21
4 Dub/D.L	37.7	38	34.9	Limerick city	32	31.3	30
Dublin City	34.9	39.2	39	Co. Limerick	30	27.5	23.3
Co. Dublin	31	34	29.7	Tipperary North	29.7	28.7	25.4
Kildare	27.9	26.5	25	Tipperary South	30.3	28.7	24.3
Kilkenny	30.7	28.2	24.6	Waterford City	32.5	30.5	32.4
Laois	27.9	26.3	24.3	Co. Waterford	30.5	27.7	25.3
Longford	27	26.5	22.3	Galway	29.6	28.5	24.7
Louth	29.4	32	34	Leitrim	26.5	26.7	22.4
Meath	26.6	27.8	26.6	Mayo	29.8	28.9	23.2
Offaly	29.5	29.9	26.4	Roscommon	26.9	27	21.5
Westmeath	28.2	8.8	25.9	Sligo	28	28	24.3
Wexford	31	27.9	24.4	Cavan	28	27.2	23.7
Wicklow	28.2	30	27.8	Donegal	31.2	30	24.4
Clare	27.5	26.6	22.2	Monaghan	31	9.5	26.5

Table 2 helps us to interpret Table 1 by letting us know if a comparatively high percentage of married women workers went hand-in-hand with high, low, or average female employment.

Notes

INTRODUCTION

1 Eavan Boland, 'What We Lost' in *Outside History* (Manchester, 1990), pp. 43–4.
2 See Chapter One.
3 J.J. Lee, *Ireland 1912–85: Politics and Society* (Cambridge, 1989), pp. 124–5, p. 193.
4 *Committee of Inquiry into Widows' and Orphans' Pensions* (1933), R.49/1; *Guide to the Social Services: A Summary Designed for the Information of Individuals and Groups* (Dublin, 1941), pp. 4–5. See also John Dunne, *Waiting the Verdict: Pensions or Pauperism: Necessitous Widows and Orphans in the Irish Free State* (n.d., c. 1928).
5 Ruth Barrington, *Health, Medicine and Politics in Ireland 1900–1970* (Dublin, 1987), pp. 113–66: *Reports of the Department of Local Government and Public Health 1925–47*, sections on Maternity and Child Welfare.
6 J.J. Lee, *Ireland*, pp. 277–85; *Guide to the Social Services* (Dublin, 1950, 1954).
7 Alan Shatter, *Family Law in Ireland* (Dublin, 1977), p. 13, 14, 242, 273, 274, *passim*.
8 Department of Local Government and Public Health/Department of Health, *National Nutrition Survey*, Parts I–VIII (1948), Compendium 1953, K.53/1–7; Central Statistics Office, *Household Budget Inquiry 1951–2* (Dublin, 1954).
9 Barrington, pp. 195–222; James Deeny, *To Cure and to Care: Memoirs of a Chief Medical Officer* (Dublin, 1989), *passim*, but particularly pp. 104–78; Noel Browne, *Against the Tide* (Dublin, 1986), pp. 141–55; Eamonn McKee, 'Church-State Relations and the Development of Irish Health Policy: the Mother and Child scheme 1944–53' *Irish Historical Studies* Vol. XXV, No. 98, (November 1986), pp. 159–94,
10 Mary Clancy, 'Aspects of Women's Contribution to Oireachtas Debate in Ireland 1922–37' in M. Luddy and C. Murphy (eds.) *Women Surviving: Studies in Irish Women's History in the 19th and 20th centuries* (Dublin, 1990), pp. 206–32; Mary E. Daly, *Industrial Development and Irish National Identity 1922–39* (Syracuse 1992), pp. 75–6, pp. 122–6, and 'Women in the Irish Free State 1922–1939: The Interaction between Economics and Ideology' in *Journal of Women's History* Vol. 6/7, Nos. 4/5, Winter 1994/Spring 1995, pp. 99–116. (Published in Ireland as J. Hoff and M. Coulter (eds.) *Irish Women's Voices: Past and Present* (1996).
11 For a full discussion see Chapters 2 and 3.
12 For a full discussion see Chapters 2 and 3.
13 For a full discussion see Chapters 2, 3 and 4.
14 M.K. Rosaldo, 'The Uses and Abuses of Anthropology' Signs: *Journal of Women in Culture and Society*, Vol. 5, No. 31 (1980) pp. 389–417.
15 Long a cliché in the Irish print media, the 'comely maidens' have gone across the water, as so many did in real life, e.g. John Lichfield, 'Ireland's Comely Maidens Are Doing It For Themselves' *Independent on Sunday* September 15 1996. See also Note 10, above, and Notes 17, 18, 19, 22, 23, 24, 26, 28, 29, 30, 31, below.
16 J.J. Lee, *Ireland*, p. 335.
17 Jenny Beale, *Women in Ireland: Voices of Change* (Dublin, 1986).
18 Catherine Rose, *The Female Experience: The Story of the Woman Movement in Ireland* (Dublin, 1975).

19 Amy Wieners, 'Rural Irishwomen, Their Changing Role, Status and Condition' *Eire-Ireland* Earrach-Spring 1994, pp. 76–91.

20 Deborah Simonton, *A History of European Women's Work: 1700 to the Present* (London, 1998), p. 214.

21 The founding texts of second wave or late twentieth-century feminism referred to here, are Simone de Beauvoir, *The Second Sex* (London, 1953), Betty Friedan, *The Feminine Mystique* (London, 1963), Germaine Greer, *The Female Eunuch* (London, 1970), Shulamith Firestone, *The Dialectic of Sex* (London, 1971).

22 Evelyn Mahon, 'Women's Rights and Catholicism in Ireland' *New Left Review* No. 166 (Nov–Dec 1978), pp. 53–78.

23 Beale, p. 140.

24 Maryann Valiulis has published extensively on this topic, see e.g. 'Defining Their Role in the New State: Irishwomen's Protest Against the Juries Act' *Canadian Journal of Irish Studies* Vol. 18, No. 1 (1992), pp. 43–60; 'Power, Gender and Identity in the Irish Free State' *Journal of Women's History* Vols. 6/7, Winter/Spring 1994–5, pp. 117–136; 'Neither Feminist Nor Flapper: The Ecclesiastical Construction of the Ideal Irish Woman' in M. O'Dowd and S. Wichert (eds.) *Chattel, Servant or Citizen: Women's Status in Church, State and Society* (Belfast, 1995), pp. 168–78.

25 This will be discussed in Chapters 2, 3 and 4.

26 'Power, Gender and Identity',p. 120.

27 The most comprehensive survey is in Gisela Bock and Pat Thane, (eds.) *Maternity and Gender Policies: Women and the Rise of European Welfare States* (London, 1991). Alice Kessler-Harris, 'Gender Ideology in Historical Reconstruction: A Case Study from the 1930s' in *Gender and History* Vol. 1, No. 1 (Spring, 1989), pp. 31–49, reminds us that some women, married and single, were among the most vociferous opponents of an unqualified 'right to work' for women. A rather unconvincing response to this article was made by Margaret Hobbs, 'Rethinking Antifeminism in the 1930s: Gender Crisis or Workplace Justice? A Response to Alice Kessler-Harris' in *Gender and History* Vol. 5, No. 1 (Spring, 1993), pp. 4–15, and Kessler-Harris's 'Response' in the same volume, pp. 16–19.

28 Catherine Rose, *passim*.

29 Regina Sexton, *A Little History of Irish Food* (Dublin, 1998), pp. 29–30.

30 Mary O'Dowd and Maryann Valiulis (eds.) *Women and Irish History* (Dublin, 1997), Introduction, p. 13.

31 Frances Gardiner, 'The Unfinished Revolution' *Canadian Journal of Irish Studies* Vol. 18, No. 1 (1992), pp. 15–39, pp. 19–20.

32 The classic accounts of the Irish suffrage movement are Margaret Ward, *Unmanageable Revolutionaries* (Dingle, London, 1983) and Rosemary Cullen Owens, *Smashing Times* (Dublin, 1984), also Cliona Murphy *The Irishwomen's Suffrage Movement and Irish Society in the Early Twentieth Century* (Brighton, 1988).

33 Bock and Thane; Martin Pugh, *Women and the Women's Movement in Britain 1919–1959* (London, 1992); Seth Koven and Sonya Michel (eds.) *Mothers of a New World: Maternalist Politics and the Rise of Welfare States* (London, 1993), and Mary Clancy, 'Women's Contribution to Oireachtas Debate', also her thesis, 'Women's Contribution to Public Political Debate 1922–37' MA, University College Galway, 1988. See also Mary McGinty, 'A Study of the Campaign for and against the Enactment of the 1937 Constitution' MA University College Galway 1978, pp. 279–303.

34 James Deeny, pp. 104–78; Correspondence between Central Midwives Board and Department of Health 16/5/49 to 8/3/50, N A S 12117, A, B.

35 Yvonne Scannell, 'The Constitution and the Role of Women' in Brian Farrell (ed.) *De Valera's Constitution and Ours* (Dublin, 1988), pp. 123–36.

36 Mary Daly, 'Women in the Irish Free State', p. 112.

37 Conversation with the late Professor T.P. O'Neill, December 1987.

38 Professor Maxine Berg pointed out in response to a conference paper I gave, 'The Women Cannot Be Blamed: Women and the Commission for Vocational Organisation' May 15–17

1993, Queen's University, Belfast, that de Valera was not reading Pinchbeck correctly if this was the impression he had. I think it is noteworthy that he was reading Pinchbeck at all!

39 Pauric Travers, 'Emigration and Gender: The Case of Ireland 1922–1960' in M. O'Dowd and S. Wichert (eds.) *Chattel, Servant or Citizen*, pp. 187–99: Peter Moser, 'Rural Economy and Female Emigration in the West of Ireland 1936–1956' *UCG Women's Studies Review* No. 2, (1993), pp. 41–52.

40 J. Fentress and C. Wickham, *Social Memory: the Construction of the Past* (London, 1988).

41 For the best collection of articles on the theory and practice of oral history, see R. Perks and A. Thomson (eds.) *The Oral History Reader* (London, 1998). See also Appendix 1: A Note on Sources.

42 M. Boxer and J. Quataert, (eds.) *Connecting Spheres* (Oxford, 1987), Introduction.

43 A good general survey of European history in this period is John Merriman, *A History of Modern Europe Vol. 2* (New York, 1996), pp. 903–914.

44 Angela John, By the *Sweat of Their Brow: Women at Victorian Coalmines* (Oxford, 1984); Mary Lynn Stewart, *Women Work and the French State 1880–1939* (Montreal, 1989).

45 It was Koven and Michel who coined the term maternalism, initially in 'Womanly Duties: Maternalist Politics and the Origins of Welfare States in France, Germany, Great Britain and the United States 1880–1920' *American Historical Review* 95 (1990), pp. 1076–1108. Those who tend towards the belief that interest in mothers was oppressive both in intent and in effect are Jane Lewis, *The Politics of Motherhood: Child and Maternal Welfare in England 1900–1939* (London, 1980); Anna Davin, 'Imperialism and Motherhood' *History Workshop Journal* 5, 1978, pp. 9–67.

46 Deborah Dwork, *War Is Good For Babies and Young Children: A History of the Infant and Child Welfare Movement in England 1898–1918* (London, 1987) takes issue with Davin and Lewis on several points; V. Fildes, L. Marks and H. Marland (eds.) *Women and Children First: International Maternal and Infant Welfare 1870–1945* (London, 1992) while it does not ignore the coercive and racialist aspect of state interest in mothers' health, emphasises the benefits to health which might have accrued from this, as does Irvine Loudon, *Death in Childbirth: An International Study of Maternal Care and Infant Mortality 1800–1950* (Oxford, 1992).

47 The impact of advertising on women's household work in the last hundred years or so is more assumed than proven, with very few historical works on this topic. Excellent and useful writers on advertising content and trends in consumption are Ruth Schwarz Cowan, *More Work For Mother: The Ironies of Household Technology from the Open Hearth to the Microwave* (London, 1989), and Christina Hardyment, *From Mangle to Microwave: the Mechanisation of Household Work* (London, 1988), while Christine Zmrocek, 'Dirty Linen: Women, Class and Washing Machines 1920s–1960s' *Women's Studies International Forum* Vol. 15, No. 2, (1992), pp. 173–85, reconstructs women as active consumers rather than as victims of advertising. As far as magazines are concerned, Jennifer Scanlon, *Inarticulate Longings: The Ladies Home Journal, Gender and the Promises of Consumer Culture* (New York, 1995) suggests new ways of approaching women's reading, including advertisments. Hugh Oram, *The Advertising Book: A History of Advertising in Ireland* (Dublin, 1986) is very informative and entertaining on Irish advertising, and invaluable to the social historian.

48 Ruth Schwarz Cowan, *More Work For Mother*; Elizabeth Ross, *A Woman's Place: An Oral History of Working-Class Women 1890–1940* (Oxford, 1984); Ellen Ross, *Love and Toil: Motherhood in Outcast London* (London, 1993); Tessie P. Liu, 'Le Patrimoine Magique: Reassessing the Power of Women in Peasant Households in 19th Century France' *Gender and History* Vol. 6, No. 1 (April, 1994), pp. 13–36; Jan Lambertz, 'Marriage Relations, Money and Domestic Violence in Working-Class Liverpool 1919–1939' and Lynn Jamieson, 'Limited Resources and Limiting Conventions: Working-Class Mothers and Daughters in Urban Scotland 1890–1925' in Jane Lewis (ed.) *Labour and Love*. Olwen Hufton's magnificent *The Prospect Before Her: A History of women in Western Europe 1500–1800* (London, 1995), especially pp. 487–507, offers such new and exciting ways of looking at women's lived experience in history that it has been a major influence on this

work, despite the fact that it deals with the early modern period. Judy Giles, *Women, Identity and Private Life in Britain 1900–1950* (London, 1995) also offers some fresh ways of approaching women's lived experience of house and family life. I also found very useful Linda Gordon, *Heroes of Their Own Lives: The Politics and History of Family Violence* (New York, London, 1988) and Beverly Stadum, *Poor Mothers and Their Families: Hard-Working Charity Cases 1910–1930* (New York, 1992).

49 Joanna Bourke, *Husbandry to Housewifery: Women, Economic Change and Housework in Ireland 1890–1914* (Oxford, 1993), *passim*, pp. 277.

50 Pat O'Connor, *Emerging Voices: Women in Contemporary Irish Society* (Dublin, 1998), pp. 136–60.

51 Discussed in Breda O'Brien, 'Caring for Children, not Ideology' *Sunday Business Post* 11 October, 1998.

52 The pitfalls of both assumptions for late twentieth-century women are set out clearly by Jayne Buxton, *Ending the Mother War: Starting the Workplace Revolution* (London, 1998).

53 Hilda Tweedy, *A Link in the Chain: The Story of the Irish Housewives Association* (Dublin, 1992).

54 Hanna Sheehy Skeffington, 'Random Reflections on Housewives, Their Ways and Works' *The Irish Housewife* Vol. 1 (1946), pp. 20–22.

55 Rev. P.S. Dineen/Peadar O Duinín, *Foclóir Gaeidhilge Agus Béarla: An Irish–English Dictionary, being a Thesaurus of the Words, Phrases, and Idioms of the Modern Irish Language* (Dublin, 1927), p. 1184.

CHAPTER ONE

1 Mary E. Daly, 'Women in the Irish Workforce from Pre-Industrial to Modern Times' *Saothar: Journal of the Irish Labour History Society* 7 (1981), pp. 74–82 remains the classic account, unsurpassed by any subsequent surveys.

2 *Census of Ireland, General Report, Vol. V*, Occupations, 1926, 1936, 1946, 1961.

3 See e.g. *Report of the Commission on Youth Unemployment* (1951), R. 82, pp. and Louie Bennett's Minority Report, pp. 51–2: see also e.g. Louie Bennett, 'The Domestic Problem' *The Irish Housewife* Vol. 1 (1946), pp. 29–30; Elizabeth Boyle, 'A Plan for the Northern Houseworkers' *The Irish Housewife* Vol. 1 (1946), pp. 31–3; 'Joan', 'The Homefront' *The Irish Housewife* Vol. 4 (1950), pp. 103–5; and the notorious recommendation by the Commission on Emigration that middle-class families be subsidised to employ servants, *Report of the Commission on Emigration and Other Population Problems 1948–54* (1956), R. 84, pp. 171–3, pp. 253–4. For a fuller discussion see Chapters 3 and 4.

4 Females in each occupational group in each province, county and county borough, classified by age-group and conjugal condition, Census of Ireland 1926 Vol. V, Table 12B: 1946, Vol. V, Table 5B: 1961, Vol. V, Table 3B.

5 Occupation tables, age-groups and conjugal conditions according to occupational groups: 1926 Census of Population, Vol. V, Part II, Table 12B: 1936 Census of Population, Vol. V, Part II, Table IB; 1946 Census of Population, Vol. V, Part II, Table IB; 1961 Census of Population, Vol. V, Part II, Table 2B.

6 See Chapters 5 and 6 for a discussion of mothers' health.

7 Mary E. Daly, 'Women in the Irish Workforce from Pre-Industrial to Modern Times' (1981).

CHAPTER TWO

1 *Bunreacht na hEireann*, 1937, Article 41.2; Minutes of evidence of the Joint Committee, comprising the Joint Committee of Women's Societies and Social Workers, the National

Council of Women, and the Catholic Federation of Secondary School Unions, to the Commission on Vocational Organisation, 23 November 1940, NLI Ms. 930, Vol. 9, 1996–7.

2 Katharine Tynan, 'A Trumpet Call to Irish Women' in *The Voice of Ireland: A Memorial of Freedom's Day by the Foremost Leaders* (New York, 1924), pp. 170–74.

3 Joanna Bourke, *Husbandry to Housewifery*, pp. 236–62; Pat Bolger (ed.) *And See Her Beauty Shining There: The Story of the Irish Countrywomen* (Dublin, 1986); Sarah McNamara, *Those Intrepid United Irishwomen: Pioneers of the Irish Countrywomen's Association* (Parteen, 1995); *The Irish Homestead*.

4 Evidence of ICA to Commission on Vocational Organisation, 21 November 1940, NLI Ms 930, Vol. 9, 2928–2948, 18333–6: Sarah McNamara, p. 9.

5 'Readers' Opinions' *Irish Independent* April 2, 1938. The original article which started this particular controversy was 'They All Say The Same; Irish Girls Can't Cook' *Irish Independent* March 30, 1938.

6 'Can Irish Girls Cook? Our Readers Reply to the Critics' *Irish Independent* April 4, 1938.

7 *Ibid.*

8 'More Opinions From Readers' *Irish Independent* April 6, 1938.

9 See note 6.

10 'Cooking in Ireland: More Views from Readers' *Irish Independent* April 8, 1938.

11 Kathleen Ferguson, *Lessons in Cookery and Housewifery: For the Use of Children* Book 1 (Dublin, 1908); *Sickroom Cookery and Notes on Sick Nursing* (Athlone, 1903); 'An Expert's View' *Irish Independent* April 8, 1938.

12 'Can Irish Girls Cook? More Opinions from Readers' *Irish Independent* April 6, 1938.

13 *Ibid.*

14 Coimisiúin Béaloideasa Eireann, Iml. 742, pp. 14–21, collected by Mary B. Dunphy N.T. 23 November, 1940.

15 'Domestic Modern Girls' *Irish Press* September 8, 1931.

16 Mary Clancy, 'Aspects of Women's Contribution to Oireachtas Debate.'

17 Annie M.P. Smithson, 'The Children of Our Slums' *Irish Monthly* Vol. LIII (October, 1925), pp. 553–6.

18 *Report on the Conference between the Department of Local Government and Public Health and Representatives of the Local Public Health and Public Assistance Authorities at Mansion House Dublin 8–9 July 1930* (Dublin, 1930), K. 29. p. 20, pp. 48–9, *passim*.

19 Brigid Redmond, 'Rural Home-makers' *Irish Monthly* Vol. LXV, (September, 1937), pp. 602–10, p. 603.

20 Mary Hayden, 'Woman's Role in the Modern World' *Irish Monthly* Vol. LXVIII (August, 1940), pp. 395–415, p. 398.

21 Dr James Deeny, 'Poverty as a Cause of Ill-Health'. Paper read, and ensuing discussion, May 31, 1940 and published in the *Journal of the Satistical and Social Inquiry Society of Ireland* Vol. XVI, 93rd session, (1939–40), pp. 75–89.

22 *Ibid.*, p. 88.

23 *Ibid.*, p. 87.

24 G. Dockeray and W.R. Fearon, 'Ante-natal Nutrition in Dublin: A preliminary survey' *Irish Journal of Medical Science* (1939), pp. 80–84.

25 Charles Clancy-Gore, 'Nutritional Standards of Some Working-Class Families in Dublin 1943' *Journal of the Statistical and Social Inquiry Society of Ireland* Vol. XVII 97th session, (1943), pp. 220–39.

26 Reverend T.F. Ryan, SJ 'Dublin's Poorest' *The Capuchin Annual* Vol. 1 (1930), pp. 12–19, p. 17.

27 Dorothy Macardle, 'Some Irish Mothers and Their Children' *Irish Press* September 14, 1931.

28 Alice Curtayne, *The New Woman: Text of a Lecture Given in the Theatre Royal, Dublin, October 22 1933, Under the Title 'The Renaissance of Woman'* (Dublin, 1933). Curtayne, born in Ireland in 1901 and educated abroad, was a novelist and journalist.

29 'Eithne', 'Can I Come With You, My Pretty Maid?' *Irish Monthly*, Vol. LIII (December, 1925), pp. 628–34.

30 *Ibid.*

31 The best explanation of this is to be found in Jane Rendall, *The Origins of Modern Feminism 1780–1860* (London, 1985), pp. 73–107, pp. 189–230, and also her edited collection, *Equal or Different* (Oxford, 1987).

32 This was part of a series addressed to the modern girl, e.g. 'Where Are You Going To, My Pretty Maid' (August, 1925), pp. 404–9; (September, 1925) pp. 458–66; (October, 1925), pp. 518–26.

33 Maryann Valiulis, 'Neither Feminist Nor Flapper'.

34 Valiulis, 'Power, Gender and Identity' p. 118.

35 'Causes and Consequences of Depopulation: Notes from France' *Catholic Bulletin* Vol. 15, June–December, 1925, pp. 911–8.

36 'General Intention for February: Recognition of the Sanctity of Marriage' *Irish Messenger of the Sacred Heart* Vol. 43, (February, 1930), pp. 95–6.

37 'Little Notes on Life' *Irish Messenger*, Vol. 50 (February, 1937), pp. 61–2.

38 Mary MacGeehin, 'A Scheme for the Rural Guilds' *Irish Monthly* Vol. LXV (December, 1937), pp. 799–813.

39 'Clarion Call of Lenten Pastoral: Clonfert' *Connacht Tribune* February 17, 1934.

40 W.F. MacDonagh, 'The Position of Woman in Modern Life' *Irish Monthly* Vol. LXVII (June, 1939), pp. 389–99.

41 *Ibid.*, p. 390, 399.

42 See note 20 above.

43 'Paternal Authority in the French Family' *Catholic Bulletin* Vol. 28, January–June, 1938, pp. 299–303.

44 *Report of the Commission on Vocational Organisation* (1943), K. 76/1.

45 J.J. Lee, 'Some Aspects of Corporatist Thought in Ireland: The Commission on Vocational Organisation 1939–43' in A. Cosgrove and D. McCartney (eds.) *Studies in Irish History: Papers Presented in Honour of R. Dudley Edwards* (Dublin, 1979), pp. 324–46; Ireland (1989), pp. 271–7.

46 John H. Whyte, *Church and State in Modern Ireland* (Dublin, 1980), pp. 62–119, and passim.

47 Ellen Hazelkorn, 'The Social and Political Views of Louie Bennett' *Saothar: Journal of the Irish Labour History Society* 13 (1988), pp. 32–44; Stephen J. Rynne, *Father John Hayes: Founder of Muintir na Tire* (Dublin, 1960), *passim*, refers to the support given by Protestant clergy and individuals to the organisation. Support was strong, e.g. among the Palatine community of county Limerick (oral evidence from Patrick J. Clear, National Secretary MnT 1981–84.)

48 'The Women Cannot Be Blamed: Countrywomen, Home-makers and the Commission on Vocational Organisation' in M. O'Dowd and S. Wichert (eds.) *Chattel, Servant or Citizen*, pp. 179–91.

49 Minutes of evidence of the ICA to the CVO: see note 4, above.

50 Minutes of evidence of Joint Committee to the CVO: see note 1, above.

51 CVO Report., p. 279.

52 *Ibid.*, pp. 279–81; pp. 414–16; pp. 346–47.

53 *Ibid.*, Addendum No. III by Máire S. Nic Aodháin (Miss MacGeehin), pp. 471–4.

54 *Ibid.*, Reservation No. II by Mr G. Crampton, pp. 481–6.

55 *Ibid.*, pp. 414–5.

56 Sarah McNamara, pp. 107–9; Geraldine Mitchell, *Deeds Not Words: The Life and Times of Muriel Gahan* (Dublin, 1997).

57 *Report of the Interdepartmental Committee on the Question of Making Available a Second Dwelling-House on Farms* (1943) NAS 13413/1. I am indebted to Pauric Travers for this reference.

58 See Chapters 8, 9 and Conclusion, for a full discussion of this.

CHAPTER THREE

1 *Dáil Debates* (hereafter *DD*)[92], 579–80, 2 December 1943: Louie Bennett, 'The Domestic Problem' *The Irish Housewife* Vol. 1 (1946), pp. 29–30.
2 'Children's Allowance Bill: Payment Proposal to Mothers Lost' *Irish Press* December 3, 1943.
3 Hilda Tweedy, *A Link in the Chain; The Irish Housewife* 1946–1986 (Dublin, 1986).
4 'Question Box' *Irish Messenger of the Sacred Heart*, Vol. LVII (August 1944), p. 127.
5 *Irish Messenger*, February 1944, p. 1.
6 Reverend E. O'Connor SJ, 'The Pope Speaks to Women Workers', *Irish Messenger*, Vol. LXIV, (May 1951), pp. 109–10.
7 Brigid Stafford, 'Equal Pay For Women', *Irish Monthly* Vol. LXXIX, (July 1951), pp. 308–14.
8 Francis Hanna, 'Family Life: the Facts' *Christus Rex* Vol. 5 (1951), pp. 20–45.
9 'Changes That Turn Women From Careers' *Irish Times* February 27, 1954.
10 Reverend G.J. Shannon, 'Woman: Wife and Mother' *Christus Rex* Vol. 5 (1951), pp. 155–74.
11 Ita Meehan, 'Woman's Place in the Community' *Christus Rex* Vol. 13 (1959), pp. 90–103.
12 Betty Friedan, *Feminine Mystique*, pp. 112–159.
13 Shannon; also Sr Mary Annetta McFeeley, PBVM, 'Education for Womanhood: An American Experiment' *Christus Rex* Vol. 5 (1951), pp. 81–93.
14 See Department of Education, *Rules and Programmes for Secondary Schools 1928–9*, pp. 38–41; *Rules and Programmes for Secondary Schools 1954–5*, pp. 52–4.
15 Department of Education, *Annual Reports: Results of Examinations 1925–61*.
16 Arland Ussher, 'The Boundary Between the Sexes' pp. 150–63 in John A. O'Brien (ed.) *The Vanishing Irish* (London, 1954), but see also the far more sympathetic articles by the other contributors – Fr John Hayes, 'Stemming the Flight from the Land', pp. 127–43; Mary Frances Keating, 'Marriage-shy Irishmen', pp. 164–75; Edmund Murray, 'The Key to the Problem', pp. 65–77.
17 Patrick McNabb, 'The Farm Worker and the Social Structure' *Limerick Rural Survey*, p. 208.
18 *Emigration Report*, passim.
19 Eoin O'Leary, 'The INTO and the Marriage Bar for Women National Teachers 1933–58' *Saothar* 12 (1987), pp. 47–52; Correspondence about the marriage bar N A S7985, A, B, C, D.
20 *Emigration Report*, p. 81; J. Newman, 'Social Provision and Rural Centrality' in Newman (ed.) *Limerick Rural Survey*, pp. 248–304, particularly p. 260.
21 Shannon, see note 10, above.
22 *Commission on Youth Unemployment*, p. 19.
23 *Emigration Report*, Addendum No. 1 by the Reverend Thomas Counihan, SJ, pp. 191–7, particularly p. 192.
24 Lucius McClean, OFM *What's The Problem?* (Dublin, 1961), pp. 57–9.
25 *Ibid.*, pp. 17–19.
26 There is by now a substantial literature on the question of family allowances; Bock and Thane, *op. cit*, Koven and Michel, *op. cit*, incorporate several articles on this topic worldwide, while *Gender and History* Vol. 4 No. 1 (1992) is a special issue on Motherhood and the Race. For a useful pan European survey see G. Bock, 'Poverty and Mothers' Rights in the Emerging Welfare States' and N. Lefacheur, 'Maternity, Family and the State' in G. Duby and M. Perrot (eds.) *A History of Women Vol. V: Toward a Cultural Identity in the Twentieth Century* (Harvard, 1996), pp. 402–51.
27 *Committee of Inquiry into Widows and Orphans Pensions, Reports* (1933), R.49/1. On recommendations, see John P. Dunne, *Waiting the Verdict: Pensions or Pauperism: Necessitous Widows and Orphans in the Free State* (n.d. c. 1928.)
28 *Commission of Inquiry into the Relief of the Sick and Destitute Poor, Including the Insane Poor*, 1927, R.27/3, p. 57.

29 *DD* (75), 383, 30 March, 1939.
30 Patrick King CC, BD 'Family Allowances' *Catholic Bulletin* Vol. 28 January–June 1938, pp. 310–12.
31 J.J. Lee, *Ireland 1912–85* (1989), pp. 277–85.
32 Correspondence on Family Allowances 13/11/39–16/3/43, and Report of Interdepartmental Committee on Family Allowances , N A S 12117 A, B.
33 *Guide To Social Services* (Dublin, 1945); 'Children's Allowance Bill: Payments to Mothers Proposal Lost' *Irish Press* December 3, 1943.
34 *Report of Interdepartmental Committee*, p. 15, p. 16. pp. 49–50. Eleanor Rathbone, *Family Allowances: A New Edition of the Disinherited Family* was reprinted in 1949 from its first printing in London 1924.
35 *SD* (26), 1001–5, 22 April, 1942.
36 *SD* (28), 442–6, 13 January, 1944.
37 *SD* (28), 418–31, 13 January, 1944.
38 *DD* (92), 223–4, 23 November, 1943.
39 *DD* (92) 59–60, 23 November, 1943.
40 *DD* (92), 591–2, 2 December, 1943.
41 *DD* (92), 206, 24 November, 1943; 598, 2 December, 1943.
42 *DD* (92), 87–9, 23 November, 1943.
43 *DD* (92), 197, 24 November, 1943.
44 *DD* (92), 204, 24 November, 1943.
45 Jane Lewis, 'Models of Equality for Women: the case for state support for children in 20th century Britain.' in Bock and Thane (eds.) *Maternity and Gender Policies*,(1991), pp. 73–92, p. 81.
46 *DD* (92), 583–6, 2 December, 1943.
47 *DD* (92), 579–80, 2 December, 1943.
48 *DD* (92), 593–4, 2 December, 1943.
49 Pamela Graves, *Labour Women: Women in British Working-Class Politics 1918–1939* (Cambridge, 1994), p. 99.
50 *DD* (92) 109–10, 23 November, 1943.
51 *DD* (92) 598, 2 December, 1943.
52 *DD* (92), 593–4, 2 December, 1943.
53 Lee, *Ireland 1912–85*, p. 280.
54 *SD* (28), 417, 13 January, 1944.
55 *Emigration Report*, pp. 97–101.
56 *Emigration Report*, p. 113.
57 On 'degeneracy', see Daniel Pick, *Faces of Degeneration: A European Disorder 1848–1918* (Cambridge, 1989); G. Stedman Jones, *Outcast London* (Oxford, 1971). Medical discourses will be discussed in more detail in Chapter 6, but the suggestion that multiparity as such did not affect child health is in J.K. Feeney, MD, MAO, FRCOG, 'Complications Associated With Grand Multiparity' *Journal of the Irish Medical Association* Vol. 32 (1953), pp. 36–55.
58 *Emigration Report*, pp. 99–100.
59 Very Reverend Cornelius Lucey, Minority Report to *Emigration Report*, pp. 335–63, in particular p. 342, 367.
60 For a brief discussion, see Chapter 5.
61 Dr W.R.F. Collis, *The State of Medicine in Ireland* (1943), section on child health.
62 *Emigration Report*, Reservation No. 1, W.R.F. Collis and Arnold Marsh, pp. 220–1.
63 *Ibid.*, Reservation No. 8, Arnold Marsh, for information on Dr Robert Collis, see Thomas A. Clarke and Thomas G. Matthews, 'The Development of Neonatal Paediatrics at the Rotunda: A Tribute to Dr W.R.F. Collis and Sister Maudie Moran' in Alan Browne (ed.) Masters, *Midwives and Ladies in Waiting: The Rotunda Hospital 1745–1995* (Dublin, 1995), pp. 121–46.
64 *Emigration Report*, Reservation No. 2, Alexis Fitzgerald, p. 222.
65 *Ibid.*, Reservation No. 6. Reverend A.A. Luce, pp. 230–1.

66 *Ibid.*, pp. 98–101; p. 341.

67 *Ibid.*, p. 221.

68 Kevin Devlin, 'Single and Selfish' *Christus Rex* Vol. 6 (1952), pp. 223–31.

69 Francis Hanna, 'Family Life; the Facts' *Christus Rex* Vol. 5 (1951), pp. 20–45, pp. 21–2 in particular.

70 Daisy Lawrenson Swanton, *Sarah Anne Lawrenson and Lucy Olive Kingston* (Dublin, 1994), p. 109.

71 Louie Bennett, 'The Domestic Problem' see note 1.

72 Helen Chenevix, 'Women's Opportunities in Local Government', *The Irish Housewife* Vol. 1 (1946), pp. 34–5.

73 Hilda Tweedy, *A Link in the Chain, passim.*

74 See Introduction.

75 'Foreword' *The Irish Housewife*, Vol. 1 (1946), p. 2.

76 Ann J. Burke and Robert M. Burke, 'The Rural Housewife and Family' *ibid.*, pp. 66–8.

77 Sheila Greene, 'Youth and Crime', *Ibid.*, pp. 36–9.

78 Helen Campbell, 'Nursery Schools' and Olivia Hughes, 'The Need for Meals for Schoolchildren in the Rural Areas' *Ibid.*, pp. 44–7. pp. 54–5.

79 Andrée Sheehy Skeffington, 'What's the Use' *Ibid.*, pp. 49–50.

80 Personal testimony from Patrick J. Clear, former member and one-time National Secretary of Muintir na Tire.

81 Vigilans, 'As I See It' *Christus Rex* Vol. 2 (1948), p. 75.

82 'As I See It' *Ibid.*, Vol. 3 (1949), pp. 64–5.

83 *Ibid.*, Vol. 4 (1950), pp. 74–5.

84 'Family Life: the Facts' *loc. cit.*

85 Francis J. Somerville, *Christ is King: A Manual of Catholic Social Doctrine* (Oxford, 1949), p. 197.

86 Hilda Tweedy, *A Link in the Chain*, p. 70, 72–3. The IHA was not a communist organisation, but Eithne MacDermott tells us that Robert and Hilda Tweedy were among a group who gathered to celebrate the 25th anniversary of the Bolshevik rising, in 1942, and that for this reason a file was kept on the IHA by the gardai. *Op. cit.*, passim.

87 Statement by Miss Louie Bennett regarding her refusal to sign the *Youth Unemployment Report*, (1951), pp. 51–2.

88 Louie Bennett, 'The Domestice Problem' see note 1.

89 Elizabeth Boyle, 'A Plan for the Northern Houseworkers' *The Irish Housewife* Vol. 1 (1946), pp. 31–3.

90 'Joan' 'The Homefront' *Ibid.*, Vol. 4 (1950), pp. 103–5.

91 W. Letts, 'Bracing Thoughts on a Universal Duty' *Ibid.*, Vol. 9 (1956), pp. 58–9.

92 *Emigration Report*, pp. 171–3, and Reservation No. 11, Ruaidhri Roberts, pp. 247–76, pp. 253–4 in particular.

CHAPTER FOUR

1 *Dublin Opinion* Vol. XX, May 1941.

2 A good and comprehensive historical survey of women's magazines and advice to women has yet to be written. Valuable introductory surveys of British women's magazines are Cynthia White, *Women's Magazines 1930–1968* (London, 1970) and Janice Winship, *Inside Women's Magazines* (London, 1987); R. Ballaster, M. Beetham, E. Frazer and S. Hebron's *Women's Worlds: Ideology, Femininity and the Woman's Magazine* (London, 1991) explores, among other things, the idea of the 'resisting reader'. My favourite study of a women's magazine, which places it in context and does not condescend to the magazine's readership, is Jennifer Scanlon, *Inarticulate Longings: the Ladies Home Journal, Gender and the Promises of Consumer Culture* (New York, London, 1995). Penny Tinkler,

Constructing Girlhood: Popular Magazines for Girls Growing Up in England 1920–1950 (London, 1995), suggests many different approaches to the subject of popular reading.

3 *Cookery Notes Prepared for use in Schools and Classes for Girls Working under Schemes of Departments of Lands and Agriculture* (Dublin, 1925, revised every two or three years or so, Dublin, 1942). A/14. Introduction.

4 *Ibid.*, pp. 60–1.

5 *Ibid.*, 1942 edition, which my aunt Nancy Clear used at secondary school in the Presentation convent, Sexton St, Limerick, in 1944.

6 Josephine Redington, *The Economic Cookery Book: Tried Recipes etc. Suitable for all Households, Schools and Domestic Classes* (Dublin, 1927; first edition 1905), p. 13. The first edition of this useful manual had a frontispiece of students merrily cooking dinner on a turf fire.

7 Redington also published *The Laundry Book* (Dublin, 1913), and her name appears on the prospecti for the Irish Training School for Domestic Economy, up to 1935. (*Prospecti Irish Training School for Domestic Economy*, 1929–42, E.T.3/1-E.T.3/12.

8 Redington, *Economic Cookery Book* (1927), pp. 1–2, passim.

9 See, *e.g.* Amalgamated Press, Ltd. *The Motherhood Book* (c. London 1933), pp. 297–349; M. Truby King, *Mothercraft* (London, 1939), pp. 221–36; John Gibbens, *The Care of Young Babies* (London, 1940, 1959), pp. 202–9 *Good Housekeeping's Baby Book* (London, 1944, 1952), pp. 98–99. On advice to mothers in Britain – and, by implication in Ireland, between the wars, see Elizabeth Peretz, 'The Costs of Motherhood to Low-Income Families in Interwar Britain' in V. Fildes *et al*, (eds.) *Women and Children First* (London, 1993), pp. 256–79.

10 Marguerite Patten, *We'll Eat Again: a Selection of Recipes from the War Years Selected by Marguerite Patten in Association with the Imperial War Museum*, (London, 1985) p. 29.

11 Margaret Roper and Ruth Duffin, *The Bluebird Cookery Book for Working Women* (Dublin, 1939), pp. 3–4, pp. 46–7. Mrs Sydney Frankenburg, *Common Sense in the Nursery* (several editions from 1927, up to 1946).

12 Women's Industrial Development Association, *The Woman At The Wheel: Household Handbook* (Dublin, 1935), p. 96. The WIDA was inaugurated in 1933, with the aim of encouraging the purchase of Irish goods and encouraging the investment of Irish capital in Irish industry, and to encourage only such Irish industries as conform to proper trade union wages and conditions. Senator Jenny Wyse Power was the President.

13 Maura Laverty, *Flour Economy (*Dublin, 1941), p. 7.

14 Josephine Marnell, Nora Breathnach, Anna Martin and Mor Murnaghan, *All In The Cooking: Coláiste Mhuire Book of Household Cookery* (Dublin, 1946), pp. 15–16, passim.

15 Ann Hathaway's Homecraft Library, *The Homecraft Book* (Dublin n.d; 1944 according to NLI), p. 9.

16 *Ibid.*, old shoes p. 83; pails p. 25; specs p. 55; matches and curtains p. 40.

17 *Ibid.*, exercise, p. 73; nicotine p. 68; neuralgia p. 80; balanced diet pp. 77–81; eggs, pp. 89–90; soup p. 92; 'war'-malade, p. 95. See Marguerite Patten, *We'll Eat Again*, for comparison.

18 Biographical information on Mary Frances Keating, in John A. O'Brien (ed.) *The Vanishing Irish*, pp. 164–5.

19 See, for example, some of the articles on house design in *The Irish Housewife* cited in notes 54–58 in the previous chapter,; 'American Home' in *Woman's Life* Vol. 28, February 24, 1951.

20 Hathaway, *Homecraft* (1944)., p. 15.

21 *Ibid.*, p. 11–12.

22 *Ibid.*, p. 13.

23 *Ibid*, pp. 9–10

24 Aunt Kaye (ed.), *The Household Guide* (London and Dundee n.d. wartime paper, c. 1947?), p. 15. Aunt Kaye's daily/weekly timetable (pp. 7–9) is almost identical to that of Ann Hathaway – it seems to have been standard.

25 Bríd Mahon, *While Green Grass Grows: Memoirs of A Folklorist* (Cork, 1997), p. 123. Mahon's information on Laverty's growing-up and early adulthood seems to be taken entirely from her two books *Never No More: The Story of a Lost Village* (London, 1942), and *No More Than Human* (London, 1944), which, while they are autobiographical, have a fictional protagonist and, Maeve Binchy claims in her introduction to the Virago edition of *Never No More* (London, 1983) a fictional grandmother, in whose existence Mahon seems to believe, p. 126. Honor Moore in her warm and loving profile of Laverty, 'Full and Plenty' *The Sunday Tribune Food and Wine '99* (29 November, 1998), pp. 14–16, does not give us any more information about Laverty's early life than is to be found in her various books, though it includes a photograph. A biography of this fascinating and, I would argue, influential woman – a founder member of the innovative but doomed Clann na Poblachta and scriptwriter for its film, *Our Country* – is long overdue. For information on Clann na Poblachta, see Eithne MacDermott, *Clann na Poblachta* (Cork, 1998), pp. 56–7, pp. 60–1.
26 Maura Laverty *Kind Cooking*, (Tralee, 1946). The story about the farmer comes from her *Full and Plenty* (Dublin, 1961), p. 113.
27 Laverty, *Kind Cooking* (1946), p. 30.
28 *Ibid.*, p. 4.
29 *Ibid.*, passim.
30 *Ibid.*, pp. 1–2; pp. 9–10; the story about the 'white church' which features in *Lift Up Your Gates* also features in *Kind Cooking* and there is also a recipe called 'Roast Rabbit à la Ballyderrig', p. 55. *Never No More* and *Lift Up Your Gates* (London, 1947); see Note 25, above.
31 Laverty, *Kind Cooking* , p. 110; pp. 87–93.
32 *Ibid.*, p. 4.
33 *Ibid.*, p. 2.
34 *Ibid.*, p. 8.
35 The phrase is from Betty Friedan, *The Feminine Mystique*, pp. 30–60.
36 Maura Laverty, *Full and Plenty*, (Dublin, 1961), passim. Laverty's *Touched By The Thorn* (published in America as *Alone We Embark*) (1944) was banned for its sympathetic treatment of adulterous characters. Brian Cleeve, *Dictionary of Irish Writers*, (Cork, 1975)
37 Bean a' Tighe, 'For Mothers and Daughters' *Catholic Bulletin* Vol. 27, (January–June 1937), pp. 558–9.
38 Bean a' Tighe, 'For Mothers and Daughters' *Catholic Bulletin* Vol. 13 (July–December 1923), p. 573.
39 Bean a' Tighe, 'For Mothers and Daughters' *Catholic Bulletin* Vol. 13 (January–June 1923), p. 186.
40 Madame Marie Jacques, 'How We Renovated Our Home', *Irish Messenger* Vol. XL (August, 1927).
41 Madame Marie Jacques, 'The Little Ones' *Irish Messenger* Vol. XLI (April 1928), pp. 221–2.
42 MSE, 'The Tierney Home' *Irish Messenger* Vol. XLIII, (February 1930), pp. 55–59.
43 *e.g. Irish Messenger*, Vol. XLV (April 1932).
44 Ethna Kavanagh, 'Household Hints, *Irish Messenger* Vol. LVIII (January 1945), p. 10; G. Holmes, 'The Woman of the House' *Irish Messenger* Vol. LX (July 1947), pp. 153–4, and April 1947, pp. 31–2.
45 Fidelma, 'Friendly Advice' *Irish Messenger* Vol. LXIV (February 1951), pp. 41–2.
46 Information on Máire Comerford from her book, *The First Dáil* (Dublin, 1969).
47 'The Housewife's Outfit' *Irish Press* 19 October, 1931; 'Pretty but Practical: Jane West Patterns' *Irish Independent* 18 October, 1943; 'An Attractive Overall: Jane West Patterns' *Irish Independent* 1 January, 1947.
48 *Freeman's Journal* 14–19 September, 1924.
49 *Irish Press* 25–30 April, 1933.
50 *Irish Independent* 21–26 August, 1950.
51 *Irish Independent* 8–13 October, 1956.

52 *Irish Times* 12–17 October, 1956.

53 *Irish Press* 9–14 March, 1959.

54 *Woman's Life: the Irish Home Weekly*, 24 September, 1949.

55 *Woman's Life* 27 August, 1938; on Madame Dionne 5 September, 1936; Mrs Simpson, 27 March, 1937; on Maureen O'Sullivan, 2 June, 1937. On working women; street-seller 20 February, 1937; packer in flour mill 5 September, 1936; secretary in trade union, 17 April, 1937; commercial traveller, 7 October, 1939; milliner, 28 October, 1939; wife and mother, 16 January, 1937; hotel receptionist, 23 September, 1939; oarswoman, 26 June, 1937; radiographer 30 September, 1939; chorus-girls 26 August, 1939.

56 'Mrs Wyse Answers Problems Woman's Life', 4 February, 1939; 'Echoes of the Constitution' *Womans Life* 12 March, 1938.

57 *Womans Life* 27 August, 1938; *Womans Life* 5 November, 1938.

58 'Is This A Tin-Opener Age' *Womans Life* 27 February, 1937 (perhaps but it is all to the good if it saves time); 'Efficiency Begins In The Kitchen', by Martha Grey, *Womans Life* 29 August, 1938; 'Marriage As A Career, by a Business Girl', *Womans Life* 5 March, 1938 ('Business-like modern girls look upon marriage less as the only thing, than as a possible career in which they might or might not succeed.') Mrs Wyse 'Where A Wife Fails' *Womans Life* 24 September, 1938 (a mother of 7, married 19 years, is sternly admonished to make time for herself).

59 'Diane's Diary: Happy the Wooing' *Womans Life* 5 November, 1938; 'Home Planning and Decoration' *Womans Life* 16 July, 1951.

60 The first issue of *Woman's Mirror: The Irish Woman's Very Own Home Weekly* appeared on 28 May, 1932. The numbering of volumes seems to suggest that this magazine was published off and on; it was certainly published in 1945. *Woman's Mirror*, February 1955 (Vol. 16, No. 2)

61 Bean a' Tighe, 'For Mothers and Daughters' *Catholic Bulletin* Vol. 19 (January–June 1929), pp. 92–3; Eileen Lacey, 'New Year Ps and Qs for Mothers' *Irish Independent* 4 January, 1947.

62 Bean a' Tighe, 'For Mothers and Daughters' *Catholic Bulletin*, Vol. 13 (July–December 1923), p. 573.

63 May Laverty, 'The Terrors of Washing-Up: Lightening the Housewife's Burden' *Irish Press* 7 September, 1935. This does not seem to be Maura Laverty under a different first name, though the style is almost identical: May refers to 'we in the North' at one stage, and Maura not only came from Kildare, but referred to it very often in her writing. Just to confuse us further, Eithne MacDermott's book has two separate entries for Maura Laverty and May Laverty, but does not distinguish between them in her text. *Op. cit*, p. 56, p. 35 and index.

64 Ann Hathaway, *Homecraft Book*, p. 15, p. 40.

65 See Chapter 7 for a fuller discussion of this.

66 Carmel Duggan, 'Farming Women or Farmers' Wives? Women in the Farming Press' in C. Curtin, P. Jackson and B. O'Connor (eds.) *Gender in Irish Society* (Galway, 1987)

67 Ann Kennedy, 'Diary of a Farmer's Wife' *Irish Times* 14 November, 1956.

68 'Letter to a Farmer's Wife' *Woman's Life* 2 January, 1937.

69 *Ibid.*, 9 January, 1937.

70 Marie O'Reilly, 'I Sketch Your World' *Irish Independent* 17 January, 1947.

71 'Countrywomen in Uniforms' *Irish Independent* 6 September, 1956.

72 Frances Enraght Mooney, 'Out of the Wind and the Rain's Way' *Irish Independent* 14 August, 1956.

73 'Grandmother Envies the Housekeeper of Today' *Irish Press* 28 December, 1938.

74 'Question Box' *Irish Messenger*, Vol. LXI (January 1948), p. 23; for the 1920s and 1930s, a short story, A. Dease, 'Those Nuns' *Ibid.*, Vol. XL, (October 1927) is about a little girl whose mother dresses her in 'immodest' clothes and who is always being criticised by the nuns for it much to the mother's chagrin; the girl grows up vain and shallow, runs off to England, has a baby and is cared for by the nuns before she and her baby die. 'Dress and

Fashion' by Maria Agnes Bauer, *ibid.*, Vol. XLIX (August 1936) was the one which mentioned Elisabeth of Thuringia.

75 Stephen Rynne, *Father John Hayes*, p. 178.
76 See, e.g. E. E. O'Donnell, (ed.) *Fr Browne's Remarkable Images: People and Places* (Dublin, 1989), *passim*, and G. Mullins and D. Dixon (eds.) *Dorothea Lange's Ireland* (London, 1996), *passim*.
77 *Woman's Life* 19 January, 1946; 8 June, 1946.
78 'Friday's Gossip Column: Women in the News' *Irish Press*, 10 April, 1959.

CHAPTER FIVE

1 See Table 5.1, this chapter.
2 Ruth Barrington, passim.
3 On the anti-medicalisation side of the debate, see Sheila Kitzinger's twenty or so books, most of which have some historical/anthropological context, especially, *Ourselves As Mothers* (London, 1992). B. Ehrenreich and D. English, *Witches, Midwives and Nurses: A History of Women Healers* (New York, 1973); Jessica Mitford, *The American Way of Birth* (New York, 1992), pp. 19–513. Boston Women's Health Collective, *The New Our Bodies Ourselves: A Book by and for Women* (New York, 1992), pp. 397–513, in its various incarnations, is the bible of the alternative childbirth lobby. Because the pro-medicalisation perspective is more mainstream, it suffices to give one example of the kind of writing, e.g. to be found in Alan Browne (ed.) *Masters, Midwives and Ladies In Waiting: The Rotunda Hospital 1745–1995* (Dublin, 1995). Typical of the tone of this excellently informative and valuable volume, is the first sentence of Mary A. Kelly, 'The Development of Midwifery at the Rotunda', in Browne, (ed.) pp. 77–117: 'Prior to the opening of the first Dublin lying-in hospital, midwifery was in the grip of ignorance, fear and superstition.'
4 For the Irish context, see Jo Murphy-Lawless, 'The Silencing of Women in Childbirth, or, Let's Hear It From Bartholomew and the Boys' *Women's Studies International Forum*, Vol. 11, No. 4, (1988), pp. 293–98; Marie O'Connor, *Birth Tides: Turning Towards Home Birth* (London, 1995), and Sandra Ryan, 'Interventions in Childbirth: The Midwives' Role' in Anne Byrne and Madeleine Leonard (eds.) *Women and Irish Society: A Sociological Reader* (Belfast, 1997), pp. 255–67. For a radical feminist critique of the 'natural childbirth' lobby, see Sue O'Sullivan (ed.) *Women's Health: A Spare Rib Reader* (London, 1987), pp. 303–17.
5 Irvine Loudon, *Death in Childbirth: An International Study of Maternal Care and Infant Mortality* (Oxford, 1992). Nicky Leap and Billie Hunter, *The Midwife's Tale: An Oral History from Handywoman to Professional Midwife* (London, 1993), corroborates Loudon's thesis.
6 Ballard, Linda May, 'Just Whatever They Had Handy' *Ulster Folklife* Vol. 31 (1985), pp. 59–72.
7 Ruth Barrington, *Health, Medicine and Politics*, 79, 105; Revised Midwives Bill 1931, N A S S 942.
8 *Department of Local Government and Public Health Reports 1925–47*: section on Maternity and Child Welfare.
9 Annual Report of the Central Midwives Board 31 March, 1935, *Department of Local Government and Public Health Report 1934–5*, Appendix XXXI.
10 *Department of Local Government and Public Health Report, 1936–7*, pp. 71–87.
11 *First and Second Reports of the Department of Health*, 1945–9, pp. 54–59.
12 *Ibid.*, pp. 58–9.
13 Ruth Barrington, *Health, Medicine and Politics*, pp. 222–50.
14 *Ibid.*, passim, and *Department of Health reports*, 1951–61.
15 The classic account of this conflict is in John H. Whyte, *Church and State in Modern Ireland* (Dublin, 1980), pp. 196–272; another angle is given by Eamon McKee, 'Church-

State Relations and the Development of Irish Health Policy: the Mother and Child Scheme 1944–1953' *Irish Historical Studies* Vol. XXV, No. 98, (November, 1986), pp. 159–94.

16 Vigilans, 'As I See It' *Christus Rex* Vol. 5 (1951), p. 297.

17 Alex Spain, ' Maternity Services in Éire', and James Quin, 'A Suggested Maternity Service for Éire ' in *Irish Journal of Medical Science: The Official Journal of the Royal Academy of Medicine in Ireland* No. 229, January 1945, pp. 1–23; Letter from P.J. Greene, Loughrea, to the *Journal of the Medical Association of Éire*, Vol. 14, No. 3 (1944), pp. 57–8.

18 *Ibid.*

19 The term 'meddlesome midwifery' was also used by S.J. Boland, 'Radiology in Antenatal Care' *Journal of the Irish Medical Association*, Vol. 36 (1955), pp. 20–1, where doctors were advised to 'hold hand and avoid' as much as possible when it came to using x-rays as diagnostic tools (they were often the only way to find out the position of the baby and the placenta, if such information were needed, before ultrasound). See also J.K. Feeney, 'Antenatal Care' *Journal of the Irish Medical Assocation*, Vol. 34, (1954), pp. 42–4.

20 Mary Kelly, 'The Development of Midwifery at the Rotunda.' pp. 100–1.

21 National Maternity Hospital Annual Report, Discussion of the Dublin Maternity Reports, *Irish Journal of Medical Science*, No. 371 (November, 1956), pp. 523–34.

22 John P. Shanley, 'The Reorganisation of the Medical Service' *Journal of the Medical Association of Éire*, Vol. 14, No. 2 (1944), pp. 40–3.

23 Correspondence (long and acrimonious) between the Central Midwives Board and the Department of Health in which the latter urged the abolition of the title midwife and the former, its retention, 16/5/49–8/3/50, N A S 14 515.

24 *Department of Local Government and Public Health Report*, 1935–6, p. 87; *Ibid.*, 1943–4, p. 63.

25 Deeny, *To Cure and To Care*, p. 116, p.115.

26 Barrington, *Health, Medicine and Politics*, p. 131.

27 Deeny, *To Cure and To Care*, p. 26. He goes on to say, 'but some were "shockers," real Sarah Gamps.'

28 Leslie Matson, *Méiní: the Blasket Nurse* (Cork, 1995), pp. 88–99 in particular.

29 Máire Ni Ghuithin, *Bean an Oiléain* (Baile Atha Cliath, 1985) transl. *The Island Woman*, p. 11 of Irish text.

30 Leslie Matson, *Méiní*, p. 94.

31 Irvine Loudon, *Death in Childbirth*, pp. 218–23.

32 Leslie Matson, *Méiní*, pp. 88–99.

33 Ruth Barrington, *Health, Medicine and Politics*, p. 105.

34 Nicky Leap and Billie Hunter, *The Midwife's Tale*, pp. 19–43.

35 Coimisiúin Béaloideasa Eireann, Iml. 1386, pp. 199–201; Iml. 1220, pp. 3–57; Iml.1210, pp. 179–91, testimony of Richard Denehan, labourer, 70 years of age, Co. Limerick.

36 Kevin Kearns, *Dublin Tenement Life: An Oral History* (Dublin, 1994), p. 48.

37 Sheila Kitzinger, *The New Pregnancy and Childbirth* (London, 1989), pp. 266–7.

38 Kevin Kearns, *Dublin Tenement Life*, pp. 115–6.

39 Sheila Kitzinger, *Ourselves As Mothers*, passim.

40 Nicky Leap and Billie Hunter, *The Midwife's Tale*, p. 27. 'Mrs G.' also used to threaten jokingly (!) to stick patients' heads in a bucket of water if they didn't shut up crying.

41 Mary Kelly, 'The Development of Midwifery at the Rotunda' p. 103.

42 Mary Ryan, Seán Browne and Kevin Gilmour (eds) *No Shoes In Summer* (Dublin, 1995), p. 89.

43 Noel Browne, *Against the Tide*, pp. 16–17.

44 See the Central Midwives Board Reports in the appendices to the Annual Reports of the Department of Local Government and Public Health. See also Editorial, *Irish Nurses Union Gazette*, No. 13, May 1925, on fears of handywomen and midwives being compromised by being compelled to be assisted by them at childbirth. Also Sandra Ryan, 'Interventions in Childbirth'.

45 Mary Healy, *For the Poor and for the Gentry: Mary Healy Remembers her Life* (Dublin, 1989), pp. 84–5. On maternal mortality in Kilkenny, see death rate tables (usually 16, 17 and 18) in the *Annual Report of the Registrar-General*, 1941–9.

46 Irvine Loudon, *Death in Childbirth*, pp. 206–33.

47 Alex Spain, 'Maternity Services in Éire', p. 8.

48 Mary Healy, *For the Poor and For the Gentry*, pp. 84–7.

49 Spain, 'Maternity Services in Éire'.

50 On Teresa Murphy, Carla Blake, 'Midwives Tales' *Cork Examiner* 9 December, 1993. Thanks to Kathleen Clear for finding this item for me at a time when I had a two-week old baby myself.

51 James P. Murray, *Galway: A Medico-Social History* (Galway, 1995), p. 134.

52 John Healy, *Nineteen Acres* (Galway, 1978), pp. 128–30.

53 Mary Healy, *For the Poor and for the Gentry*, pp. 86–7. On horror stories of women being left alone in labour, see Sheila Kitzinger, *Ourselves as Mothers*, pp. 133–156; Jessica Mitford, *The American Way of Birth*, pp. 60–1, passim. Fashions change; Erna Wright's highly influential natural childbirth bible, *The New Childbirth* (London, 1964), pp. 112–13, presents the scenario where the woman is left alone 'to get on with it' as natural and sensible.

54 Dorothy Harrison Therman, *Stories from Tory Island* (Dublin, 1989), pp. 76–8.

55 Mary Healy, *For the Poor and for the Gentry*, p. 84.

56 Mary Kelly, 'The Development of Midwifery at the Rotunda' pp. 107–8; Leap and Hunter, *The Midwife's Tale*, pp. 158–88.

57 *Department of Local Government and Public Health Report* 1930–1, p. 57; Alexander Humphreys, *New Dubliners*, p. 120.

58 See Note 55.

59 *Department of Local Government and Public Health Report*, 1935–6, p. 81.

60 Stanley Lyon, 'Natality in Dublin in the Years 1943, 1944 and 1946' (Paper read on Friday 28 May, 1948) *Statistical and Social Inquiry Society of Ireland* Vol. XVIII, 1947–8, pp. 57–77.

61 Central Statistics Office, *Vital Statistics for 1955* (1958), T.3/35, p. 140; *Ibid.*, for 1956 (1958), T.3/36, p. 139; *Ibid.*, for 1959 (published 1960), T.3/39, p. 126.

62 Marie O'Connor, *Birth Tides*, pp. 7–13.

63 Eleanor Holmes, 'The Social Work Department' in *Clinical Report of the Rotunda Hospital* 1 November 1954–31 October 1955, pp. 3–8, in *Irish Journal of Medical Science* No. 371, (November, 1956).

64 Alexander Humphreys, *New Dubliners*, pp. 186–7.

65 Michael Solomons, *Pro-Life*, pp. 8–9.

66 Dr John O'Connell, *Doctor John: Crusading Doctor and Politician* (Dublin, 1989), p. 27.

67 Noel Browne, *Against the Tide*, p. 69.

68 James Deeny, *To Cure and To Care*, p. 27.

69 Kevin Kearns, *Dublin Tenement Life*, and Maire Ni Ghuithin, *Bean an Oileain*.

70 G. Connolly, Resident Obstetrician, 'Extract from the Annual Report 1947' in Medical Missionaries of Mary, *The First Decade: Ten Years' Work of the Medical Missionaries of Mary 1937–47* (Dublin, 1948), pp. 41–3.

71 Kevin Kearns, *Dublin Tenement Life*, pp. 115–6.

72 John O'Connell, *Doctor John*, p. 26.

73 Amalgam ated Press, *The Motherhood Book*, p. 740–1, p. 744–5.

74 All the figures for maternal mortality are taken from the Office of the Registrar-General, Annual Report 1923–52, up to 1949, Table 10, 15 or 17 (variously), Marriage, Birth and Death Rates by Provinces, Counties and County Boroughs. Thereafter, there was no longer a regional breakdown. Information from 1953 thereafter from Central Statistics Office, *Vital Statistics 1953* (1955) T.3/33, Table XXVII, Deaths of women in 1953, caused by pregnancy, childbirth and the puerperal state, p. xxxv. In this year maternal mortality was at the lowest it had ever been, and it continued to fall (see *Vital Statistics 1954* (1957) T.3/34, p. xxxiii; *Vital Statistics 1955* (1958) T.3/35, p. xxx; *Vital Statistics 1957* (1960), p. xxxi, Table XXVII, and so on.

75 Dr Alex Spain, 'Beginnings' in Medical Missionaries of Mary, *The First Decade*, pp. 26–7. Alex Spain, 'Maternity Services in Éire' (1945), p. 2.

76 James Quin, 'A Suggested Maternity Service for Éire', p. 11–12.

77 John O'Connell, *Doctor John*, p. 2.

78 Irvine Loudon, *Death in Childbirth*, passim.

79 *Department of Local Government and Public Health Report*, 1936–7, pp. 71–2.

80 Discussion of the Dublin Maternity Reports, (1956), *loc. cit.*, pp. 524–5, passim.

81 Alex Spain, 'Obstetric Emergencies' *Journal of the Medical Association of Éire* Vol. 27, (1950), p. 62.

82 J.G. Gallagher, 'Causes of Maternal Mortality' *Irish Journal of Medical Science* 6th series 1941, pp. 497–50, where obstetric shock is plausibly (to the lay-woman who has experienced childbirth) described as caused by delay in delivering the placenta and rough attempts at its removal and manual expulsion; anaemia and malnutrition were thought to be important factors.

83 G.C. Dockeray and W.R. Fearon, 'Ante-Natal Nutrition in Dublin: A Preliminary Survey' *Irish Journal of Medical Science*, No. 175 (1939), pp. 80–4.

84 On causes of toxaemia, see Miriam Stoppard, *Woman to Woman*, p. 329. *National Nutrition Survey*, Table 22, Numbers of certain nursing and expectant mothers in Dublin classified by occupational group of husband, parity/size of family and nutritional state, and comment p. 23.

85 *Department of Local Government and Public Health Report*, 1930–1, p. 57.

86 G. Connolly, 'Extract from the Annual Report' *The First Decade*; Discussion of the Dublin Maternity Reports, (1956) *loc. cit.*, p. 528.

87 James Deeny, *To Cure and To Care*, p. 26; Irvine Loudon, *Death in Childbirth*, passim.

88 All the information on maternal mortality rates up to 1949 comes from note 74; information on public assistance in Kildare, from Tables in the *Annual Reports of the Department of Local Government and Public Health 1923–40*; on Kildare and Mayo and the differences between them, from T.W. Freeman, *Ireland: Its Physical, Historical, Social and Economic Geography* (London, 1950).

89 Irvine Loudon, *Death in Childbirth*, passim.

90 Mary E. Daly suggested this to me.

91 On numbers of doctors and midwives in Kildare and Mayo, *Census of Population 1926*, 'Preliminary Report' Table 3, pp. 18–26; Vol. 2, 'Occupations' Table 5, pp. 32–93; *Census of Population 1936*, 'Preliminary Report', Table 2, pp. 23–8; Vol. 2, 'Occupations' Table 5, pp. 34–99; *Census of Population 1946*, 'Preliminary Report', Table 2, pp. 19–25; Vol. 2, 'Occupations', pp. 34–91. On the attempt to attract nurses back from Britain, see Deeny, *To Cure and To Care*, pp. 104–23.

92 Appendix XIX 'Maternity and Child Welfare Grant' in *Department of Local Government and Public Health Annual Report* 1929–30, pp. 183–5; Appendix XXI, 'Maternity and Child Welfare Grant' in *Ibid.*, 1933–4, pp. 240–2; Appendix XV, *Ibid.*, 1937–8, pp. 179–81; Appendix XVII, *Ibid.*, 1942–3, pp. 170–171. *First and Second Reports of Department of Health*, 1945–9, pp. 54–49.

93 Barrington, Health, *Medicine and Politics*, p. 105.

94 Loudon, *Death in Childbirth*, passim.

95 For example, in 1936–7, there were no deaths from puerperal sepsis in Meath, Tipperary N., or in Limerick City, while there were high death rates in Dublin City, Waterford, Wicklow and Louth. *Department of Local Government and Public Health Report*, 1936–7, p. 71.

96 *National Nutrition Survey*, Part II, Part III, Part IV 'Farm Workers' Families'.

97 Cormac O Gráda, *Ireland: A New Economic History* (Oxford, 1994), pp. 218–25; Brendan M. Walsh, *Some Irish Population Problems Considered* ESRI Paper 42 November 1968; Robert J. Kennedy Jr, *The Irish: Emigration, Marriage and Fertility* (California, 1973), pp. 173–205.

98 Central Statistics Office, *Vital Statistics 1959* (1961?), Table XXXI, p. xvi.

99 Michael Solomons, *Pro-Life?*, pp. 5–6.

100 John O'Connell, *Doctor John*, p. 30.

101 J.K. Feeney, Master, Coombe hospital, 'Complications Associated With High Multiparity: A Clinical Survey of 518 Cases' *Journal of the Irish Medical Association*, Vol. 32, (1953), pp. 36–55. Australian doctor Derek Llewellyn-Jones, *Everywoman: A Woman's Health Guide for Life* (London, 1982 edition), p. 290, mentions that this term (which he calls the 'grande multigravida') 'was first used in Dublin to describe those women who have had at least four (sic) previous pregnancies'. His information might not be accurate but his sense of the provenance of the definition is significant.

102 J.K. Feeney, 'Complications'.

103 A.P. Barry, D. Meagher and E. O' Dwyer, ' Heart Disease in Pregnancy' *Journal of the Irish Medical Assocation* Vol. 38 (1956), pp. 82–3.

104 Irvine Loudon, *Death in Childbirth*; Michael Solomons, *Pro-Life?*, p. 14.

105 Solomons, *Pro-Life?*, p. 6.

106 John O' Connell, *Doctor John*, p. 30.

107 *Report of the Registrar-General*, 1936, Abstract V: Causes of Death in Saorstát Éireann by Sexes, Ages and Places of Occurence; *Report of the Registrar-General for 1950* (1953), Table 20, Deaths in 1950 Classified by Cause Showing Place of Occurrence.

108 Brendan Walsh, *Some Irish Population Problems*, p. 36.

CHAPTER SIX

1 Infant mortality rates for the period are taken from *Statistical Abstracts* 1923–61; actual numbers from *Registrar-General Reports*, 1923–52, and *Vital Statistics*, thereafter. For Senator Tierney's comments and source thereof, see Chapter 3.

2 For a detailed discussion on infant mortality for the period up to 1950, see Central Statistics Office *Report of the Registrar-General 1950* (1953) T.3/30, pp. xlvii–lvii.

3 *Department of Local Government and Public Health Report*, 1931–2, pp. 55–59.

4 James Deeny, *To Cure and To Care*, pp. 92–9. See also Robert Collis, *The State of Medicine in Ireland* (n.d. c. 1943) and 'Infant Mortality in Éire and the Proposed Mother and Child Scheme' in *Journal of the Medical Association of Éire*, Vol. 23 (1948), pp. 82–5, where he admits that full credit for the decline in infant mortality in any country and in Ireland in particular lies not with developments in paediatrics but with 'civil servants' – officials of the Department of Health and their public health initiatives. A very interesting and lively account of the career of Dr Collis and some of his contemporaries in paediatric health can be found in T. Clarke and T. Matthews, 'The Development of Neonatal Paediatrics at the Rotunda' in A. Browne, (ed.) *Masters, Midwives and Ladies-in-Waiting*, pp. 121–46.

5 Deeny, *To Cure and To Care*, pp. 92–9.

6 Kevin Kearns, p. 206; Deeny, p. 94.

7 See notes 1, 2 and 3.

8 Deeny, pp. 92–9.

9 See note 2, above.

10 Olivia Hughes, 'The Need for Meals for Schoolchildren in the Rural Areas' *The Irish Housewife* Vol. 1 (1946), pp. 44–7

11 James Quin, 'A Suggested Maternity Service for Éire' p. 17.

12 Deeny, p. 94.

13 Kevin Kearns, *passim*.

14 *Irish Messenger* Vol. LVII, (April 1944), p. 59.

15 *Irish Messenger* Vol. LVII, (July 1944), p. 108.

16 *Irish Messenger* Vol. LIV, (May 1951), p. 108.

17 There are several useful discussions on reading silences in oral evidence, see e.g. Joan Sangster, 'Telling Our Stories: feminist debates and the use of oral history' *Women's History Review* Vol. 3 No. 1 (1994), pp. 5–28; Sherna Berger Gluck, 'Feminist

Methodology and Women's Oral History: from celebration to critical analysis' paper read at Internationale Tagung der Historikerinnen und Historiker der Arbeiterinnen und Arbeiterbewegung (ITH) Linz, Austria, 18.9.1992. I am indebted to Mary Clancy for this last paper. Robert Perks and Alastair Thomson (eds.) *The Oral History Reader* (London, 1998) is an indispensable collection of essays on all aspects of oral history; Luisa Passerini, 'Work, ideology and consensus under Italian fascism', pp. 53–62, emphasises the importance of silence in contributions to oral history. See *A Note on Sources* for a fuller discussion of all this.

18 *Department of Local Government and Public Health Annual Reports* 1923–47; section on maternity and child welfare.

19 *Emigration Commission*, p. 113.

20 *Woman's Life* 1936–39, 'Happy Irish Babies' column.

21 A Trained Children's Nurse, 'Your Baby's First Year: On It Depends His Future Health' *Irish Press* July 9, 1934.

22 Redington, *Economic Cookery Book*, p. 21; Roper and Duffin, *Bluebird Cookery Book*, pp. 46–47.

23 D.B. Jelliffe and E.F. Jelliffe, *Human Milk in the Modern World* (London, 1978); Gabrielle Palmer, *The Politics of Breastfeeding* (London, 1989); Sheila Kitzinger, *The Experience of Breastfeeding* (London, 1978), Chapter One, passim.

24 La Leche League, *The Womanly Art of Breastfeeding* (London, 1975), Kitzinger, *Experience of Breastfeeding*.

25 M. Truby King, *Mothercraft*, pp. 58–89; Amalgamated Press, *The Motherhood Book*, pp. 121–44.

26 Maire Mullarney, *What About Me? A Woman For Whom One Damn Cause Led To Another* (Dublin, 1992), pp. 114–15.

27 Gabrielle Palmer, *The Politics of Breastfeeding*; strange to say, there is no one history of this huge social change, though Fildes, Marks and Marland, (eds.) *Women and Children First*, Ellen Ross, *Love and Toil*, Valerie Fildes' own book, *Wet-Nursing* (London, 1989), and Jane Lewis, *The Politics of Motherhood*, all contribute somewhat to our knowledge of the conditions under which mothers could, or would, breastfeed, and the attitudes of health professionals to them.

28 'Duties of the Health Visitor' *Irish Nurses' Union Gazette* No. 32, January 1930.

29 Michael Curtin, 'Failure to Breastfeed: A Review of the Feeding History of 1,007 Infants' *Irish Journal of Medical Science* No. 346 (1954), pp. 447–56.

30 Alex Spain, 'Maternity Services in Éire', p. 5.

31 Despite the fact that the dangers of overlying have been played down in recent years – notably in an authoritative guide like Hugh Jolly, *Book of Child Care: The Complete Guide for Today's Parents* (London, 1987), p. 103 – Thomas A. Clarke and Thomas G. Matthews, 'The Development of Neonatal Paediatrics at the Rotunda: A Tribute to Dr W.R.F. Collis and Sister Maudie Moran' in Alan Browne (ed.), *Masters, Midwives and Ladies-in-Waiting*, p. 127. remarks that the characteristic swing cots of the Rotunda obviated the danger of overlying, 'a not altogether uncommon occurrence in the history of the hospital'.

32 Conversation with Mrs J. Finlay, (b. Dublin City 1918) 38 Jamestown Road, Inchicore, Dublin 8, October 1990, who had her two children in the Rotunda in the later 1930s.

33 Ruth Barrington, *Health, Medicine and Politics*, pp. 145–46.

34 J.K. Feeney, 'Complications Associated With High Multiparity'.

35 Maire Mullarney, *What About Me?*, p. 114.

36 C.F.V. Coyle, MBMAO, (Tutor in Obstetrics, National Maternity Hospital), 'Breast-feeding and Some of its Difficulties' *Journal of the Medical Association of Éire*, Vol. 17, July 1945, pp. 86–88. On nipples and nailbrushes, see M. Truby King, *Mothercraft*, pp. 18–19; 'Mother and Baby' in *Aunt Kaye's Household Guide*, p. 127; and 'Health Hints by "Torcy"', A Tip For Expectant Mothers' in *Irish Messenger* Vol. LX, Nov. 1947, p. 246, a highly frank and technical article about breastfeeding.

37 *Department of Local Government and Public Health Report 1931–2*, pp. 55–58.
38 Chris Curtin and Tony Varley, 'Children and Childhood in Rural Ireland: A Consideration of the Ethnographic Literature' in C. Curtin, Mary Kelly and Liam O'Dowd (eds.) *Culture and Ideology in Ireland* (Galway, 1984), pp. 30–45.
39 Leslie Matson, *Meiní*, pp. 72–3.
40 Nancy Scheper-Hughes, *Saints, Scholars and Schizophrenics: Mental Illness in Irish Culture* PhD University of California, Berkeley (1976), passim, and p. 176; John Charles Russell, *In the Shadows of Saints: Aspects of Family and Religion in a Rural Irish Gaeltacht* University of California San Diego, PhD (1979), pp. 121–5.
41 James Deeny, 'Infant Mortality in the city of Belfast 1940–41' *Journal of the Statistical and Social Inquiry Society of Ireland* Vol. XVII, 1943–4, pp. 220–39.
42 Coimisiún Béaloideasa Éireann, Iml. 42, p. 33. Charleville District, John McAuliffe (76), 1935.
43 Coimisiún Béaloideasa Éireann, Iml. 259, p. 416, Co. Port Láirge (Waterford), Liam O Caoimh, pinsinéar, 1936.
44 Arensberg and Kimball, *Family and Community in Ireland*, p. 197.
45 Michael Curtin, 'Failure to Breastfeed:' *loc. cit.*
46 Survey cited by Tony Farmar, *Holles St 1894–1994*, pp. 136–7. On Lourdes hospital, Drogheda, oral evidence from Professor Mary E. Daly, Department of History, University College, Dublin. On Dublin artisans, Alexander Humphreys, *New Dubliners*, p. 145.
47 Ann Kennedy, 'Diary of a Farmer's Wife' *Irish Times* 14 November, 1956.
48 Curtin, 'Failure to Breastfeed', p. 453–4.
49 John D. Sheridan, 'Nine, Thank God' in *Half in Earnest* (Dublin, 1948), pp. 16–20; Croistóir O'Flynn, *There Is An Isle: A Limerick Boyhood* (Cork, 1998), Chapters 3, 4 and 5.
50 This will be discussed more fully in the succeeding chapters.
51 O'Flynn, passim.
52 *Census of Population* 1946, Vol. IX, Fertility of Marriage, Table 9, pp. 74–89; *Census of Population* 1961, Vol. VIII, Fertility of Marriage, Table 9, pp. 67–87; *Census of Population* 1981, Vol. XI, Fertility of Marriage Table 8B, p. 65. For a fuller discussion see Caitriona Clear, 'Women of the House 1921–1961: Discourses, Experiences, Memories' PhD thesis, UCD (1997), pp. 246–9.
53 John Dobbing, 'Medical and Scientific Commentary on Charges Made Against the Infant Food Industry', in J. Dobbing (ed.) *Infant Feeding: Anatomy of a Controversy 1973–1984* (New York, 1988), pp. 9–27, p. 16.
54 Una Claffey, *The Women Who Won: Women of the 27th Dáil* (Dublin, 1993), p. 15.
55 Both my mother, Kathleen Clear (née Synnott) and my mother-in-law (Bríd Lenihan née O'Flaherty) who had babies in small, intimate nursing homes in provincial towns and cities between 1951 and 1968, remember that everything for the baby (changing, feeding, bathing) was done for them by staff, during a two-week lying-in period.
56 'Health Hints by "Torcy": a Tip for Expectant Mothers', *Irish Messenger* Vol. LX, November 1947, p. 246.
57 Maura Laverty, *Lift Up Your Gates* (London, 1946), pp. 110–21.
58 Maura Laverty, *No More Than Human* (London, 1944, original edition) pp. 71–3; *No More Than Human* (London, 1945, Irish edition), pp. 71–3; on the abortion, pp. 130–31, (1944 edition) and 133–34 (Irish edition). The pagination is slightly different in any case because the 1944 print and pages are smaller.
59 See discussion of Maura Laverty in Chapter 4, and notes.
60 Terence Brown, *Ireland: A Social and Cultural History 1922–1985*, (London, 1985), pp. 196–7. The objection to *The Tailor and Ansty* was not so much the frank references to sex, but the fact that the reproductive activity of humans and of animals were referred to almost in the same breath, and that this was done in a rural setting. Maura Laverty's *Never No More* (London, 1942) was not banned in Ireland or the cause of any furore, and it contains many quite frank references to the sexual activity of rural people, and people getting away with sexual transgressions.

61 This was suggested to me by Margaret Hogan, born and reared in a rural area in the 1940s and 1950s, from Birr, Co. Offaly, Women's History Association of Ireland conference, University of Limerick, 19 September 1998.

62 See note 53, above.

63 Margery Spring Rice, *Working-class Wives: Their Health and Conditions* (London, 1939), p. 98, p. 97.

64 Gabrielle Palmer, *The Politics of Breastfeeding* (London, 1988, 1991), pp. 144–6.

65 See, e.g. Kitzinger, *Experience of Breastfeeding*, pp. 33–44, p. 189; Palmer, pp. 28–31, and Penelope Leach, *Children First: What Society Must Do – And Is Not Doing – For Children Today* (London, 1994), p. 58.

CHAPTER SEVEN

1 John Healy, *Nineteen Acres*, p. 103.

2 Maura Laverty, *No More Than Human* (1944), p. 182.

3 Joanna Bourke, *Husbandry to Housewifery*, pp. 212–13.

4 Ann Hathaway, *Homecraft Book*, p. 51; on water, 1946, Michael Shiels, *The Quiet Revolution: The Electrification of Rural Ireland* (Dublin, 1984), Chapter 17.

5 Patrick McNabb, 'Family Roles', p. 230, in J. Newman (ed.) Limerick Rural Survey.

6 Mary Healy, *For The Poor and For the Gentry*, p. 60.

7 Joe O'Reilly with fifth class, convent school, Edenderry, (ed.) *The Pauper's Graveyard* (Edenderry, 1993), p. 15.(An excellent collection of older people's life-stories.)

8 Maura Laverty, *Never No More*, p. 5.

9 Christine Zmroczek, 'Dirty Linen: Women, Class and Washing Machines 1920s–1960s' *Women's Studies International Forum* Vol. 15, No. 2 (1992), pp. 173–85.

10 Kevin Kearns, *Dublin Tenement Life*, pp. 121–2.

11 Zmroczek, 'Dirty Linen', p. 177.

12 Máire Ní Ghuithín, *Bean an Oileáin*, transl., p. 52 of Irish text.

13 *Household Budget Inquiry* 1951–2 (CSO 1954), pp. xxxix–xxxxi.

14 Advertisment, *Woman's Life* 24 February, 1951

15 Kevin Kearns, *Dublin Tenement Life*, p. 28.

16 Dorothy Macardle, 'Some Irish Mothers and Their Children' *Irish Press* 4 September, 1931.

17 Joe O'Reilly *et al.*, (eds.) *The Pauper's Graveyard*, p. 202. Kevin Kearns, *Dublin Tenement Life*, passim.

18 Croistóir O'Flynn, *There Is An Isle: A Limerick Boyhood* (Cork, 1998), Chapters 3, 4, 5.

19 Michael Shiels, *The Quiet Revolution*, pp. 206–7

21 John Healy, *Nineteen Acres*, p. 12.

22 Mary Healy, *For the Poor and for the Gentry*, p. 37.

23 Kevin Kearns, *Dublin Tenement Life*, p. 138.

24 John Healy, *Nineteen Acres*, p. 22

25 Ruth Barrington, *Health, Medicine and Politics*, pp. 139–40.

26 John Healy, *No-one Shouted Stop, formerly Death of an Irish Town* (first published Cork, 1968, Achill, 1988), pp. 87–91.

27 *Household Budget Inquiry* 1951–2, Table 3A Detailed Weekly Expenditure by Income Group pp. 18–23.

28 Shiels, *The Quiet Revolution*, pp. 206–07.

29 Kathleen Donnelly, 'What Rural Electrification Means In Our Home' *Irish Countrywomen's Association, Our Book* 1st Issue (1954), pp. 17–18.

30 John Healy, *Nineteen Acres*, p. 22.

31 Michael Shiels, *The Quiet Revolution*, p. 162, p. 166.

33 Michael Hartnett, *Maiden Street Ballad* (Newcastle West, 1980), p. 13.

34 Alice Taylor, *Quench the Lamp*, pp. 60–64.

35 *Ibid.*, p. 62.
36 Department of Agriculture, *Cookery Notes*, p. 60.
37 Alice Taylor, *Quench the Lamp*, pp. 42–4; Larry Kiely, interview transcript.
38 *National Nutrition Survey*, General Report, p. 15. Olive Ashmore, 'An Irishwoman's Diary' *The Irish Times* 1 December, 1998.
39 Noel Browne, *Against the Tide*, p. 13.
40 Francis McManus, *Flow On Lovely River* (Cork, 1966), p. 15.
41 *Household Budget Inquiry*, 1951–2., pp. xlvii–li.
42 Bríd Mahon, *Land of Milk and Honey* (Dublin, 1991, Cork, 1998), p. 87.
43 Maura Laverty, *Kind Cooking*, p. 71; Máire Ní Ghuithín, *Bean an Oilein*, transl. chapter, 'Cooking in the Blasket Kitchen'.
44 *National Nutrition Survey*, General Summary, Part II, and General Summary, Farm Workers' Families, Part IV.
45 OHA Hughes, 'The Need for Meals for School-Children in Rural Areas' *The Irish Housewife* Vol. 1 (1946), pp. 27–28. Hughes was a longstanding and office-holding member of the ICA.
46 Darina Allen, *Irish Traditional Cooking*, pp. 6–7.
47 Miss Walsh's evidence on behalf of the ICA to the Commission on Vocational Organisation, 21 November, 1940, NLI 930, Vol. 9, 18252–4.
48 Letter from Kate Rohan, *Irish Independent* 8 April, 1938.
49 Maura Laverty, *Kind Cooking*, pp. 29–30.
50 Darina Allen, *Irish Traditional Cooking*, pp. 6–10; see also Myrtle Allen, *The Ballymaloe Cookbook* (Dublin, 1977).
51 Kevin Kearns, *Dublin Tenement Life*, p. 212.
52 Darina Allen, *Irish Traditional Cooking*, p. 120, pp. 124–39.
53 Letter from 'One of the Bad Ones' *Irish Independent* 8 April, 1938.
54 Ruth Schwarz Cowan, *More Work For Mother*, pp. 20–25.
55 Maura Laverty, *Never No More*, p. 15, pp. 52–4; p. 71–2.
56 Máire Ní Ghuithín, *Bean an Oileáin*, transl. 'Cooking in the Blasket Kitchen' – manual dexterity.
57 Theodora Fitzgibbon, *Irish Traditional Food* (Dublin, 1983), cites (pp. 243–4) the memories of Jane Spence, Letterkenny,
58 Ní Ghuithín, *passim.*
59 *Household Budget Inquiry*, p. xxxii; Table 3A; Average Weekly Expenditure by Income Group, pp. 18–23.
60 Mary Ryan *et al.*, (eds.) *No Shoes In Summer*, p. 16.
61 Alice Taylor, *Quench the Lamp*, pp. 42–4; pp. 93–5.
62 'Mrs Wyse Answers Problems', *Woman's Life* 24 September, 1949.
63 Betty Friedan, *The Feminine Mystique*, Chapter 1.
64 See note 11.
65 Kathleen Donnelly, 'What Rural Electrification Means in Our Home' gives a graphic and detailed description of the amount of cleaning needed by oil lamps.

CHAPTER EIGHT

1 For the socio-historical perspective on women's status in contemporary Ireland, see Catherine Rose, *The Female Experience*; Jenny Beale, *Women in Ireland*; Evelyn Mahon, 'Women's Rights and Catholicism in Ireland'; Frances Gardiner, 'The Unfinished Revolution'; Ailbhe Smyth (ed.) *An Irish Women's Studies Reader*, and the articles written by Maryann Valiulis, cited in Chapter One. These writers all seem to have been heavily influenced by the sociological trends of early 1970s, which is evident particularly in the contributions to *Social Studies: An Irish Journal of Sociology* (December 1973), Vol. 2, No.

6. (D. Hannan, 'Changes in Family Relationship Patterns', pp. 559–63; Brendan Walsh, 'Married Women, Employment and Family Size', pp. 565–72.

2   Interdepartmental Committee on the Question of Making Available A Second Dwelling House on Farms, 1943, N A S 13413/1. I am indebted to Pauric Travers' article, 'Emigration and Gender: the case of Ireland 1922–1960' in O'Dowd and Wichert (eds.) *Chattel, Servant or Citizen*, pp. 187–99, for this reference.

3   Arensberg and Kimball, *Family and Community in Ireland*; C. Curtin and P. Gibbon, 'The Stem Family in Ireland' *Comparative Studies in Society and History* Vol. 20, No. 3, July 1978, pp. 429–53; for a useful and readable summary of sociological perspectives on the Irish family, see Tony Fahey, 'Family and Household in Ireland' in Patrick Clancy (ed.) *Irish Society: Sociological Perspectives* (Dublin, 1995), pp. 206–33.

4   Eileen Kane, 'The Changing Role of the Family in a Rural Irish Community' *Journal of Comparative Family Studies*, Vol. X No. 2, (1979), pp. 146–50: John Charles Russell, 'In The Shadow of Saints' p. 103; Alexander Humphreys, *New Dubliners*; Hugh Brody, *Inishkillane: Change and Decline in the West of Ireland* (New York, 1974), Chapter 4; Dr Peter Birch, 'The Irish Family in Modern Conditions' in *Social Studies: An Irish Journal of Sociology* Oct./Nov. 1973, Vol. 2, No. 5, p. 486.

5   Patrick McNabb, pp. 226–7, *Limerick Rural Survey*.

6   Elizabeth Brennan, 'Fine China', *The Irish Countrywoman* 1963–4, pp. 23– 7.

7   Dower-House Committee, letter from Land Commission Inspector W.H. O'Brien, 3/1/44; letter from Patrick Toohall, 3/1/44.

8   NLI Ms.930, Vol. 9, 18271–4. Bishop Browne was not at all happy with this, arguing that surely it was in the nature of things for the older to guide the younger, but was assured, 'They [young and old] agree beautifully, my Lord.'

9   CBE, Iml. 1100, p. 42.

10 Patricia O'Hara, *Partners in Production: Women, Farm and Family in Ireland* (Oxford, 1998), p. 74; Dower-House Committee, letter from Patrick Tohall, 3/1/44.

11 O'Hara, p. 74; Margaret Horne, 'The Almoner's Work in a Maternity Hospital' *Journal of the Irish Medical Association*, Vol. 34 (1954), pp. 105–7.

12 Mary Healy, *For the Poor and for the Gentry*, pp. 30–31.

13 Tony Fahey, 'Family and Household in Ireland' provides a very useful summary of the sociological and anthropological literature here.

14 Alexander Humphreys, *New Dubliners*, p. 206.

15 Mary Healy, *For the Poor and for the Gentry*, passim, especially the first four chapters.

16 Kevin Kearns, *Dublin Tenement Life*, p. 92.

17 *Ibid.*, pp. 106–7, pp. 49–51.

18 Mary Healy, *For the Poor and for the Gentry*, p. 22.

19 Hugh Leonard, *Home Before Night* (London, 1980), p. 15.

20 Marilyn Silverman, '"A Labouring Man's Daughter": constructing respectability in South Kilkenny' in C. Curtin and T. Wilson (ed.) *Ireland From Below: Social Change and Local Communities* (Galway, 1987), pp. 109–27.

21 Seán O Súilleabháin, in his *Handbook of Irish Folklore* (Dublin, 1963; Detroit, 1970), p. 138, takes for granted that this practice existed traditionally at least, in rural Ireland: 'What names were applied locally to this habit of night-visiting . . . What was said of those who over-indulged in it, or of those who "never stirred out"?': Arensberg and Kimball, *Family and Community in Ireland*, pp. 181–94.

22 Alexander Humphreys, *New Dubliners*, pp. 184–5.

23 Alexander Humphreys, *New Dubliners*, p. 141.

24 Charles Clancy-Gore, 'Nutritional Standards of Some Dublin Working-Class Families 1943' p. 251.

25 Patrick McNabb, 'Family Roles' pp. 228–9, *Limerick Rural Survey*.

26 Alexander Humphreys, *New Dubliners*, p. 99.

27 Clancy-Gore, 'Nutritional Standards of Some Dublin Families' p. 247.

28 *Dáil Debates*, (92), 581–2, 2 December, 1943.

29 Alexander Humphreys, *New Dubliners*, p. 203.

30 Kevin Kearns, *Dublin Tenement Life*, p. 118; Patrick McNabb, p. 228, *Limerick Rural Survey*; Patricia O'Hara, pp. 120–24.

31 Ethel R.'s testimony was written, that of the others, spoken.

32 Damian Hannan, 'Changes in Family Relationship Patterns'; see also his 'Patterns of Spousal Accommodation and Conflict in Traditional Farm Families' *Economic and Social Review* 10, No. 1 (1978), pp. 61–84.

33 John Charles Russell, ' In the Shadows of Saints', p. 142; Arensberg and Kimball, *Family and Community in Ireland*, pp. 45–58.

34 Eileen Kane, 'The Changing Role of the Family in a Rural Irish Community', p. 150.

35 Alexander Humphreys, *New Dubliners*, p. 98; also, p. 141, where a man doing housework was considered a 'molly'.

36 CBE, Iml. 1100, pp. 27–8.

37 Croistóir O'Flynn, *There is An Isle*, passim.

38 Alexander Humphreys, *New Dubliners*, p. 141.

39 Mary Healy, *For the Poor and For the Gentry*, pp. 83–4, pp. 89–90, pp. 91–???

40 Myles na Gopaleen/Flann O'Brien, (Brian O'Nolan), *The Best of Myles* (London, 1968; 1975), pp. 295–6.

41 Pat O'Connor, *Emerging Voices*, pp. 153–4.

41 Damian Hannan, 'Patterns of Spousal Accommodation'.

42 Hugh Brody, *Inishkillane*, Chapter 4 and passim; Patrick McNabb, pp. 228–31, *Limerick Rural Survey*.

43 Damian Hannan, 'Patterns of Spousal Accommodation'.

44 Nuala O'Faoláin, *Are You Somebody? The Life and Times of Nuala O'Faoláin* (Dublin, 1996), p. 89.

CONCLUSION

1 Margery Spring-Rice, *Working-Class Wives*, pp. 97–8.

2 Hartnett, *Maiden Street Ballad*; O'Flynn, *There Is An Isle*.

3 John McGahern, *Amongst Women* (London, 1990).

4 *Census of Ireland* 1926, 1936, 1946, 1961: Occupational Tables.

5 Patricia O'Hara, *Partners in Production*, pp. 128–32.

6 Penny Summerfield, *Reconstructing Women's Wartime Lives: Discourse and Subjectivity in Oral Histories of the Second World War* (Manchester, 1998), pp. 252–86, and passim; Judy Giles, *Women, Identity and Private Life in Britain 1900–1950* (London, 1995), pp. 27–8.

7 Joanna Bourke, *Husbandry to Housewifery*, p. 277, and pp. 25–200.

8 Judy Giles, p. 7, on Vera Brittain, Winifred Holtby and domestic service; this assumption was also implicit in many Irish feminist discussions of women's work, see Chapter Three.

9 E.P. Thompson, *The Making of the English Working Class* (London, 1963), p. 12: 'I am seeking to rescue the poor stockinger, the Luddite cropper, the "obsolete" hand-loom weaver, the "utopian" artisan . . . from the enormous condescension of posterity.'

APPENDIX ONE

1 See Appendix 2 for appeal and questionnaire, and bibliography for short, pseudonymous biographies of contributors.

2 For example, the fact that almost all were from lower-middle class or working-class or medium to small-farming backgrounds, and that whatever men there were, were almost all from all-male families of origin, or families with a preponderance of boys where the mother was widowed early. See Chapters 7, 8 and Conclusion.

3 Luisa Passerini, 'Work Ideology and Consensus Under Italian Fascism' in R. Perks and A. Thomson (eds.) *The Oral History Reader* (London, 1998), pp. 53–62. My conduct of interviews and my own 'composure' as an interviewer owes a lot to Stephen Caunce, *Oral History and the Historian* (London, 1992).

4 Penny Summerfield, *Reconstructing Women's Wartime Lives: Discourse and Subjectivity in Oral Histories of the Second World War* (Manchester, 1998), pp. 16–23. Judy Giles, *Women, Identity and Private Life in Britain 1900–50* (London, 1995), p. 27–8, also talks about women's composures in interviews.

5 For example,transcripts Tom and Joan K., Seamus and Annie R., Anne D., Josephine E.

6 Summerfield, p. 15, who cites Graham Dawson, *Soldier Heroes: British Adventure and the Imagination of Masculinities* (London, 1994) as one of the originators of this idea.

7 For example, the distribution of money within families, the relationship with co-resident (after marriage) parents and in-laws, the division of labour between cooperative couples. See Chapters 7 and 8, and Conclusion.

8 For example, when both Josephine E. and Olive A., from two entirely different backgrounds, defined comfort and ease for the woman of the house as having time and money to put cream on one's face, this led me to wonder if aspiration to luxury items like this was a feature of women's lives in the 1950s, and something that applied to women of different ways of life. The stepped-up advertising of cosmetics in newspapers and magazines in the 1950s and the increase in the number of hairdressers, as well as evidence from photographs, seemed to corroborate this. Much more work needs to be done, of course, but there is enough evidence for a suggestion. Similarly, I was always puzzled that women claimed never to have read any magazines or women's pages, or could not remember these very clearly when they had done so, until I read Penny Tinkler, *Constructing Girlhood: Popular Magazines for Girls Growing Up in England 1920–1950* (London, 1995), and she found the same in her research, which led her in the end to a content analysis rather than the impossible task, under the circumstances, of finding out how readers had 'read' these magazines.

9 Raphael Samuel, *Theatres of Memory: Vol. 1 of Past and Present in Contemporary Culture* (London, 1994), p. 15.

Bibliography

A. PERSONAL TESTIMONY, SOLICITED

See Appendices for letter which solicited evidence and questionnaire sent to some contributors, also tape and letter transcripts.

Names and Addresses, Personal Details (pseudonyms only)
'Personal contact' means that the contributors were known to the researcher other than by responding to the newspaper appeal.

1. MADGE C. Born Dublin City 1933, father an insurance salesman. Trained as a teacher and married 1960. Interview July 13, 1995.

2. BRENDAN McN. Born on 60–70 acre farm, Clare, 1914. Interview June 12, 1995. Galway. Took notes.

3 and 4. TOM AND JOAN K. TOM, b. c. 1924, 16 acre farm, Mayo, five brothers, two sisters, mother widowed early; Joan b. c. 1924, nine siblings, large farm, Wexford. Married 1951, lived all married life in Dublin City. Tom a bus driver till he retired, Joan an office worker before she married. Five children, b. 1952–1960. Interview May 30, 1995 plus 2 long letters written by Tom.

5. LARRY K. Born in a town in Co. Laois, 1914. Five brothers. Married 1940. Railway worker in the Laois-Kildare area, moved to Co. Galway 1950s as station-master. Wife, Noreen, a Dublin City woman. Four children, born in 1940s. Interview May 11, May 17, 1995. Died October 1995.

6. KATHLEEN B. Portlaoise, Co. Laois. Born 1932, one of four children, big farm. Mother born 1898: letter mostly about mother's life. Long letter, written May 1, 1995.

7. MAUREEN T. Born Co. Louth, 1921, rural but not farming, eldest of family of seven. Wrote a long letter, May 5, 1995.

8. EILEEN K. Born 1942 in small town in south-west; father a Garda, moved around a bit. Mother married 1930. Two long letters.

9. EAMONN B. Born 1933, town in north Tipperary; father a National teacher, mother a shopkeeper. Two brothers. Retired public servant. He himself made a long tape about his home of origin and his father's people in Clare where he used to go on holidays as a child.

10. ANNA A. Born Co. Sligo 1940: farm about 10–12 acres, belonging to grand-aunt, worked by parents and grand-aunt, three sisters and two brothers. Filled in questionnaire and interviewed, November 1995.

11. OLIVE A. Born c. 1929, Cork City. Office worker before marriage; husband had a business. Married 1951. Six children. Trained as elocution teacher late 1960s. A long letter and an interview August 1995.

12. LUCY O'S. Born 1932, father National teacher, rural area. One sister. Mother kept hens and a cow as well as keeping house. Married 1960. Long letter and interview, June 1995.

13. GRETTA M. Born 1952, upper-middle class Cork family, one of five children. Solicitor. Long letter, May 1995.

14. SEAN C. Born 1911, 'belonging to a large family'. Farming since 1949, two sons. Questionnaire.

15 and 16. FRANK AND MARGARET Q. Married 1954: Margaret worked in a factory before her marriage; Frank, in British navy, later worked in an oil refinery, Co. Cork. Seven children. Long interview June 1995. Frank died September 1995.

17. JANE S. Born 1906, worked at home on farm, Cavan, married 1928, farmer, eight children. Successful poultry business 1950s. Interview July 1995.

18. MARIAN B. No personal details at all, except 'brought up in countryside', and has details of the work of the house 1932–1960 but lots of information on farm women's work long ago. Very interesting, useful as perception and informative.

19. MAUREEN O'R. Born 1937 in a 'working-class family', eldest of eight. Sizeable Cork town. Father casual labourer, mother a small regular home-based income. Long letter and interview August 1995.

20. ITA O'C. Born 1921, eldest of a large family, midlands town. Mother widowed when family was young. Seem to have had reasonable standard of living, though always short of money. Long, vivid letter June 1995.

21. JIM D. No personal details, but refers to work of mother on small Mayo farm (10–20 acres) in the 1950s, nine children, three at home 1950s.

22. ANNE D. Born rural Sligo, 1922, 'the third youngest in a family' and the eldest girl, it seems; father a blacksmith, small farm. Married 1942 onto a farm. Detailed and lyrical description of work processes pre-electrification, everything from flour-bags to home-made dyes, over two 7–8-page letters.

23. JOSEPHINE E. Born 'on a very small farm' Mayo, 1928, one brother who died of TB in 1947. Went working in local town early 1940s and thence to England, where she married 1957, returned 1959 to look after mother, run small farm while husband got building work locally, four children. No water or electricity till 1970. Long letter and interview June/July 1995.

24. JACK R. Born 1911, mother married 1916. Mainly about her life, vivid letter on work processes received June 1995.

25. AINE Uí G. No personal details but a lot of information about matchmaking. Letter.

26. MARY ELLEN D. Born 1928, big farm, Roscommon. Worked on farm until marriage in 1951, to farmer in midlands. Nine children. Long interview and dinner, September 1995.

27. JIMMY O'M. Born 1927 in a coastal Waterford town. Long and vivid letter about daily work of his mother, 1927–1950.

28. LILY G. Born Mayo 1923, went teaching to England, returned 1948, married 1950, inherited small farm and husband working, seven children. Interview October 1995. Lily died April 1996.

29. MICHAEL E. Born in 1920s, eight siblings, father an ex-Anzac on pension, helped by relatives, had a nanny and a maid, but fierce struggle to make ends meet. Mother worked very hard also, constant mending etc. Two long and very descriptive letters, June 1995.

30. ANN C. 'Over 75 years'. Long and informative letter about the work of the woman of the house on a farm pre-electrification and aquafication in Roscommon.

31. AGGIE D. Born 1914 on a 'big farm', Co. Limerick. Married?, husband died when only 11 years married, three boys. Two long and descriptive letters about aspects of life on and around farms in Limerick. Went to domestic economy college.

32. NOREEN L. Born 1939, two younger brothers, parents 'victims of an arranged marriage'. Trained as psychiatric nurse from 1957. Very vivid and bleak letter about conditions as she remembers them.

33. ETHEL R. Born 1944, Cork town. Three sisters. Father a bank manager. Active in ICA as was her mother. Questionnaire.

34. CARMEL C. Born 1921, east Galway, twelve acre farm, married a farmer and went in with a mother-in-law. Very valuable and vivid letter.

35. T. J. McD. Born Cavan, 70 acre farm, low-lying, c. 1935–40. Three brothers. Mother widowed 1944. Ran farm. Questionnaire and letter, very informative.

36. DELIA R. Born 1921, Limerick City, fourth eldest (third surviving) of nine children, father an artisan, mother a farmer's daughter. Lived with paternal grandmother in small south-eastern town from age 8 until age 14. Remembers both family economies vividly. Long interview August 1995. Personal contact.

37 and 38. SEAMUS AND ANNIE R. Seamus born 1917 (brother of D., above), Annie in 1921, 70 acre farm west Limerick, two sisters and two brothers. Seamus reared till age 8 by maternal grandparents on small Offaly farm. Annie also reared in early childhood by grandparent and aunts. Married 1956. Seamus a book-keeper in family firm; Annie an office worker before marriage. Interview August 1995. Personal contact.

39. HANNAH C. born Co. Sligo 1918, father a quarry owner and road-maker with small farm. Went to England as a nurse 1940s, married and settled in Mayo 1953. Interview December 1992 and written testimony. Personal contact.

40. BETTY S. Born 1932, in Dublin; married 1954 ('Dublin middle-class' is how she describes her social milieu), five children. Long and detailed letter about breastfeeding in September 1998, after having heard the writer give a paper on the subject. Personal contact.

B. MANUSCRIPTS INCLUDING STATE PAPERS

Coimisiúin Béaloideasa Eireann, evidence collected 1930–1960. Microfilms in James Hardiman Library, UCG, of mss in the Department of Folklore, University College, Dublin.

Correspondence between Department of Education and Irish National Teachers' Organisation, 14/3/32–15/11/32, N A S 7985, A, B, C D.

Revised Midwives Bill (1933), N A S S 942.

Correspondence between Department of Lands and Department of Finance on employment of women as Land Commission Inspectors, 30/7/34–24/8/34. N A S 6 664.

Correspondence on Family Allowances, 13/11/39–16/3/43, and Report of Interdepartmental Committee, 1943, N A S 12117, A, B.

Correspondence between Central Midwives Board and Department of Health, 16/5/49–8/3/50, N A S 14 414.

Minutes of Evidence of INTO to Commission on Vocational Organisation, 1940, NLI Ms. 920, Vol. 2.

Minutes of Evidence of Irish Countrywomen's Association to Commission on Vocational Organization, 1940, NLI Ms. 930, Vol. 9.

Minutes of Evidence of Joint Committee of Women's Organisations (the National Council of Women in Ireland, the Joint Committee of Women's Societies and Social Workers, the Catholic Federation of Secondary School Unions) to Commission on Vocational Organisation, 1940, NLI Ms. 930, Vol. 9.

Memorandum of ICA to Commission on Vocational Organisation, NLI Ms. 941, Vol. 20, No. 196.

Memorandum of Joint Committee of Women's Organisations to Commission on Vocational Organisation, NLI Ms. 941, Vol. 20, No. 200, 200B.

Report of the Interdepartmental Committee on the Question of Making Available a Second Dwelling-house on Farms (1943), N A S 13413/1.

C. GOVERNMENT PUBLICATIONS

Report of the Commission on Emigration and Other Population Problems 1948–54 (1956) R.84.

Report of the Commission on Vocational Organisation (1943) K.76/1.

Department of Health, National Nutrition Survey Parts 1–VII, (1948). K.53/1–6

Central Statistics Office, *Household Budget Inquiry 1951–2* (1954).

Report of the Commission on the Relief of the Sick and Destitute Poor including the Insane Poor (1927) R.27/3.

Report of the Commission on Youth Unemployment 1951 R./82.

Guide to the Social Services: A Summary Designed for the Information of Individuals and Groups (Stationery Office, 1941, 1945, 1955).

Department of Local Government and Public Health, *Report of the Conference between the Department of Local Government and Public Health and Representatives of the Local Public Health Authorities held at the Mansion House Dublin 8th and 9th July 1930* K.29.

Report of Committee of Inquiry into Widows' and Orphans' Pensions, Reports 1933 R.49/1.

Department of Agriculture, *Cookery Notes Prepared for use in Schools and Classes for Girls Working Under Schemes of Departments of Lands and Agriculture* (Dublin 1925, revised every two or three years or so, Dublin, 1942) A/14.

Censuses of Population, 1926, 1936, 1946, 1951, 1961.
Reports of the Department of Local Government and Public Health, 1923–47.
Reports of the Department of Health 1948–61.
Annual Reports of the Registrar-General, 1923–52.
Department of Health/Central Statistics Office, *Vital Statistics, 1953–61.*
Dáil Debates, 1923–1944.
Seanad Debates, 1937–1944.
Department of Education, *Rules and Programmes for Secondary Schools, 1927–1959.*
Department of Education, *Annual Reports and Results of Examinations, 1925–61.*
Department of Education, *Prospecti Irish Training School of Domestic Economy 1929–42.*

D. ARTICLES AND BOOKS PUBLISHED 1921–61

Anon. 'An Attractive Overall: Jane West Patterns' *Irish Independent* Jan 1, 1947.
Anon. 'Attempted Murder Echo: Old Lady Sues Daughter-in-Law: Judge Imposes Fine' *Connacht Tribune* Jan 27. 1934.
Anon. 'Changes that turn women from careers' *Irish Times* Feb 27, 1954.
Anon. 'Clarion Call of Lenten Pastoral: Clonfert' *Connacht Tribune* Feb 17, 1934.
Anon. 'Countrywomen in Uniforms' *Irish Independent* Sept 6, 1956.
Anon./'Darina', 'Friday's Gossip Column: women in the news' *Irish Press*, 1957–59.
Anon. 'Diane's Diary: Happy the Wooing' *Woman's Life* Nov 5, 1938.
Anon. 'Domestic Modern Girls' *Irish Press* Sept 8, 1931.
Anon. 'Duties of the Health Visitor' *Irish Nurses' Union Gazette* No. 32, January 1930.
Anon. 'Echoes of the Constitution' *Woman's Life* March 12, 1938.
Anon./'Eithne', 'Can I Come With you, My Pretty Maid?' *Irish Monthly* Vol. LIII, No. 630, December 1925, pp. 628–34.
Anon. 'Grandmother Envies the Housekeeper of Today' *Irish Press* December 28, 1938.
Anon. 'Home Planning and Decoration' *Woman's Life* July 16, 1951.
Anon. 'Is This A Tin-Opener Age.' *Woman's Life* Feb 27, 1937.
Anon./'Joan', 'The Homefront' *The Irish Housewife* Vol. 4 (1950), pp. 103–5.
Anon. 'Letter to a Farmer's Wife' *Woman's Life* Jan–Jun 1937.
Anon. 'Pretty but Practical: Jane West Patterns' *Irish Independent* Oct 18, 1943.
Anon. 'Question Box' *Irish Messenger of the Sacred Heart* 1927–55.
Anon. 'The Housewife's Outfit' *Irish Press* October 19, 1931.
Anon. 'Torcy', 'A Tip For Expectant Mothers' in *Irish Messenger* Vol. LX, Nov. 1947, p. 246.
A Trained Children's Nurse, 'Your Baby's First Year: On It Depends His Future Health' *Irish Press* July 9, 1934.
Amalgamated Press, Ltd. *The Motherhood Book* (c. London, 1933).
Arensberg, C. and Kimball, S. *Family and Community in Ireland* (Harvard, 1940, other date please).
Aunt Kaye (ed.), *The Household Guide* (London and Dundee, n.d. wartime paper, c. 1947).
Barry, A.P., Meagher, D. and O' Dwyer, E. 'Heart Disease in Pregnancy' *Journal of the Irish Medical Assocation* Vol. 38 (1956), pp. 82–3.
Bauer, Maria Agnes 'Dress and Fashion' *Irish Messenger of the Sacred Heart* Vol. XLIX (Aug 1936) 87.

Bean a'Tighe, 'For Mothers and Daughters' *Catholic Bulletin 1923–38.*

Bennett, Louie 'The Domestic Problem' *The Irish Housewife* Vol. 1 (1946), pp. 29–30.

Blanshard, P. *The Irish and Catholic Power* (London, 1954).

Boland, S.J. 'Radiology in Antenatal Care' *Journal of the Irish Medical Association,* Vol. 36 (1955), pp. 20–1.

Boyle, Elizabeth 'A Plan for the Northern Houseworkers' *The Irish Housewife* Vol. 1 (1946), pp. 31–3.

Brown, Reverend Stephen J. 'Little Notes on Life' pp. 61–2; *Irish Messenger*, Vol. 50, No. 2.

Burke, A.J. and Burke, R.M. 'The Rural Housewife and Family' *The Irish Housewife* Vol. 1 (1946) pp. 66–8.

Business Girl, A 'Marriage As A Career, by a Business Girl, *Woman's Life* March 5, 1938.

Campbell, Helen 'Nursery Schools' *The Irish Housewife* Vol. 1 (1946), pp. 44–7.

Carroll, Paul Vincent 'The Mystical Irish' in John A. O'Brien (ed.) *The Vanishing Irish* (1954), pp. 54–64.

Cellen, E.M. 'Good News for Housewives' *The Irish Housewife* Vol. 9 (1956), pp. 92–3.

Chenevix, Helen 'Women's Opportunities in Local Government' *The Irish Housewife* Vol. 1 (1946), pp. 34–5.

Clancy-Gore, Charles 'Nutritional Standards of Some Working-class Families in Dublin, 1943.' *Journal of the Statistical and Social Inquiry Society of Ireland* 97th session, Vol. XVII, pp. 220–39.

Collis, Dr W.R.F. *The State of Medicine in Ireland* (1943).

Collis, Robert (W.R.F.) 'Infant Mortality in Eire and the Proposed Mother and Child Scheme' in *Journal of the Medical Association of Eire*, Vol. 23 (1948), pp. 82–5.

Coyle, C.F.V., MB MAO, (Tutor in Obstetrics, National Maternity Hospital), 'Breastfeeding and Some of its Difficulties' *Journal of the Medical Association of Éire* Vol. 17 (1945), pp. 86–8.

Coyne S. J., Edward, J. 'Mother and Child Service' *Studies* Vol. XL (1951), pp. 129–40.

Cullen, Bee 'It's a continental custom and I'll leave it there' *Irish Independent* August 8, 1956.

Curtayne, Alice *The New Woman: text of a lecture given in the Theatre Royal, Dublin, October 22 1933, under the title: 'The Renaissance of Woman'* (Dublin, 1933).

Curtin, Michael 'Failure to Breastfeed: a review of the feeding history of 1007 infants' *Irish Journal of Medical Science* No. 9 (1954), pp. 447–56.

de Cléir, Sean S.J. 'Marriage and Family in Irish Life' *Christus Rex* Vol. 6 (1952), pp. 303–13.

Deeny, James 'Infant Mortality in the city of Belfast 1940–1' *Journal of the Statistical and Social Inquiry Society of Ireland* Vol. XVII, 1943–4, pp. 220–39.

Deeny, James 'Poverty as a Cause of Ill-Health' Paper read May 31 1940 and published in the *Journal of the Statistical and Social Inquiry Society of Ireland* Vol. XVI, 93rd session, 1939–40, pp. 75–89.

Devlin, Kevin 'Single and Selfish' *Christus Rex* Vol. 6 (1952), pp. 223–31.

Dineen, Reverend P.S. (Peadar O Duinín), *Foclóir Gaeidhilge agus Béarla: an Irish-English dictionary, being a thesaurus of the words, phrases and idioms of the modern Irish language* (Dublin, 1927).

Dockeray, G.C. and W.R. Fearon, 'Ante-natal Nutrition in Dublin: a preliminary survey.' *Irish Journal of Medical Science* Vol. ? (1939), pp. 80–4.

Donnelly, Kathleen 'What Rural Electrification Means in Our Home' *Irish Countrywomen's Association, Our Book*, 1st Issue (1954), pp. 17–18.

Duff, F. *Miracles on Tap* (New York, 1961).

Dunne, John P. *Waiting the Verdict: Pensions or Pauperism: Necessitous Widows and Orphans in the Free State* (n.d. c. 1928).

Eithne, 'Where Are You Going To, My Pretty Maid' *Irish Monthly*, Vol. LIII, No. 626, August 1925, pp. 404–9, and No. 627, September 1925, pp. 458–66, and No. 628, October 1925, pp. 518–26.

Enraght Mooney, Frances 'Out of the Wind and the Rain's Way' *Irish Independent* August 14, 1956.

Feeney, Dr J.K. 'Antenatal Care' *Journal of the Irish Medical Assocation*, Vol. 34, (1954), pp. 42–4.

Feeney, Dr J.K. Master, Coombe hospital, 'Complications Associated With High Multiparity: a clinical survey of 518 cases' *Journal of the Irish Medical Association*, Vol. 32, (1953), pp. 36–55.

Ferguson, Kathleen *Lessons in Cookery and Housewifery: for the use of children Book I* (Dublin, 1908).

Ferguson, Kathleen *Sickroom Cookery and Notes on Sick Nursing* (Athlone, 1903).

Fidelma, 'Friendly Advice' *Irish Messenger* Vol. LXIV (February 1951), pp. 41–2.

Fischer, Jo 'Nine To Five' (cartoon), *Irish Independent* 1950–1956.

Fox, R.M. *Louie Bennett: Her Life and Times* (Dublin, 1957).

Freeman, T.W. *Ireland: Its Physical, Historical, Social and Economic Geography* (London, 1950).

Gallagher, Dr J.G. 'Causes of Maternal Mortality' *Irish Journal of Medical Science* 6th series 1941, pp. 497–50.

Gibbens, John *The Care of Young Babies* (London, 1940; 1959).

Good Housekeeping's Baby Book (London, 1944, 1952).

Gossip by Finola, *Woman's Life* July 16, 1951.

Greene, Dr P.J. 'A Suggested Health Scheme' *Journal of the Medical Association of Éire*, Vol. 14, No. 3 (1944), pp. 57–8.

Greene, Sheila 'Youth and Crime', *The Irish Housewife* Vol. 1 (1946), pp. 36–9.

Grey, Martha 'Efficiency Begins In The Kitchen', *Woman's Life* August 29, 1938.

Hanna, F. LLB, MP 'Family Life: the Facts' *Christus Rex* Vol. 5 (1951), pp. 20–45.

Hathaway, Ann *Ann Hathaway's Homecraft Library, The Homecraft Book* (Dublin, 1944).

Hayden, Mary 'Woman's Role in the Modern World' *Irish Monthly* Vol. LXVIII August 1940, p. 398.

Hayes, John 'Stemming the Flight from the Land' in John A. O'Brien (ed.) *The Vanishing Irish* (1954), pp. 127–43.

Holmes, Eleanor 'The Social Work Department' in Clinical Report of the Rotunda Hospital, *Irish Journal of Medical Science* No. 371, (Nov 1956), pp. 3–8.

Holmes, G. 'The Woman of the House' *Irish Messenger* Vol. LX (July 1947), pp. 153–4, and April 1947, pp. 31–2.

Horne, Margaret 'The Almoner's Work in a Maternity Hospital' *Journal of Irish Medical Association* Vol. 34 (1954), pp. 105–7.

Hughes, Olivia 'The Need for Meals for School Children in Rural Areas' *The Irish Housewife* Vol. 1 (1946), pp. 27–8.

Hughes, Olivia 'The Need for Meals for School Children in the Rural Areas' *The Irish Housewife* Vol. 1 (1946).

Jacques, Madame Marie 'How We Renovated Our Home' *Irish Messenger* Vol. XL (August 1927), pp. 623–4.

Jacques, Madame Marie 'The Little Ones' *Irish Messenger* Vol. XLI (April 1928), pp. 221–2.

Kavanagh, Ethna 'Household Hints, *Irish Messenger* Vol. LVIII (January 1945).

Keating, Mary Frances 'Marriage-shy Irishmen' in John A. O'Brien (ed.) *The Vanishing Irish* (1954), pp. 164–75.

Kelly, Gerald S.J., *Medico-Moral Problems* (Dublin, 1949).

Kennedy, Ann 'Diary of a Farmer's Wife' *Irish Times* Nov 14, 1956.

King, Patrick CC, BD 'Family Allowances' *Catholic Bulletin* Vol. 28 Jan–Jun 1938, pp. 310–12.

Knaggs, J. F. 'Natality in Dublin in the year 1955' *Statistical and Social Inquiry Society Journal* Vol. XX (1957–8), pp. 37–55.

L'Observateur, 'Causes and Consequences of Depopulation: Notes from France' *Catholic Bulletin* Vol. 15, Jan–Dec 1925, pp. 911–18.

L'Observateur, 'Paternal Authority in the French Family' *Catholic Bulletin* Vol. 28, Jan–June 1938, pp. 299–303.

Lacey, Eileen 'New Year Ps and Qs for Mothers' *Irish Independent* January 4 1947.

Laverty, Maura *Flour Economy* (Dublin, 1941), p. 7.

Laverty, Maura *Full and Plenty* (Dublin, 1961).

Laverty, Maura *Kind Cooking* (Tralee, 1946).

Laverty, Maura *Lift Up Your Gates* (London, 1946).

Laverty, Maura *Never No More: The Story of a Lost Village* (London, 1942).

Laverty, Maura *No More Than Human* (London, 1944, original edition; 1945, Irish edition).

Laverty, May 'The Terrors of Washing-Up: Lightening the Housewife's Burden' *Irish Press* Sept 7, 1935.

Letts, W. 'Bracing Thoughts On A Universal Duty' *The Irish Housewife* Vol. 9 (1956), pp. 58–9.

Lyon, Stanley 'Natality in Dublin in the Years 1943, 1944 and 1946' (Paper read on Friday 28th May 1948) *Statistical and Social Inquiry Society of Ireland* Vol. XVIII, 1947–8, pp. 57–77.

M.S.E., 'The Tierney Home' *Irish Messenger* Vol. XLIII, (February 1930), pp. 55–9.

Macardle, D. 'Adoption' *The Irish Housewife* Vol. 4 (1950).

Macardle, Dorothy 'Some Irish Mothers and Their Children' *Irish Press* September 4, 1931.

Macardle, Dorothy 'Some Irish Mothers and Their Children.' *Irish Press* September 14, 1931.

MacDonagh, W.F., SJ 'The Position of Woman in Modern Life' *Irish Monthly* Vol. LXVII (June 1939), pp. 389–99.

MacGeehin, M. 'A Scheme for Rural Guilds' *Irish Monthly* Vol. LXV, December 1937, pp. 799–813.

Macken, Mary 'In Memoriam: Mary T. Hayden' *Studies* Vol. XXX (1942), pp. 369–71.

MacNeill, Josephine 'Give a Hand to the Women' in *Muintir na Tire Official Handbook* (Dublin, 1941), pp. 51–3.

Maguire, Florence 'The Girl Who Lives In A Suitcase; that's you, Nurse!' *Irish Independent* June 4, 1947.

Manning, Susan 'Foreword' *The Irish Housewife* Vol. 1 (1946).

Marnell, Josephine; Breathnach, Nora; Martin, Anna and Murnaghan, Mor *All In The Cooking: Coláiste Mhuire Book of Household Cookery* (Dublin, 1946).

McClean, Fr Lucius OFM, *What's The Problem?* (Dublin, 1961).

McFeeley, Sr Mary Annetta, PBVM, 'Education for Womanhood: An American Experiment' *Christus Rex* Vol. 5 (1951), pp. 81–93.

Medical Missionaries of Mary, *The First Decade: Ten Years' Work of the Medical Missionaries of Mary 1937–1947* (Dublin, 1948).

Meehan, Ita 'Woman's Place in the Community' *Christus Rex* Vol. 13 (1959), pp. 90–103.

Moffett, Margot 'That Ideal Home' *The Irish Housewife* Vol. 1 (1946), pp. 44–7.

Mrs Wyse Answers Problems *Woman's Life*, February 4 1939.

Mrs Wyse 'Where A Wife Fails' *Woman's Life* September 24, 1938.

Murray, Edmund 'The Key to the Problem' in John A. O'Brien (ed.) *The Vanishing Irish* (1954), pp. 65–77.

O'Brien, John A. (ed.) *The Vanishing Irish* (London, 1954).

O'Reilly, Marie 'I Sketch Your World' *Irish Independent* January 17, 1947.

Patten, Marguerite *We'll Eat Again: a selection of recipes from the war years selected by Marguerite Patten in association with the Imperial War Museum*, (London, 1985).

Quin, Dr James 'A Suggested Maternity Service for Éire '*Irish Journal of Medical Science: the official journal of the Royal Academy of Medicine in Ireland* No. 229, January 1945, pp. 1–23.

Redington, Josephine *The Economic Cookery Book: tried recipes etc. suitable for all households, schools and domestic classes* (Dublin, 1927; first edition 1905).

Redington, Josephine *The Laundry Book* (Dublin, 1913).

Redmond, Brigid 'Rural Home-makers' *Irish Monthly* Vol. LXV, September 1937, pp. 602–10.

Roper, M. and Duffin, R. *The Bluebird Cookery Book for Working Women* (Dublin, 1939).

Ryan, Reverend T.F. SJ 'Dublin's Poorest' *The Capuchin Annual* Vol. I (1930), pp. 12–19.

Rynne, Stephen J. *Father John Hayes: Founder of Muintir na Tire/People of the Land* (Dublin, 1960).

Shanley, John P. 'The Reorganization of the Medical Service' *Journal of the Medical Association of Éire*, Vol. 14, No. 2 (1944), pp. 40–3.

Shannon, Reverend G.J., CM 'Woman: Wife and Mother' *Christus Rex* Vol. 5 (1952), pp. 155–74.

Sheehy Skeffington, Hanna 'Random reflections on housewives, their ways and works' *The Irish Housewife* Vol. 1 (1946), pp. 20–2.

Sheehy-Skeffington, Andrée 'What's the Use' *The Irish Housewife* Vol. 1 (1946), pp. 49–50.

Sheridan, John D. *Half in Earnest* (Dublin, 1948).

Smithson, Annie MP 'The Children of Our Slums' *Irish Monthly* Vol. LIII, October 1925, pp. 553–6.

Spain, Dr Alex 'Maternity Services in Éire' *Irish Journal of Medical Science: the official journal of the Royal Academy of Medicine in Ireland* No. 229, January 1945, pp. 1–23

Spain, Dr Alex ' Obstetric Emergencies' *Journal of the Medical Association of Éire* Vol. 27, (1950), pp. 62–3.

Stafford, Brigid 'Equal Pay For Women' *Irish Monthly* Vol. LXXIX, No. 937, July 1951, pp. 308–14.

Stone, Abraham and Hannah *A Marriage Manual: a Practical Guide-Book to Sex and Marriage* (London, 1940).

Struther, Jan *Mrs Miniver* (collection of journalism late 1930s, edited by Valerie Grove, London 1989).

Truby King, M. *Mothercraft* (London, 1939).

Tynan, K. 'A Trumpet Call to Irish Women' in *The Voice of Ireland: a memorial of freedom's day by the foremost leaders* (New York, 1924), pp. 170–4.

Vigilans 'As I See It' *Christus Rex* Vol. 4 (1950), pp. 74–5.

Vigilans, 'As I See It' *Christus Rex* Vol. 2 (1948), p. 75.

Vigilans, 'As I See It', *Christus Rex* Vol. 3 (1949), pp. 64–5.

Vol. LIII, Oct. 1925, pp. 553–6.

White, G. M. 'Some Problems of a Country Housewife' *The Irish Housewife* Vol. 1 (1946) pp. 64–5.

Women's Industrial Development Association, *The Woman At The Wheel: Household Handbook* (Dublin, 1935).

Wood, Ethel M. 'The Women's Group on Public Welfare' *The Irish Housewife* Vol. 8 (1955), pp. 33–5.

Yvette, 'Hearth and Home' *Irish Messenger* Vol. LXI, No. 1, January 1948, pp. 7–8.

E. SECONDARY WORKS: BOOKS, ARTICLES, THESES PUBLISHED/ISSUED SINCE 1961

Allen, Darina *Irish Traditional Cooking* (Dublin, 1995).

Allen, Myrtle *The Ballymaloe Cookbook* (Dublin, 1977).

Ballard, Linda May 'Just Whatever They Had Handy' *Ulster Folklife* Vol. 31 (1985), pp. 59–72.

Barrington, R. Health, *Medicine and Politics in Ireland 1900–1970* (Dublin, 1987).

Beale, J. *Women in Ireland: Voices of Change* (Dublin, 1986).

Berry, P. and Bishop, A. (eds.) *Testament of a Generation: the journalism of Vera Brittain and Winifred Holtby* (London, 1985).

Birch, Dr Peter 'The Irish Family in Modern Conditions' *Social Studies: an Irish Journal of Sociology* Vol. 2, No. 5, Oct–Nov 1973, pp. 485–92.

Blake, Carla 'Midwives Tales' *Cork Examiner* December 9, 1993.

Bock, G. and Thane, P. (eds.) *Maternity and Gender Policies: Women and the Rise of the European Welfare States* (London, 1991).

Bolger, P. (ed.) *And See Her Beauty Shining There: the story of the Irish Countrywomen* (Dublin, 1986).

Boston Women's Health Collective, *The New Our Bodies Ourselves: a book by and for women* (New York, 1992).

Bourke, J. *Husbandry to Housewifery: Women, Economic Change and Housework in Ireland 1890–1914* (Oxford, 1993).

Boxer, M. and Quataert, J. (ed.) *Connecting Spheres* (Oxford, 1987).

Brown, T. *Ireland: A Social and Cultural History* (London, 1985).

Browne, Alan (ed.) *Masters, Midwives and Ladies In Waiting: the Rotunda Hospital 1745–1995* (Dublin, 1995).

Browne, Noel *Against The Tide* (Dublin, 1986).

Buxton, Jayne *Ending the Mother War: Starting the Workplace Revolution* (London, 1998).

Byrne, Anne and Leonard, Madeleine, (eds.) *Women in Irish Society: A Sociological Reader* (Belfast, 1997).

Caunce, Stephen *Oral History and the Historian* (London, 1992).

Claffey, Una *The Women Who Won: Women of the 27th Dáil* (Dublin, 1993).

Clancy, M. 'Aspects of Women's Contribution to Oireachtas Debate in Ireland 1922–37' in M. Luddy and C. Murphy (eds.) *Women Surviving: studies in Irish women's history in the 19th and 20th centuries* (Dublin, 1990), pp. 206–32.

Clarke, T.A. and Matthews, T.G. 'The Development of Neonatal Paediatrics at the Rotunda: a tribute to Dr W.R.F. Collis and Sister Maudie Moran' in Alan Browne, *Masters, Maids and Ladies in Waiting* (1995).

Clear, Caitriona 'The Women Cannot Be Blamed: 'Home-makers', 'Countrywomen' and the Commission on Vocational Organization in the 1930s and 1940s' in M. O'Dowd and S. Wichert (eds.) *Chattel, Servant or Citizen? Studies in Women's History* (Belfast, 1995), pp. 179–86.

Clear, Caitriona 'No Feminine Mystique: Advice to Women of the House in Irish Publications in the 1930s, 1940s and 1950s' in M. O'Dowd and M. Valiulis (eds.) *Women and Irish History* (Dublin, 1997), pp. 189–205

Clear, Caitriona 'Women of the House: Women's Household Work in Ireland 1923–1961: Discourses, Experiences, Memories' PhD Thesis Department of History, University College Dublin, 1997.

Clear, Caitriona Section on Women and Household Work in M. Luddy *et al.* (eds.) *Field Day Anthology of Writing about Women* (forthcoming 1999).

Cleeve, Brian *Dictionary of Irish Writers*, (Cork, 1975).

Comerford, Máire *The First Dáil* (Dublin, 1969).

Cowan, Ruth Schwarz *More Work For Mother: the ironies of household technology from the open hearth to the microwave* (London, 1989).

Cullen Owens, R. *Smashing Times: A History of the Irish Women's Suffrage Movement* (Dublin, 1984).

Cullen, M. (ed.) *Girls Don't Do Honours: Irish Women and Education in the 19th and 20th centuries* (Dublin, 1987).

Curtin, C. and Gibbon, P. 'The Stem Family in Ireland' *Comparative Studies in Society and History* Vol. 20, No. 3 (July 1978), pp. 429–53.

Curtin, C. and Varley, T. 'Children and Childhood in Rural Ireland: a consideration of the ethnographic literature' in C. Curtin, Mary Kelly and Liam O'Dowd (eds.) Culture and Ideology in Ireland (Galway, 1984), pp. 30–45.

Daly, M.E. 'Women in the Irish Workforce from pre-industrial to modern times' *Saothar 7* (1981), pp. 74–82.

Daly, M.E. 'Women, Work and Trade Unionism in Ireland' in M. MacCurtain and D. O Corrain (eds.) Women In Irish Society: the historical dimension (Dublin, 1978).

Daly, M.E. *Industrial Development and Irish National Identity 1922–39* (Syracuse, 1992).

Daly, M.E. 'Women in The Irish Free State 1922–1939; the interaction between economics and ideology' in *Journal of Women's History* Vol. 6/7, Nos. 4/5; Winter/Spring 1995, pp. 99–116.

Davidoff, L. (ed.) *Gender and History* Vol. 4, No. 3 (1992), Special Issue on Motherhood, Race and the State in the Twentieth century.

Davin, Anna 'Feminism and Labour History' in R. Samuel (ed.) *People's History and Socialist Theory* (London, 1981).

Davin, Anna 'Imperialism and Motherhood' *History Workshop Journal 5*, 1978.

Deeny, James *To Cure and To Care: Memoirs of a Chief Medical Officer* (Dublin, 1989).

Devine, Francis 'Women in the Irish Trade Unions; a note' *Oibre: Journal of the Irish Labour History Society* No. 2 (1975).

Dineen, Reverend P.S. (Peadar O Duinín), *Foclóir Gaeidhilge agus Béarla: an Irish-English dictionary, being a thesaurus of the words, phrases and idioms of the modern Irish language* (Dublin, 1927).

Diner, H. *Erin's Daughters in America: Irish Immigrant Women in the 19th century* (Baltimore, 1983).

Duggan, Carmel 'Farming Women or Farmers' Wives? Women in the farming press' in C. Curtin, P. Jackson and B. O'Connor (eds.) *Gender in Irish Society* (Galway, 1987).

Dwork, D. *War Is Good For Babies and Young Children: a history of the infant and child welfare movement in England 1898–1918* (London, 1987).

Ehrenreich, B. and English, D. Witches, *Midwives and Nurses: a history of women healers* (New York, 1973).

Fahey, Tony 'Family and Household in Ireland' in Clancy, P., Drudy, S., Lynch K. and O'Dowd, L. (eds.) *Irish Society: Sociological Perspectives* (Dublin, 1995), pp. 206–33.

Fanning, R. *Independent Ireland* (Dublin, 1983).

Farmar, Tony *Holles St 1894–1994: The National Maternity Hospital – a centenary history* (Dublin, 1994).

Farrell, B. *Chairman or Chief: the Role of Taoiseach in Irish Government* (Dublin, 1971).

Fentress, J. and Wickham, C. *Social Memory: the construction of the past* (London, 1988).

Fildes, V., Marks, L., and Marland, H. (eds.) *Women and Children First: international maternal and infant welfare 1870–1945* (London, 1992).

Fildes, Valerie, *Wet-Nursing* (London, 1989).

Fitzgibbon, Theodora *Irish Traditional Food* (Dublin, 1983).

Friedan, Betty The Feminine Mystique.(New York, London, 1963).

Gardiner, F. 'The Unfinished Revolution' *Canadian Journal of Irish Studies* Vol. 18, No. 1 (1992), pp. 15–39.

Giles, Judy *Women, Identity and Private Life in Britain 1900–1950* (London, 1995).

Gittins, D. *The Family In Question: changing household and family ideologies* (London, 1993).

Gluck, Shena B. and Patai, Daphne (eds.) *Women's Words: The Feminist Practice of Oral History* (London, 1991).

Goodwin, Joanne 'An American Experiment in Paid Motherhood: The Implementation of Mothers' Pensions in early 20th-century Chicago' *Gender and History* Vol. 4, No. 3 (Autumn 1992), pp. 323–42.

Gordon, Linda *Heroes of Their Own Lives: the politics and history of family violence* (New York, London, 1988).

Graves, Pamela M. *Labour Women: women in British working-class politics 1918–1939* (Cambridge, 1994).

Greer, Germaine *The Female Eunuch* (London, 1970).

Hannan, Damian 'Changes in Family Relationship Patterns' *Social Studies: an Irish Journal of Sociology* Vol. 2 No. 6 (Dec 1973), pp. 559–63.

Hannan, Damian 'Patterns of Spousal Accommodation and Conflict in Traditional Farm Families' *Economic and Social Review* Vol. 10, No. 1 (1978), pp. 61–84.

Hardyment, Christina *Perfect Parents: babycare advice past and present* (Oxford, 1995).

Hardyment, C. *From Mangle to Microwave: the mechanisation of household work* (London, 1988).

Harris, Lorelei 'Class, Community and Sexual Divisions in North Mayo' in Curtin, C. *et al.* (eds.) *Culture and Ideology in Ireland* (Galway, 1984), pp. 154–71.

Hartnett, Michael *Maiden Street Ballad* (Newcastle West, 1980).

Hazelkorn, E. 'The social and political views of Louie Bennett' (1870–1956), *Saothar 13* (1988), pp. 32–44.

Healy, John *Nineteen Acres* (Galway, 1978).

Healy, John *No-one Shouted Stop: formerly The Death of an Irish Town* (Cork, 1968; Achill 1988).

Healy, Mary *For the Poor and for the Gentry: Mary Healy remembers her life* (Dublin, 1989).

Hearn, Mona *Below Stairs: Domestic Service in Dublin and Beyond, 1870–1940* (Dublin, 1993).

Hobbs, Margaret 'Rethinking Antifeminism in the 1930s: Gender Crisis or Workplace Justice? A Response to Alice Kessler-Harris' in *Gender and History* Vol. 5, No. 1 (Spring 1993), pp. 4–15

Hobson, Barbara 'Feminist Strategies and Gendered Discourses in Welfare States: Married Women's Right to Work in USA and Sweden' in Koven, S. and Michel, S. (eds.) *Mothers of a New World* (1993), pp. 396–430.

Hufton, Olwen *The Prospect Before Her: a history of women in western Europe* Vol. 1 (London, 1995).

Humphreys, Alexander J. *New Dubliners: Urbanisation and the Irish Family* (London, 1966).

Jamieson, Lynn 'Limited Resources and Limiting Conventions: working-class mothers and daughters in urban Scotland 1890–1925' in Lewis, J (ed.) *Labour and Love* (1986), pp. 49–69.

Jelliffe, D.B. and Jelliffe, E.F. *Human Milk in the Modern World* (London, 1978).

John, A. *By the Sweat of their Brow: Women workers at Victorian coalmines* (Oxford, 1984).

Jolly, Hugh *Book of Child Care: the complete guide for today's parents* (London, 1987).

Jones, M. *Those Obstreperous Lassies; the Irish Women Workers' Union* (Dublin, 1988).

Kane, Eileen 'The Changing Role of the Family in a Rural Irish Community' *Journal of Comparative Family Studies* Vol. X, No. 2 (1979), pp. 146–50.

Kearns, Kevin *Dublin Tenement Life: an oral history* (Dublin, 1994).

Kelly, Mary A. 'The Development of Midwifery at the Rotunda', in A. Browne, (ed.) (1995) pp. 77–117.

Kennedy Jr, R. *The Irish: Emigration, Marriage and Fertility* (California, 1973).

Keogh, D. *Twentieth-century Ireland* (Dublin, 1994).

Kessler-Harris, A. 'Gender Ideology in Historical Reconstruction: a case study from the 1930s' *Gender and History* 1 (1989), pp. 31–49.

Kitzinger, Sheila *Ourselves As Mothers* (London, 1992).

Kitzinger, Sheila *The Experience of Breastfeeding* (London, 1978).

Kitzinger, Sheila *The New Pregnancy and Childbirth* (London, 1989).

Koven, Seth and Michel, Sonya (eds.) *Mothers of a New World: Maternalist Politics and the Rise of Welfare States* (London, 1993).

Koven, S. and Michel, S. 'Womanly Duties: Maternalist politics and the origins of Welfare States in France, Germany, Great Britain and the United States 1880–1920' in *American Historical Review 95* (1990), pp. 1076–108.

Lake, Marilyn 'A Revolution in the Family: the challenge and contradictions of Maternal Citizenship in Australia' in Koven and Michel (eds.) *Mothers of a New World*, (1993), pp. 378–95.

La Leche League, *The Womanly Art of Breastfeeding* (London, 1975).

Lambertz, Jan 'Marriage Relations, Money and Domestic Violence in working-class Liverpool 1919–39' in Lewis, J (ed.) *Labour and Love* (1986), pp. 195–219.

Leap, N. and Hunter, B. *The Midwife's Tale: an oral history from handywoman to professional midwife* (London, 1993).

Lee, J.J. *Ireland 1912–85: Politics and Society* (Cambridge, 1989).

Lee, J.J. *The Modernisation of Irish Society 1848–1918* (Dublin, 1973).

Lee, J.J. 'Some Aspects of Corporatist Thought in Ireland: the Commission on Vocational Organization 1939–43' in A. Cosgrove and D. MacCartney (eds.) *Studies in Irish History* (Dublin, 1979) pp. 324–46.

Lewis, Jane *The Politics of Motherhood: Child and Maternal Welfare in England 1900–1939* (London, 1980).

Lewis, Jane 'Gender, the family and women's agency in the building of 'welfare states' *Social History* Vol. 19. No. 1 (January 1994), pp. 37–55.

Lewis, Jane (ed.) *Labour and Love: Women's Experiences of Home and Family 1850–1940* (Oxford, 1986).

Lewis, Jane 'Models of Equality for Women: the case of state support for children in 20th-century Britain' in Bock, G. and Thane, P. (eds.) *Maternity and Gender Policies* (1991), pp. 73–92.

Lichfield, J. 'Ireland's "Comely Maidens" Are Doing It For Themselves' *British Independent on Sunday* 15 September, 1996.

Liu, T.P. 'Le Patrimoine Magique: Reassessing the Power of Women in Peasant Households in Nineteenth-century France' *Gender and History* Vol. 6, No. 1 (April 1994), pp. 13–36.

Llewellyn-Jones, Derek *Everywoman: A Woman's Health Guide for Life* (London, 1982 edition).

Loudon, I. *Death In Childbirth: an international study of maternal care and maternal mortality 1800–1950* (Oxford, 1992).

Mahon, Bríd *Land of Milk and Honey: A History of Irish Food* (Cork, 1997).

Mahon, Bríd *While Green Grass Grows: memoirs of an Irish folklorist* (Cork, 1998).

Mahon, Evelyn 'Women's Rights and Catholicism in Ireland' *New Left Review* No. 166 Nov–Dec 1978, pp. 53–78.

Mahon, Evelyn 'From Democracy to Femocracy: the women's movement in the Republic of Ireland' in Clancy, P., Drudy, S., Lynch, K. and O'Dowd, L. (eds.) *Irish Society: Sociological Perspectives* (Dublin, 1995), pp. 675–708.

Matson, Leslie *Meiní the Blasket Nurse* (Cork, 1995).

MacDermott, Eithne *Clann na Poblachta* (Cork, 1998).

McGinty, Mary 'A Study of the Campaign for and against the Enactment of the 1937 Constitution' MA thesis (UCG) 1987.

McKee, Eamonn 'Church-State relations and the Development of Irish Health Policy: the Mother and Child Scheme 1944–53.' *Irish Historical Studies* Vol. XXV, No. 98, (November 1986).

McManus, Francis *Flow On Lovely River* (Cork, 1966).

McNamara, Sarah *Those Intrepid United Irishwomen: Pioneers of the Irish Countrywomen's Association* (Parteen, 1995).

Merriman, J. *A History of Modern Europe* Vol. 2 (New York, 1996).

Mitford, Jessica *The American Way of Birth* (New York, 1992).

Moore, Honor 'Full and Plenty' *The Sunday Tribune Food and Wine* 99 29 November 1998, pp. 14–17.

Moser, Peter 'Rural Economy and Female Emigration in the West of Ireland 1936–56' *UCG Women's Studies Centre Review* (2) 1993, pp. 41–52.

Mullarney, Máire *What About Me? A Woman For Whom One Damn Cause Led To Another* (Dublin, 1992).

Mullins, G. and Dixon, D. (eds.) *Dorothea Lange's Ireland* (London,1996).

Murphy, Cliona *The Irish Women's Suffrage Movement and Irish Society in the Early Twentieth Century* (Brighton, 1988).

Murphy, John A. *Ireland in the Twentieth Century* (Dublin, 1975).

Murphy-Lawless, Jo 'The Silencing of Women in Childbirth, or, Let's Hear It From Bartholomew and the Boys' *Women's Studies International Forum*, Vol. 11, No. 4, (1988), pp. 293–8.

Murray, James P. *Galway: A Medico-Social History* (Galway, 1995).

na Gopaleen, Myles/O'Brien, Flann *The Best of Myles* (London, 1968, 1975).

Nash, Mary 'Pronatalism and Motherhood in Franco's Spain' in Bock, G. and Thane, P. (eds.) *Maternity and Gender Policies* (1991), pp. 160–77.

Newman, Reverend J. (ed.) *The Limerick Rural Survey 1958–64* (Tipperary, 1964).

Ni Ghuithin, Máire *Bean an Oiléain* (Baile Atha Cliath, 1985).

O'Brien, Breda 'Caring for Children, Not Ideology' *Sunday Business Post* October 11, 1998.

O'Connell, Dr J. *Doctor John: Crusading Doctor and Politician* (Dublin, 1989).

O'Connor, Emmet *A Labour History of Ireland* (Dublin, 1992).

O'Connor, Marie *Birth Tides: Turning Towards Home Birth* (in Ireland) (London, 1995).

O'Connor, Pat *Emerging Voices: Women in Contemporary Irish Society* (Dublin, 1998).

O'Donnell, E.E. (ed.) *Fr Browne's Ireland: Remarkable Images of People and Places* (Dublin, 1989).

O'Dowd, Mary and Valiulis, Maryann (eds.) *Women and Irish History: Essays in Honour of Margaret MacCurtain* (Dublin, 1997).

O'Dowd, Mary and Wichert, Sabine (ed.) *Chattel, Servant or Citizen? Studies in Women's History* (Belfast, 1995).

O'Faoláin, Nuala *Are You Somebody? The Life and Times of Nuala O'Faoláin* (Dublin, 1996).

Offen, Karen 'Body Politics: women, work and the politics of motherhood in France 1920–1950' in Bock, G. and Thane, P. (eds.) *Maternity and Gender Policies* (1991), pp. 138–59.

O'Flynn, Croistóir, *There Is An Isle: A Limerick Childhood* (Cork, 1998).

O Gráda, C. *Ireland: A New Economic History* (Oxford, 1994).

O'Hara, *Patricia Partners in Production: Women, Farm and Family in Ireland* (Oxford, 1998).

O'Leary, E. 'The INTO and the marriage bar for women national teachers 1933–58' *Saothar 12* (1987) pp. 47–52.

O'Reilly, Joe with 5th class convent school, Edenderry (ed.) *The Pauper's Graveyard* (Edenderry, 1993).

O'Sullivan, Sue (ed.) *Women's Health: A Spare Rib Reader* (London, 1987), pp. 303–17.

O Súilleabháin, Seán *A Handbook of Irish Folklore* (Dublin, 1963 Detroit; 1970).

Oakley, Ann *Housewife* (London, 1974).

Oram, H. *The Advertising Book: The History of Advertising in Ireland* (Dublin, 1986).

Paglia, Camille *Sex, Art and American Culture* (London, 1993).

Palmer, G. *The Politics of Breastfeeding* (London, 1989).

Passerini, Luisa 'Work Ideology and Consensus under Italian fascism' in R.Perks & A.Thomson (eds.) *The Oral History Reader* (London, 1998).

Peretz, Elizabeth 'The Costs of Motherhood to Low–Income Families in Interwar Britain' in V. Fildes *et al.* (eds.) *Women and Children First* (1992), pp. 256–79.

Perks, Robert and Thomson, Alastair (eds.) *The Oral History Reader* (London, 1998).

Pick, D. *Faces of Degeneration: A European Disorder 1848–1918* (Cambridge, 1989).

Piehl, Mel *Breaking Bread: The Catholic Worker and the Origin of Catholic Radicalism in America* (Philadelphia, 1982).

Pugh, Martin *Women and the Women's Movement in Britain 1919–1959* (London, 1992).

Rendall, Jane *Equal Or Different* (Oxford, 1987).

Rendall, Jane *The Origins of Modern Feminism 1780–1860* (London, 1985).

Riegle Troester, R. (ed.), *Voices from the Catholic Worker* (Philadelphia, 1993).

Roberts, Elizabeth *A Woman's Place: An Oral History of Working-Class Women 1890–1940* (Oxford, 1984).

Rose, C. *The Female Experience: The Story of the Woman Movement in Ireland* (Dublin, 1975).

Ross, E. *Love and Toil: Motherhood in Outcast London* (London, 1993).

Rozaldo, M.K. 'The Uses and Abuses of Anthropology' *Signs: Journal of Women in Culture and Society* Vol. 5, No. 31, pp. 389–417.

Russell, John Charles 'In the Shadows of Saints: Aspects of Family and Religion in a Rural Irish Gaeltacht' (University of California San Diego, PhD, 1979).

Ryan, Mary, Browne, Sean and Gilmour, Kevin (eds) *No Shoes In Summer* (Dublin, 1995).

Ryan, Sandra 'Interventions in Childbirth: The Midwives' Role' in A. Byrne and M. Leonard (eds.) *Women and Irish Society: a Sociological Reader* (Belfast, 1997), pp. 255–67.

Saraceno, Chiara 'Redefining maternity and paternity: gender, pronatalism and social policies in fascist Italy' in Bock, G. and Thane, P. (eds.) *Maternity and Gender Policies* (1991), pp. 196–212.

Samuel, Raphael *Theatres of Memory: Past and Present in Contemporary Culture* (London, 1994).

Sangster, Joan 'Telling Our Stories: feminist debates and the use of oral history' *Women's History Review* Vol. 3 No. 1 (1994), pp. 5–28.

Scanlon, J. *Inarticulate Longings: The Ladies Home Journal, Gender and the Promises of Consumer Culture* (New York, 1995).

Scannell, Y. 'The Constitution and the Role of Women' in Brian Farrell (ed.) *De Valera's Constitution and Ours* (Dublin, 1988), pp. 123–36.

Scheper-Hughes, Nancy 'Saints, Scholars and Schizophrenics: Mental Illness in Irish Culture' PhD University of California, Berkeley (1976).

Seip, Anne-Liese and Ibsen, Hilde 'Family Welfare, Which Policy? Norway's Road to Child Allowances' in Bock, G. and Thane, P. (eds.) *Maternity and Gender Policies* (1991), pp. 40–59.

Sexton, Regina *A Little History of Irish Food* (Dublin, 1998).

Shanklin, Eugenia 'Sure and What Did We Ever Do But Knit: women's lives and work in south-west Donegal' *Donegal Annual* No. 40 (1988), pp. 40–54.

Shatter, A. *Family Law in Ireland* (Dublin, 1977).

Sheehy-Skeffington, Andrée *Skeff: A Life of Owen Sheehy-Skeffington* (Dublin, 1991).

Shiels, Michael *The Quiet Revolution: The Electrification of Rural Ireland* (Dublin, 1984).

Silverman, Marilyn, ' "A Labouring Man's Daughter": constructing respectability in South Kilkenny' in Curtin, C. and Wilson, T. (eds.) *Ireland From Below: Social Change and Local Communities* (Galway, 1988), pp. 109–27.

Simonton, Deborah *A History of European Women's Work From 1800* (London, 1998).

Sklar, Kathryn Kish 'The Historical Foundations of Women's Power in the Creation of the American Welfare State' in Koven, S. and Michel, S. (eds.) *Mothers of a New World* (1993), pp. 43–73.

Smyth, Ailbhe (ed.) *Irish Women's Studies Reader* (Dublin, 1993).

Solomons, Michael *Pro-Life? The Irish Question* (Dublin, 1992).

Stadum, Beverly *Poor Mothers and Their Families: Hard-Working Charity Cases 1910–1930* (New York, 1992).

Stedman Jones, Gareth *Outcast London* (Oxford, 1971).

Stewart, Mary Lynn *Women, Work and the French State 1880–1939* (Montreal, 1989).

Stoppard, Dr Miriam *Pregnancy and Birth Handbook* (London, 1987).

Stoppard, Dr Miriam *Woman to Woman: The Comprehensive Practical Guide for Women that puts you in Control of your Body and its Health* (London, 1988).

Summerfield, Penny *Reconstructing Women's Wartime Lives: Discourse and Subjectivity in Oral Histories of the Second World War* (Manchester, 1998).

Swanton, Daisy Lawrenson *Emerging From The Shadow: The Lives of Sarah Anne Lawrenson and Lucy Olive Kingston* (Dublin, 1994).

Taylor, Alice *Quench the Lamp* (Dingle, 1990).

Thane, Pat 'Visions of Gender in the Making of the British Welfare State' in Bock, G. and Thane, P. (eds.) *Maternity and Gender Policies* (1991), pp. 93–118.

Therman, Dorothy Harrison *Stories from Tory Island* (Dublin, 1989).

Tinkler, Penny *Constructing Girlhood: Popular Magazines for Girls Growing Up in England 1920–1950* (London, 1995).

Travers, P. 'Emigration and Gender: the case of Ireland 1922–60' in M. O'Dowd and S. Wichert (eds.) *Chattel, Servant or Citizen: Women's Status in Church, State and Society* (Belfast, 1995) pp. 187–99.

Tweedy, Hilda *A Link In The Chain: The Story of the Irish Housewives 1942–1992* (Dublin, 1992).

Ungerson, C. (ed.) *Women and Social Policy: A Reader* (London, 1985).

Valiulis, Maryann 'Defining Their Role In The New State: Irishwomen's Protest Against the Juries Act 1927' *Canadian Journal of Irish Studies* Vol. 18, No. 1, (1992), pp. 43–60.

Valiulis, Maryann 'Neither Feminist nor Flapper: The Ecclesiastical Construction of the Ideal Irish Woman' in M. O'Dowd and S. Wichert (1995), *Chattel, Servant or Citizen*, pp. 168–78.

Valiulis, Maryann 'Defining Their Role in The New State: Irishwomen's Protest Against the Juries Act' *Canadian Journal of Irish Studies* Vol. 18, No. 1 (1992), pp. 43–60; and 'Power, Gender and Identity in the Irish Free State' *Journal of Women's History* Vols 6/7, Winter/Spring 1995, pp. 117–36.

Wallich-Clifford, Anton *Caring On Skid Row* (London, Dublin, 1974).

Walsh, Brendan 'Married Women, Employment, and Family Size' *Social Studies: An Irish Journal of Sociology* Vol. 2 No. 6 (Dec 1973), pp. 565–72.

Walsh, Brendan M. *Some Irish Population Problems Considered* ESRI Paper 42 November 1968.

Ward, M. *Unmanageable Revolutionaries: women and Irish nationalism* (Dingle, 1983).

Whyte, J.H. *Church and State in Modern Ireland* (Dublin, 1980).

Wieners, A. 'Rural Irishwomen, their changing role, status and condition' *Éire-Ireland* Earrach-Spring 1994, pp. 76–91.

Winship, Janice *Inside Women's Magazines* (London, 1987).

Wolf, Naomi *The Beauty Myth* (London, 1990, 1991).

Wright, Erna *The New Childbirth* (London, 1964).

Zmroczek, Christine 'Dirty Linen: Women, Class and Washing Machine 1920s–1960s' *Women's Studies International Forum* Vol. 15 No. 2 (1992), pp. 173–85.

Index